Laila El-Haddad helps us navigate and experience a world far beyond our own and unknown to us, of what it means to own "a passport that allows no passage." Perhaps most critically, this book does what few do: It allows us to understand Palestinians as we understand ourselves and in so doing affirms our common humanity. An extraordinary, eloquent work.

—Dr. SARA ROY
Center for Middle Eastern Studies, Harvard University

Gaza Mom is humanly moving and politically explosive, vividly illuminating the cruelties of everyday life for Palestinians living under occupation for decades. Laila El-Haddad writes with disciplined passion and conveys a powerful sense of authenticity. This book should become required reading for Americans who have yet to comprehend the prison-camp conditions that prevail in Gaza.

—Prof. RICHARD FALK
Professor of International Law Emeritus, Princeton University
Special Rapporteur for the OPTs, UN Human Rights Council

El-Haddad's assessment of the personal and collective impacts of Israel's occupation policy—from trudging through the endless bureaucratic labyrinths of identification papers and travel restrictions, to her everyday conversations with people picking up the pieces of their lives after a bombing—and the piercing analysis of her own personal journey has created a text not often found in current literature on Palestine. It is exactly the kind of documentation that is needed in these times of dehumanization of the Palestinian people.

—NORA BARROWS-FRIEDMAN
Writer, *Electronic Intifada* and *Al Jazeera*

Other titles from

JUST WORLD BOOKS
"TIMELY BOOKS FOR CHANGING TIMES"

This title, like most of our titles, is being published first in paperback, and will later be released as a hardcover, in two or more e-book versions, and in a number of overseas editions. Please check our website for updates on the publishing plans, and to buy the books:

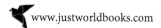 www.justworldbooks.com

Our Fall 2010 schedule includes initial publication of the following additional titles:

America's Misadventure in the Middle East
Chas W. Freeman, Jr.
(October 2010)

Afghanistan Journal: Selections from Registan.net
Joshua Foust
(November 2010)

A Responsible End? The United States and Iraq, 2005-2010
Reidar Visser
(November 2010)

GAZA MOM

2/23/12

Peace. Justice. Equality

In Solidarity,

Laila

To Yousuf and Noor. Thank you for always
helping me to put things in perspective.
I hope one day this will all make sense.

Gaza Mom

Palestine, Politics, Parenting, and Everything In Between

Laila El-Haddad

With photographs by the author
and a Foreword by
MIRIAM COOKE

JUST WORLD
BOOKS

Charlottesville, Virginia

Chapter 22 includes "Athens Airport" by Mahmoud Darwish, from *Unfortunately, It Was Paradise: Selected Poems* (Berkeley: University of California Press, 2003). Reprinted by permission of the publisher.

Publisher's Cataloging-in-Publication
(Provided by Quality Books, Inc.)

El-Haddad, Laila M.
Gaza mom : Palestine, politics, parenting, and
everything in between / by Laila El-Haddad ; with
photographs by the author ; and a foreword by Miriam
Cooke.
p. cm.
LCCN 2010937075
ISBN-13 978-1-935982-00-5
ISBN-10: 1-935982-00-1

1. El-Haddad, Laila M.—Blogs. 2. Palestinian Arabs
—Biography. 3. Palestine—Social conditions.
4. Palestine—Social life and customs. 5. Gaza Strip—
Social conditions. 6. Palestine—Foreign relations—
21st century. 7. United States—Foreign relations—21st
century. 8. Israel—Foreign relations—21st century.
I. Title.

DS126.6.E39A3 2010   956.9405'4'092
                          QBI10-600205

Contents

Foreword

For the past five years, Palestinians have been blogging from inside Gaza. Some wrote asking for help, some sought to attract attention to a catastrophe the world was ignoring, and Laila El-Haddad blogged to inform and educate.

Like Riverbend's chronicling of the 2003 American invasion of Baghdad, Laila takes us into the thick of things in Gaza. Unlike Riverbend, Laila is married with two children. She started the blog in December 2004 to keep her Palestinian husband, Yassine, informed about how his wife and newborn baby, Yousuf, were faring in a Palestine he is not allowed to enter. Born in a refugee camp in Lebanon, Yassine does not have permission to step on Israeli-controlled Palestinian soil. When Laila visits her parents who live in Gaza, she has to go without him.

Throughout the past six years and in this extraordinary book, Laila balances her multiple roles as wife, mother, daughter, and journalist for *Al Jazeera*. That's when she's inside Gaza. When she leaves, two more identities come into play: Palestinian and Muslim. She follows events with the keenness of an observer obliged to report to the world—but always also to Yousuf—the truth of life in a region so crowded, so crushed, and so surveilled that it has become known as the world's largest open-air prison, 350 densely populated square miles with often one exit only: the Rafah crossing that the Israelis and Egyptians take turns in closing.

Laila's matter-of-fact narration lies lightly on the terror pervading every instant of her life and that of her compatriots in Gaza. She is often terrorized, as when Israeli F-16s fly so low and fast that they break the sound barrier and create sonic booms so thunderous that they feel as though a bomb has exploded in the house. But she is not afraid in the sense of being in awe of the people and institutions. She interviews leaders—the head of Mossad, the head of the Fateh so-called Death Brigades, and so forth—responsible for crimes that they never acknowledge. It is always someone else who started it, whatever "it" was that time. She criticizes anyone who acts unjustly, whether they are Israelis or members of Fateh or Hamas.

Like other Arab women who have written about the wars they have survived during the past 50 years, her commitment is to justice, and justice demands a multiple critique, a relentless pursuit of those in power who do not put the interests of the people above their own. To criticize an out-of-control Fateh or Hamas militiaman does not mean betrayal; it means that this person has betrayed his people by targeting them. Like other Arab women writers, Laila affirms that war today scorns the binary paradigm that used to characterize its space and activities. There is no special place for warriors and another for civilians. All are targets at the front that is everywhere. But the civilians carry the added burden of caring for the helpless in their charge. Her parents, both retired physicians, are drawn back into medical practice as the number of casualties soar and outstrip the ability of hospital staff to care for them.

The informal tone, especially at the beginning, gives the impression of being in a conversation that is routinely interrupted by the unexpected, sometimes from Yousuf and sometimes from the outside. The reader is brought into the intimacy of a Gazan home, with Yousuf initially more afraid of the sound of a vacuum cleaner than of the distant F-16s whose noise is part of the ambient atmosphere.

Formal reportage for *Al Jazeera* mixes with the sardonic commentary of a down-to-earth witness who keeps a careful check on her language so that it is not hysterical and never out of control. A child is killed, and Laila knows that if she does not report this death, it will go unnoticed. Each day is blogged as it happens, without the hindsight wisdom of other genres. Hers is the wisdom of a seasoned, rational participant-observer who has survived wars in Saudi Arabia and again and again in Gaza.

Checkpoints figure importantly with their routine of civilian suffering, Israeli sadism, and Palestinian defiance. We wait with Laila for hours, days, and sometimes weeks when she is stuck with one or more family members at some border. A mother caring for an infant has to be brave, and Laila is always brave for Yousuf. He gives her courage to stand up to the most vicious soldiers. With time, she mentions her parents more often than Yousuf, because she in the United States, cut off from her family and their ordeal. We listen in on daily phone conversations, with her father Skyping as soon as he can. When this usually calm, strong man calls with fear quaking his voice, we know how terrifying the situation has become, and we stay on the line with Laila until dawn brings a break in the black of night and endless electricity cuts.

But we also learn the details of Palestinian history from the 1948 *Nakba* to today in an intense way that is not possible with works of history, political science, anthropology, and even economics, where the same itinerary of dispossession and oppression has to be retrod again and again. This book is far from repetitive, because even the most familiar events resonate with the intensity of Laila's particular experience and the constant need to cope for Yousuf but also for her job. She has to package every event in its historical context but also in a new way that will give it a chance to make it to the top of the editor's pile of articles. Laila's writing stands out as eloquent eyewitness accounts of moments in the attempted destruction of a people, their genocide.

But Laila rarely uses such words; the first time she mentions the word "genocide" is late in the book, when she is quoting a progressive Israeli intellectual. Her text is not inflammatory. It is rational, sensible, sometimes tender, sometimes indignant, but always insistent on the heartbreaking facts—physical, emotional, economic, and social disintegration—and on the mandate for the world to pay attention. Palestinians make up one-third of the world's total refugee population, but the world is tired of hearing about them.

Laila seems confident that she can break through this indifference. Ironic humor, sometimes at her own expense, is a way to make this terrible saga not only *not* same old, same old but enticing and compelling. You want to read how Laila is going to manage tomorrow; will it be funny in the midst of tragedy so that you will have to read and not want to just skip the bad parts? So vivid and immediate is the writing that we feel that we are with her stuck either inside or outside Gaza. We measure time by the occasional reminder of Yousuf's age.

And in the midst of all the deprivations and bombings and utter misery, Laila, like her compatriots, finds moments of joy, hope, and unimaginable optimism. Elections promise autonomy; disengagement and the removal of the loathed settlers from Gaza fill the people with hope. And when the hope turns out to be another betrayal, Yousuf comes to the rescue with something outrageous that breaks the vicious cycle.

Reader, even if you think you know all the details of Gaza's history, you have not read this before. *Gaza Mom* is new, fresh. My hope is that this passionate book will shake readers, make them understand the crimes that have been committed against a people who are struggling to survive brutality with a dignity that seems impossible to understand unless one has been there. And thanks to Laila El-Haddad, we have virtually been there.

miriam cooke
Doha, Qatar
September 2010

Preface

The blog that was the source of much of the material in this book came about largely by happenstance. It was originally named "Raising Yousuf" and later became "Gaza Mom." I started it in the fall of 2004, not even knowing what the word "blog" meant and with no idea of where this new adventure would take me.

That year was a testing time for my husband and me: We were recently married and living with our first child in Boston, where we had met shortly before I finished graduate school at Harvard's Kennedy School of Government.

Just one year earlier, in August 2003, I had gotten my first real break as a journalist with the newly launched *Al Jazeera English* website. In 2004, that position would take me back to do some reporting from Gaza, my family's beloved home city. But my husband Yassine could not come with us. As a Palestinian with refugee status, Yassine was denied the right to enter or even visit Gaza or any other part of the occupied Palestinian territories (OPTs) or modern-day Israel—despite the fact that Palestine is his homeland and that of his wife and child (now, children). Yassine is denied any version of "the Right of Return" to his ancestral homeland. This, while Israel gives Jewish people from anywhere in the world—or anyone who can trace his Jewish ancestry back to several generations earlier or is a spouse, grandchild, or child of such a person—the immediate "right" to reside in any of the areas it controls, even if their immediate ancestors have never lived in the area.

Yassine was born in the UN-administered refugee camp of Baalbek in Lebanon. Until shortly before his birth, his family had been living in a refugee camp in Beirut, Lebanon, called Tel al-Zaatar, "Hill of Thyme," that was a flashpoint in the internecine fighting of the Lebanese civil war. (His uncle was killed in the anti-Palestinian massacre perpetrated in Tel al-Zaater in 1976.) Yassine grew up amid the civil war that continued to rage throughout Lebanon in the 1980s. Thirty-five years earlier, during the Nakba, or the Palestinian exodus,[1] his grandparents had been driven out of their homes in historic Palestine, their lives displaced and their property lost, just as the State of Israel was established. The villages from which two of his grandparents fled in the face of Jewish paramilitary and later Israeli troop advances were both destroyed in their entirety by the Israeli authorities, soon after 1948. . . .

In 1993, Yassine won a scholarship to attend high school in the United States. From there, he made his way to college and eventually to Harvard Medical School. I had also done all my college studies in the United States; it was while he was at medical school that we met.

My parents were both medical doctors. When I was born in the late 1970s, they were among the scores of thousands of Palestinian professionals working in Kuwait. I was born in Kuwait and passed most of my youth living primarily in the Gulf kingdoms of Saudi Arabia and Bahrain; however, my brothers and I would spend our summers, springs, and sometimes our winters in Gaza. I remember that at the height of the first Palestinian Intifada in around 1990, we kids were mocked in my mother's hometown of Khan Yunis, just south of Gaza City, for not knowing the difference between the insignia of the two main Palestinian movements, Fateh and Hamas! My parents tried to keep our lives as far away from politics as possible. But our existence as Gaza Palestinians was itself inescapably political.

Because I am a Gaza Palestinian, I hold a Palestinian Authority (PA) "passport" and the all-important identification or residency card, known as a *hawiya*, that is issued by the Israeli military authorities who still control the population registries of the Gaza Strip and the West Bank. The *hawiya* is the document by which we Palestinians from the OPTs live and die. It was a document that, when I was growing up in the 1980s, we struggled hard to preserve and renew, because Israel threatened to take it away from Gazans living outside the occupied Gaza Strip, just as today it still tries to take it away from Palestinian residents of East Jerusalem. Even when we were children, we endured annual, 24-hour journeys to Gaza by land, complete with strip searches at the hands of young Israeli soldiers, uncertain periods of waiting, arbitrary procedures and interrogations, and generally humiliating treatment, such as being asked to collectively retrieve our shoes and socks from a large pile after the strip search was complete—all so we could hang on to our *hawiyas*.

But the *hawiya* is the ultimate Catch-22. The Israelis still, today—despite their much-vaunted "withdrawal" from Gaza in 2005—control all the Gaza Strip's markers of sovereignty, including its borders, airspace, sea, and (crucially) the population registry. So long as I have a *hawiya*, Israel considers me to be a "legal resident" of Gaza. And thus, so long as the only land crossing, at Rafah, is open, the Israelis (jointly with the Egyptians) will graciously "allow" me to travel to my hometown, Gaza. But they forbid most other people—even Palestinians from the nearby West Bank or refugee Palestinians who grew up in exile, such as my husband, let alone any of my American or European friends who might want to visit me—from doing so. The *hawiya* is also used to prevent me from traveling to other areas Israel controls, such as the West Bank, Jerusalem, or "1948 Palestine" (that is, modern-day Israel). It even bars me from the kind of access to those areas that other, non-Palestinian journalists have. As an Israeli Army officer once explained to me, "We consider you as Palestinians, and therefore security threats, first; as journalists, second." All those kinds of restrictions intensified after the conclusion of the Oslo Accords in 1993. (Go figure.)

The Israeli military has imposed the *hawiya* system on the indigenous (and therefore legitimate) residents of the West Bank and Gaza Strip continuously throughout all the 43 years since it first occupied these territories back in 1967, long before I was born. From the mid-1990s on, possession of a *hawiya* has also entitled its holder to obtain a passport issued in the name of the PA—though Israel still maintains and controls the whole system. But the *hawiya* system lies at the heart of the tight-knit mechanism by which Israel controls Palestinian movement, residency, and life in general. It allows Israel alone to decide which "Arabs" it will recognize as "Palestinian," which couples it will recognize as "families" that qualify for "reunification" and thus residency, and who is allowed to move where and at what point—all inside our own homeland. As the pioneering Israeli journalist Amira Hass has explained:

> This control allowed Israel to deprive hundreds of thousands of Palestinians of their residency status after 1967. It allowed the continuation of marital, social, economic, religious, and cultural ties between Gaza and the West Bank until 1991—and then, it severed those ties. This control allows Israel to prevent the addition of foreign residents to the population registry; it allows Israel to intervene in, and even decide, the choice of a partner, place of study, type of medical treatment, address, quality time with children, participation in celebrations and funerals, the writing of wills and distribution of family property. Israel has the authority to ban the entry of friends or family members who are not Palestinian residents—not just their entry into Israel, but also into the West Bank and Gaza Strip.[2]

After Israel occupied the West Bank (including East Jerusalem) and the Gaza Strip in June 1967, it issued *hawiyas* only to those Palestinians it found in residence there during a door-to-door census. Palestinians who had been driven out of, or fled, their homes in either the 1948 war or the 1967 war were excluded, as were any Palestinians who, at census time, were abroad for whatever reason—studying, working, visiting family, or vacationing. An exception was made for Palestinian physicians, for whom there was a desperate need. My parents were both completing their medical internships in Egypt at the time. They grabbed the opportunity to return to Gaza (and, in my father's case, cut an internship short), traveling in Red Cross ambulances with blackened windows that whisked them through the closed military zones of the newly occupied Sinai.

Then in 1975, my father had a sharp argument with the head of the Israeli medical military unit, who had come to meet with leading Palestinian doctors in Gaza to assess the needs of the main hospital there. The Israeli officer arrived with a predetermined opinion: The hospital had no further needs. My father, a person who tells it like it is, staunchly disagreed. He told the officer that the hospital was substandard, ranking at only "negative 2 on a scale of 1 to 10," and that "we run out of antibiotics by the first week of the month!" The other Palestinian doctors panicked, pleading with my father to stay quiet, but he continued. Israeli promises to build a new hospital never materialize, he continued.

"So we're liars?" asked the Israeli official.

"Take it anyway you like," my father replied.

The Israeli official forwarded my father's file to Israeli intelligence, where he was then summoned on a weekly basis. He was advised to leave Gaza to seek work elsewhere or face imprisonment, so he and my mother left. . . . Many years later, when their careers in the Gulf came to an end and when Israel was no longer directly involved in the Palestinian health administration, my parents decided to retire back home in Gaza City.

When I started traveling to Gaza for my job in 2004, I took my son, Yousuf, then 9 months old and still nursing, with me. Yassine stayed behind in the United States. A tech-savvy cousin suggested I should start a blog to help Yassine keep in touch with our travels and with Yousuf's development. My first reaction was that I knew nothing about creating or maintaining websites! "You don't need to," she replied. "Just create a title, and you're off."

And so I did. In the fall of 2004, "Raising Yousuf" was born while we were visiting Boston. The idea was to write strictly about, well, raising Yousuf. I created a separate blog in which I commented on all things purely political, often in a satirical manner. But in December 2004, as I traveled back to Gaza with Yousuf, I was faced with the very real prospect that I would be unable to return to the Strip, and I would have no recourse for appeal against that decision. I was stuck in Cairo, a city that I barely knew, waiting to make the arduous land journey to the Rafah crossing, which was (and still is) the only way Gazans who had left the Strip for any reason could get back in. Israel announced it was indefinitely closing the Rafah crossing as punishment after a bomb killed several of its soldiers there. That closure stranded 1.5 million Palestinians inside the Strip and tens of thousands of others (including us) outside it. It continued for 55 days, leaving Yousuf and me beached in Cairo. I came to understand then, as I would a hundred times over in the years that followed, that as a Palestinian you cannot separate the personal from the political. Our identity surfaces with particular intensity on international borders!

In 2006, I left Gaza to spend more time with Yassine in the United States, though I remained determined to return as frequently as I could. My parents stayed behind in their apartment in central Gaza City. At that point, I had to face a different challenge: the pain of being stranded outside my homeland when it was under siege. I struggled to explain our complicated lives to Yousuf—and later to his little sister, Noor, born in early 2008: Palestine and Gaza; border crossings and closures; the right of return and occupation; civil unrest and Palestinian division. Who were "the bad guys"? Why were the Israelis, who created so many of the miserable experiences Yousuf had, never visible? Why couldn't we travel like ordinary people, when we wanted and how we wanted? Why could the children's beloved *Baba* (Daddy) never travel to Gaza with us, anyway?

I managed to visit Gaza twice more in 2007. But in 2009, after Gaza had been under prolonged closure, my attempts to go back failed. In April 2009, the Egyptian authorities, which were colluding closely with Israel to keep Gaza completely closed, held my children and me in Cairo airport for 30 hours before they finally expelled us back to the United States. Finally, in early summer 2010, responding to pressures raised by the Israel's lethal showdown with the Turkish-led aid flotilla, Egypt loosened the siege—just a little. In July 2010, I was able to go back to Gaza for a two-month visit.

The chapters that follow cover this six-year period—from fall 2004, when the second Intifada was still raging and Israel's systematic demolitions of homes along Gaza's southern border was at a peak, until the very recent past. They chronicle in intimate detail such historic events as Israel's highly misleading "disengagement" from Gaza, which ended up repackaging its occupation in more insidious forms; the first truly democratic Palestinian parliamentary elections, held in 2006—and the Western-backed, Israeli-enforced boycott and bloody intra-Palestinian feuds that ensued; and ultimately, Israel's "Cast Lead" assault on Gaza, which still left Israel's crippling siege of the Strip in place despite the many new needs for reconstruction that became clear once that assault's ruins could be surveyed. Today, much of the optimism and hope I saw during critical moments like the Palestinian elections also lie in ruins. But its people go on living.

If there is any lesson to glean from this book or from covering and living the conflict for this period of time, it is the consistency and constancy of Israel's Palestinian policies—regardless of who rules in Gaza or the West Bank. So long as those in power in Palestine are not willing collaborators in their own imprisonment, the consequences will be fierce: Institutions will be destroyed, development and prosperity will be blocked, and the pretext will always be security. The Israelis will always argue that Palestinian violence, rather than Israeli occupation, colonization, and violence, is the stumbling block to "peace." For decades, the Israeli authorities have used such strategies to deliberately forestall any prospect for viable Palestinian statehood. The late Israeli sociologist Baruch Kimmerling referred to this overriding policy as "the politicide of the Palestinian people, a gradual but systematic attempt to cause their annihilation as an independent political and social entity."[3] Indeed, an Israeli government document released in September 2010 showed publicly for the first time that Israel's objective was to create two separate Palestinian political entities.[4]

Throughout the book, you will be introduced to many of the people in my life. Chief among them are my children: Yousuf, now 6 years old, and Noor, who turns 3 in January 2011; my husband, Yassine, who has now completed his medical training in the United States; my parents, Maii El-Farra, a pediatrician, and Moussa El-Haddad, a retired obstetrician gynecologist (OB/GYN).

The tone and style of writing changes continuously throughout the book, as do the space, the setting, the content, and the situation. In the book, you will see me trying to navigate the always varied terrain of different identities and spaces: of being a reporter and a mother, a Palestinian under occupation and a Palestinian in exile—and navigating many other complexities and details as well. I try to guide you through these aspects of my life with as much fluidity and clarity as possible!

Journalists who have covered the Palestinian-Israeli conflict at great length often note that that headlines written five or even 10 years ago could have been written today. Readers finish reading articles or listening or watching news programs feeling more confused than before and left with a sense of hopelessness that the conflict will ever be resolved. Such headlines as "more violence in the Middle East" or "Palestinian terror" have become mainstays of the American nightly news—and of the average American's perceptions of the conflict. Such statements are mistakenly attributed to a vague and misleading notion of "cyclical violence" that seems to have no end and no clear beginning, while most mainstream media fail to delve deeper, to ask why the conflict has persisted for so long, what forces are driving the "violence," or what kinds of lives people can live underneath it all.

This book does not claim to explain Gaza comprehensively or to speak for all its residents. It is a singular account within the dizzying multiplicity of experiences and existences that constitute the Palestinian experience as a whole. It is a window into Gaza during some of its most turbulent years and into the violated but resilient lives we live as Palestinians. It is a story about mothering, homeland, identity—and survival.

Laila El-Haddad
Gaza and Maryland
October 2010

NOTES

1. The *Nakba* ("Catastrophe") refers to the 1948 Palestinian exodus, when some 725, 000 Palestinians were expelled from, or fled, their homes in historic Palestine during the 1948 Arab-Israeli war. Shortly thereafter, the first Israeli government enacted several laws that barred the expelled Palestinians from returning to their homes or claiming their property.
See http://en.wikipedia.org/wiki/1948_Palestinian_exodus.
2. Amira Hass, "What a Strange 'Abroad,'" *Haaretz*, February 14, 2007, archived at http://bit.ly/caaM1C.
3. Baruch Kimmerling, "The Politicide of Palestinians," *Dissident Voice*, June 11, 2002, archived at http://bit.ly/cXi6dR.
4. An English-language version of this government document can be found at http://bit.ly/alptVv.

PART I

Gaza Life as Israel (Partially) Withdraws

December 2004–December 2005

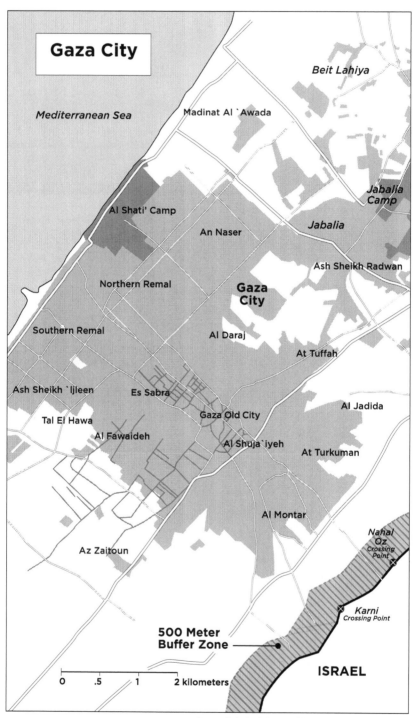

Gaza City

Mediterranean Sea

Beit Lahiya

Madinat Al `Awada

Jabalia
Camp

Al Shati' Camp

An Naser

Jabalia

Ash Sheikh Radwan

Northern Remal

Gaza
City

Southern Remal

Al Daraj

At Tuffah

Ash Sheikh `Ijleen

Es Sabra

Al Jadida

Tal El Hawa

Gaza Old City

Al Fawaideh

Al Shuja`iyeh

At Turkuman

Al Montar

Nahal
Oz
Crossing
Point

Az Zaitoun

Karni
Crossing Point

500 Meter
Buffer Zone

ISRAEL

0   .5   1   2 kilometers

Cartography by Lewis Rector and © 2010 Just World Publishing, LLC

Chapter 1

Going Home to Gaza

December 2004–February 2005

This book begins in the fall of 2004 during a trip I was making back to Gaza from the United States with my son, Yousuf, then 9 months old. We had been back and forth multiple times before this date, twice with Yousuf in utero. But this time was different. The birth of my blog coincided with a forced stay of exile in Egypt for both of us as Israel sealed the border to Gaza for an indefinite period of time. And so suddenly surfaced the complications and contrasts of being a Palestinian, a mother, and a journalist—striving for survival, sanity, and the stories behind the news.

It was the beginning of what would become a recurrent theme of the labyrinthine nature of travel and movement for our family, as it has long been for Palestinians in the broader sense. The chapter also includes a piece I wrote for Al Jazeera about the sniping death of a young schoolchild in southern Gaza. In Gaza, existence was as jarring and strenuous as untimely death was commonplace. As in the text, the routines of mothering (which continue, even in a war zone) were frequently interrupted by field reporting in that same war zone.

Stuck in Egypt[1]
Cairo, Egypt, December 25, 2004

Was on my way back to Gaza to work after a brief hiatus to the U.S. to see Yassine, when wouldn't you have it, the Israelis closed the Rafah border crossing—the only route into Gaza—after a gigantic explosion killed five of their troops there. Well that means Yousuf and I have been stuck here for over two weeks now and counting.

An Egyptian friend of my mother's, who trying to be good-natured, made the comment that, "It's not a big deal, you must be used to this by now," meaning of course, the constant border closures.

How can one EVER get used to the uncertainty of Palestinian existence? To being prevented from entering one's own homeland arbitrarily, spontaneously? To being in absolute lack of control of one's life—that is, to have another be in absolute control of your every movement? You cannot. And as Palestinians we do not. We live, for the most part, in a state of constant temporality, and this, more than anything else, has come to define us.

And on We Grow . . .[2]
Cairo, Egypt, December 28, 2004

Today, I came to the realization that Yousuf is growing—whether I like it or not. Sadly, I had to retire many of his six-to-nine-month clothes after my friend Hoda made the comment that his bum seems to be sticking out of all his pants. I think I was in denial. I had to come to terms with the fact that he would never fit into any of the darling little six-to-nine-monthers again—*ever!* Next thing you know, as his daddy says when I complain about this cling-to-me-like-a-fly-to-honey-phase, he won't want to spend time with his embarrassing mother. *Sigh* Maybe I'm being a little melodramatic, but I'm stuck in Cairo alone with a 9-month-old in an unfurnished flat, so cut me some slack here.

Standing on My Own (Sort of . . .)[3]
Cairo, Egypt, January 8, 2005

Yes, unfortunately, we are still in Cairo. But we're trying to make the best of it. Here's an excerpt from article I've published on it at *Al Jazeera English*, "Palestinians Stranded at Border Crossing":

> With the world's focus on the Palestinian elections, Palestinians stranded at the closed Rafah-Egypt border feel they have been forgotten.
>
> One such victim of the Israeli measure is Yasmin and her groom who held their engagement celebration in a Cairo hotel.
>
> For the Palestinian couple from Gaza it was supposed to be a momentous occasion that was months in the planning—the celebration of the beginning of a lifetime together.
>
> But the ceremony was bittersweet, and the dance floor empty save for the bride and groom. The majority of their guests, after all, could not attend.[4]

Meantime, Yousuf is growing: He stood up on his own the other day for a few fleeting seconds! I couldn't get it on film though.

He's also developed an appetite for popcorn (thanks to *Seedo*).

Unfortunately he's still not sleeping well at night, which means neither am I!

A True Gazan Palate[5]
Cairo, Egypt, January 12, 2005

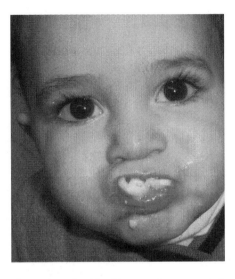

Yet further proof that Yousuf has picked up more of my Gazan roots than his father's Haifawi ones: He wolfed down a plate of chicken livers, Gaza-style, today. That means *lots* of chilies (those who have been a foot away from a Gaza chili can relate). And he didn't seem to mind them one bit. On the other hand, when I attempt to feed him any dairy product (the staple of the North), even if disguised in other foods, he will spit it out in disgust.

Another thing I think he picked up from Gaza (besides his voracious appetite) is his manners! He found a tangerine on the floor and ripped it apart—quite literally, before stuffing it in his mouth. *Sigh* I think we have our work cut out.

On another note, his hair is getting out of control. I mean it. Yassine is insisting I let it grow until he seems him again, hopefully next month.

Shards of Glass and Murphy's Law[6]
Cairo, Egypt, January 20, 2005

Add to the list of highly unusual, toxic, and dangerous things Yousuf has managed to put in his mouth during these forty days of imposed exile: a shard of glass!! I noticed him attempting to chew on something, which he then spit out only to realize it was a piece of glass from a chili sauce bottle that shattered the previous day . . . oops.

He's also, during the past week, become very attached to his *seedo*. He has learned how to wave "Bye Bye" (although he pronounces it "beh beh") when he sees his granddad approaching the door.

On another note, the Rafah border will *finally* open on Friday, *Inshallah*. We all plan to journey to al-Arish Friday afternoon, then attempt to make our way to Gaza Saturday along with thousands of others. Murphy's law? Yesterday I decided to stop buying things in minute amounts in anticipation of the border opening "any day now," and wouldn't you have it, the border opens.

Killing of Palestinian Girl Shatters Family[7]
Gaza City, Palestine, February 5, 2005, *Al Jazeera English*

Nuran Dib went to school as ecstatic as any schoolgirl should be. But this crisp winter day was special: She would receive her bi-annual report card.

As it turned out, she passed with flying colours, which meant a gift from her parents, who had been saving up their dwindling funds for this occasion. The teacher's comment on top of her report read: We predict a very bright future for Nuran.

But Nuran would have no such future, and her gift lies abandoned in a corner of her family's grieving home. On the afternoon of 31 January 2005, Israeli sniper fire ripped through her face as she stood in her school's courtyard, lining up for afternoon assembly.

The last thing Nuran's mother remembers of her daughter before she left for school that morning was hearing her say her morning prayers, during which she recited a verse about God having created death—and life—as a test for mankind.

In retrospect, Nuran's mother believes it was a premonition of what was to come.

"Then she left for school. She was a completely selfless child. She was thinking of her sisters till the last second. She came back after she had left the house, and said: 'Mommy, it's cold—please put some sweaters on my sisters before they leave,'" her mother said.

"What more can I say except that she was a breath of fresh air in these hard times? Her name was Nur [light] and that's exactly what she was."

Her death has many here questioning Israel's commitment to a ceasefire amid a one-sided truce and virtual period of calm.

"We extended an olive branch to them and instead of reciprocating they cut our hand off," Nuran's mother cried, sitting in an unpainted cement-block bedroom with nothing but thin foam mattresses on the ground.

"What did she ever do to deserve such a fate? Or her sister, who saw Nuran die in front of her? Every night she wails out in her sleep: 'Bring me my sister, bring me my sister.'"

Fifth child killed

Nuran was the fifth Palestinian child to be shot dead or maimed by Israeli occupation forces while on the premises of their UN-flagged schools in the past two years. She was also one of 172 children killed in Gaza this year alone—and one of 644 killed in Gaza since the start of al-Aqsa Intifada in September 2000.

Two girls were shot dead in separate incidents in Rafah and Khan Yunis last year while sitting at their desks, and a little girl was permanently blinded in March 2003.

According to UNRWA's spokesperson, Paul McCann, the UN relief organisation has repeatedly protested against the Israeli military's indiscriminate firing into civilian areas in the occupied Palestinian territory.

Nuran's school, which is about 600m away from the border, has been hit on numerous occasions since the start of the conflict, he said. This is the first time the shots have had tragic consequences.

"We want to ask the world: Was Nuran holding an explosive belt around her waist? Was she toting a Kalashnikov? She knew no politics, only love," her aunt Iktimal Husayn asked rhetorically.

"She was supposed to bring home her report from school, but instead she brought home her death certificate."

. . . Witnesses say the children were clapping their hands and singing the national anthem when the firing started.

One bullet pierced the hand of Aysha Isam al-Khatib, while the other hit Nuran in the head. She fell to the ground at once.

Bystanders say they assumed she was unconscious until they noticed the pool of blood beneath her shattered skull.

A third bullet hit a young girl's book bag, and was stopped in its tracks by one of her folders, just inches away from her spine.

Eleven-year-old Salwa al-Khalifa was next to Nuran when the bullets struck. She described with disturbing composure well beyond her years the details of that bloody hour.

"A bullet went in through her nose and came out of her neck. We all ducked. Several other bullets hit the window and school wall over there."

A day after the incident, Israeli authorities said their initial investigation indicated it was fire from jubilant Palestinian police celebrating the return of Hajj pilgrims, not Israeli sniper fire, that killed Nuran.

But the pockmarked wall of the UNRWA school, which stands 600m away from an Israeli sniper tower and far away from residential blocks, tells a different story.

"There is nothing around us here, and there were no pilgrims that we know of celebrating that day. There is just an outpost a few hundred metres away—one from which sniper fire has frequently hit our school," school principal Siham al-Ghoff said.

Al-Ghoff says if the fire was indeed Palestinian, the bullet would not have hit Nuran in the face but rather landed on top of her head, as rifles fired in celebration usually point upwards.

Both Palestinian security sources and UN officials confirm the account, saying that the way the bullets were scattered, along with witness testimonies, point to Israeli gunfire.

"Everything is pointing to the fact that it was the Israelis. There were a number of shots, and the way they were scattered gives us an indication of the direction where they came from, and that corresponds with witness reports that the firing came from an [Israeli] APC or tank in the area," one official said.

School goes on

Meanwhile, in Nuran's school, life goes on. Girls who received top marks this term were rewarded with tins of toffee that they passed out enthusiastically to all visitors, a step taken by school counsellors to attempt to normalise an abnormal situation.

But in Nuran's fourth-grade classroom, the mood was far from celebratory.

"The children are too afraid to go out for their recess, and many simply go to the bathroom and weep all day," principal al-Ghoff said.

Counsellors have been trying to help the children work through the trauma of recent days. When asked to portray their classmate's death, most drew tanks and Apache helicopters invading their school.

"I thought there's a truce now, something like this would never happen. Now we're trying to pick up the pieces," al-Ghoff added.

The Palestinian Authority has filed a formal complaint with the Israeli side about the girls' shooting, but it is unlikely Nuran's family will ever get answers about their daughter's death.

Back in her family's home, Nuran's mother sat gazing in disbelief at her daughter's report card, while her father, Iyad, stood weeping silently.

Nearby, an Israeli tank shell rattled the windows of the room, which together with young Nuran's death served as a reminder that if there is any calm it has not yet reached Rafah.

Student working next to memorial.

"When Nuran died, a part of me died also," her mother said.

"She was a bright light that was extinguished. For me, there can be no more peace.

Help! A Vacuum Cleaner![8]
Gaza City, Palestine, February 14, 2005

Most children living in a strip of land overrun by trigger-happy soldiers, Merkava tanks, and sewage might be afraid of loud noises and machine gun ricochets (that and putrid-smelling water). Not Yousuf. Those he tackles fearlessly, having become accustomed to F-16s swooping overhead and the pounding of shells (even while in the womb).

His latest phobia: vacuum cleaners. My father was cleaning the carpets today, and the boy crawled to save his life, wailing in horror, fingernails clenched deep within mother's back. Tanks, bad . . . vacuum cleaner, good, I tried to explain. Perhaps it was an incident of friendly fire. But how will I explain this to his therapist years from now?

Rap Finds New Voice in Occupied Gaza[9]
Gaza City, Palestine, March 15, 2005 (reported late February), *Al Jazeera English*

Far away from its roots in the Bronx of New York, rap is finding a new voice as a group of young Palestinians sing about the frustrations of life under occupation in the Gaza Strip.

As I enter the small sound-proof recording room in central Gaza, I am greeted by something rather unexpected. . . . It is rap; it is potent; and it is in Arabic.

Sitting in front of the recording equipment is 22-year-old Nadir Abu Ayash, a member of Gaza's first ever hip-hip group PR (Palestinian Rappers), who provides many of the song's identifiable background sounds—with no special effects.

"Rap is our way of resisting the occupation, it's our weapon," he explains . . .

"Do you remember, or do you choose to forget/that your army, against us, aggressed/My voice will continue to echo, you'll never forget/You call me terrorist, when I'm the one who's oppressed," he raps in one of their latest songs.

The band, which first starting rapping two years ago, believe that hip-hop provides them with an alternative way to voice their resistance to and frustrations with the Israeli occupation.

The young rappers, Nadir Abu Ayash, Mutaz al-Huwaisi (Mezo), Muhammad al-Fara (DR), and Mahmud Fayad (Bond), pour all their emotions into their work. And they don't need to go far for inspiration.

Abu Ayash lives in the refugee camp of Maghazi and all around are constant reminders of the Israeli occupation, whether by way of a demolished home, an orphaned family, or the enduring poverty that has taken hold over 57 years of dispossession.

Fellow band-member Muhammad al-Fara lives in one of the most volatile areas of the Gaza Strip, just 5km away from the refugee camp of Khan Yunis. Three years ago he was shot in the arm by Israeli snipers situated in one of the nearby Jewish settlements.

"With the situation and the events around us, it's not difficult to come up with songs. It expresses itself inside us. Whenever you are affected by something you see, you write," al-Fara said.

A few months ago, the group was unable to leave Gaza to perform at a concert in France because of an Israeli policy banning young men between the ages of 16 and 35 from traveling.

. . . The band members say they dream of one day meeting with all of the hip-hop groups in Palestine to rap together in a large concert. They would especially like to rap with the Arab-Israeli group DAM, who they consider their idols, and whose song "Who's the Terrorist?" put them on the musical map.

They are hopeful it won't remain merely a dream. The lyrics of one their song declares, "the night is bound to leave and day will come upon us."

Happy Birthday!![10]
Gaza City, Palestine, March 6, 2005

Yay for Yousuf! He officially turned 1-year-old on Saturday. Something very bittersweet about that day though—I felt my grip slowly beginning to loosen, and that Yousuf was graduating into toddlerhood . . . never again will he unexpectedly roll off the bed and land crashing on the porcelain floor, or wail bloody murder every hour if the milking station was not open for service, or eat my mother's hormone replacement pills . . . oh wait, he did that yesterday. I suppose I have much to look forward to after all.

CHAPTER NOTES

1. The full original text of this post is archived at http://www.gazamom. com/2004/12/stuck-in-egypt/, shortened to http://bit.ly/bk0aop.
2. Archived at http://bit.ly/caeJbc.
3. Archived at http://bit.ly/cPt2EI.
4. Laila El-Haddad, "Palestinians Stranded at Border Crossing," *Al Jazeera English*, January 8, 2005, archived at http://bit.ly/dyo6Ge.
5. Archived at http://bit.ly/akPFDB.
6. Archived at http://bit.ly/cSoATt.
7. Laila El-Haddad, "Killing of Palestinian Girl Shatters Family," *Al Jazeera English*, March 10, 2005, archived at http://bit.ly/aCPDcN.
8. Archived at http://bit.ly/ai3Jff.
9. Laila El-Haddad, "Rap Finds New Voice in Occupied Gaza," *Al Jazeera English*, March 15, 2005, archived at http://bit.ly/a2Slmb.
10. Archived at http://bit.ly/bTTK1Q.

Chapter 2

Palestinian Life in Lebanon and the West Bank

March–July 2005

This chapter sees Yousuf and me reunited with Yassine in Lebanon, where his family, descendants of refugees from the 1948 Nakba, reside in a refugee camp. Yassine had some rare time off after finishing medical school in Boston. Because he is forbidden from traveling to Gaza, we decided to meet up in Lebanon instead. While there, I wrote various stories exploring the situation of the Palestinian refugees living in Lebanon. Yousuf and I returned to Gaza in early May 2005.

It was the first time either of us met Yassine's family. And though I was lucky to enjoy a "relative" degree of freedom of movement denied to many other Palestinians (like Yassine's own family, forbidden from entering Palestine), the journey was far from easy or assured. It took more than two months to arrange the proper single-entry permit I required to enter Lebanon.

While I could eventually get to both Lebanon and Syria on this visit, I was unable to travel to the West Bank (see "The Crushed Citizen"), despite its proximity to Gaza and its status as supposedly part of the same territory. Pieces I reported about the West Bank, such as "Road Signs Get Remade," had to be reported by phone, because Israel banned most Palestinians from traveling between Gaza, the West Bank, and East Jerusalem.

It is also worth noting that though the Rafah crossing was often tortuous to cross in 2005, some Palestinians were still able to cross in and out of Gaza much more easily then than we could in subsequent years, after Israel's much-lauded "Disengagement" from Gaza.

And Off We Go . . . Again[1]
Cairo, Egypt, March 18, 2005

Once more Yousuf and I have braved the labyrinths of Rafah crossing, with all that entails of hours upon hours of waiting in cramped buses surrounded by occupation soldiers who never fail to remind you who's in charge. Of course, to Yousuf it was just another journey of the many he has taken—and the soldiers who control our lives behind the glass screens other faces to giggle at.

Anyhow—we made it safely to Cairo after 14 hours. And tonight we depart to Beirut (we are both excited that this entails an airplane, as opposed to three buses, four taxis, two donkey carts, and endless hours of uncertain waits that preceded our arrival here). In addition to doing some reporting on the condition of the Palestinian refugees in Lebanon, and on the current political events there, we will meet up with Yassine, who is ever so anxious to see his little trouble-making baby incredible. Yousuf has absolutely exhausted every iota of sanity I thought I had left in me. The boy is a human Energizer bunny—may God protect him.

To Baalbeck, and Beyond![2]
Baalbek, Lebanon, March 21, 2005

So, it finally happened. Yousuf (and I) met Yassine's family for the first time, as we journeyed to his refugee camp in Baalbek, deep in the heart of Lebanon's Beqaa Valley. As we arrived, Syrian forces that controlled the area for more than 29 years began to depart to the Syrian border, not far from where we were.

As for Yousuf: Suffice to say, you can sure take the boy out of the refugee camp,

but you can't take the refugee camp out of the boy. Yousuf found his flock, and boy did he fly. As the Arabic saying goes, "He is a pot that found its cover." It wasn't long before baby incredible was waddling his way around Wavel's winding alleyways, making friends with everyone (i.e., the butcher, the baker, and the Internet café owner—and yes, there are Internet café's in refugee camps—illegal, but that's another story), and getting to know his new (and many, I might add) aunts, uncles, and cousins.

And of course, one of the highlights of our still-nascent trip: Yousuf finally got his hair cut!! It involved lots of tears (and an equal amount of hair—boy are those billowy curls deceiving) but the results were well worth it—I found my little boy again!

Trouble at the (Syrian) Border[3]
Damascus, Syria, May 5, 2005

We're on the move again, this time to Syria. For a moment (well, I'll be honest, it was more like nine hours of moments), we didn't think we were going to get through (seems like a running theme by now, doesn't it?). Yousuf had an Israeli stamp in his passport from the first time he traveled to Gaza with me (when he was 2 months old, no less) certifying that his mother has Palestinian residency and that she would add him to her *hawiya*, or identity card (that's the Israeli way of keeping track of their cows).

The Syrians wouldn't have it.

"It's not an Israeli visa," I tried to explain. "What fault is it of ours that we are under occupation? In order to enter Gaza, I have to pass through Israeli border control."

But logic has no place in Syria, where the government purports to be an Arab nationalist party yet denies Palestinians the right to visit.

After approximately nine hours of waiting in the bitter mountain cold, lots of pleading, shaming, finger pointing, and a number of phone calls to a matrix of Syrian security agencies, we were allowed through. Yassine was on edge and very worried I'd be thrown into a Syrian prison. I already live in one large prison, I told him, think I'm used to it.

Incidentally, we left for Syria alongside masses of Syrian military vehicles withdrawing from Lebanon as per Resolution 1559.[4]

Safeguarding Palestine's Past[5]
Tyre, Lebanon, May 7, 2005 (reported in March 2005), *Al Jazeera English*

Hidden away in a squalid Palestinian refugee camp is a historical treasure trove that keeps the dreams of many alive.

In a corner of the Palestinian refugee camp of Mashook in southern Lebanon, 68-year-old Muhammad Dakwar shows the way into a dusky two-room gallery that he guards with his life.

Inside, ragged pieces of traditional Palestinian garments hang on thin metal racks; decades-old clay pottery and copper plates are neatly arranged on shelves amid a mélange of traditional Palestinian household items.

Rustically preserved samples of Palestinian earth—soil, rocks, and olive tree branches—are displayed on poster boards, crudely taped and labelled according to city or village of origin.

All are part of what Dakwar says is the only Palestinian museum in exile, and by some estimates, the only Palestinian heritage museum in the world.

Personal sacrifice

Dakwar, a retired school teacher with UNRWA (the UN Relief and Works Agency for Palestine Refugees in the Near East), founded the museum 15 years ago and has run it at his own expense ever since, refusing to charge any entry fee to visitors. It is a cause that has driven him near to the point of financial ruin.

Most of the items in the museum have been generous gifts from Palestinians and philanthropists the world over, but many are purchased out of Dakwar's own pocket.

"I've spent my entire retirement bonus to keep the museum running. I am almost broke, but I am prepared to beg in order to keep this museum open to the public," he says, admitting he has had to shut down the museum's website due to the lack of funds.

The museum was established in 1989, but not officially recognised by the Lebanese government until eight years later . . .

It is also a treasure trove of Palestinian currency used during the British mandate, and coins from as far back as the Roman period. The gallery also includes a library with more than 10,000 books and journals, many of them rare editions . . .Dakwar insists on using the year 1948—the date of the Palestinian Nakba, or catastrophe—as a benchmark for dating items on display.

"This is no coincidence, to centre the museum around 1948," he explains eruditely. "I want to make sure people forever remember this date and what it means for Palestinians. This is part of the museum's purpose."

Palestine partitioned

In 1948, Jews declared their state in Palestine after the United Nations voted to partition Palestine, and hundreds of thousands of Palestinians were made homeless and forced to flee in the process, their villages subsequently destroyed or depopulated.

Dakwar was one such refugee, hailing from the Palestinian village of Qadeetha near the city of Safad.

He sought refuge in Lebanon with his family at the tender age of 11. His village was depopulated by Israel in the aftermath of the 1948 war. The museum and Dakwar's refugee camp are only 15km away from the border of his Palestine.

On clear mornings from high rooftops in the camp, one can see the Palestinian town of al-Naqura, not far from his own village.

But the distance may as well be 50,000km away. As a refugee, Dakwar is denied the right to return to his home.

And so he has made it his mission in life to preserve Palestine in his refuge away from home, something he regards as his personal contribution to the Palestinian struggle.

He hopes one day to gift the museum to Palestine—when there is a Palestinian government he trusts enough to take care of it, he says.

For now, it will remain an exhibit in exile for Lebanon's some 400,000 Palestinian refugees, "so they will never forget where they came from, and to where they hope to one day return."

It's a Bird, It's a Plane . . . It's an Israeli Apache[6]
Gaza City, Palestine, May 18, 2005

You know things ain't right when a child has become so accustomed to warplanes that he confuses them with birds.

Today we went to my father's farm, and on the way we stopped by a local *souk* in the central Gaza Strip. I bought Yousuf two little chicks to play with. (They later died, I'm sorry to say . . . though through no fault of my little chick-choker, thank you very much.) He chased after them gleefully, waving his hands, screaming "*Jaja! Jaja!*" ("Chicken! Chicken!"). . . . I can only imagine the fear that overtook those poor birds, rest their souls.

Later that evening Israeli helicopter gunships appeared overhead from the nearby Netzerim settlement, on their way to attack Palestinian fighters in Khan Yunis. I didn't notice until Yousuf began pointing to the sky, asking (confirming?) "*Jaja? Jaja?*" *sigh* . . . How do you explain this one to a 1-year-old?

Chips and Charcoal . . . Not a Good Combination[7]
Gaza City, Palestine, May 22, 2005

The other day, one of my editors sent me an e-mail asking me how I do it—being a mommy and a journalist who's practically on call 24 hours a day. Sometimes I wonder that same thing myself, I told him—usually around the time I'm conducting an important interview on the phone and Yousuf crawls onto my lap, pulls up my shirt, and starts uncontrollably chirping "*Azzah, azzah!*" (Translation: "Boobie, boobie!")

It's been particularly challenging this week because my parents are out of town for 10 days so I'm watching Yousuf on my own. Today, in between the phone ringing off the hook and my trying to get a story in on time, Yousuf popped open a bag of chips, and found his way to a box of quick-lighting charcoal. Everything became black and salty within the span of five minutes. And they say the Israeli army has an enormous destructive potential . . .

Relax, You're under Occupation[8]
Gaza City, Palestine, June 2, 2005

After a brief five-day visit to the Egyptian border town of al-Arish, we are back in Gaza. Yousuf and I left rather suddenly to meet up with my parents and my brother Tariq, who had come from the U.S. for a brief visit. He was afraid if he came across the border to Gaza, he'd get stuck due to an Israeli travel ban on Palestinian men and boys between the ages of 16 and 35 from leaving the Strip.

So once again Yousuf and I tackled the nightmare that is Rafah crossing (or, as a remade signpost mockingly renamed, the "Rafah border tourist resort"). Leaving wasn't so bad. And the three days we spent in a rental on the beach were incredibly relaxing. Coming back though, was a blast (no pun intended).

The highlight of the return journey (besides having to change Yousuf's poopy diaper on an open sidewalk with inept Egyptian soldiers behind me and Israeli tanks in front of me) was a conversation I had with an Israeli soldier after four hours of waiting in a bus crammed to capacity.

It went something like this:

MY MOTHER: Why are you making my husband wait for so long while you search a small carry-on bag?

SOLDIER: It's for your protection. What if there was a bomb in there?

MY MOTHER: Has there ever, in all the time you've been here, been a bomb smuggled into luggage on the crossing??
[Silence]

SOLDIER: Why are you so angry? Aren't you comfortable here on the Israeli side? Its air-conditioned you know.

ME: You do realize we just spent four hours in a decrepit, un-air-condtioned bus with a 14-month-old baby?

SOLDIER: Yes, but that's not our fault, we would never subject you to such conditions here on the Israeli side. Here, you can relax.

ME: Are you aware that the reason we wait in that horrible bus in the blazing heat for hours on end is because you so command it? We aren't allowed out of the bus, or through to the Israeli side, or even to crack a window open, until the Egyptians get your approval.

SOLDIER: Oh . . .

ME: And isn't it true that on certain days, when it suits your fancy, you let as many buses as you can through as quickly as possible, but on other days, like today, you let the people suffer and marinate in there?

SOLDIER: That's true . . .

ME: Why???

Soldier: I really don't know.

Soldier's superior [in **Hebrew**]: Come here and stop talking to her. And tell her to get off the search table she's sitting on. It's not proper.

Soldier: He says to get off the search table. He says, "It's not proper."

Me: *Not proper???* Where do I begin with what's "not proper"? Is making 100 sick children, elderly folks, men, women, and infants wait in a 60-seat bus for four hours without allowing them out for air proper???
[Laila walks away irate, chasing after Yousuf, who has made a game out of the baggage conveyor.]

End of conversation.

Israeli Road Signs Remade[9]
Gaza City, Palestine, June 12, 2005

Okay, this is by far the most original piece of political resistance I've seen here: A group of activists changed a number of Israeli road signs on a major highway leading to illegal settlements to reflect the "political realities on the ground." An excerpt from my *Al Jazeera* coverage of the event:

> A sign pointing to Ariel, the largest settlement in the northern West Bank, built on land belonging to the Palestinian villagers of Salfit, now marks the way in Hebrew, Arabic and English to "stolen land."
>
> Another sign that indicates the distance to Ariel from an Israeli checkpoint 12km away reminds drivers of the ongoing occupation and of the separation wall being built around Palestinian towns. "1967: Occupation; 2005: Apartheid Wall in Salfit" read the signs.
>
> Signs of Truth, a group of Israeli and international activists acting in solidarity with local Palestinians, altered the signs on Saturday to coincide with the 38th anniversary of the occupation of the West Bank and Gaza Strip in 1967.[10]

And Life Goes On . . .[11]
Gaza City, Palestine, June 18, 2005

There is nothing quite like summer in Gaza, when the Strip's million and a half some Palestinians head to the beach, their only outlet under this collective prison they call home. It is a perplexing scene, at once heartrending and uplifting.

Shabab donning greasy hairdos, look-cool shades, and European-style jeans, occasionally accessorized with a Palestinian *Kaffiya*, strut their stuff as they keep a subtle eye out for the girls. Woman (*abayas* and all), men, and children all submerged at once as the wild Gaza Mediterranean swallows and regurgitates them time and again.

Vendors trying to make a living, whether by way of selling chips, candied apples, roasted sweet potatoes, summer corn (Israeli and *baladi*), and even *mulukhiya* leaves, all on local horse-drawn carts. Ponies, camels, and Arabian stallions. Children making games out of an empty cola bottle and a piece of string, or flying their dreams on handmade kites, which crowd the lonely Gaza sky. A persistent windsurfer, ignoring the lifeguards' futile pleas to mind the current and waves today.

In the background, the dull thud of home-made mortars can be heard landing in a nearby settlement, in retaliation, we would later learn, for the beating and shooting that four Palestinians, enjoying what would have otherwise been a similar afternoon on the beach, took from extreme-right Jewish settlers. For Gaza's Palestinians, life goes on.

Sunset in Gaza[12]
Gaza City, Palestine, June 19, 2005

"Take me to the beach at sunset, so I may hear what the beach says; when it returns to itself quietly, calmly."
—Mahmud Darwish

A Room with a View, Please[13]
Gaza City, Palestine, June 22, 2005

It's interesting to read the news from this perspective. I mean, when you are the news, or when you are living the news that is being reported, and while all the while you write the news.

On Monday I visited the Khan Yunis refugee camp, the target of many an attack by Israeli forces, to talk to Palestinian refugees there, to hear their thoughts on Israeli disengagement (the subject of a forthcoming article).

It was quite an incongruous—and bleak—scene, as is often the case in Gaza. Crumbling refugee homes with pockmarks the size of apples stand like carcasses in front of the Neve Dekalim settlement, part of the Gush settlement bloc. It is shaded with palm trees, red-roofed Mediterranean-style villas, and the unspoiled pristine sands of the Khan Yunis beach, accessible to all but the Palestinians now.

Abo Ahmed is one of the refugees I met. The view from the second floor of his home on the edge of the camp overlooking Neve Dekalim, and an Israeli sniper tower, is to die for (no pun intended). The military base aside, there is nothing but the clear blue of the lonely Khan Yunis Mediterranean. "Nice view, right?" he told me jokingly, the wall behind him pockmarked like a piece of Swiss cheese from the hundreds of Israeli shells and bullets that have hit it. "One of those holes could have been in me." It was the first time Abo Ahmed has been able to enjoy this view since he built this house a few years ago.

His neighbor's children, living under a zinc sheet covered with torn blankets, giggled when they saw me. "Please take our picture," asked a little girl, Siham. So I did. Maybe it would help them forget the daily reality they face, that children should never have to face. Overhead, a drone whirred menacingly, and a helicopter gunship cruised the coast. "See those planes, they come and shoot missiles at us," they explained expertly. Planes they have seen too many times before. War has been their teacher.

Nearby, a group of Palestinians who live in the Mawasi enclave—completed sealed off from the rest of Gaza by Israeli forces—sat under the shade of a hand-made palm-leaf canopy waiting for the Tufah checkpoint to open, so they could return home. A day before, three of Mawasi's residents were brutally beaten by Jewish settlers from the Gush bloc.

Meanwhile, the children trotted off into the horizon, dangerously close to the Israeli sniper tower, trying to fly a rustic paper kite one of the older boys folded together. Next to them, a group of boys cooled off in a pool of salty wastewater that pours into a sand pit here from the settlements, the byproduct of an Israeli desalination plant. This is their playground. Soon, the Israelis call the Palestinian District Coordination Office (DCO) to warn them off.

On my way to Gaza City, I would learn that 17-year-old Iyad al-Nabaheen was shot dead by Israeli snipers as he was catching birds with his friend north of the Breij refugee camp. I couldn't help but think that could have been Siham. Or one of the other boys wading in the water. Or my own son, Yousuf. But Iyad's death didn't make the news anywhere. His obituary could be found in the seventh or eighth paragraph of an article talking about an attempted female suicide bombing at Erez, and the killing of an Israeli settler in the West Bank. Rest in peace, Iyad. May your soul fly higher than little Siham's kite.

Palestinians Keep Dream of Return Alive[14]
Gaza and Lebanon, June 24, 2005, *Al Jazeera English*

Um Muneer Utoor fought back tears through wistful eyes as she told of a dream in which she was returning home to Palestine.

In it, the 67-year-old refugee was going back to her house just behind a young almond tree on a small, breezy hill in the village of Jish.

"Just the way I remember it when I was little," she recalled. And for a moment, Um Muneer's eyes were not so sad.

Then she woke up.

"It was so real. After 57 years in exile, I was finally returning home."

Um Muneer, who is known in Arabic as the mother of Muneer, one of two sons who were killed in the region's wars, left Jish with her family in 1948, terrorised by massacres by Israeli forces in Palestinian villages, including her own.

The family sought refuge with thousands of fellow Palestinians in southern Lebanon. From there, they moved to a camp in Aleppo, Syria, then to Beirut's Burj al-Barajneh camp, and finally to Baalbeck's Wavell camp, popularly known as al-Jaleel (Galilee), where she lives today.

Like Um Muneer, about 400,000 Palestinian refugees in Lebanon and 4 million throughout the Arab world dream of returning to their homes in Palestine.

Rising numbers

According to the United Nations High Commissioner for Refugees, the world's refugee population has declined by 4 percent to 9.2 million this year, the lowest total in almost a quarter of a century.

But the number of Palestinian refugees like Um Muneer, who are not included in UNHCR statistics, continues to rise in the absence of a real solution to their plight.

Fifty-seven years ago, about 750,000 Palestinians were forced from their homes by Jewish forces, seeking refuge in Syria, Lebanon, Jordan, Egypt, and in what would later become the Gaza Strip and West Bank. Most of their villages were destroyed as part of official Israeli policy.

Today, the number of Palestinian refugees is equivalent to one-third of the world's refugee population.

Lebanese camps

While they no longer reside in tents, the situation of Palestinian refugees is abysmal, and the conditions in conflict-strewn Lebanon are the worst of the lot.

Their camps are effectively ghettos, "large group prisons" as one Lebanese politician put it, with winding, narrow alleyways, wall-to-wall cement block shelters, seeping sewers, and leaky zinc-sheet rooftops.

Camps are crowded, and a lack of public electricity and polluted drinking water are constant health hazards.

Lebanon has the highest percentage of Palestinian refugees who are living in abject poverty and who are registered under the United Nations Relief and Works Agency for Palestine Refugees (UNRWA) "special hardship" program.

Improvements stopped

But Lebanese authorities have vetoed the reconstruction of camp housing, and until recently the UNRWA had largely frozen funding improvement of the camps, leading many of the refugees to say they are neglected and to stage protests on 20 June, the UN's World Refugee Day, which is marked this month.

Hoda Samra, public information officer for Lebanon's UNRWA field office, said that since 2003, the UNRWA has stepped up its role in the camps. "UNRWA has not frozen its funding for infrastructure in the camps, rather the contrary. The agency is implementing since 2003 a major environmental health project in five out of the 12 camps in Lebanon funded by the European Union in the amount of 8.75 million euros. It includes construction of sewerage and storm water drainage systems and provision of safe and adequate quantities of water," she told AlJazeera.net.

But for Lebanon's refugees, the issue is not merely one of basic survival needs.

They lack physical security, freedom of movement, and access to government services, such as health care and education. They are denied the right to work in dozens of professions by Lebanese authorities, to receive social security, or to own or inherit property.

Third generation

Abdullah Kayed, 23, is one such refugee. His family was forced to flee in 1948 from their village of Lubya in Northern Palestine.

Unlike Um Muneer, Kayed is a third-generation refugee and has never set foot in Palestine. Nevertheless, he demands his right to return.

"If I were given the option, I would definitely return to Palestine. Why? Because it is my country—Lebanon will never be my country. We never knew Palestine, but it has always been in our hearts."

Though a recent graduate of pharmacology, Kayed has been unemployed for almost a year.

"Even if we were naturalised, and the [Lebanese] government gave us our complete civil rights, I would not want to live here. It's about the principles. It's about our right to return home," said Kayed.

Representation

Palestinian refugees in Lebanon complain that they have no official to represent them in negotiations, though there are a number of non-governmental organizations that work to further their cause.

Ali Hweidi is the London-based Palestine Return Center's representative in Lebanon and a Palestinian refugee himself. Like others, he calls on the Lebanese government to ease civil and political restrictions on Palestinians. "The very least that we demand from the Lebanese government is to provide us with our basic civil rights, which are non-existent for Palestinians in Lebanon, so we can fight for our right to return to Palestine, not for our ability to survive," he says from his office in the Bus refugee camp in southern Lebanon.

One of the problems facing refugees is that they can't expand their living space horizontally, Hweidi says.

"Keep in mind that the number of refugees in Lebanon has increased by more than 300 percent since 1948, and this has clear social ramifications. As the number of refugees grows, the space to house them in diminishes," he said.

The walls of his office, like most refugee households here, are plastered with maps of historic Palestine, labeled with the lost villages of 1948.

"In every house you will find something that reminds you of Palestine: A map, a key, a title deed," he says, waving a copy of a key from one of his camp's elders and pointing out framed copies of original title deeds to lands in Palestine belonging to refugees in the Ain al-Hilweh camp a few kilometers away.

Right of return

Hweidi said that establishing peace in the region is inextricably linked to the refugees' right of return.

"The refugee problem has an immense humanitarian and political horizon," he said.

"But we refuse to accept other options, such as naturalization or being sent to a third country."

Hweidi is uncertain about what's to come, but he is certain that a solution must be found.

"I can't say I have an accurate scenario for what will happen, but what I do know is that while it is our future at stake, we will not be given a choice in it. They deal with us as if we are things, not human beings. There has been no consultation with us so far, and no formal representative assigned us.

"But so long as there is justice, we are hopeful a solution will be found."

The Crushed Citizen[15]
Gaza City, Palestine, July 1, 2005

I was invited to attend a reception in Ramallah last month by my former scholarship sponsors, the Academy for Educational Development. They said they'd take care of the permit, though no guarantees were made. A few days ago I received word my permit was one of several that were approved. "Congratulations, you're going to Ramallah."

I am excited—it's been four years since I've been to Ramallah. Though it is only an hour away, permits are rarely, if ever, issued to Gazan Palestinians wishing to travel to the West Bank, let alone those between the ages of 16 and 35. I call up all my friends, relatives, and colleagues there. I even wonder if I can make it to Jerusalem on Friday. We leave early Thursday, around 7 a.m., from Gaza City. In the van, the other girls I'm traveling with joke, share anecdotes about their time in America.

As we approach Erez, the ruckus dies down, turns into hushed whispers. "What's that?" asks one girl, who hasn't been to Erez in several years. "It's a tank, silly," responds another bluntly.

We enter Erez, popularly known as the cow pen here for the kilometer-long, fenced-in corridor that passengers must walk through to pass through to the other side. We are forbidden from entering the Israeli side without first receiving approval from the Israelis, via walkie talkie to the Palestinian DCO. It is all part of Gaza's invisible occupation. We wait, and one hour turns into two, then three, then four.

There are people waiting in different groups, for different reasons. Some wait for approval to enter and visit their loved ones in Israeli jails. Others to receive medical treatment. There are also foreign journalists and humanitarian aid workers attempting to make it through to Gaza. Israel has increasingly made this difficult for them. Oftentimes they are denied entry, with the footnote, "It's for your own protection."

As we sit, we discuss Gaza, and the complete hopelessness of people there that always seems to be highlighted on borders. One of the girls recalls a caricature in a magazine she read growing up called the "the Crushed Citizen"—a scrawny, balding man, hunched over, head facing the ground, dejected, demoralized. "That's what we are in Gaza now, crushed citizens," she said. "Completely powerless, hopeless, impoverished—everything is against us."

A Palestinian officer approaches and calls out names that Israelis have denied entry. "Don't ask me why your permit was refused, it just was. Israelis don't give reasons, it's all in the name of security," he tells the crowd of anxious Palestinians. "Samhiri, Ahmed, Hillis, El-Haddad . . . "

"Why am I not surprised?" I tell one of the girls. It's not the first time I've been denied entry to the West Bank. The officer suggests I try to make some inquiries, so I make a few calls, and re-submit my ID card to the Palestinian DCO. The rest of the group is given the go-ahead and proceeds to the Israeli side, then to Ramallah.

After several more hours of waiting, surrounded by barbed wire, empty cola cans, and in the horizon, the land that I cannot reach, I learn that there is in fact no permit—at least that's what the Israelis say. The American who applied on my behalf insists it was approved. "It's probably their way of justifying your denial of entry, don't worry about it" she assures me.

I call an Israeli friend with some connections. He makes a few calls and ends up with the same answer: There is no permit. "As a Jew, I am sorry for this," he says.

I later learn that my permit was first approved, then, upon reaching a higher security authority in Erez, was rejected—I figure since you can't deny something that has already been approved, they made up an explanation for how it went missing (the only rational way to explain how it could be there, but not there, at the same time). Then, logic has no place in the Israeli security matrix, I think to myself.

Exhausted, hungry, and a little bit "crushed," I return to Gaza. Home sweet home, of 1.5 million crushed citizens.

CHAPTER NOTES

1. The full original text of this post is archived at http://www.gazamom. com/2005/03/and-off-we-go-again/, shortened to http://bit.ly/ayop41.
2. Archived at http://bit.ly/c7ACwQ.
3. Archived at http://bit.ly/bVrzyD.
4. UN Security Council Resolution 1559, passed in early September 2004, called for the withdrawal of Syrian troops from Lebanon.
5. Laila El-Haddad, "Safeguarding Palestine's Past," *Al Jazeera English*, May 7, 2005, archived at http://bit.ly/cmfBqy.
6. Archived at http://bit.ly/cCcJRo.
7. Archived at http://bit.ly/cD2EGD.
8. Archived at http://bit.ly/bNBlyH.
9. Archived at http://bit.ly/9jEwRS.
10. Laila El-Haddad, "Israeli Signs Get Activist Makeover," *Al Jazeera English*, June 5, 2005, archived at http://bit.ly/bBL4rp.
11. Archived at http://bit.ly/8YjZf3.
12. Archived at http://bit.ly/ajOwNd.
13. Archived at http://bit.ly/bwFHl4.
14. Laila El-Haddad, "Palestinians Keep Dream of Return Alive," *Al Jazeera English*, June 5, 2005, archived at http://bit.ly/bBYSb5.
15. Archived at http://bit.ly/bbSAop.

Chapter 3

A Long Hot Summer in Gaza

Mid-July 2005

This chapter is about (largely Israeli-imposed) suffering and its many manifestations—mental, physical, psychosocial. It covers the beginning of the Palestinian lawlessness and factional infighting that would culminate in June 2007. But it is also about the resilience of people under occupation, who make their happiness under the toughest and most intrusive of circumstances.

For much of this period, there was also a tenuous unilateral Palestinian-initiated cease-fire. The situation was relatively calm as Israeli Prime Minister Ariel Sharon's government prepared for its unilateral disengagement from Gaza.

Sharon had first announced his disengagement plan at the 2004 Herzliya Conference. (It included plans for an economic disengagement from Gaza as well.) The Israeli government officially adopted it on June 6, 2004, and preparations for it were well underway by the end of this chapter. Palestinians on all levels, including governmental, were meanwhile kept largely in the dark about the details, and the vast majority did not how the disengagement would unfold until it was over.

Interview with the Settler[1]
Gaza City, Palestine, July 7, 2005

Before leaving for his six-week vacation (that's right, six weeks! I didn't even know six-week vacations existed anymore!), my editor at *Al Jazeera* begged me to look into writing an article from the Gaza settlements. Of course, seeing as how this is physically impossible, due to Jewish-only Israeli access (see: Apartheid) laws, unless I tunneled my way in, I did some research and came up with a settler I could interview by phone instead. His name is Avi Farhan; he is originally from Libya;

he founded a settlement in Sinai before it was evacuated, then founded Eli Sinai ("Towards Sinai") in Gaza, and now says he wants to become a Palestinian citizen. Interested? Confused? Read on. Here's an excerpt:

> **FARHAN:** All I want to do is remain, as a Jewish settler, in Eli Sinai in Gaza, just like Palestinians who live in the Um al-Fahem in Israel.
>
> **ME:** Um al-Fahem is a Palestinian village. Eli Sinai is an illegal colony built on occupied land.
>
> **FARHAN:** We are a village, too. The word "settlement" is merely a lexicon—just a figure of speech. It just means settling down in one place. It's not the way the world is saying—that we conquered the territory. They made it into a negative word. Um al-Fahem is a settlement just like Eli Sinai.
>
> **ME:** Israeli settlements are racist by their very nature—only Israeli Jews can live there. Palestinians from Gaza cannot live there. On the other hand, you can live in Um al-Fahem.
>
> **FARHAN:** I can't even walk by Um al-Fahem—I'll get shot.
>
> **ME:** Theoretically speaking . . .
>
> **FARHAN:** A few hundred meters away from me, there are Arabs living here. But there still isn't enough goodwill for them to live inside the settlement. I'm sorry to see things this way, but it's not a one-sided problem.

If you'd like a laugh (or are just really interested in what settlers have to say), my complete interview with Eli Sinai ("Towards Sinai") leader Avi Farhan was published by *Al Jazeera English*.[2] Farhan insists he ain't moving from Gaza, even if that means becoming a Palestinian citizen. Of course, the interview is also riddled with contradictions—he insists all this land is God-given to the Jews, including Sinai, yet he goes on to say it's 2005 and things have changed now—for the Palestinians.

Ordinary Lives, Extraordinary Circumstances[3]
Gaza City, Palestine, July 8, 2005

At long last—my new camera has arrived, via a friend of mine who came from the U.S. to the West Bank, and from her to another French friend who works for Medecins du Monde and was kind enough to bring it over from Jerusalem (things ain't so easy when you are a prisoner in Gaza).

In case I didn't mention it before, my other camera broke (according to the fellow who tried in vain to fix it, it took one too many falls . . . *oops* . . . between

Yousuf and me, and countless trips to Rafah and Jabaliya . . . I can see how). I have been trying to take more pictures of life in Gaza . . . of regular people living ordinary lives under extraordinary circumstances (of course, this means many quizzical looks from passersby: "Hello . . . hello? You are foreign?" "No, no . . . she is Gazan."). Meandering about, taking random pictures of people on the beach, in the souk, etc., isn't so simple here.

Pat the Bunny[4]
Gaza City, Palestine, July 11, 2005

Yousuf has picked up a new, nasty habit: He has taken to swatting me ferociously with his hand at every available opportunity, and he seems to enjoy it. I wanted to pinpoint the source of his questionable habit du jour—was life in Gaza finally getting to him, is a therapist already in order (for this, and his vacuum-cleaner phobia), or was he mimicking something he saw?

As I mulled over the problem in his play corner, I saw him punch a large, freakish pink bunny with glowing red eyes he received as a gift for his first birthday. (Why someone would design such a bunny for a child is another story.) The bunny, in theory, is supposed to sing a nice song when you move it. Instead, what you get is the indiscernible voice of a child singing in a language which I have concluded to be a mélange of Chinese and Arabic slang.

"Not like that Yousuf," I explained calmly, in Arabic. "Gently rub its tummy . . . pat the bunny . . . er . . . like this . . . "

bam bam bam!

Suffice to say, I think I see where the problem is now. It's the bunny. That's right—there is a violent bunny in our midst. A bunny that teaches children to hit it to get what they want. The bunny, in essence, rewards violent behavior. Am I beginning to sound like a certain occupation army?

The moral of the story is that, contrary to popular belief, Palestinians do not teach—nor encourage—their children to be violent. Tanks, armored bulldozers, Apaches, and, occasionally, deranged pink bunnies do that for us.

Chaos and Uncertainty in Gaza[5]
Gaza City, Palestine, July 16, 2005

It was all-out chaos in Gaza City yesterday, as factional infighting claimed the lives of three teenage boys after drawn-out battles between security forces and Hamas activists in northern Gaza spread to the city (just a street down from my house), keeping most residents indoors on Friday, and Israeli helicopter gunships left six Hamas men dead.

Within the span of 24 hours, it seemed like all hell had broken loose here, and things reverted back to the way they were five months ago: The Strip has been split into three, dividing families all over; Rafah crossing, an official just told me, has been once again sealed off to Palestinian men and boys between the ages of 16 and 35; and tanks are amassing near Jabaliya, preparing for an offensive.

In the midst of all this, my family and I went out to visit and congratulate a cousin of mine who passed his *Tawjihi* exams, and Yousuf got a chance to play with the ducks and geese they keep in their backyard (childhood . . . eh?). Their house is located a block over from the site of yesterday's assassination. The streets were eerily empty, save for Palestinian police officers attempting to "keep the peace," cordoning off certain streets and directing traffic. Smoke from burning tires, which is said to "blind" the all-seeing eye of the unmanned Israeli drone, filled the air, a practice usually reserved for refugee camps, and the site of Israeli offensives, like Jabaliya and Rafah.

Today, in scenes reminiscent of a few months ago, funeral processions for yesterday's victims were held. Thousands of Palestinians marched through the streets from different factions in a show of solidarity, as Hamas activists vowed revenge by way of more Qassam rockets on the settlements.

Analysts and officials I've spoken to insist the "truce" (if this is a truce . . .) is not in tatters, and that neither side, strategically speaking, will want to officially abandon it. At the same time, neither side is defining its "red line." It's simply easier to be vague, politically speaking, I guess.

We can only wait and see what will happen tonight.

Lawlessness at Midnight[6]
Gaza City, Palestine, July 16, 2005

A quick post on the situation before I head to bed: It's a bit crazy here. Fateh people, from what I can tell, *shabab* with nothing better to do, are out on the main city streets in a show of force, banging their rifles every which way, in response to yesterday's incidents.

I'm crawling into bed and suddenly I hear the all-too-familiar darts of bullets spraying into the air. I look out the kitchen window (note to self: Never look out glass window when Fateh men are firing haphazardly) and see several hundred Fateh men marching down the street, chanting "*kata'ib*" in reference to the Fateh-linked al-Aqsa Martyrs' Brigades.

OK, now the rundown: No idea why (1) they chose midnight to do this, (2) they are endangering innocent bystanders' lives with their emotions run wild (though perhaps they may argue that is why they chose midnight . . .), and (3) the police, under the auspices of the Ministry of the Interior, are not doing anything about this but are all-too-anxious to shoot at Hamas folks.

Just today, a spokesperson for the Ministry assured me that "no one is above the law," which they would enforce equally, without discrimination or hesitation. My take on it is that there are simply *way* too many unlicensed weapons on Gaza's streets. I mean, anyone who's no one can get hold of a gun.

There's something rather unsettling about a lot of fed-up, stressed-out people locked in a 350-square-mile open-air prison with a bunch of guns in their hands. Let's not even talk about road rage. And by the way, all of these are real psychosocial implications of the occupation, according to a Gaza psychiatrist I interviewed in late 2003. That article is right below here.

Intifada Takes Physical and Mental Toll[7]
Gaza City, Palestine, December 6, 2003, *Al Jazeera English*

As the Intifada enters its fourth year, scant attention has been given to the thousands of Palestinians who have been injured and handicapped for life.

Little notice has been given to the long-term physical, mental, and social health effects of this ravaging conflict, particularly on children and young adults.

An estimated 30,000 Palestinians have been injured during the second Intifada.

According to the Red Crescent, initial studies indicate that nearly 5,000 of these have shifted from the category of injured to that of temporarily or permanently handicapped.

In al-Wafa Medical Rehabilitation Hospital, the only hospital in Gaza with in-patient services for the disabled and a meagre 50 beds, the scene is grim.

Some, such as Rifat Shaeir, 45, have no more future to speak of.

Rifat has been comatose since he was hit by a tank shell on his way to the Rafah middle school in the occupied Gaza Strip where he used to teach.

The tank shell took off half of his skull and a portion of his brain. He had left behind seven children and an unemployed wife.

"His family used to visit him every day, but now they hardly come once a week because of the costs of travel.

"For them, it comes down to deciding whether they want to use this money for visiting their father or for buying food," said Dr. Khamis al-Essi, director of the hospital.

Others, like Abd al-Rahman Tayyam, 15, count themselves amongst the lucky.

Tayyam had to have his leg amputated after being injured in a massive Israeli air attack against the Nusseirat refugee camp last month. The heads of the Israeli army later admitted to concealing the types of munitions used in the strike.

Ramzi Attaf, 20, took two 8mm bullets to the head in Rafah during the Israeli incursion of the camp in October and is now wheelchair-bound and missing part of his skull.

Shooting to kill

According to al-Essi, 70 percent of the patients treated here are 15 to 29 years old, and more than 75 percent of the injuries are located in the upper part of the body.

"This demonstrates that the goal of the Israelis is not merely to disable, but to kill. They are shooting with a purpose to kill," he said.

Most of the patients that come in to the hospital suffer from severe spinal cord injuries and are now paraplegic. Al-Essi attributes this to the type of bullet being used, which shatters the target upon contact.

Huda Naem Darwish, 12, was shot in the head while sitting in her classroom in Rafah. A CT scan revealed metallic fragments in her brain at the point of impact. Darwish suffered a severe brain injury and is now blind.

"During this Intifada, the types of disabilities are more varied and more severe," said al-Essi.

"We have patients with multiple injuries . . . spinal and internal organ damage for example . . . so we face difficulties in classifying their injuries."

Surviving the odds

According to al-Essi, al-Wafa was not operational in the last Intifada.

"Most patients were forced to stay at home, or if they were lucky enough to have a contact in the government, they could go to the West Bank for treatment. There was not a single hospital in Gaza to deal with the disabled."

From the start of the Intifada until now, the hospital has managed to treat 206 Intifada victims in its inpatient clinic and 188 others in its outpatient clinics.

Due to frequent closures between the northern and southern ends of the Gaza Strip, many patients in Rafah and Khan Yunis—areas most affected by the conflict—have been unable to receive the vital services they need.

As a result, the hospital has established two satellite clinics and two outreach programs that work with the patients in their homes. Approximately 2,270 patients have been treated in these clinics.

Psychosocial deterioration

In addition to the physically disabled, the Intifada has resulted in a vast number of psychosocial debilitations, according to Dr. Taysir Diab, of the Gaza Community Mental Health Program.

Diab says he has seen an increase in post-traumatic stress disorder, bed-wetting, anxiety disorders, depression, and drug abuse as well as domestic and physical violence.

"I believe the Intifada is leading to the deterioration in the psychosocial status of our people. I also think there are immeasurable long-term effects especially in terms of mental illnesses, but also on the level of a new generation regarding their models of conflict resolution."

"A lot of people have developed disorders [and] the behavior of people in the street reflects this—people shout at each other for no reason and are easily provoked and there a general situation of stress," said Diab.

He says children particularly have been affected.

According to a report published by Diab earlier this year, about two in three children have seen a family member being injured or killed, 95 percent of children have witnessed funerals, and 83 percent have witnessed shootings.

Such exposure to traumatic events, said Diab, had created an alarming increase in post-traumatic stress disorder—or PTSD—symptoms in children. Some 82 percent of children interviewed for the study suffered from acute or moderate levels of PTSD.

Setbacks

Rabah Jabir, director of the Palestinian Red Crescent Society's Rehabilitation Department, said handicapped Palestinians in general—pre- and post-Intifada—had suffered serious setbacks because of the military occupation.

"More important than the injuries themselves is the negative impact the Intifada has had on the ability of the handicapped to get to rehabilitation centers," said Jabir.

"A large number of patients, especially in the remote areas of Hebron and Nablus, are unable to get to rehabilitation centres in the cities because of the curfews, sieges, and checkpoints," said Jabir.

Unlike its predecessor, this Intifada brought with it severe economic strain and suffering, he said. When it comes to deciding between food and treatment, physical rehabilitation was the clear loser.

"If they had to choose between paying 20 shekels [$4.50] for their son's rehabilitation and using this money to buy bread, they will buy the bread," said Jabir.

Regression

"[The handicap's] situation should have evolved, but it hasn't. We have gone backwards. The negative social and mental consequences have multiplied. They end up staying at home and being isolated from family and society," added Jabir.

In the end, the damage done to an entire generation of youth and to Palestinian society in general by the Israeli army will only truly become clear years from now, said al-Essi.

"In the past, we used to define disability in purely medical terms.

"But now we realise the long-term effects are not only on one person but on the whole society, especially since the overwhelming majority of the victims are under 29 years old and the rest are no older than 50.

"If these people are being incapacitated, the whole family will fall below the poverty line."

"We don't see these effects immediately. They will be visible years from now when we see hundreds of people walking on crutches or moving around in wheelchairs."

The Sky's the Limit[8]
Gaza City, Palestine, July 17, 2005

This picture was taken the evening after chaos erupted in Gaza (see previous posts), on a small playground by the beach. It was desolate, save for a few families, with most people opting to stay indoors, for fear of an impending Israeli attack.

There were a few boys playing on this swing set, and they took Yousuf along with them. Their happiness struck me, and their childhood innocence shined through despite all that was happening around them.

When Will It End?[9]
Gaza City, Palestine, July 18, 2005

I spent much of today talking to Palestinians trying to cross the Netzarim check-point today. It is basically a 6m-deep trench dug deep into Gaza's coastal road, which has, in recent days, been ripped apart by nocturnal armored bulldozers that come out from behind the lone sniper in the distance and disappear before dawn when their work is done.

The checkpoint, along with one farther south at Abo Holi, has divided Gaza into three isolated segments for over five days now: Rafah and Khan Yunis in the south; Deir al-Balah, Maghazi, and Nseirat refugee camps in the central Gaza Strip; and Gaza City, Beit Hanoun, and Jabaliya in the north.

It was a painful site, as I heard testimony after testimony of the hardship endured in what would otherwise be a daily routine. Commercial trucks, donkey carts, fruit vendors, taxis, all attempting to make it down the trench and across to the other side. Young women heading to college carrying textbooks, walking over 3km around the checkpoint; women with infants; elderly Palestinians trudging across on canes through mounds of sand; and, most heartbreaking of all, a man who was suffering from Parkinson's and had come back from al-Shifa Hospital with a bag full of medicine and a medical transfer to Egypt, though he would be unable to travel there because, farther south, Abo Holi checkpoint was completely sealed off to commuters.

I heard accounts of "close calls," of bullets just missing commuters' heads, fired in "warning" by the lone sniper overlooking the checkpoint, and when it was over I headed home, relieved that none of those bullets had been fatal, satisfied with a job well done, and wrote the story out.

I made it home in time to meet with a colleague from the BBC (and former boss of mine at *Al Jazeera*) who was here on assignment for a radio program. "I just heard a 14-year-old boy was shot at Abo Holi, but the IDF hasn't yet confirmed it," she said.

I checked my sources. I called the hospitals, the families in Dair al-Balah, and sure enough, 14-year-old Ragheb al-Masri was brutally killed as he was waiting with his family in a taxi at Abo Holi.

But the world's media was too busy covering a press conference Palestinian President Mahmoud Abbas was holding and a meeting between Hamas and Egyptian delegates on the "ceasefire."

I immediately called an Israeli Army spokesperson for an explanation. They dodged my phone calls, and finally, late in the night, they called me back, only to inform me the matter was "under investigation."

"All we know is that Palestinian cars attempted to cross the checkpoint by force, so the soldiers fired warning shots into the air, not at the cars, and we have not received word of any injuries—there wasn't even an ambulance there."

Suddenly, all I could think about was Tom Hurndall.[10] And Rachel Corrie.[11] Iman al-Hams.[12] Nuran Dib.[13] And her mother's tears. And her father's silent anguish. And the lies.

The doctor who examined Ragheb's body said the bullet hit him in the back and came out through his chest, tearing his fragile heart apart. There is no chance this bullet was fired into "open air."

Now I think to myself as I head to bed, having just submitted a news story on the tragic incident, after rewriting my initial story that merely talked about the closure's impact (how could I know the impact would be so deadly?), I feel a sense of emptiness inside.

I compiled the facts and snapped the photos and wrote them out, nicely arranged, on a page, on a site, that soon will be forgotten. Along with Ragheb. Along with all the innocent angels that have fallen. And I think to myself, when will it end?

"K" Is For . . .[14]
Gaza City, Palestine, July 23, 2005

Time for a Yousuf update. While I was busy helping a BBC World Service crew here on assignment from London, Yousuf made that long-awaited realization that what comes out of his bum, and stays snugly in his diaper, actually belongs in the toilet. Or so I think. At least it seems he's made that verbal link . . . he actually said "*kaka*" yesterday! A milestone in the El-Haddad household here in Gaza, whose diaper purchases alone have probably helped the struggling economy stay afloat.

Of course, the timing was less than opportune. We were having dinner with guests down at our farm (finally accessible now that the coastal road is once again open and re-surfaced), discussing the future of Gaza's economy after withdrawal, and as I was feeding Yousuf, he blurted out "*kaka!*" to make sure everyone sitting could hear him.

Needless to say, I didn't let the impropriety of it all curb my excitement. "*Kaka?!* Did you hear that? He said *kaka!*" Of course, it may have been his mouth was simply full of rice and he was trying to say "*tata,*" short for "*shokolata.*" You never know with these things. Why is it that house training cats takes less than a day, but with kids . . .

On another note, my friend Deema, who was visiting from Jerusalem, taught Yousuf how to "fly" like an airplane. He didn't waste time putting his new-found skills to practice, as he "flew" throughout the house, knocking down everything with his "wings." Suffice to say, my mother was not pleased. Based on the nose dive he took off my bed the other day, it may take him a while to figure out he can't actually "lift off" into the air, though.

Gaza Summers
July 2005

CHAPTER NOTES

1. The full original text of this post is archived at http://www.gazamom. com/2005/07/interview-with-the-settler, shortened to http://bit.ly/cCAd9T.
2. Laila El-Haddad, "Interview: Israeli Settler Avi Farhan," *Al Jazeera English*, July 4, 2005, archived at http://bit.ly/cE9PG6.
3. Archived at http://bit.ly/9cyvWq.
4. Archived at http://bit.ly/brhJLu.
5. Archived at http://bit.ly/c2uMVK.
6. Archived at http://bit.ly/d0Kopz.
7. Laila El-Haddad, "Intifada Takes Physical and Mental Toll," *Al Jazeera English*, December 6, 2003, archived at http://bit.ly/bYYFkv.
8. Archived at http://bit.ly/d1sdki.
9. Archived at http://bit.ly/9s6wN2.
10. Thomas "Tom" Hurndall was a British photography student and an activist against the Israeli occupation of the Palestinian Territories. On April 11, 2003, he was shot in the head in the Gaza Strip by an Israeli Army sniper, Taysir Hayb. Hurndall was left in a coma and died nine months later. See http://en.wikipedia. org/wiki/Tom_Hurndall.
11. Rachel Aliene Corrie was an American college student and member of the International Solidarity Movement (ISM). She was crushed to death in the southern Gaza Strip by an Israeli Army bulldozer as she was kneeling in front of a local Palestinian's home, attempting to protect it from demolition.
12. Iman Darweesh al-Hams was a 13-year-old Palestinian girl killed by Israeli sniper fire near a military observation post in Rafah in the Gaza Strip on October 5, 2004. The Israeli commander who was accused of shooting her 17 times as she lay wounded on the ground was found not guilty on all charges by an Israeli military court.
13. Nuran Iyad Dib was a 10-year-old Palestinian schoolchild killed by Israeli fire as she lined up for her school's afternoon assembly on January 31, 2005.
14. Archived at http://bit.ly/cpAzzj.

Chapter 4

Waiting for Israel's Pullout

End of July through mid-August 2005

The summer of 2005 was an exciting and uncertain time in Gaza. With the Israeli disengagement—details of which Palestinians knew very little—looming on the horizon, much hope and anxiety surrounded the future. More than 5,000 international journalists descended upon the tiny strip to cover the historic event—mainly from within Israel or the settlements.

Palestinians factions, some propped up with large sums of money from the United States, vied for credit over the pullout of Israeli troops ahead of the Palestinian parliamentary elections that were scheduled to take place some months later, in January 2006. And ordinary Palestinians, particularly those whose homes were sandwiched between Israeli settlements and isolated by checkpoints and constant closures, looked in anticipation to the day they could roam freely within Gaza.

But as preparations continued to get underway, Palestinians from across the spectrum warned presciently of the perils a postdisengagement Gaza would face if access and free movement of people and goods were not guaranteed by Israel and the international community. After all, what would it matter that Israel was no longer in Gaza, if it was still controlling its goods and its people's lives and livelihoods from the outside without granting them any real sovereignty? Economist Muhammad Samhouri, whom I interview in an article included in this chapter, reminds us that Gaza is not viable on its own. "When we talk about the future of Gaza, it has to be as part of the Palestinian entity, including the West Bank and Jerusalem," he told me.

Meanwhile, in the West Bank, Palestinians protested the Separation Barrier's continued construction, the annexation of their land, and illegal settlement expansion that persisted under what they referred to as the "smokescreen of the disengagement" from Gaza, on one occasion symbolically burning tires along the path of the wall.

A Bleak Forecast[1]
Gaza City, Palestine, July 24, 2005

I was busy last week assisting a BBC World Service crew here on assignment from London and working on my own article, pondering the economic impact following disengagement.

The BBC crew wanted to better understand the lives of Palestinians in Gaza, and how they may, or may not, change after disengagement. I spoke to fisherman, real estate agents, businessmen, politicians, and farmers.

What I heard from them was not promising: As long as the problem of "access" is not resolved, nothing will change for Gazans. In fact, it may only get worse. This is according to Salah Abdel Shafi, an economic consultant for the Palestinian Authority (PA), and Mohammad Samhouri, the head of the technical committee in charge of withdrawal. One of the major challenges they are facing is planning for the future: In 20 years, Gaza will house some three million people, it is predicted.

We also visited the fisherman's port. The two men I spoke with told me how for months, their boats had been docked in the harbor, due to Israeli restrictions that bar them from reaching the "good" catches; how they were shot at by the Israeli Navy, splashed with cold water, thrown overboard.

Real estate agents told me that there will be a surplus of farm land after withdrawal, and many Palestinians who owned land within the settlements, which they will finally be able to access, will be anxious to sell it quickly, but the purchasing power is simply not there to buy it as it was in the '90s. Besides, if you can't export your tomatoes, hundreds of hectares more of them become worthless.

Interestingly, I learned that the Gaza Strip is the number-one producer of cherry tomatoes in the world, but that more often than not, they are labeled "Israel" in EU markets. This from a Belgian European Commission projects consultant.

The funniest anecdote of all that he shared with me: Gaza municipalities only have the capacity to treat 20,000 cubic meters of sewage water a day. Currently, 35,000 cubic meters are produced. "Which means that 15,000 cubic meters of shit are going directly into the sea each day."

And with that, ladies and gentlemen, I leave you to ponder the future of Gaza after disengagement.

It's a Conspiracy, I Tell You![2]
Gaza City, Palestine, July 25, 2005

I'm convinced. Yousuf has secret ties with the Israeli government. How else would Israeli Prime Minister Ariel Sharon have known my mother was in Khan Yunis visiting my grandmother and closed the Abo Holi checkpoint to coincide with her visit there?

It was sealed off to all Palestinian traffic three days ago, after Palestinian fighters killed two settlers traveling on the road above it to the illegal Kissufim settlement. The problem is that the closure is a form of collective punishment, as we are reminded by a large sign posted near Abo Holi: "Terror has negative repercussions on Palestinian society." Of course, the sign could just as well read, "Occupation has negative repercussions in Israeli society."

Abo Holi divides northern Gaza, where we live, from southern Gaza, where my grandmother lives. Thousands of Palestinians have been stranded on either end as a result and prevented from attending university, jobs, and hospitals, while settler traffic continues uninterrupted.

At the end of the day, it's all in Yousuf's interest, of course. The boy's energy has no bounds, I tell you. Without my mother's help, I could hardly keep up with his mischief (and my work), as he emptied the kitchen cupboards to make an ideal hiding space, hosed down the bathroom walls, and colored his face red (war paint perhaps?) with a marker he conveniently found tucked away in the corner of my desk—all within the span of one hour. I can just see Sharon snickering smugly in his Negev ranch now. *Sigh*

Back to Gaza City, Closed in Again[3]
Gaza City, Palestine, July 26, 2005

So my mother made it back to Gaza City, finally. That means I have rejoiced, and Yousuf's menacing can once again be put in (arguable) check. Unfortunately her trip back from Khan Yunis, where she was stuck for three days while visiting her mother, after the Israelis closed down the Abo Holi checkpoint, was not so easy.

The Israelis announced they would be opening Abo Holi for one-and-a-half hours last night, from 7–9:30 p.m. Thousands of stranded Palestinians fled to the checkpoint to try to make it back to Gaza City in time, including my mother. She was stuck in a car for four hours, with a five-months-pregnant woman who began to have abdominal pains from waiting so long and most likely miscarried her baby later on, according to my mother, who is a physician.

The Israelis were only letting through five cars at a time, which resulted in an immense backlog of cars, people, and goods. We didn't hear from her for four hours and were afraid something had happened—the invisible soldiers in the outpost guarding Abo Holi often shoot haphazardly at commuters (last week they killed a 14-year-old boy). Thank God she made it home alive, and, once again, we are sealed into Gaza. Abo Holi was closed again today.

"Disengagement from Justice"[4]
Gaza City, Palestine, July 28, 2005

My op-ed in the *Washington Post* on the same subject [disengagement], featuring (well, citing) Yousuf is excerpted below. I'm excited this got published where it did. I just hope it has some effect on Washington policymakers.

> Like the much-maligned Oslo peace process before it, which for 10 years was just that, a process and nothing more, this disengagement cannot yield a lasting peace unless it brings justice for the Palestinian people. So long as the Bush administration continues to turn a blind eye to illegal settlements in the West Bank and Israel maintains its control of Gaza's borders—including its sea and air space and land crossings—the disengagement will suffer a fate similar to that of Oslo.[5]

Interview: Mohammad Samhouri on the Gaza Disengagement[6]
Gaza City, Palestine, July 31, 2005, *Al Jazeera English*

In less than two weeks, Israeli Prime Minister Ariel Sharon will begin the evacuation of 21 illegal settlements from the Gaza Strip, built during Israel's occupation of the impoverished territory since 1967.

What follows that process for the Palestinians is less clear.

. . . Mohammad Samhouri has been assigned the task of coordinating the withdrawal on the Palestinian side.

Samhouri, a U.S.-educated economist by training, oversees a team of 40 experts who are handling the postdisengagement process, including what's to be done with the evacuated land and remaining assets.

AlJazeera.net spoke to Samhouri in his Gaza office about the disengagement that is set to start on August 15, the importance of free access for Palestinians and the future of Palestinian economy.

MOHAMMAD SAMHOURI: . . . Basically we are working on three main blocks of issues.

The first block is land and assets that supposedly the Israelis will evacuate in a couple weeks. We need to figure out what these assets are—agricultural, industrial, electricity, power, roads, infrastructure, housing units—and what to do with the debris and rubble when they are demolished, and what mechanism we should adopt in order to go ahead and get those assets. So the transfer mechanism—this is one block—preparations for technically being ready for the transfer of land assets when Israel evacuates.

The second major block of issues is related to access and movement, border crossings, all ports, territorial link between Gaza and the West Bank, and internal closures within the West Bank.

The third major block of issues is related to what to do with the land in the long term. We are gaining back 25 percent of the Gaza Strip's land, with a population of 1.5 million that is increasing by 4 percent yearly. So this is a major challenge—how to use everything here optimally.

To what extent is there coordination with the Israelis?

It is minimal. We still didn't get a single bit of information about what exists in the settlements. All that we have is information you can easily get when you do a Google search.

. . . Their plan doesn't speak [to] anything about access, sovereignty, or a West Bank–Gaza link. All they want is to get the settlers and army out of Gaza and keep overall control over the place. That's not our vision.

So in terms of coordination, it is a long, tedious, silly, nonproductive process so far, although there is some international pressure on the Israelis to get their act together and do what is needed.

What specific changes would you like to see?

We desire coordination to gradually ease up restrictions for cargo and individuals and go back to plans for building a sea port and reconstruct the airport and have it fully operational in due time.

What we want is secure and fast trade. Security dictates everything of importance to us and to them.

We want to end once and for all the "back to back" system of cargo delivery at Karni, which entails reloading the goods from one truck to another, because everything says this is not giving a chance for the private sector.
We are asking for door-to-door delivery instead and a bigger terminal for Palestinian laborers at Erez crossing.

The controls on the border are killing the Palestinian economy. The technology exists to remove these restrictions, but the Israelis are not convinced to use them.

This is our concept of coordination. It's not just to make life easy for the Israeli settlers and army, but also for us.

What will happen to Gaza's airport after disengagement?

Nothing has really been agreed upon. Whenever we bring it up, the [Israelis] say, "We'll talk about it later."

And the sea port?

Israel initially agreed to the idea. The Oslo Accord gave us that right. But beyond a general statement, we haven't been given clear answers when we attempt to discuss details, though the sea port is not as big a problem as the other ports.

What of the commodities that will be left behind in the settlements?

Palestinians are mainly concerned about the greenhouses. Some of them are being dismantled. But even in the best case scenario, if they are left intact, the marketing channel is an issue.

What makes agricultural products profitable is direct access to the end consumer. If agricultural products are not delivered on time, if they are stuck for even one day at Karni [industrial crossing], they are of no use.

If there is no free access to Israel and the outside world for all products, the greenhouses and other commodities left behind will be of no value to us.

. . . Can you create a viable Palestinian economy in a tract of land less than 350 sq. kilometers in size, given all the challenges you've mentioned?

This question has an obvious political dimension. We are talking here about the viability of a Palestinian state. We can't just focus on Gaza or we are playing the Israeli game.

Often while discussing the disengagement and what will happen is that we forget this, that we are also dealing with the wall in the West Bank, and with settlement growth there. All of this is killing viability of a Palestinian entity. When we talk about the future of Gaza, it has to be as part of the Palestinian entity, including the West Bank and Jerusalem.

What about the future of the Rafah crossing?

Rafah depends on talks with Egypt.

. . . All in all, are you optimistic about Gaza's future following disengagement?

You cannot say, in many issues, whether you are optimistic or not. In this case it depends on three things: first, how much we understand what we want in terms of access. If there is no easy access, disengagement will not be successful. We have to understand this, because sometimes we focus on the smaller issues. It is about A-C-C-E-S-S. If you don't have it, it is a big problem.

For Israelis, the issue is to realize that in the long term, it is in their interest to understand the implications of maintaining this stupid policy of closure and restrictions. In the long term, it will fire back because you are putting pressure on an impoverished, overcrowded people, and, sooner or later, it will get back to you.

And finally, the international community must understand it is not money that will solve the problem. Giving us a couple of billion dollars is necessary, but not sufficient. They need to put political pressure on the Israelis.

A Gem of an Idea?[7]
Gaza City, Palestine, August 2, 2005

As the Israeli withdrawal from Gaza nears, so too do preparations for anticipated victory celebrations. The "Palestinian Withdrawal Committee" has begun to hang banners throughout Gaza City, proclaiming proudly, "Today Gaza, tomorrow the West Bank and Jerusalem."

Now, according to the latest press release from the Palestinian Authority (PA):

> "We plan to wave 20,000 Palestinian flags during the evacuation. This will be a time for Palestinians to join together under one banner—the Palestinian flag," the PA Minister of Civil Affairs, Muhammad Dahlan, commented.
> "Thousands of T-shirts, pants, and hats are also being made in factories all throughout the Gaza Strip, employing 1,800 Palestinians. These clothing articles will be worn by thousands of Palestinians during the course of the evacuation."

OK, I'm going to pause here for a moment. Pants?! Did I just read that correctly? Is it just me, or is it difficult to imagine thousands of Palestinian men wearing pants that read something like . . . "Reclaiming my gem"?[8] Yikes.

Gaza Fishermen's Livelihood on the Line[9]
Gaza City, Palestine, August 3, 2005, *Al Jazeera English*

Though one of Gaza's oldest active fishermen, Suheil Sa'dallah spends most of his time loitering around Gaza's makeshift fisherman's port, where dozens of docked boats, including his own, bob gently in the sea.

In the face of stringent Israeli restrictions on Palestinian fishing zones, and in the absence of a modern industrial port, many fishermen there, like Sa'dallah, can no longer make a living.

He talks about the days their catches exceeded 700kg a day "of every fish your heart desires," when the only limit on fishing zones were as far as the eye could see.

A new port would mean better equipment, modern storage facilities for importing and exporting fish, and, assuming Israeli restrictions are lifted, improved catches. An agreement to build the port was reached between the two sides on September 21, 2000, one week before the eruption of the second intifada.

Israel has since frozen the project. The land that was set aside for it is now a cabbage farm not far from the Netzarim settlement, set to be evacuated beginning August 15. The Israelis have given initial approval for construction to resume after the evacuation of settlements and troops from Gaza, but as with most issues related to post-disengagement coordination, nothing has been officially agreed upon.

"The Israelis have agreed to the construction. The Oslo Accord, after all, gave us that right. But beyond a general statement, we have nothing. They don't give us clear answers when we try to discuss details with them," says Mohammad Samhouri, general coordinator of the Palestinian technical committee following the withdrawal.

Top priority

The European Union has said it is willing to invest up to half a billion dollars in Gaza after disengagement. The port is their "priority of priorities," according to Seamus Dunne, senior social development officer for the EU's International Management Group. He says the port would include facilities for medium-sized boats that would allow export of fish to as far away as Cyprus and Italy.

"The EU is extremely interested in the fisherman's port because it's a small investment with big potential. It could be operational in as little as six months, for about $15 million, and will create a host of employment opportunities for Palestinians," Dunne said. "But whether [Israel] will continue to search and harass fishermen at sea, I cannot say."

Gaza fishermen are restricted from accessing the southern coastline, adjacent to the Gush Katif bloc of settlements, and can only fish within a 10km in-sea zone. In addition, the fishermen say they face harassment from Israeli Navy vessels. "We are regularly shot at, ordered to strip down, to jump overboard. We've had cold water thrown on us, our boats have been damaged, and many of us have been imprisoned," said Sa'dallah, his colleagues confirming the incidents with collective nods.

Israeli control

Dunne says a port will be useless if Israeli restrictions on Palestinians exports are not removed. "We have to be realistic. The whole export structure is under Israeli control. They can even go so far as to force nations to stop buying Palestinian goods.

"Israeli exporters often delay the exit of Palestinian products. The Palestinians need to have their own points of exit—whether this is a sea port or an airport," he said. "Politically, pressure must come from the Quartet to resolve this issue," Dunne said, referring to the group made up of the United Nations, European Union, United States, and Russia trying to negotiate a Palestinian-Israeli peace deal through a road map they drew up in 2003.

Without the freedom to export freely, all the fish in the sea are worthless to Palestinians, Samhouri said. "If they are not delivered on time, if they are stuck for days at Karni, if there is not free access to Israel or outside markets, they will not add value to us."

Palestinian officials have made the issue of access their mantra in recent weeks. A June 2004 report published by the World Bank warned that if the Israeli closure policy was not changed, the Palestinian economy would not revive, and poverty and alienation would deepen. Israel controls all access points to the impoverished strip of 1.5 million people.

Agricultural assets

It is not clear whether that will change after Israeli Prime Minister Ariel Sharon's planned pullout from Gaza later this month. According to the original plan, Israel will maintain control over Gaza's air, sea, and land space.

Salah Abdel Shafi, an economic consultant for the Palestinian Authority (PA), says the problem of access applies equally to agricultural assets, such as greenhouses, that may be left behind in the evacuated settlements. "There is exaggeration on the issue of assets and the ability to take advantage of them. Right now, there are about 13,000 greenhouses in Gaza.

"Sixty percent of their production cannot be marketed due to the Israeli closure regime. Adding another 4,000 [greenhouses] from the settlements will only be a burden, unless Israel facilitates the export of the products," he said.

"If the access issue is not resolved, if they turn Gaza into a large prison, it will be a disaster, and disengagement will not lead to economic recovery. That's why most of the coordination going on has to do with the ports." The PA is calling for modern screening techniques that will make passage of goods more efficient and secure to satisfy the needs of both sides.

Modern security checks

At the Karni industrial crossing with Israel, the PA seeks to replace the "back-to-back" system of export with a "door-to-door" system, says Abdel Shafi. In the back-to-back system, goods must be reloaded from one truck to another on the Israeli side after a series of security checks. Many perishable items, such as dairy products and fish, spoil in the process.

The EU has proposed a modern system of security checks. Goods would be transported in sealed containers embedded with traceable electronic chips. The system would allow products to be delivered quickly and securely to their destinations.

As with everything related to post-disengagement coordination, however, there has only been agreement "in principle," says Abdel Shafi. "In principle, the Israelis have agreed to change the system. But once you get into the details—and the Israelis kill you in the details—it's a different story."

In the meantime, Sa'dallah and his fellow fishermen say all they can do is pray for better times. "I hope things will change. It's all in God's hands," he said. "But really, I am not optimistic."

Celebrate with White and Blue[10]
Gaza City, Palestine, August 4, 2005

OK, I've now learned that those mystery "victory pants" will actually be blue jeans, to be worn with white T-shirts. Um . . . were the collective PA heads screwed on right when they thought this color scheme up?

> For the victory rallies, the government will give away to its supporters 128,000 pairs of blue jeans along with white T-shirts.

Meanwhile, Abbas has forbidden any factions from displaying their flags during the celebrations (except the yellow Fateh flags of course, which have covered the Legislative Council in anticipation of a big "victory festival" today).

Revelers at a Fateh-sponsored Gaza "liberation festival" after the official start of the Israeli disengagement.

More Color Scheming[11]
Gaza City, Palestine, August 5, 2005

It came to my attention through the blog "Rafahpundits" that there is some confusion about the orange flags being waved in the picture I posted of the Gaza "liberation festival." Those are actually the new (formerly black and white) flags of Fateh's al-Aqsa Martyrs' Brigades. They were redesigned apparently so they wouldn't be confused with the black (and gold) of the Islamic Jihad flag. Even worse, now they are confused with the orange of the Israeli anti-disengagement movement!

As "Rafahpundit" commented:

> Just to be clear then, the residents of Gaza are going to celebrate disengagement dressed in the colours of the Israeli national flag, waving flags in the colour of the [Israeli] ANTI-disengagement protestors. It is ironic right?! No wonder we call it Disneygagement™.

I couldn't have said it better myself.

Palestinian Factions Vie for Gaza Credit[12]
Gaza City, Palestine, August 5, 2005, *Al Jazeera English*

With less than two weeks left before Israel evacuates the Gaza Strip, Palestinian factions are gearing up for celebrations with publicity campaigns that are equally intended to win Palestinian votes.

The Palestinian Authority (PA), which is spending an estimated $1.7 million on withdrawal celebrations, kicked off its campaign on Thursday with an event it called a liberation and evacuation festival, held in front of Gaza City's Legislative Council.

Prime Minister Ahmed Qurei, also called Abu Alaa, addressed the crowd, calling upon the Palestinian people to preserve national unity and fight against "all acts which harm our people and cause dissipation."

. . . Thousands of mainly young supporters donning Fateh memorabilia showed up to the event to hear Minister of Civil Affairs Mohammad Dahlan speak.

He made only a momentary appearance, however, before being whisked away by throngs of security guards, who fired their rifles into the air to disperse the crowd.

. . . The PA's publicity campaign is not without its critics, however.

Hamas considers the victory preparations a propaganda show intended to boost the Palestinian Authority's ruling Fateh party's popularity prior to upcoming parliamentary elections in January of 2006, and regards them with contempt for claiming the Gaza "victory" as their own.

"They want to show that negotiations and international pressure is what forced the Zionist enemy to withdraw from Gaza, not military resistance.

"We in Hamas—as well as, I would say, the Palestinian people—find this absolutely ridiculous. We proved that through resistance and sacrifice only was Gaza liberated," said Mushir al-Masri, spokesperson for Hamas.

. . . In the end, the battle over the hearts and minds of ordinary Palestinians may well be fought over the issues that matter most to them.

"I am the mother of a martyr, and of a Palestinian prisoner," said 55-year-old Fatimah Draini, as she left the "liberation festival," holding up framed pictures of her two sons.

"I cast my vote for whoever can bring the Palestinian prisoners home [from] Israeli jails, for whoever can bring tangible improvement to our lives."

Who Exactly Is in Charge Here?[13]
Gaza City, Palestine, August 8, 2005

Though this title may equally apply to Yousuf, who has yet to learn that crawling up on a table and scavenging for food with his hands is not normal human behavior, I am referring to the Gaza judicial system, whose members are on strike for the third day in a row.

The strike is in protest over attacks against Gaza's chief justice and attorney general, with judges threatening to suspend their work until the Palestinian Authority (PA) addresses the continuing state of lawlessness in Gaza.

Just to put things in perspective—imagine a country (well, or a semi-autonomous government ruling over a still-occupied series of Bantustans) whose entire judicial system has been put on hold. The entire system comes to a standstill.

This all started when Zuhair Sourani, the chairman of the Palestinian Authority's Higher Judicial Council, announced his resignation on Saturday, days after a hand grenade was lobbed at his home by a group of masked gunmen. Talk about taking the law into your own hands.

The funny thing is, a spokesperson for the Ministry of the Interior insists that the PA security apparatus has a "91 percent success rate" when it comes to resolving cases and apprehending criminals. Kind of reminds me of the 99 percent approval rating of Egypt's Hosni Mubarak. Where do they come up with these figures?

One's thing's for certain: With withdrawal just days away, opposition groups jockeying for credit and power ahead of January elections, and lawlessness plaguing Gaza, PA President Mahmoud Abbas is one man I do not envy.

The Little Things[14]
Gaza City, Palestine, August 12, 2005

Am I becoming a militant mother? First, I go around chasing down truck drivers throughout Gaza to secure some end-of-the-season oranges for Yousuf. Now, I argue my way into a hotel pool that didn't allow "males" in on women's day, issuing a few threats in the process.

I had been preparing to take Yousuf to one of two (clean) pools in Gaza for several weeks now, making sure I would have the whole day off, nothing to disturb us. Women's-only day is just once a week, and at 35 shekels [$9.00] a pop, not exactly cheap. Still, it's not something we do often, so I figured it's worth it.

So when I learned from the hotel receptionist that "no males are allowed in" (never mind the fact that the "male" accompanying me was 17 months old), you can bet I was furious. Nothing, and I mean nothing, was going to spoil my special day with Yousuf. I had to calmly, casually, relay this message to Osama, the receptionist. But all I got from him was an enthusiastic waving of the finger at a sign on his desk—"See—no males allowed! And this is *non-negotiable.*"

Worse: "Unless you are from the Mortaja family, you can't take him in." Hello? The Mortaja family? "Wait, so this pool is only for Gaza's who's who? Am I not special enough for you to make exceptions?" I considered asking if he wanted a bribe, just to see if that's what he was getting at.

I later learned that the Mortajas are the hotel owners. But I also learned that families of ministers actually can "reserve" the entire pool for themselves.

"So this pool is exclusive, despite the fact that we pay a hefty fee to get in?" I asked, angrily.

In the end, one of his superiors intervened and let me in, Yousuf in hand, though I couldn't help feeling humiliated, like an unwelcome guest. I thought, this is something I would have never done for myself, even though we paid the full fee. But for Yousuf . . . I have learned to cross all the boundaries. Yet I couldn't help feeling miserable. Being yelled at is no fun.

Later that day, we went to the farm and Yousuf, as usual, reminded me that it's the little things that matter. Together, we watched ants crawling through the sand. We tracked the stars. And we laughed until our sides ached playing hide-and-go-seek. No matter what a miserable day I've had, how many mean hotel receptionists yell at me, or snobbish government officials snub me, I always have Yousuf there to remind me of what really matters. His big goofy smile and wet smooches makes it all better. I love him. He is my world. And though it may make me selfish, having him around makes things all better. I think I need him just as much as he needs me. Or more.

Layers upon Layers Of . . .[15]
Gaza City, Palestine, August 13, 2005

My dad went out sailing with an old college friend of his on Friday, who is big in Gaza's NGO circles. The friend, whom I am not at liberty to identify, but whom I'll refer to as "E," is close with President Mahmoud Abbas. It's interesting to hear, according to E, what Abbas had to say.

In a recent conversation he had with him, Abbas explained his dilemma: "I want to change things in Gaza. But I look to the layer of Fateh and PA people surrounding me, and I see shit. So I look to the layer beyond that, and again, all I see is shit. And the layer beyond that, and yet more shit. In all honesty, I just don't know what to do, and how to rid myself of these layers of shit that I am surrounded by." E, who is as secular as they come, suggested his only way out is to ally himself with Hamas and Co. in a strange-bed-partners sort of way, because in the past they have been known for their finesse in ridding Gaza of its shit. Talk about a deep dirty mess.

Disen-what-ment?[16]
Gaza City, Palestine, August 15, 2005

I don't know how many times I've said that word today. What does that mean anyway? I feel like my speech has become a series of edited and re-edited sentences with all the same buzzwords.

Disengagement . . . freedom . . . access . . . prison . . . anxiety . . . hope.

Still, I return to what comes after diseng . . . oh, you know. With word of a kidnapped French-Algerian reporter last night, we return once again to, yet more buzzwords, "lawlessness and chaos," after withdrawal. Usually, these terms are uttered in unison with Hamas (just as Gaza is teamed with "hotbed of terror," courtesy of Sharon's speech tonight).

However, the trained observer will tell you it's really a problem within the ranks of the ruling PA's Fateh party itself, with a corrupt system of patronage and payoffs, and hundreds of former guerillas to incorporate into the system. Tonight, we received yet another reminder of the problems that Abbas will have to, at some point, face: Hundreds of fighters from the al-Aqsa Martyrs' Brigades marched through Gaza's city streets shooting their weapons, not in celebration, but to make a point. "We will never give up our weapons so long as a single Israeli soldier remains," they shouted. What's interesting is that they don't disassociate themselves from or criticize the PA. They also shouted "Fateh . . . Fateh . . . Fateh."

Just another card to throw into the pile, to make things more fun. After all, we could all use a good laugh about now (and I could use a good night's sleep . . . so off I go).

CHAPTER NOTES

1. The full original text of this post is archived at http://www.gazamom.
   com/2005/07/a-bleak-forecast/, shortened to http://bit.ly/aYGSMZ.
2. Archived at http://bit.ly/9Jb8jt.
3. Archived at http://bit.ly/cnvWch.
4. Archived at http://bit.ly/9JtAK4.
5. Laila El-Haddad, "Disengagement from Justice," *Washington Post*, July 28, 2005,
   archived at http://bit.ly/dnJbQ8.
6. Laila El-Haddad, "Interview: PA's Pull-out Coordinator," *Al Jazeera English*, July
   31, 2005, archived at http://bit.ly/bAySGu.
7. Archived at http://bit.ly/aN432N.
8. "Reclaiming our gem" was one of the promotional slogans used by the Palestinian
   Withdrawal Committee in a UNDP-funded disengagement poster series.
9. Laila El-Haddad, "Gaza Fisherman's Livelihood on the Line," *Al Jazeera English*,
   updated September 6, 2005, archived at http://bit.ly/aw1H6H.
10. Archived at http://bit.ly/bsTVvK.
11. Archived at http://bit.ly/aQLq1V.
12. Laila El-Haddad, "Palestinian Factions Vie for Gaza Credit," *Al Jazeera English*,
    August 5, 2005, archived at http://bit.ly/cYiLOK.
13. Archived at http://bit.ly/cqmapz.
14. Archived at http://bit.ly/c7VXyU.
15. Archived at http://bit.ly/cchc44.
16. Archived at http://bit.ly/ddxxg7.

Chapter 5

The Occupation
Goes Remote Control

Mid-August through mid-September 2005

This chapter covers the period during, and immediately after, Israel's disengagement from Gaza. The actual implementation of Israel's pullout of its soldiers and settlers was off limits to Palestinian journalists. Thus, my coverage was largely from the Palestinian perspective, written from within Gaza city, not from inside the settlements or within Israel. The process of disengagement stretched out over several weeks. The moments leading up to the start of it were tense and exciting for Palestinians, and the days directly afterward absolutely intoxicating as Gazans basked in their newfound internal freedom.

This would quickly end. An analogy was frequently drawn to a hamster being released from one cage with an obstacle course in it to another without the obstacle course: At the end of the day, he was still in a cage. As one resident of an isolated Palestinian village whose residents had for many long years prior to the disengagement been forbidden from swimming at the beach just a few meters away from them—it was reserved exclusively for Jews—reminded me at the time, "If it was just about having access to a beach, we would go to Gaza City. It's about our right to live freely. It's about occupation, which will continue even after they withdraw."

Meanwhile in the West Bank, in 2005 alone, Israel's expansion of settlements created housing for 30,000 new settlers, just as 5,000 settlers were being "disengaged" from Gaza. That prompted the Palestinian Negotiation Unit to dub it a "re-engagement in the West Bank." Worse, the fate of the much-dreaded Rafah crossing was being decided. It turned out the crossing would remain (even if only indirectly) in Israel's hands. The Israeli authorities could decide when to open the crossing by ordering the E.U. observers posted there to go to their posts or withdraw; and the Israelis would monitor the crossing remotely via surveillance cameras, allowing passage only to Palestinians carrying the much-loathed (and Israeli controlled) hawiyas. The travel ban from Gaza to the West Bank or East Jerusalem—both less than an hour away—was also kept in place. It was Occupation 2.0.

Zero Hours[1]

Gaza City, Palestine, August 15, 2005

So D-day has finally come. It's like a zoo here, what with thousands of journalists flown in from around the world, spread across every inch of Gaza, every settlement, refugee camp, border crossing, with satellite linkup, Internet, radio, you name it (*Al Jazeera* TV has a revolving 3-D model of the Gaza Strip and has chosen *the* weirdest '80s theme music for its special coverage). I can only imagine how different covering something like, say, the fall of the Berlin Wall was.

So far it's been anticlimactic, but I'll admit, I couldn't help but stay up and watch the end of the Palestine Satellite Channel ticker marking down the "days till liberation." Or the hoards of journalists and photographers who were massed at Kissufim crossing, waiting for midnight, when the once-golden settler-only gates would finally close for good (as my dad commented, it's the first time a crossing has been closed for Israelis, as opposed to Palestinians . . . hah).

Of course, I did my own reporting but tried to steer clear of the news-hungry correspondents parachuted in for the occasion, all waiting in unison for the big moment, and for any observable moment at that.

I observed life around Gaza City and also drove to the northern village of Siyafa, sandwiched between the settlement triangle of Nisanit, Dugit, and Eli Sinai (Siyafa is Mawasi's lesser-known cousin, so to speak).

Palestinians there prepared for what they were told would be a month-long closure of their community, as they stockpiled food, water, and cooking gas and waited for Israeli approval to enter their fenced-in village. In the background, the soon-to-be evacuated red-roofed villas of Dugit were visible amid swaths of razed farmland. This area was once known for its lush strawberry fields. Looming overhead used to be a tank and a camera operated by remote control, hooked to an observation room in a sniper tower that forebodingly overlooked the troubled village. The tower was dismantled last week.

When I got too close to the gate of the village to take pictures and interview residents, a soldier shouted at me to back off or he would not let in any of the residents. They told me they dream of the quickly approaching day when they will no longer have to wait in front of this gate, when they will be able to move freely in their own land. But still, they are anxious and uncertain of what the future holds.

. . . Near midnight, sporadic protests erupted throughout Gaza, and Palestinian mosques called on worshippers to come and pray a communal prayer of thanks.

Gazans Cautious, but Eager for Pullout[2]

Khan Yunis, Gaza Strip, Palestine, August 16, 2005, *Al Jazeera English*

At the edge of the Khan Yunis refugee camp in the southern Gaza Strip, crumbling refugee homes face off with the red-roofed seafront villas of the Neve Dekalim settlement.

The settlement, one of 21 chosen for evacuation in coming months, has been the source of much grief—and now speculation—for Palestinians here.

Abo Ahmed's home stands directly across from Neve Dekalim, the largest and most ideologically extreme of the Gush Katif settlements, a bloc established in 1970—three years after Gaza was captured and occupied by Israel.

Not far from the settlement is an Israeli sniper tower, placed there along with hundreds of soldiers to protect the illegal settlers from their Palestinian neighbours, the original inhabitants of the land. Gunfire from the tower has left pockmarks the size of apples in the wall of Abo Ahmed's second-floor living room.

Aside from this, the view from the window of the abandoned room is striking.

"It's beautiful, right?" he said, laughing, looking back at his cratered wall. "If only we could enjoy it."

For several years, Abo Ahmed had not ventured up to this room for fear of becoming a target. And though the beach is a five-minute walk away, it is off limits to Palestinians.

Anxious

Like most refugees here, Abo Ahmed is anxiously waiting for the day Jewish settlers leave Gaza and for his life to return to semi-normality. "The settlements are one of the biggest obstacles for us, and we feel it more than anyone here on the front lines. We suffer on a daily basis," he said.

"All I remember from the past few years is that there were always martyrs, always injuries, and always tanks down the street," he recalled.

His sister-in-law, Zakiya Musa, held a nursing 3-month-old in her arms. "I just can't wait for them to leave, so we can relax, for our children's sake. They are terrified of the sniper fire they hear every night," she said.

Palestinian Authority

How the settlers will leave and what role the Palestinians will have in all this remains a mystery to most, including the Palestinian Authority (PA). Until now, Israeli Prime Minister Ariel Sharon has largely refused to coordinate his withdrawal from Gaza with the Palestinians, said Palestinian Deputy Prime Minister Nabil Shaath.

"There is very little coordination going on. . . . [T]he Israelis only talk about coordination, but it hasn't happened," Shaath told AlJazeera.net.

. . . Abo Walid, whose brother was killed by an Israeli sniper two years ago in the camp, says the first thing he will do after the settlers leave is head to the beach.

His friend Abu Khalid, a teacher in the nearby elementary school, is quick to point out that it is not just about enjoying the beach.

"If it was just about having access to a beach, we would go to Gaza City. It's about our right to live freely. It's about occupation, which will continue even after they withdraw," he said.

"Remember, they will still control Gaza's borders, airspace, and sea. And they are relocating all the settlements to the West Bank. They are simply restructuring the occupation."

For others in Khan Yunis, the question of what should be done after disengagement is simpler.

"We want to be able to have fun without the fear of getting shot, to go on outings and play, to go to the seashore," said 10-year-old Kifah Abu Ibayd.

She and some other children trotted off into the horizon, close to the sniper tower, trying to fly a handmade paper kite.

Mawasi enclave

Nearby, Mawasi resident Subhi Astal, 57, waited for Israeli forces to open the Tufah checkpoint. Mawasi, a Palestinian enclave within the Gush Katif bloc, has been sealed off from the rest of the Gaza Strip for more than four years.

Special permits must be obtained to pass the checkpoint, and Palestinian residents often wait for days before they are allowed to enter. "The settlers are leaving in the right time. There is nothing left for them here. They took everything and have completely abused the area's resources.

"They overdrilled the area for water wells such that the water salinity has increased in Gaza. They are even taking our earth," said Astal, pointing out several trucks of golden Gaza sand being transported, at 2000 shekels ($437) a load, to Israel for construction purposes.

"I would like to see things improve in Gaza. I think they should turn the settlement lands into a tourist area and some of it into agricultural land. I think the land should be returned to the people, and the returns should be distributed fairly. But I guarantee this won't happen," Astal said.

Preparations

Shaath insists the postdisengagement process will be transparent and that the Palestinian Authority has bigger things to worry about after disengagement.

"I don't think [corruption] is a danger, but rather the chaos that political factions are creating under this pretext. We are worried of a 'hurry up everyone take a piece of land for yourself before they do because we deserve it' scenario. Our fear is of something that might resemble Iraq or Algeria postindependence—this is what we want to prevent," he said.

The PA has established a new security service of 5,000 police officers to take control of the evacuated land and to prevent "hostile takeovers."

Though details of postdisengagement are far from ironed out, Palestinians seem to agree on one thing.

"Everyone looks forward to withdrawal. We want the occupation to end. We want to live like regular human beings," said Abo Walid, looking over to the palm-shaded settlement.

"Every May, we see their fireworks display from the roof of our house, celebrating their independence day, and our catastrophe. All we feel now is pain and misery. We wish one day to see our independence being celebrated."

WSS: Weepy Settler Syndrome[3]
Gaza City, Palestine, August 18, 2005

I've had it. I think I've seen one too many images of weepy settler theatrics (and weepy settler questions on radio interviews) for my own sanity. I mean, I don't even know where to start with this. Two thousand (by some estimates, 6,000 . . . and shame on every one of them) journalists from around the world, and the image dominating this entire period is that of weepy settlers (not, I might add, of wacko settlers shooting to death four Palestinian workers in the West Bank).

The story is *not* about settler surfers having to leave the beautiful seashore they crave; or dismantling prized organic orchids or whatever the hell it is the settlers grow; or weeping over the agony of leaving their paradise on earth that God, according to them, said was theirs and theirs alone.

It is about 30,000 Palestinians who lost their homes (and many times, their lives), sometimes with less than two minutes' notice, sometimes with no notice at all, to armored Israeli bulldozers—all for the sake of these "weepy settlers" who are being "forcefully evicted" from the "only homes some ever knew," to quote a recent article in the *Los Angeles Times*.

Sharon talks about the pain he feels upon seeing these images. I wonder if he felt any pain when he destroyed the lives of those refugees in Rafah. Or when his soldiers shot Iman al-Hims 17 times; or when they shot Nuran Dib while she was lining up for school; or when they ran over Rachel Corrie with their bulldozers.

The settler enterprise is unlawful, cruel, racist, perverse, and violent, to name a few.

It is wrong. It must end. In their name, millions of Palestinians lives' have been crippled, roads torn apart and sealed off, thousands of homes destroyed, hundreds of innocent lives lost; acres upon acres of fertile farm land, of trees that had been hundreds of years growing in this land, razed to the now-scorched earth.

Yes, I see a lot of things to weep about in Gaza. Settlers being "evicted" from their "homes" is not one of them.

Save Our Sons[4]
Gaza City, Palestine, August 18, 2005

Grieving Palestinian mothers protested their sons' imprisonment in Israeli jails yesterday after hijacking a scheduled press conference for the Palestinian foreign minister and lamenting the fact that the media's attention is "disengaged" from the truth. "A Separation Barrier, like the one in the West Bank, is being built around the issue of the 8,000 Palestinian political prisoners" they cried.[5]

Closed in, Again[6]
Gaza City, Palestine, August 20, 2005

I've had a long week. In between covering the "other side" of withdrawal, combating a mystery stomach illness, and trying to potty train Yousuf (unsuccessfully— see: poopy stain on Dad's Persian rug), I thought I needed a break yesterday, seeing as how it was Friday.

Instead, I decided to head down to Rafah and Khan Yunis. I felt obligated to revisit the issue of house demolitions, to speak again with some of the thousands of Palestinians who lost their homes in Rafah, all in the name of security for the settlers. But just as I was about to head out the door, I decided to check whether Abo Holi was open. "I heard you're opening all of Friday and Saturday," I asked the Palestinian police officer near the Israeli-controlled checkpoint over the phone.

"You mean closing all of Friday," he replied. Apparently, Israeli forces reneged on their promises to keep Abo Holi open on Friday, the Muslim holy day, during disengagement (it's been closed the rest of the week, with the exception of about two hours in the middle of the night). Israeli forces also began digging an 8m-deep trench around Gush Qatif "to keep Palestinians out for premature celebrations," an army spokesperson told me. What are these, some kind of sick parting gifts?

A day earlier, Gaza settlers continued to disrupt Palestinian life as they attacked villagers near Kfar Darom and burned down their storage sheds (these very villagers warned me a day earlier that settlers might attack them, but their calls fell on deaf ears; the media thought it more apt to write about surfer settlers having to find new shores instead).[7]

I decided to take my father's advice and take a break. We went to the beach and had tea as we watched the sun set over a freer, more beautiful Gaza and bought fragrant *Zanbaq* flowers from young boys for a shekel. The flowers grow in the wild near the enclosed area of Mawasi, in Khan Yunis. I've always found something so stark yet beautiful about flowers that grow in an area subject to the some of the darkest manifestations of human behavior.

Bye Bye Bye . . .[8]
Gaza City, Palestine, August 22, 2005

So, after 38 years of occupation (more, in the case of Kfar Darom, an Israeli settlement situated in the middle of the Palestinian town of Dair al-Balah, whose Palestinian families I visited today, the subject of tomorrow's entry, I hope), the settlement era has finally come to an end in Gaza.

To think, Netzarim, the isolated and vulnerable settlement that Sharon once famously declared was as important to him as Tel Aviv, the once towering symbol of strength of the Israeli settler movement in Gaza, is gone!

For Palestinians, of course, it was one of the most hated and visible symbols of the occupation—a combat boot that stood on the neck of Gaza, tearing the strip apart into two strategic halves.

It is also the site where 12-year-old Muhammed al-Dura, the central icon of the second Palestinian uprising, was killed by an Israeli sniper as he was cowering in his father's arms in front of a television camera, at the beginning of the second Intifada.

As the Israeli army declared the end of the evacuation, 30,000 Palestinians waving green Hamas flags rallied through Gaza City Monday night in the largest celebration so far since the beginning of Israel's withdrawal from the Gaza Strip.

The rally also marked the anniversary of the attempted burning of the al-Aqsa Mosque in Jerusalem in 1969 and the assassination of moderate Hamas leader Ismail Abo-Shanab.

During the rally, the Islamic Resistance Movement's political leader, Ismail Haniyeh, gave a speech, declaring five main "priorities" of the movement following the withdrawal from Gaza—the right to retain arms and continue the resistance, preserving national unity, participation in politics, nation building, and defending and protecting the Palestinian cause.

Haniyeh also spoke to fears of many Palestinians that some corrupt government officials may try to claim some of the liberated land as their own.

"We want to emphasize that the land that is liberated is the property of all the Palestinian people, not just Ziad or Amr," continued Haniyeh, sending a clear message to the Palestinian Authority.

"This is the beginning of the end of the settlement enterprise for Israel," he concluded.

Re-engagement[9]
Gaza City, Palestine, August 22, 2005

A map (at right) published by the Palestinian Negotiation Affairs Department shows how the Gaza "disengagement" translates into a West Bank "engagement." While the focus of the WSS-infected media this past week has been on the "historic" withdrawal from Gaza, we forget that settlement expansion this year alone in the West Bank has created room for 30,000 more illegal settlers. Bravo, Sharon, for the greatest theatrical performance pulled off by a head of state since, well, I'm tempted to say since Bush's Iraq . . . but really, since ever.

Dinner and a Kidnapping[10]
Gaza City, Palestine, August 25, 2005

Forget about SNAFUed radio programs (as in, my live Open Source Radio Interview in the wee hours of Tuesday morning, where the phone line kept getting disconnected)—let's talk about SNAFUed dinner parties.

I had invited a few friends of mine, along with a European Commission consultant I had the pleasure of meeting through some work-related interviews, to dinner at my parents' place. When I visited Antoine's office for an article I was writing on the economy and the future of Gaza, I saw a *zibdiah* on his desk, a small clay pot used to make a famous Gazan hot tomato dill salad (called *dagga*) and to bake a spicy shrimp dish. He got it as a gift and didn't know what it was used for (he made a pencil holder out of it), so I promised him dinner, along with his colleague, to show them.

So we wrapped our grape leaves, stuffed our squash, clay-potted our *dagga*, and set the table—only to receive a phone call from Antoine informing us that he had "good and bad news."

"We just received a warning from the security forces that all foreigners are not to move from their locations—there are armed groups prowling around the city looking to kidnap someone."

The warning was repeated every five minutes until, finally, there was an attempted kidnapping by two gunmen of a foreign woman in front of her beachside hotel, but she got away safely (as did the gunmen).

I wasn't so mad about all the hard work we put into the dinner party, but at the fact that some moron who thinks this is the way to address his grievances—mainly because no one is telling him otherwise or doing anything to stop it—threatened the safety of my friends and continued to propagate this image of Gaza as a lawless, free-for-all place.

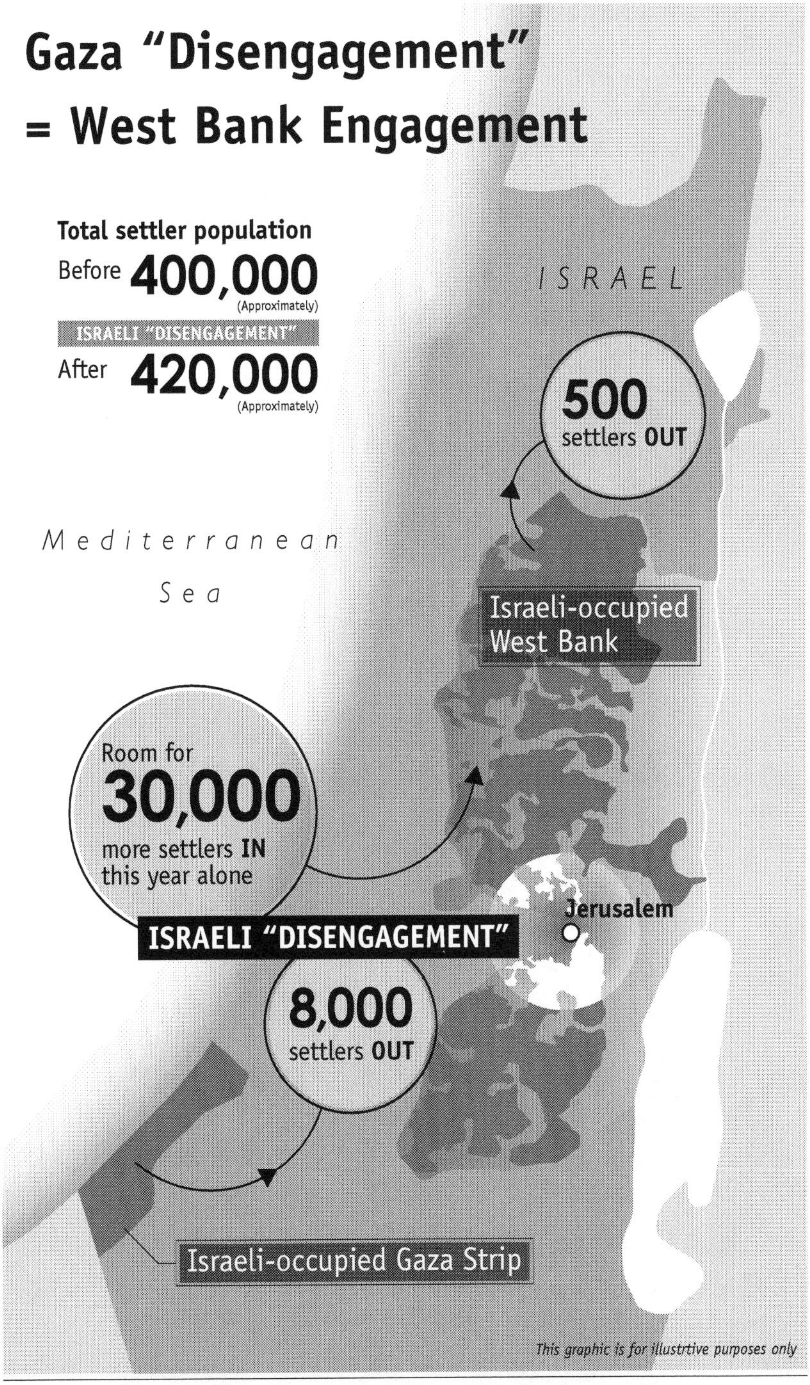

Gaza "Disengagement"
= West Bank Engagement

Total settler population

Before **400,000**
(Approximately)

ISRAELI "DISENGAGEMENT"

After **420,000**
(Approximately)

ISRAEL

500
settlers **OUT**

Mediterranean

Sea

Israeli-occupied
West Bank

Room for
30,000
more settlers **IN**
this year alone

ISRAELI "DISENGAGEMENT"

Jerusalem

8,000
settlers **OUT**

Israeli-occupied Gaza Strip

This graphic is for illustrtive purposes only

SOURCE: Palestinian Negotiation Affairs Department 2005

While not identified this time, the alleged kidnappers have in the past been disgruntled members of the PA's security forces themselves, not unidentified "armed groups" threatening Mahmoud Abbas's authority. It's his own party threatening his authority, which is why it doesn't get much publicity in the local press.

Everybody knows everybody, so it's hard to conceal something like a kidnapping in Gaza.

It's becoming a sad reality that many people—including the PA—are not coming to grips with. To their credit, this was the first time they put out a "warning" like this and actually *prevented* a kidnapping. That's a good first step, although the conspiracy theorist in me thinks the whole event may have been staged to bolster the appearance of a competent Palestinian security force. Tonight, there is a Palestinian vigil protesting the incident (also sponsored by the PA) and the continued lawlessness in Gaza. I suppose they are trying to project the image that this is a taboo, not a norm, in our society.

The good news is, we wrapped up the food and took it along with our other guests to Antoine's place. We got to have dinner after all.

My Top 10 List[11]
Gaza City, Palestine, August 27, 2005

As the Israeli disengagement from Gaza draws to a close (we've still got those pesky soldiers watching over us like guardian angels), I've reflected on my time here, Yousuf in hand (and in womb at one point) as I covered every aspect of Gaza (and I mean that . . . from rowing refugees, to Gazan rappers, to archeological digs, to assassinations, to home demolitions, to artificial insemination). I've come up with a tentative list of my top 10 most memorable moments of the past two years, in no particular order:

1. Having to spend the night in Rafah in a stranger's home during an Israeli siege of the area, while five months' pregnant, with shells flying over my head and sniper fire all around, because Israeli forces had sealed off the crossing and I was unable to return to Gaza (at least not the same way I came in . . . sneaking through someone's farm under a rain of fire).

2. Chasing down Sheikh Ahmed Yasin (before he was assassinated) amid throngs of Hamas supporters in a rally of 10,000 people on Gaza City's streets, while eight months' pregnant, in my maternity jeans and sneakers. When I finally caught up with him, heaving, sweaty, and ready to fall over, I was invited into his simple home and given a seat and an open-ended interview. Yasin was unassuming and answered my questions, oddly enough, with verses of

poetry. "Aren't you afraid of being assassinated?" I asked forebodingly. "A swimmer is never afraid of drowning," he replied.

3 . Being lifted up into the air on a rooftop by an enthusiastic resident of Jabaliya during Operation Days of Penitence, who, while trying to be helpful, put my life in danger so he could show me an Israeli helicopter gunship that appeared out of nowhere and began firing at his neighbors a few meters away from us. More than 120 Palestinians were killed during the brutal attack, nearly one-third of them children.

4. Riding a donkey cart down a rocky slope and across the beach to bypass the closed-off Netzarim checkpoint, with a then-4-month-old Yousuf strapped to my side in a baby carrier, to make it to Rafah crossing on our way to the U.S., on a trip that would stretch out to more than 48 hours. Israeli forces had sectioned Gaza into three parts, closing off the coastal road in front of Netzarim to all traffic. Then, waiting four more hours in the August heat for a very fickle Israeli soldier to open the Abo Holi crossing. Letting Yousuf crawl loose in the nude because it was so hot.

5. Seeing my mother lose her sanity at the fence at Rafah crossing separating us from the Israelis, threatening to walk out in front of the Israeli watchtower with her hands raised in the air if we weren't allowed through. Seeing the expression of the Palestinian officers—who seemed more scared of my mother than of the Israeli soldiers.

6. Despite all this, seeing Yousuf giggle at Israeli troops stamping our passports at Rafah crossing, and my mother's joking response, "No, no, Yousuf dear, don't giggle, that's the enemy."

7. Spending 55 days of imposed exile in Cairo with a jet-lagged, crawl-crazy Yousuf after Israel closed down Rafah crossing the night we arrived back from a trip to the U.S.

8. After the crossing finally opened, yelling at an Israeli soldier after waiting five hours in that stinkin' border bus with my face smashed against a window and having to change Yousuf's poop-bomb on the ground in a no-man's land with tanks in front of us and receiving no response when I asked why the delay if the terminal was practically empty. Then, being told by his superior officer that my behavior was "not proper."

9. Forgetting my role as a journalist for a moment and crying alongside the grieving parents of 10-year-old Nuran Dib, whose life was taken by an Israeli sniper as she stood waiting in line, singing with her classmates, waiting to enter her classroom in the besieged town of Rafah.

10. Thinking of my own son every minute of every day. Knowing he was always there at the end of the day to give me his little koala hug and wet smooches, no matter how many terrible things

have happened. Being unable to imagine my life without him. Knowing how wonderful life is, now that he's in the world . . .

Look Who's Looting Now[12]
Gaza City, Palestine, September 1, 2005

According to IsraelReporter.com, it seems some of the settlers who have returned to Gaza to do some belated packing are actually looting under the guise of gathering up their property. Apparently no one checks the settlers on their way out, and all they need to do to reenter Gaza is send a fax to the Disengagement Authority in Israel.

Once inside, no one checks that the mover is moving only the specific property for which he was sent. A senior worker in the former Gaza Beach Regional Council revealed that citizens have been able to loot from private homes and from communal institutions without any problems, even though the army is theoretically guarding those possessions.

This is in addition to the looting by soldiers themselves, which reminds me of the countless tales I've heard from Palestinians in Rafah of soldiers stealing their possessions during house raids (including those prized African parrots in the ill-fated Rafah zoo).

More on Looting[13]
Gaza City, Palestine, September 2, 2005

According to *Haaretz*,[14] and in confirmation of my last post, there has been massive looting of the Gaza settlements by public agencies, nonprofit organizations, individuals, and even other local councils (not "Arab truck drivers". . . why do people insist on reducing us as Palestinians in our entirety to a bunch of violent, lawless, barbaric thugs?) ever since the settlements were evacuated. The Gaza settlement council's liquidator filed a complaint with the police about the matter on Thursday.

Some of the big items, such as trash cans and lampposts, are thought to have been stolen by other local councils inside Israel, on the theory that the evacuated settlers no longer need this equipment and it should not be left for the Palestinians. However, the liquidator is supposed to be selling such items to settle the disbanded regional council's debts. Government ministries are also suspected of having looted certain items, including kindergarten equipment.

Rafah: More of the Same[15]
Gaza City, Palestine, September 3, 2005

Israeli and Egyptian officers signed an agreement Thursday to deploy 750 lightly armed Egyptian troops along the border with the Gaza Strip in an effort to prevent weapons-smuggling into Gaza.

Following the announcement, one could hardly flip through a paper or browse an online news site without finding something that didn't tout the agreement as the end of the miserable border regime that is Rafah crossing; a bunch of other articles I came across even spoke of the reunion of Egyptian and Palestinian Rafah, split apart after the 1967 war.

I was speaking to a friend of mine yesterday—a freelancer based in Ramallah who is here visiting Gaza—and I remarked in frustration, "It seems like these people are living in some sort of parallel universe." "That's because they are," he said.

We say that because, in the end, nothing will change. Ultimate control over the border—the only route to the outside world for Gaza's 1.4 millions Palestinians (that oft-repeated statistic includes Yousuf and me)—will remain in Israeli hands . . .

The Remote-Controlled Occupation[16]
Gaza City, Palestine, September 7, 2005

Well, just when I though it was all over, here I am, stuck once again in the cozy disengaged confines of Gaza City. I wish I could say in the confines of "Gaza Strip," but then I'd be lying. Israel has split Gaza into two parts, closing off the Abo Holi checkpoint in central Gaza to all Palestinian movement, and today it announced the indefinite closure of Rafah crossing, the only route to the outside world for me, Yousuf, and 1.4 million others.

The closure, following the trend of disengagement, was a unilateral Israeli move.

Of course, this is all the more significant given the fact that we are due to travel in about a week to the United States to visit my husband, Yousuf's baba, via Rafah crossing and Cairo. It's even more painful for Palestinians requiring medical visits in Egypt, coming back from abroad to begin school, or—even worse—needing to bury their dead.

One of our best family friends was killed today in a car crash in Egypt, along with her husband and adopted daughter (only the second daughter, the 12-year-old girl, survived). They were there seeking cancer treatment for the father that is unavailable in Gaza. Now the family who survives them in Gaza cannot go to Egypt and bring the bodies back to be buried here or bring the surviving child with them. This is the harsh daily reality for Palestinians. This is the reality that I fear will not change if we are not allowed control over Rafah crossing.

The fanfare in recent days about the "deal" reached over Rafah is vastly overstated. The agreement signed between Egypt and Israel basically gives Egyptian troops the right to—get this—redeploy on their own border. What a breakthrough.

Better yet, the "Egyptian compromise" over border control that the Israeli government is "leaning toward accepting" will have Israel controlling a new terminal for the passage of goods and Israeli surveillance cameras monitoring Palestinian movement through the current Rafah crossing, which will be operated jointly by Egyptians and Europeans (with Israeli oversight, of course). Right. It all makes sense now. A remote-controlled occupation.[17]

Over and OUT . . .[18]
Gaza City, Palestine, September 11, 2005

It's almost midnight. In a few hours, they will be gone—they, of course, being the soldiers who have for so long made our lives miserable here. Already, sporadic celebrations are taking place in Gaza—these celebrations feel much more real than the "manufactured" ones, when disengagement first began several weeks ago. People are out on the streets, singing, dancing, lighting firecrackers. They are gathering near settlements—everyone wants a peek of what's inside (not much, I hear from PA and E.U. officials who visited some of the sites earlier today).

According to them, everything has been destroyed, uprooted, ripped out, or looted. Sabri Saidam, minister of Telecommunications, compared it to the Hurricane Katrina disaster zone. A European official I spoke with said even the greenhouses—for which the settlers were *paid* something like $40 million to keep—were dismantled: Only the tarp and wire were kept intact, with everything *in* the greenhouses destroyed or taken back. He told me some settlers came back and offered to "resell" the machinery that kept the greenhouses going.

Everything was taken out, even light sockets. The official also told me how he saw so-called sewage treatment facilities: "Basically, it was one big septic tank—the sewage was dumped onto Gaza dunes and filtered into the Coastal Aquifer."

Of course, besides causing the total destruction of all infrastructure that could have been used by Gaza's Palestinians, Israel has also left unanswered the question of control over borders. So yes, they *have* left Gaza as one big prison. They left and quite literally locked the door on their way out. All border crossings are now closed indefinitely. No one can leave or come in.

In a press conference held Sunday afternoon in Gaza City, Minister of Civil Affairs Mohammad Dahlan accused Israel of imposing a solution upon the Palestinians regarding the Rafah crossing.

"Everyone knows Israel has a clear plan to force us to agree on the Israel proposal to close the Rafah crossing and move it to Kerem Shalom. There has been no agreement on the issue of border control yet, and we blame Israel fully for leaving Gaza imprisoned," he said.

. . . More tomorrow, I hope, after I finally get a chance to tour the vacated settlements . . .

My Settlement Tour: Katrina Meets Alice's Wonderland[19]
Gaza, Palestine, September 12, 2005

It's almost 2 a.m., and I'm very tired. I've spent the entire day touring the settlements—a tour of the surreal. I just don't know how else to describe it, but I'll try. Here's a rough draft and a more extended version of an article I wrote for *Al Jazeera*:

Using roads that had been previously blocked off to them, Palestinians from all walks of life—the young and the old, men, women, children, and families, resistance fighters and security forces, slowly filtered into the former colonies after daybreak to take a glimpse of what was inside.

In the infamous colony of Netzarim, which had strategically split Gaza into two sections and was, for so long, a pillar and much-hated symbol of the occupation, nothing was left untouched by departing Israeli forces. Trees were uprooted,

electricity lines were cut, and vegetation inside greenhouses and around the land had not been watered in more than 15 days, leaving a dry and dead landscape.

Palestinians salvaged what they could from the rubble, including copper wires and scrap metal, which sells for 8 shekels [$2] a kilo in this impoverished territory.

Some children picked large mangos off a razed tree, while others took to scavenging for leftover toys and books; some found Jewish skullcaps and wore them while posing, oblivious to the irony, next to Hamas flags. Others tied orange antidisengagement ribbons to their heads. All were elated and awestruck, expressing relief and excitement at seeing the occupation depart. Everybody wanted a souvenir.

"We can finally move freely throughout Gaza and play without anyone shooting at us," said 14-year-old Abdullah Yunis, as he surveyed the remains of a ploughed-over sniper tower that had overlooked his refugee camp.

Amid the curious crowds, a Palestinian photojournalist walked around in a vest stapled with pictures he took of Palestinian martyrs killed by Israelis forces in years past, including the youngest victim, 4-month-old Iman Hijju of Khan Yunis.

"I want them to witness this historic moment with me. I want to also make sure that people never forget what they died for," he said.

Palestinians wandered around in disbelief, trying to absorb the scene and the moment. For some, like 26-year old Omar Budran, who lost a leg to an Israeli helicopter gunship that fired at a group of Palestinians not far from the settlement, in the crowded Nusseirat refugee camp two years ago, the day was particularly poignant.

"It's an incredible day for me. I am overwhelmed with happiness, and I am optimistic [about] what the future might bring," he said.

Palestinian forces could do little to stop the largely curious crowds from touring the settlements, though officials say they will take control of the areas in coming days.

"No one in the world can prevent people from expressing their joy at seeing an occupation depart," said one Palestinian security official futilely guarding the gates to the infamous former colony, adding that security forces were making sure the flimsy tarp and wire remains of the greenhouses were kept intact.

Many Palestinian boys, backpacks still on shoulders, skipped school in favor of the exploratory visits to the abandoned colonies that for so long were a source of their grief and misery.

In the former colony of Kfar Darom, young refugee children from the camp of Dair al-Balah played in an abandoned playground.

"It's the most fun we've ever had—there's nothing like this in our refugee camp," laughed 12-year-old Reem Idayn, as she slid down a slide.

Nearby, Palestinian security officers, who had been up since 3 a.m. for the handover of the settlement lands, dozed off under the shade of a large mulberry tree, while young children clamored for a photo opportunity in an abandoned but not-yet-demolished sniper tower that overlooked a pockmarked UN school.

Across the now-flattened electric fence of the former colony, 53-year-old Sulayman Tawaysha continued to watch the scenes in disbelief, along with his six children. The entire family had been up since 3 a.m. to see the soldiers leave, at which point they erupted in ululations of joy and put on a fireworks display.

"I feel free, for the first time—we all feel free," said Tawaysha, as his youngest daughter, Buthoor, served coffee and date cookies to celebrate. Her mother, a newly hired headmistress, was at a local school trying in vain to convince schoolchildren to attend classes.

"Tonight will be the first time we can sit outside after sunset without the fear of being shot at by the nearby troops," added Tawaysha.

The Tawayshas' house was occupied more than 20 times by Israeli forces throughout the Intifada; 17 donoms of their land and three buildings they owned, worth $600,000, were razed to the ground.

Farther south, Palestinians drove past the Abo Holi checkpoint for the first time in six years without having to stop and wait for orders to pass, though a traffic jam ensued as Palestinian forces took down a watchtower that Israeli forces had abandoned but not dismantled.

"I can't believe it—I spent so many miserable nights sleeping here at the checkpoint, waiting for it to open, suffering at their whim," said taxi driver Samir Dogmosh as he drove through unhindered.

In Neve Dekalim, in southern Gaza, the large synagogue in the shape of a Star of David, built in "memory" of the former settlement of Yamit, in Sinai, was still standing. Flags of Palestinian factions were hoisted on top. Inside, charred antidisengagement literature and flyers advertising "tours" to Gush Katif as "New Zionism Plus Torah True Living in Action" littered the vacated, and mostly undemolished, former settlement stronghold, juxtaposed against the impoverished Khan Yunis refugee camp. "Let us help you to sense the magic being felt daily in this beautiful part of our homeland," read the flyer.

. . . Everything was intact, including the settlement "town centre," the school, and the marketplace. Israeli antidisengagement graffiti was hastily spray painted over, and posters of Palestinian Marwan Barghouthi were put up instead.

Beyond the former colony, Palestinians swarmed the Khan Yunis beach in the fertile and formerly fenced off enclave of Mawasi, which had been off limits to them since the start of the second Intifada.

"Today I am here to enjoy this historic day with my only son, Abdullah," said Khan Yunis resident Um Abdullah as she sat under a tin-sheet shelter erected by the seaside, her son playing in the sand nearby. "I came to swim," explained her 4-year-old son.

Young boys surfed on broken refrigerator doors, children ran boisterously around abandoned sea shacks and flew kites, and families took the day off to picnic.

I had an urge to jump in the sea, to scream and laugh and run unrestrained all at once, just like those children. It was, for a people long deprived of it, the sweet and intoxicating taste of freedom.

But in the end, somehow, I couldn't help but feel like a small hamster that was released from the confines of a small decrepit cage with a vexing obstacle course to maneuver around to a more spacious, less-restrictive one—basking in the elation of its newfound freedom and forgetting, for just a moment, that it was still walled in from all sides.[20]

Across the Killing Field[21]
Gaza-Egypt Border, September 15, 2005

Yesterday, I joined thousands of Palestinians who streamed across the once-impermeable and deadly wall that divided this battered border town into two to visit family and friends they had not seen in decades, to shop, or simply to see Egypt for the first time.

It was yet another journey into the surreal. There I was, after all, standing in the Dead Zone known as Philadelphi corridor by Israelis and the killing field by Palestinians—the very location where Israeli tanks once nested, awaiting orders to pound this refugee camp, their tracks still freshly imprinted in the sand, the Palestinian homes they destroyed spread out like carcasses in the background. The once deadly frontline of the Israeli army had become a porous free-for-all.

Rafah was divided into two parts by a fence—and later an iron wall—under the 1982 peace treaty between and Egypt and Israel, which returned the occupied Sinai Peninsula to Egypt.

Thousands of Palestinian families were separated as a result.

The Israeli withdrawal has given them the brief opportunity to reunite, many for the first time in decades, as they clambered over and through the barriers, overcome with emotion.

As a Gush-Shalom ad in *Haaretz* said:

> In 1989, the masses breached the wall in Berlin. Relatives who had not seen each other for decades embraced in a storm of emotions. The whole world applauded. So did we. In 2005 the masses breached the wall in Rafah. Relatives who had not seen each other in decades embraced in a storm of emotions. The Israeli government immediately started to shout: A scandal! A violation of agreements!
>
> But when you cut a town into two, no wall will endure. Not in Berlin. Not in Rafah. Not anywhere.

"How are you?! How is the family? I missed you all so much," cried one man, Ibrahim Turbani, to a cousin he had not seen in 28 years, from the Palestinian side, as they hugged in the middle of the sandy no-man's land where Israeli tanks once nested.

The scenes were repeated all along the border area, with tearful and emotional reunions between mothers and daughters, brothers and cousins.

Some Palestinians simply went as first-time tourists, curious to find out what was outside their war-torn Gaza Strip.

"I came to see this other world I heard about. I've never left Gaza in my life—in fact, I've barely left my refugee camp—and this was my opportunity to do so," said 20-year-old Sameera Gashlan, a nursing student in a Gaza university and resident of the Nuseirat refugee camp in central Gaza.

Nearby, two small boys from the formerly besieged Rafah neighbourhood of Tal al-Sultan whispered and pointed out people from behind a blown-off portion of the wall, as they tried to identify who was Egyptian and who was Palestinian.

"See, I told you silly, that's a Palestinian, not an Egyptian," said one to the other.

"It's something new for them—they've never seen people others than Gazans in their life," one young man explained.

Many Gazans were reunited with their families that they were otherwise unable to visit in years past due to Israeli restrictions on travel that have prevented some 90 percent of Palestinians from leaving Gaza.

"I'm going to see my mother, who is very ill, in al-Arish and try and bring her back to Gaza," explained Saleh Areef, who has been unable to leave Gaza since 1999.

"I left Kuwait to come live in Gaza, but the Israelis froze the family reunion and residency permits after I arrived, and I've been a prisoner in my own land ever since."

Palestinians were critical of the calls to seal off the border again, saying Rafah was once one town and should remain that way, citing as the real problem the lack of a systemic means of access out of and into the Gaza Strip.

"If they just opened Rafah as an international border with normalized access for Palestinians, then there would be no reason for all of this madness," one Palestinian woman told me.

"The reason people are flooding the border is that they aren't allowed through in a normalized way—there is no system to allow that kind of access. They have families, and they are going to want to cross. The bigger problem is that there isn't normalized procedure to cross the border."

The Rafah border terminal, which Israeli forces have vacated but still control, was shut down indefinitely last week, leaving 1.5 million Palestinians in Gaza stranded.

The unofficial—and illegal—border passages have been their only means to leave or enter Gaza in the meantime.

Amid the surreal scenes that, to the untrained eye, seemed like a mass exodus of refugees, Palestinians herded goats and sheep they had bought for a fraction of the price in the Egyptian town of al-Arish, after first hauling them over a part of the border fence.

Egyptian visitors to Palestinian Rafah and Gaza City, of which there were thousands, carried back bags of apples—a staple of northern Gaza, but difficult to find and expensive in Egypt—along with wool blankets and trays of sweets, as moneychangers took advantage of the unexpected market, exchanging shekels for Egyptian pounds, and vice versa, at high rates for anxious visitors.

"Who would have ever believed it—there were actually Egyptians in my store this morning—in Gaza City!" a Palestinian boutique owner, downstairs from my house, exclaimed.

"I wish the border would never close—business has never been so good, and people can finally visit their families," said Egyptian shopkeeper Mohamamd Gumbaz, who owns a herb and spice store just across the border that, like many nearby shops, had sold out of most items.

Despite the intoxicating festivity, several Israeli drones whirred menacingly overhead on the Palestinian side of Rafah, creating a cacophonous, if not disturbing, symphony with nearby celebratory wedding drums and the baa-ing of newly purchased Egyptian sheep.

They monitored the movement along the border from afar, serving as an eerie and foreboding reminder that Israeli troops were never far away for residents of this battered town.

"They're never going to leave us alone," said one young Rafah resident, whose home had been demolished and brother killed during one of the deadly Israeli offensives into the area.

"They will continue to make our lives miserable, if not with tanks, then with unmanned drones."

CHAPTER NOTES

1. The full original text of this post is archived at http://www.gazamom. com/2005/08/zero-hours/, shortened to http://bit.ly/cb66Pa.
2. Laila El-Haddad, "Gazans Cautious, but Eager for Pullout," *Al Jazeera English*, August 16, 2005, archived at http://bit.ly/aTdPbk.
3. Archived at http://bit.ly/aFgSKz.
4. Archived at http://bit.ly/dgjvWU.
5. Also see Toufic Haddad's account of this same incident, "Real News: Disengaged in Gaza," *Electronic Intifada*, August 22, 2005, archived at http://bit.ly/cuH9PL.
6. Archived at http://bit.ly/bUafLY.
7. See "Palestinians under Withdrawal Curfew," *Al Jazeera English*, August 16, 2005, archived at http://bit.ly/cioopr, to read about the threats to Palestinian lives and livelihoods in the midst of the with drawal. See "Gaza Surfers Will Be Forced to Find New Waves," *MSNBC.com*, August 10, 2005, archived at http://bit. ly/9sDHn4, to see an example of some of the U.S. and international coverage of the withdrawal.
8. Archived at http://bit.ly/dzjmdX.
9. Archived at http://bit.ly/d9AwCr.
10. Archived at http://bit.ly/apw6LV.
11. Archived at http://bit.ly/bvMwuP.
12. Archived at http://bit.ly/aAmKm3.
13. Archived at http://bit.ly/9Q1Y1Z.
14. The original report is archived at http://bit.ly/9uvbwX.
15. Archived at http://bit.ly/bUGEPQ.
16. Archived at http://bit.ly/cwSHVE.
17. To read more about the "Egyptian compromise" on control of Rafah cross-ing, see "Israel to Seal Rafah Crossing on Thursday as a Part of Gaza Pullout," *Haaretz*, September 7, 2005, archived at http://bit.ly/bJKcHn.
18. Archived at http://bit.ly/dnXb8J.
19. Archived at http://bit.ly/cqRQEG.
20. See frontline pictures of the disengagement at http://bit.ly/cdbG1y.
21. Archived at http://bit.ly/daiCm1.

Chapter 6

The Empire Strikes Back

Mid-September through December 30, 2005

September 2005 saw the beginning of a new era in Gaza. We were no longer under any rosy illusions about what a postdisengagement Gaza might look like—we were living it in terrifying detail. There were no more settlements or soldiers on the ground and no arbitrary stoppages at internal checkpoints dividing Gaza. But now, new military tactics never used during the days of the settlements were being employed. Gaza City was subjected to "phantom air raids"—low-flying fighter jets intentionally breaking the sound barrier to terrorize the civilian population as "punishment" for the hand-made, wildly inaccurate rockets that were being fired into Israel (and that were themselves a response to continued Israeli political assassinations and detentions). Meanwhile, northern Gaza was being pounded by a daily barrage of Israeli tank and artillery fire from the border.[1]

Gaza's crossings, too, remained largely closed and under effective Israeli control in spite of the complicated, U.S.-brokered Agreement on Movement and Access (AMA), which had promised otherwise. And critically, Israel maintained control over the Palestinian population registry, enabling it to continue determining who is a Palestinian national and who could enter or leave Gaza.[2] The occupation had not ended—it had just been restructured. It was being run remotely, with minimal consequences (or obligations) for the Israelis, though UN officials stated time and again that Israel remained responsible, as the occupying power, for ensuring public order and the health and welfare of the Palestinian population.

Meanwhile, ever-increasing acts of lawlessness by the ruling Fateh party and its many offshoots began to aggravate the Palestinian population and increased the popularity of Hamas's "Change and Reform" party as the parliamentary elections scheduled for January 2006 came nearer. "At least Hamas can control their members. At least they can provide some calm," one Gaza woman observed.

Closed in, Again. Closed in, Again. Closed in, Again.[3]
Gaza City, Palestine, September 19, 2005

Am I beginning to sound like a broken record? If so, that should be a telling statement regarding the situation in Gaza after disengagement. It's the same old, same old. And predictions about Gaza becoming a prison have very much materialized.

I had to cancel my ticket reservations from Cairo to the United States, where Yousuf and I were supposed to meet up with Yassine, whom we haven't seen for five months (and who isn't allowed into Gaza by Israel, because he is a Palestinian with refugee papers from Lebanon, not Gaza). Israel refuses to give in on the Rafah crossing, and it remains closed for the near future in the meantime.

There is literally no way out of here for Gaza's 1.5 million Palestinians, save for an agreement to issue 50 high-priority (and difficult to obtain) permits a day through the Erez crossing. It is noteworthy to mention that nearly 90 percent of Gaza's Palestinians are refused permits through Erez, based on blanket "security reasons" (including myself . . .). I'm trying to come up with a list of all sorts of threatening things I could do that might account for this security denial—"Stop, or I'll throw his dirty diaper in your face! I'm serious . . . not one step closer."

I'm beginning to feel like I'm part of this 1981 Disney movie called *Night Crossing*, where two families (attempt, successfully, to escape walled-in East Berlin in a hot- air balloon.[4] Hmmm. I can picture that now, Yousuf and I floating across Philadelphi, dodging (probably not for long . . .) Israeli drones and radars. Hey, we've careened across the Gaza coast in a donkey cart during closures of the (area formerly known as) Netzarim Junction, I think we can handle that.

The Right to Die[5]
Cairo, Egypt, September 25, 2005

Well, the good news is, I write this from an Internet cafe in Cairo, with Yousuf sleeping soundly in his stroller by my side. We made it out of Gaza—just barely, within the span of the 24 hours that the Rafah crossing was reopened on Friday to allow out hundreds of thousands (and I'm not exaggerating here) of trapped students; expatriate Palestinians; sick men, women, and children who need treatment in Egypt and beyond; and so on, in a trip that took just as long. Those were the only categories of Palestinians allowed out of Gaza, with a select 50 more a day allowed out (that doesn't include me—I am a "security threat") through Erez.

We literally did not know whether the crossing would open or not until pre-dawn on Friday, with Israeli forces reportedly (according to a senior Palestinian security official) threatening to bomb passenger buses if the PA and Egypt operated the crossing without its approval. All pressure tactics, says Diana Butto, legal advisor to the Palestinian withdrawal committee, to force Palestinians to accept an Israeli-imposed solution (a circuitous route through a crossing called Kerem Shalom) to Palestinian movement that would render our freedom of movement—and sovereignty—null and void.

Local newscasts kept flip-flopping as to whether or not the crossing would open: First it was yes, but then it was no, indefinitely, then it was yes, then no again, and finally, "yes, for 48 hours."

That was of course, cut short to just around 30 hours, after all hell broke loose in Gaza—which I watch from a distance with great pain—and Israel decided to collectively punish all of Gaza's Palestinians (a violation of Chapter Four of the Geneva Convention, also a hallmark of an occupying power) by shutting down all crossings indefinitely again, right as we left. (Wait, I thought the occupation was over? Israel was no long in control of the borders? Er . . .)

. . . We left Gaza at 6 a.m. and arrived in Cairo at the same time the next day. It was, to put it mildly, a journey through hell. Much of the problem was due to delays because of the backlog of people trying to get through before the crossing would close again, and logistical delays—the Israelis yanked out all the computers and baggage conveyors to make sure that the Palestinians do not operate the crossing unilaterally (that word should be familiar to them . . .). Still, the Palestinian border officials were quite speedy and efficient, and everyone seemed pleased with their efforts given their minimal capabilities. The same cannot be said for the Egyptians, for whom I will reserve a separate blog rant.

Meanwhile, thousands of other Palestinians who were not as lucky as we were remain behind in Gaza and Egypt. I have spoken to Palestinian families in Gaza whose loved ones died waiting to get medical treatment and others here in Cairo who were unable to transport the bodies of their recently deceased relatives to be buried with dignity in their homeland, in Gaza. One right the Israelis have granted us: the right to die.

Give Me Your Tired . . .[6]
Columbia, Maryland, October 6, 2005

What is it about kids (and hijabi women) that manages to clear a row of passengers in an airplane faster than the plague? Don't get me wrong—I didn't mind the eye-rolling and huffs and puffs of agitated (and clearly childless) passengers one bit (including the snazzy Italian couple perusing through fashion magazines, who snapped at Yousuf for taking their empty plastic bag). It meant Yousuf and I got a whole row to ourselves. And despite the ceaseless wailing of the children in front of us (responding to the mother's vain attempts to read *Barney Goes to the Zoo*

20 different ways), Yousuf was an angel—I guess compared to Rafah crossing, this was a five-star hotel.

In case it's not clear already, my family and I have safely made it to the United States to visit my husband and brothers. It's taken me nearly a week to recover from the hellish journey across Rafah crossing (which is still closed off, sealing 1.5 million Palestinians in Gaza), bombs dropping behind us (which managed to shatter our living-room windows, along with those of several nearby schools), and F-16s swooping down into Gaza's skyline.

I still can't believe we made it across. I keep having nightmares that I am stuck in the crossing with Yousuf, sitting on the floor with thousands of others, being told I can't get across.

While in transit, in London's Heathrow Airport, our flight coincided with a flight headed to Tel Aviv. The bus that transported us from one terminal to another was full of holiday-happy Israelis, chatting nonchalantly in a Hebrew that I half-understood, arms laden with shopping bags from London boutiques.

I wondered if they had ever met a Palestinian, if they had the slightest idea what I had to go through to get here or how it felt to cross Rafah with an 18-month-old child; or if they did but simply preferred to screen out that ugly reality for which their country is responsible from their lives. That is what their government's Gaza policy is about, after all. Out of sight. Out of mind. In less than a few hours they would be back to their homes, flying carefree to the same area of land from which it had taken me weeks in waiting to begin to travel across, 24 hours to cross, several more days to rebook my flight, and another week to recover. That is the daily irony of our existence.

For now, I am just trying to enjoy my time here, to observe Ramadan, to recover, to take in the past few months. Every now and then I hear a helicopter, innocuously monitoring traffic, and I duck for cover. I am still jittery and on edge. The jagged transition from battered Gaza to picture-perfect suburbia, U.S.A., is mentally taxing.

Back Blogging, back in Gaza![7]
Gaza City, Palestine, December 14, 2005

So, I am officially back from the dead (the same cannot be said for Yousuf's stroller, which was mangled at the hands of British Airways baggage handlers on my way to Egypt). It has been a long and much-called-for hiatus, which involved among other things, tropical islands, fall pumpkin festivals, petting zoos, and Eid and Ramadan festivities. And I think (I hope) I am ready to get writing and blogging again—though I likely need a vacation from my vacation.

As an aside: Why on earth is it that Iraqis the world over are being allowed to vote in their parliamentary elections, but the same exception was not made for Palestinians—even those with residency permits who were stuck outside because of the then–border closure, like myself—in presidential elections last year?[8] Hmm . . . I wonder if this has anything to do with refugees and the right of return . . .

Anyway, now that I am back, I can officially report on the "new" Rafah crossing, which I just passed through two day ago (minus my stroller—note to self: Never cross into Gaza via Rafah without stroller). To backtrack, when I left Gaza in late September, it was amidst throngs of Palestinians clamoring to get out within a 30-hour period, after which the crossing was closed again until last week. A somewhat murky deal was reached, whereby the crossing would be Palestinian-Egyptian run, European observed, and Israeli monitored. I'm not quite sure if that's through cameras, a joint control room, or a list of all people who pass through that is handed to the Israelis.

Either way, if one ignores this notable blemish and the fact that the crossing is still not sovereign—as well as the blue-bereted European observers trying desperately, but futilely, not to stand out—the crossing is a drastic improvement. The Egyptians have also officially opened a brand-spanking-new terminal on their side, complete with marble flooring and—*gasp*—computers instead of thick, dusty folders. Now maybe someone can convince them to change those decrepit buses.

Overall, I was pleased—because for the first time in my life crossing Rafah, I felt like a human being. I don't want this to get too long. There is much to say, as usual: from Fateh pre-election infighting, to Israeli missile strikes in northern Gaza, to the continuing military and economic strangulation of the West Bank. So I'll stop here.

Fear and Terrorism: The Israeli War on Gaza Continues[9]
Gaza City, Palestine, December 15, 2005

I am writing this entry as my heart is pounding, my fingers trembling, my eyes in tears . . . so forgive me if I sound irrational. I thought it was over, I really did. Was I naive? Perhaps. But hopeful. Always hopeful. Now I simply feel stupid, and very, VERY afraid.

I was in the kitchen tonight at around 11 p.m. Gaza time, putting away a late dinner I had with my mother after filing a story for Pacifica Radio on a lawsuit filed against former Israeli Army Chief of Staff Moshe Ayalon for war crimes. The suit came a week after a similar complaint was filed against Avi Dichter for bombing a civilian neighborhood in Gaza using F-16s. How ironic that I file a story about F-16s bombing Gaza, thinking to myself—even making an argument to dinner guests—about this being a long-gone era. International pressure would never allow Israel to use such disproportionate force again in such densely populated areas. "True," argued a guest, "now they are simply focusing on resistance leaders as targets in assassinations."

The guests left, and just as my mother and I were chatting nonchalantly, putting away the small plates of za'tar, olive oil, goat cheese, and persimmons, an enormous explosion erupted, followed by the loud swoops of fighter jets—unlike *anything* I had ever heard—shaking our kitchen windows off the their hinges. The sound of Israeli fighter jets breaking the sound barrier over Gaza is a psychological war of terror.

I cannot begin to describe the sound, except to say it penetrates into your very heart. Our whole building shook. I ran outside the kitchen, fell down to the ground crying in hysterics, then started screaming. My father woke up and held me tight, saying, "It's OK, it's OK," as my mother tried to calm me down. "What's happening, what's happening?" I remember repeating hysterically. "We are being bombed, we are being bombed!"

It is that feeling of uncertainty, of vulnerability and fear in the face of an unseen, seemingly formidable force, of feeling that death is at your doorstep that gets to you . . . that strikes morbid fear in your heart and soul.

"It's nothing, it's an F-16 sound bomb, please calm down," said my father. Nothing but a sound. It sounds so harmless; what is sound after all, compared to munitions? In Arabic, they even call them "fake bombings." That is what I always thought to myself. Having experienced both, I think I can safely say the former has the possibility to inflict far more intense psychological damage in a shorter period of time.

I ran like a crazy woman to check on Yousuf—last time this happened, while we were in the U.S., far, far away, enjoying fall leaves and pumpkin patches, the windows shattered. So today, I immediately moved his crib away from the window and cracked the window open to relieve the vacuum, then called my cousins and turned the radio on. They assured me that although this is the loudest sonic boom they had ever heard (which means the F-16 was the lowest flying ever), it happened with far more frequency last month. The bombings were decried by the international community.

But now, they have continued. The planes are still overheard. They are swooping low.

My question is: why? Why *punish* all of Gaza's Palestinians? Is it to make us all so afraid we can't close our eyes? To make us beg for mercy? To make us want it to stop at any expense? It is cruel. It is inhumane. It is collective punishment. It is psychological terror and torture in its rawest, most disturbing form. And so the war on Gaza continues. Terror and torture.

Israel's Terror Tactics in Gaza Continue[10]
Gaza City, Palestine, December 16, 2005

After my last post, I tried in vain to go to sleep after taking a Benadryl. I brought Yousuf to sleep with me (who now, if asked what sound a plane makes, says "BOOM!"). Exactly at *fajr* call to prayer, it started again—two more insane sonic booms. I cry now when I think of them. I can't get near the windows, I'm too afraid to be alone . . .

I have been face-to-face with Israeli helicopter gunships on rooftops in Jabaliya; I have been fired at by sniper towers in Rafah and Dair al-Balah; I have been tear-gassed and even exposed to stun grenades in Ramallah protests; I lived through the daily and constant shelling of Beit Hanoun and Jabaliya, the daily thuds of which could be heard clearly from the main road where we live. But none of those things compares to what I heard yesterday. It wasn't just "bombing"—I've been under bombing attack before, many, many times. These "shock waves" generated from supersonic flights are disorienting, nerve-wracking, and torturous. It's like being in the middle of an earthquake and being under heavy bombardment all at once. It's like being shaken in a simulator, like being slammed against a wall.

As I searched online today for more information on sonic booms—to make sure I wasn't crazy, I wasn't over-reacting—I found this description by someone who has also experienced them: "You never get used to it if you're not prepared for the fly-past. It's the scream of a thousand banshees, which comes immediately before the crash that unnerves. If you believe the aircraft is gonna attack, you're completely disorientated."

In fact, last month, miscarriages increased sharply and children were driven to panic by Israeli jets systematically breaking the sound barrier over Gaza, according to a petition filed in the High Court by the Palestinian Centre for Human Rights and Israel's Physicians for Human Rights, with a medical opinion from renowned psychiatrist Dr. Eyad Sarraj.

Would the Israeli Army have ever dared to use such tactics when their precious settlers were occupying Gaza? I don't think so. Which makes me afraid for what the future might hold.

I also found that Israel is the *only* country to have used sonic booms deliberately, as a weapon of war against a civilian population. When I spoke to the Israeli Army's spokesperson today for an investigative piece I have decided to write on the matter, he explained that the intent is to harm the Palestinian population in Gaza, so they may put pressure on the fighters to stop firing rockets. Asked whether this wasn't collective punishment, he bluntly said, "We don't consider it so."

Article 33 of the Geneva Convention:

> No protected person may be punished for an offence he or she
> has not personally committed. Collective penalties and likewise

all measures of intimidation or of terrorism are prohibited. . . .
Reprisals against protected persons and their property are prohibited.

The Banshees Strike Again[11]
Gaza City, Palestine, December 18, 2005

I have come to learn to fear the night. I am a grown adult. I am a mother. But
yesterday, I am not ashamed to say, I had my mother sleep with me in bed, and
we clung to each other like frightened children as Israeli F-16s once again shook
the earth we live on.

Exactly one second before the dawn call to prayer, it began. My head hurts
thinking about them now, so I'm going to make this brief. I have severe migraines
now that won't go away. Yesterday evening I developed cramps and nausea. If
there was ever a way to expose an entire civilian population to torture, this is it.

These shock waves—these bomb simulations—come out of nowhere. At night
before we slept, I heard the swoops of F-16s in the distance, but I knew that meant
there would be no immediate sonic booms, because you cannot hear the planes
before they bomb (they are going faster than the speed of sound). That is what is
frightening. There is deafening silence, especially in the middle of the night, then
BOOOM, your entire house shakes like a mega-ton bomb was dropped on it.

Over and over again. Then it stops, and you think that's the end of it. There
are no air raid sirens to signal the beginning or end of the raid, as there were in
Lebanon, as there were in Sderot, as there were in Dhahran, Saudi Arabia, where I
lived during the Gulf War.

It is like a million sledgehammer-carrying banshees hanging over your shoulder, ready to strike anytime.

Dumb and Dumber[12]
Gaza City, Palestine, December 21, 2005

Today, *Haaretz* announced that the Israeli Army intends to cut off the Gaza Strip's
electricity supply if the Qassam rockets keep coming (I guess that sonic boom thing
isn't really working).

Apparently, this was supposed to happen yesterday, but "implementation was
indefinitely postponed to give the main Palestinian hospital in Gaza time to pur-
chase emergency generators." I see. It is a sort of humane collective punishment.

Reeeally smart move—exposing the entire population to deafening shock waves in absolute darkness is sure to improve security.

This idiotic (but not surprising) suggestion on the part of Minister of Defense Shaul Mofaz has tied for this week's Dumb Move of the Day award (DMD) with the kidnapping of schoolteachers in Gaza by armed gunmen. It's not clear why they kidnapped the Belgian and Australian teachers from the American International School, but reports indicate they are disgruntled gunmen who want "in" on the fringe benefits of the Fateh party.

Cutting off electricity for 1.5 million civilians, or kidnapping schoolteachers for political ends? Who wins this week's DMD? The verdict's in: dumb and dumber.

Now excuse me while I go get my flashlights and earplugs ready.

It's Raining Men . . .[13]
Gaza City, Palestine, December 23, 2005

Well, not really. But it is raining. And what do you do on a rainy day in Gaza with a 21-month-old stir-crazy boy? *Nothing.* People are too scared to go anywhere after dark here, and they get lazy in the winter ("winter" meaning a very temperate 17°C [63°F]), even lazier when it's raining, so we were stuck indoors.

I tried and tried to think of interesting things to do (climbing on Mommy's desk and destroying her CD drive was not one of them) and exhausted what little creative cells I had left in my brain. We danced, we finger-painted, we colored (the couches, inadvertently) with crayons, we watched *Finding Nemo* (in Arabic, Egyptian dialect) five times. (If I see that little wide-eyed clown fish one more time today, I think I'll fry him for dinner.) We made castles out of the couch cushions, we took pictures, we even watched a Hamas rally go by (well, it's hard to avoid— living on the main street and all can be very strategic for a journalist and somewhat annoying for a family), and, of course, we drank coffee. Needless to say, Yousuf was bouncing off the walls for a good two hours (quite literally).

Here's to more rainy days alone with Yousuf.

Rainy Days in Gaza Mean . . . [14]
Gaza City, Palestine, December 25, 2005

Tea and sweet potatoes on the grill (equivalent of "chestnuts roasting on an open fire").

The Empire Strikes Back[15]
Gaza City, Palestine, December 27, 2005

I got very little sleep last night. Yes, the Empire struck back. Funny, because yesterday was the first night in a week I decided not to cover Yousuf's crib with a sheet in case, Heaven forbid, the windows were to shatter on him from the force of a sonic boom. I also closed all the windows because it's been particularly cold in our usually temperate little Gaza this week. Wouldn't you know it, Murphy's does it again.

I had just finished a midnight call with my husband, when around 1 a.m. —- BOOM, rattle, and shake. Thank God no windows broke. Interestingly, this time I was relatively well composed. My heart was racing, yes, but I think I have finally confronted the fear of the attacks (on which I wrote an article for *Al Jazeera*).[16] Or maybe I was too tired or dazed to fully comprehend them. Or maybe the suggestions of my dentist helped. (He said I was grinding my teeth at night because of the stress, causing migraines, and suggested I engage in stress-relieving exercises.)

The same cannot be said for my mother, whom I called out to frantically four times before eliciting a response. She was literally scared stiff. I ran to check on Yousuf, who woke up, and decided to put him to sleep with me. The aerial assault on northern Gaza continued all night, and we could hear Israeli aircraft pounding streets and buildings in the distance. Around 6:30 a.m., my windows rattled once again from another sonic boom. Yousuf seemed OK in the morning—how little toddlers comprehend of men and war.

I then scanned *Haaretz*, which reported that the Israeli Army will begin enforcing their 5km "no-go" zone tonight (which covers two major northern

Gaza towns) and advised Palestinian residents to either "shut themselves up in their homes" or flee before they strike: "The army will warn residents that leaving their homes will mean putting themselves in danger." The warnings will be given through thousands of flyers dropped by Israeli aircraft.

Well, at least they are being humane about all this. I wonder what the fliers will say. "Hi there! We're going to destroy your neighborhood today, possibly your house. Just a head's up. Have a great day!"

I was then greeted by the hammering of Kalashnikovs a few streets over—courtesy of your friendly, neighborhood "disgruntled" gunmen (there seem to be a lot of "disgruntled" gunmen these days). Yet again, armed al-Aqsa Martyrs' Brigades members took over government buildings, "demanding jobs" (for me, that translates into "we want payoffs"), and yet again, it was somehow quickly resolved.

The frequency of these events is making me doubt more and more the future of the Fateh party and of Mahmoud Abbas's grip on Gaza. I do not think either will last after elections, which are scheduled for late January. Meanwhile, more and more, I hear people—including Christian friends—talk about how Hamas is gaining respect and popularity with every passing idiotic Fateh incident. As one guest put it today, "At least they can control their members, at least they can provide some calm." And sometimes, that's all people really want.

Hand Me Those Earplugs[17]
Gaza City, Palestine, December 28, 2005

Well, it seems that after a minor lull, the Israeli Air Force has decided to officially step up its use of the terrorizing sonic attacks today and the next few days, according to *Yediot* newspaper. I figured as much when last night we were shocked awake four times throughout the night, from shortly after midnight all the way to 6 a.m. The sonic attacks continued with ferocity over Gaza City, each larger and louder than the previous. The last one had my ears ringing and was particularly terrifying in its strength—I could feel the waves. I'm trying to figure out if there is some pattern to it all, some method in this madness. So far, I gather not.

Under Siege[18]
Gaza City, Palestine, December 30, 2005

It's 10:40 p.m. now, and northeastern Gaza is under serious bombardment. We can hear powerful thuds every few seconds here from Gaza City, which are rattling our windows. The shelling is very close to civilian homes, according to local correspondents located in the region.

There's Your Solution![19]
Gaza City, Palestine, December 30, 2005

I don't usually highlight highly idiotic statements that politicians or people make, for one reason or another, dismissing an entire people or race, but this time, I felt compelled to. Yesterday, the mayor of Sderot, speaking to *Ynet*, said that Israel should "wipe Beit Hanoun off the map." To quote the seagull in *Finding Nemo*, "Niiiice." That suggestion should definitely bring about a lasting peace.

It goes hand-in-hand with a "humane occupation," I guess.

Fall Bounty[20]
Gaza City, Palestine, December 30, 2005

A 72-year-old farmer from Beit Hanoun sells her fall crops (pumpkin and bell peppers) in a vegetable market near Gaza City, with Israeli helicopter gunships looming overhead.

An elderly Palestinian woman farmer from Beit Hanun sells her fall crops (pumpkin and bell peppers) in a vegetable market near Gaza City, with Israeli helicopter gunships looming overhead.

CHAPTER NOTES

1. From September 2005 through May 2007, Palestinian armed groups fired roughly 2,700 rockets into Israel, killing four Israeli civilians, according to the United Nations Office for the Coordination of Humanitarian Affairs (UNOCHA). During 2006 alone, Israel fired over 14,000 artillery shells into Gaza, killing 59 people, almost all of them noncombatants. According to a report, "Indiscriminate Fire," published by Human Rights Watch, "Hamas, Islamic Jihad, al-Aqsa Martyrs' Brigades (AMB), and the Popular Resistance Committees (PRC) have all claimed responsibility for firing rockets into Israel, though Hamas largely complied with self-imposed halts to such attacks" during this time period. "These groups have justified their attacks as actions of self-defense and reprisals for Israel's actions against the Palestinians." To find out more about UNOCHA's findings, visit http://www.ochaopt.org/documents/CAS_Aug07.pdf. To find out more about the Human Rights Watch report, visit http://www.hrw.org/en/node/10911/section/1.

2. According to a report published by Gisha, an Israeli nonprofit organization, Israel's disengagement resulted not in the relinquishment of Israeli control "but rather [removal of] some elements of control while tightening other significant controls." Gisha goes on to note, "Israel is bound to respect the rights of Gaza residents in its control of Gaza's borders, population registry, tax system, and other areas, and it also owes positive duties to permit and to facilitate the proper functioning of civilian institutions in Gaza, pursuant to international humanitarian law." To read more of Gisha's 2007 report, "Disengaged Occupiers: The Legal Status of Gaza," visit http://www.gisha.org/UserFiles/File/Report%20for%20the%20website.pdf.

3. The full original text of this post is archived at http://www.gazamom. com/2005/09/closed-in-again-closed-in-again-closed-again/, shortened to http://bit.ly/96xmmW.

4. The film is based on the true story of the Strelzyk and Wetzel families.

5. Archived at http://bit.ly/bEzY3J.

6. Archived at http://bit.ly/dxUGWt.

7. Archived at http://bit.ly/adlDRR.

8. Iraq's first general elections after the 2003 invasion occurred December 15, 2005. The International Organization for Migration (IOM) organized voting for Iraqi expatriates around the world. The International Foundation for Electoral Systems reported that approximately 290,000 Iraqis had registered to vote, including 26,000 in the United States. For more information, see "Council of Representatives Election Composite Report: Iraq," International Foundation for Electoral Systems, December 15, 2005, archived at http://bit.ly/cZcHl8. Palestinian presidential elections took place January 9, 2005. According to the Carnegie Endowment for International Peace, not only were Palestinians outside the Occupied Territories (OT) not allowed to vote; even some within the OT, specifically in Jerusalem and outlying villages, were hindered from registering and casting their ballots. For more information, see Nathan Brown, "Frequently (And Less Frequently) Asked Questions about Palestinian Presidential Elections," Carnegie Endowment for International Peace, January 10, 2005, archived at http://bit.ly/cqDt4f.

9. Archived at http://bit.ly/cUnMeZ.

10. Archived at http://bit.ly/cCJCK2.

11. Archived at http://bit.ly/apH0Ld.

12. Archived at http://bit.ly/dufWeJ.

13. Archived at http://bit.ly/9fKRPf.

14. Archived at http://bit.ly/cYP0U3.

15. Archived at http://bit.ly/czHabo.

16. Laila El-Haddad, "Israeli Sonic Booms Terrorising Gaza," *Al Jazeera English*, updated January 2, 2006, archived at http://bit.ly/dC2L6v.

17. Archived at http://bit.ly/cGKmg2.

18. Archived at http://bit.ly/ac8v8K.

19. Archived at http://bit.ly/aa49nK.

20. Archived at http://bit.ly/c3l6NJ.

PART II

Elections—and Punishing the Electorate

January–December 2006

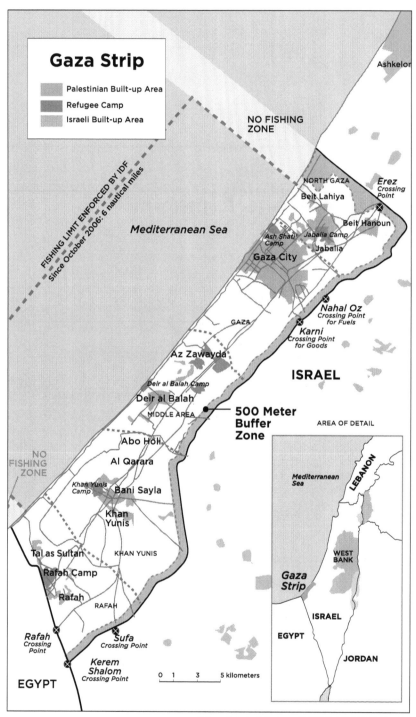

Gaza Strip

- Palestinian Built-up Area
- Refugee Camp
- Israeli Built-up Area

Ashkelon

NO FISHING ZONE

FISHING LIMIT ENFORCED BY IDF
Since October 2006: 6 nautical miles

Mediterranean Sea

NORTH GAZA

Erez Crossing Point

Beit Lahiya

Beit Hanoun

Ash Shati' Camp

Jabalia Camp

Jabalia

Gaza City

GAZA

Nahal Oz Crossing Point for Fuels

Karni Crossing Point for Goods

Az Zawayda

ISRAEL

Deir al Balah Camp

Deir al Balah

MIDDLE AREA

500 Meter Buffer Zone

AREA OF DETAIL

Abo Holi

NO FISHING ZONE

Al Qarara

Mediterranean Sea

LEBANON

Khan Yunis Camp

Bani Sayla

Khan Yunis

WEST BANK

Tal as Sultan

KHAN YUNIS

Rafah Camp

Gaza Strip

Rafah

RAFAH

ISRAEL

Rafah Crossing Point

Sufa Crossing Point

EGYPT

JORDAN

EGYPT

Kerem Shalom Crossing Point

0 1   3   5 kilometers

Cartography by Lewis Rector and © 2010 Just World Publishing, LLC

Chapter 7

Palestine's Elections Drama

January 2006

January 2006 marked what many considered to be the first truly free and fair democratic elections in Palestine and in the larger Arab Middle East.

Voter turnout was 84 percent, according to the Central Elections Commission. The elections were also notable for the participation and diversity of political parties and independent candidates from across the spectrum. Women played a particularly active role in campaigning door to door.

The results took the entire world by surprise—including the parties involved. What I remember clearly about this time was how palpable the disbelief—and in many cases joy— was throughout Gaza; people felt that they had some agency in their own lives for once and were able to catalyze change in what had been a seemingly predetermined existence, where every aspect of their lives was subject to absolute outside control.

All the while, and specifically in the weeks before election day, Israel continued to impose draconian restrictions on the movement of people and goods, unilaterally and arbitrarily shutting down Gaza's commercial crossings for extended periods. The result was millions of dollars in losses to the agricultural sector. Thousands of Palestinian farmers were out of work.

According to the United Nations, less than 4 percent of the season's harvest was exported.[1]

This period also saw the establishment of a so-called Israeli no-go zone in northern Gaza, accompanied by Israeli Army open-fire regulations permitting soldiers to shoot to kill any moving object within 150m of the zone (this regulation has since been expanded to 300m).[2] A village included in the buffer zone was Siyafa, formerly sandwiched between three Israeli settlements, isolated and locked in once again after enjoying only a fleeting few months of internal freedom of movement.

Moving Up in the World[3]
Gaza City, Palestine, January 2, 2006

I finally got myself to put Yousuf in a nursery—not because I needed someone to watch him, but because I wanted him to be exposed to some other children his age a few times a week. (OK, who am I kidding? I needed someone to watch him while I worked.) I realized the time had come for him to make contact with the outside world when he began banging his head against our kitchen wall in a state of advanced boredom. I'm kidding, of course. But really, the kid needs some friends. So I searched and searched, and the more nurseries I saw, the more worried I became. Finally, I found a cute—and clean—little place nearby that doesn't resort to sedating toddlers with food and sleep. Today is officially his second day, and he's loving it—perhaps more than I. I miss his morning banter and desperate pleas to rescue him from my mother as I'm working at my desk. But I'm sure it's for the best. Next thing you know, he'll be graduating from college. My little boy is growing up.

Apaches Overhead[4]
Gaza City, Palestine, January 2, 2006

I'm working late tonight. As I'm typing, I can hear helicopter gunships hovering above our home in Gaza City. They are not distant but rather directly overhead. I'm waiting for an inevitable missile to go flying over our house. So far, that hasn't happened, but the signs do not bode well. Last night, the booms continued at odd hours of the night: one shortly after 2 a.m. and another after 6 a.m.

Here come the helicopters again. I'd better duck and cover, just in case . . . and brace for the night ahead.

Let the Games Begin![5]
Gaza City, Palestine, January 3, 2006

I made it safely through the night, I'm pleased to report. The Apaches eventually dispersed, perhaps after being unable to find their intended target. For them to be hovering so low over Gaza City's Remal neighborhood was rather unusual—and very frightening.

Instead, I woke to the marching of campaigning Palestinians with their various electioneering accessories, including megaphones blasting out campaign messages and drums being banged throughout the streets (one group even had two clowns and a *dabke* troupe—quite a sight, like an election-circus parade, which Yousuf enjoyed thoroughly).

Today, of course—as I was reminded rather intrusively—marked the first official day of legislative council elections campaigning.

Gaza's main city square was literally plastered with posters and banners hanging every which way, which sprang up almost overnight. Some were for local independent candidates promising to "serve Gaza's people." But the most prominent banners so far were those of Hamas, which is clearly building its campaign on its reputation of honesty and its promise to combat corruption, all while standing up to Israel (its election insignia is "A hand that builds, and a hand that resists").

As one of its banners read (roughly translated), "al-Islah [literally 'reform' and also the name of the party] means security, and our party means business [or 'and our party guarantees it']." Another banner simply stated, "Hamas: Faith. Work. Change. Reform." A Hamas election float traveling through Gaza City declared by megaphone, "Vote for List Three, the List of the Inner Jihad," a reference to the struggle for self, societal reform, and improvement, as advised by the Prophet Mohammad.

Also making a prominent showing was Mustafa Barghouthi's "Independent" party list, which is building its campaign on similar promises of combating corruption and providing a just and democratic alternative to the ruling party (though it is not nearly as popular as Hamas, it does seem to have a lot of campaigning money from expatriate Palestinians, or so I've heard).

I haven't yet seen Fateh start full-fledged campaigning, although—given its reputation for over-the-top fanfare and excessive spending in past municipal elections—it should be big and interesting to see how it will combat its increasingly sour reputation.

People here can hardly keep track of the different parties (six off the top of my head) and lists of independent candidates. Perhaps I'll do a rundown in another entry.

When It Rains, It Pours[6]
Gaza City, Palestine, January 4, 2006

Boy, when it rains here in our troubled little part of the world, it really does pour. Fateh militants plough through the Egyptian border and riot with Egyptian police. The Palestinian election committee resigns in protest of ongoing anarchy. All while Qassams fall near Ashkelon, and Ariel Sharon suffers a major, likely irreparable stroke (hours after Israeli papers report an election corruption file will be reopened).

Off to get my umbrella.

United We Stand![7]
Gaza City, Palestine, January 6, 2006

I first heard members of Hamas announcing this news over a loudspeaker in Gaza City, and "Rafahpundit" confirmed it: Six Palestinian factions (specifically, their military wings) have come together to form a "Special Joint Force" (SJF) to steal from the rich and give to the poor, à la Robin Hood . . . no, I'm kidding (but close).

The SJF "will act totally independently from the official [Palestinian Authority (PA)] Security Forces" to preserve law and order and to protect Palestinian civilians, given the ever-increasing security lapse in Gaza (i.e., to do what the PA hasn't).

The Ministry of the Interior spokesperson Tawfiq Abo Khosa dismissed the idea, saying, "Nobody whatsoever is entitled to take the law into his own hands by claiming that the Palestinian Authority is not doing its job. There are many obstacles, and those *militant groups* are one of these obstacles."

Militant groups? How about *one* group, Mr. Abo Khosa, your very own al-Aqsa Martyrs' Brigades?

Interesting to see how this one will work out, given that they are all heavily armed. On the other hand, it may just work if there is some kind of balance of power. Guess who was missing from the lineup? (Mainstream Fateh.)

The Evangelical "Right of Return"[8]
Gaza City, Palestine, January 6, 2006

I'm speechless. The Israeli government—which never ceases to amaze—has now reached a new nadir. While Palestinian refugees, like my husband, continue to be denied the right of return to their own land, the Israeli government prepares to give a large slice of that land to Pat Robertson & Co. for an evangelical Disneyland of some sort.

. . . So let me see if I have this straight: I'm denied entry to the West Bank because I'm from Gaza. Yassine is denied entry to his own home because his grandparents were driven from their homes in Palestine. And evangelical Christians pick up the pieces. Yassine, have you thought about joining forces with the Christian right? It just might be your ticket home.

What Will He Say?[9]
Gaza City, Palestine, January 8, 2006

As Sharon lies on his deathbed, good wishes and prayers have poured in from around the world for the "man of peace," as President George W. Bush put it; the man who "could never be stopped," to quote the "liberal" *Haaretz*.

Before Yasser Arafat died, he was decried as an "obstacle to peace," and post-mortem, there was a "new window of opportunity." The world was considered a better, safer place.

But Sharon? Well, Sharon is Sharon. He is a man of peace. Of peace. A piece of this, a piece of that makes a whole, I guess. A whole lot of peace.

Peace. Like how peaceful, I think, those souls he crushed must be now. Those souls of Sabra and Shatilla. Of Qibya and Breij. Of Rafah and Jabaliya, Jenin and . . .[10]

Now, I'm sure people are saying—yes, but people change. Sure. Change. Change is the only constant, right?

Ask Iman Hims's family, who picked up her pieces. Her peace. Or Nuran Dib. Or, or, or. . . .

. . . And I think, will he meet those pieces on his final day?

And when he meets his Maker, what, then, will he say?

A Very Gaza Eid[11]
Gaza City, Palestine, January 11, 2006

Eid, specifically Eid al-Adha (the Festival of Sacrifice), in Gaza means many things. First and foremost, it means *meat* (some here jokingly call it "Eid al-Lahma" . . . the Eid of meat), because it is recommended that Muslims who can afford to should slaughter sheep or cows to remember Abraham's sacrifice and distribute the meat to the poor, to neighbors, and to family. Many people insist on doing it "the old-fashioned way" (i.e., slaughtering the animals [though in a humane manner] near their homes, which means streets streaming full of blood (thank God, it rained). Let's just say it was enough to make me consider becoming vegetarian.

Besides the meat, Eid here also means the usual—dressing up or buying new outfits; gifts and "eid-iyya" for the kids (some bonus gift money they get from each visiting relative); candy and chocolates and Eid cookies with date filling; crazy mini–metal Ferris wheels that suddenly pop up on Gaza's streets, offering rides for a shekel a pop (I call them death traps because they are so insanely dangerous); and, of course, something so uniquely Gazan that even a West Banker wouldn't know it—*Sumaqiyya!* (pronounced in true Gazan dialect as "Sumaggiya").

I guess you could call it one of Gaza's national dishes. Made on special occasions, it basically consists of chunks of tender meat, cooked with chard, tahini (sesame paste), dill, garlic, chilies, chickpeas, and, of course, Sumac (from which it derives its name), and it is eaten with Arabic bread. Many people have a love-hate relationship with it. I guess you could call it an acquired taste, but it is definitely one of those dishes you won't find anywhere but Gaza!

Sumaqiyya, one of Gaza's "national dishes" often served during Eid al-Adha.

Israel to Pat Robertson: Deal Is a No-Go[12]
Gaza City, Palestine, January 11, 2006

Well, apparently, Pat Robertson's comments about Sharon's stroke being an act of God struck a raw nerve in the Israeli Tourism Ministry (after all, why should Palestinians be upset?). His "steal-of-a-deal" was nixed. According to *Haaretz*, the $50-million tourism partnership where a Zio-Christian Disneyworld would have been built on land (cleared of its indigenous Palestinian inhabitants who are, 50 years on, denied the right to return to this empty land) leased for free in al-Jaleel is a no-go because of Robertson's rash bashin' of Sharon (doctors are apparently trying to stimulate his sense of smell by placing shawarmas by his bedside, according to Israeli radio).

I guess God does work in mysterious ways.

The Election Dance—in the *Guardian*[13]
Gaza City, Palestine, January 13, 2006

As Eid comes to an end, election campaigning has swung back into full gear here, with the big day less than two weeks away.

In the midst of the campaigning, I've created a basic guide to the elections, published on the *Guardian*'s website. Here's a brief excerpt:

The elections will be based on a mixed electoral system that combines district voting and proportional representation, or "lists" (each list must consist of at least seven persons). The 132 seats of the Palestinian legislative council are divided equally between the two systems. There are 16 electoral districts (11 in the West Bank and five in the Gaza Strip), with each allocated several seats according to its population.

I'm having trouble keeping all the electoral lists apart, so I've made a simple user's guide. In all, there are 11 parties, referred to as "lists" here, contesting 66 seats for the national district:

The usual suspects
The Palestinian National Liberation Movement (Fatah)
The Change and Reform list (Hamas)

Middle runners
The Popular Front for the Liberation of Palestine (Martyr Abu Ali Mustafa list)
The Alternative list (a coalition of leftist parties)
The Third Way list (led by technocrat Salaam Fayad and Hanan Ashrawi)
National Initiative list ("Independent Palestine"; led by former presidential candidate Mustafa Barghouthi)
The National Coalition for Justice and Democracy—"Wa'ad" ("Promise"; led by renowned Gaza psychiatrist Eyad Sarraj)

Say who?
Martyr Abu al-Abbas list
Freedom and Social Justice list
Freedom and Independence list
The Palestinian Justice list

Confused yet? Don't worry, so are we. Who is coming up with these party names? I think Sharon's "Kadima" somehow inspired it all. Or what about their election insignia? The ruling party Fatah, in an apparent attempt to brighten its downcast image here, opted for a sunflower with a Palestinian Kaffiya in the shape of a tie sticking out of it.[14]

Somewhere, Over the Rainbow . . . [15]
Gaza City, Palestine, January 14, 2006

A rainbow forms an incongruent beam of beauty over the Gaza Strip yesterday after several days of musky rain.

The Fateh Hotline[16]
Gaza City, Palestine, January 18, 2006

As an electioneering strategy aimed at helping it come clean about its tarnished image, the Fateh party has set up a toll-free hotline for queries about candidates, which it has advertised in the daily papers with the tagline, "We promise an answer to every question."

I decided to give the number a shot.

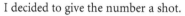

ME: How do you propose to combat corruption and keep the streets safe? [concerned as any good citizen should be]

YOUNG MAN: What a beautiful and nice question. Here at Fateh, we don't deny we made mistakes. We all make mistakes. But we're bringing in new faces. The wrongs can be rectified. Our election program is well known, we want to protect pluralism. And, as a sign that democracy is thriving, remember that Mahmoud Abbas only won by 62 percent, not 99 percent like in some countries, right? And also, freedom for all Palestinian prisoners is not just a slogan for us—it's one of our top priorities. I'm sure you have relatives in Israeli jails.

ME: Er, and the lawlessness?

YOUNG MAN: Sure, sure . . . chaos, and weapons, and the rule of law. Well, as you know, they were on Abu Mazen's list of priorities when he ran for president. These aren't just words; we mean it. Now tell me, who are you voting for?

ME: I haven't made up my mind yet.

YOUNG MAN: How can you not have made up your mind? There's no time left! Isn't the decision obvious?

[Silence, as I contemplate the potential of outsourcing call centers to Gaza.]

YOUNG MAN: Wait wait, don't hang up, let me tell you about corruption. If a mischievous boy is alone in his house, he is bound to wreak havoc. But if his brothers are there with him, they will put him in his place. That's how we view the parliament. All of the parties have some corruption in them. We want to include the whole family in the decision-making process.

[More silence.]

YOUNG MAN: We've been part of the struggle for liberation for 40 years now! We shouldn't take the actions of a few people to represent all of the party. So we have a few rotten apples. . . .

ME: I really have to go now. But thank you for taking my call.

YOUNG MAN: Please, please. Call again with any questions, and we promise to provide an answer.

[End of conversation.]

For more, check out my second blog installment in the *Guardian*.[17]

Return of the Drones[18]
Gaza City, Palestine, January 19, 2006

It's late, but I can't sleep. Israeli drones are whirring incessantly, forebodingly, overhead.

Mostly, I think, it's an intimidation tactic, like the sonic booms (which have ceased during the past week, but which the Israeli High Court said last week that the army could continue using). The drones are unmanned and often carry missiles and are controlled remotely from some operation room, where army commanders can, in the privacy of their own barracks, view what's going in Gaza from above. You can't help but feel like some macho young Israeli soldier is getting a kick out of playing a real-life video game tonight; it's our own sick reality show. "Smile Gaza, you are *all* on Army TV!"

You feel like the noise enters your brain after a while. Whirrrrrrrrrrrrrrrrrrrrrrrrrr . . . then it gets a little louder and more intense if the plane gets lower or focuses in on a target . . .

WHIRRRRRRRRRRRR . . . then dies down a bit . . . whirrrrrrrr. Like a very large, menacing mosquito, right above your head, but, of course, with more deadly consequences. You almost want that rocket to get launched somewhere, just so the whirring will stop. Oh. Now there are two of them, or are they three?

They are particularly eerie in the dead of night when the only other noises are an occasional car screeching past or late-night election-poster plasterers attempting to stick something up on our apartment building wall. Well, back to bed I go, or so I guess.

Countdown to Crunch Time[19]
Gaza City, Palestine, January 21, 2006

It's crunch time. With four days left until the big day, postprayer in Gaza Friday afternoon saw dozens of election rallies and "festivals," complete with colorful (if tacky) banners, fervent partisan politicking, folk music, revolutionary songs, and *dabke* dances.

Things are getting heated between the frontrunners, Hamas and Fateh, which have been exchanging blows over credibility during the past few days. Polls show a dead heat between the two parties.

In the northern part of the Strip, young-guard Fateh icon Mohammad Dahlan tried to rally a crowd of 20,000 in a last-ditch effort to win the northern Gaza districts.

"Are you going to allow Hamas to take the north as they say they will?" he asked, in response to defiant cheers of his supporters. He added that Hamas should apologize to Fateh for calling the 1996 elections "treason" and "admit" that the Fateh plan—negotiations based on the Oslo Accords—ultimately "triumphed" (um . . . yeah . . history lesson anyone?).

I guess even in battered Gaza, one cannot escape the deluge of dirty election politics.

For more, check out my latest post in a five-part series for the *Guardian*. Here's an excerpt:

> Hamas held a large (very green) afternoon rally of its own in Gaza City—so large, in fact, that most streets in the city had to be shut down because of the sheer numbers in attendance (50,000 at the very least). But it exerted little effort at firing back, except to remind voters of its "clean record" in newspaper ads.
>
> Everything seems to hinge on these elections some way or another, from the resumption of negotiations, to the receipt of foreign aid, to relations with the United States, to security on Gaza's streets.
>
> It represents, I think, a real turning point for Palestinian politics as well. Of course, where we will turn to is a different matter.[20]

Let's Vote Already![21]
Gaza City, Palestine, January 24, 2006

With less than 12 hours left until voting begins, Palestinian security and international observers have deployed, campaigning has (finally!!!!) ended, and everyone is waiting in anticipation for the big day finally to end already!

To help the voting process go smoothly, the Central Elections Committee published a page-long ad explaining to voters how to cast their ballots properly—the ABCs of Palestinian voting, if you will. Any aberrations, they warned, will disqualify your vote.

. . . Personally, I just want the elections to be over and done. Our walls have been disfigured, and our privacy invaded (recently with SMS messages). And Gaza resembles a horribly decorated circus (I pity the custodial workers come Thursday morning), what with the banners, flags, and incessant campaign trolleys perusing down the city streets, blasting music and messages. *Yallah khalsoona!* (Get it over with already!)

"A Democratic Wedding"[22]
Gaza City, Palestine, January 25, 2006

That's the popular phrase in Palestine these days to describe the elections, which have finally occurred. I'll make this post brief, as I'm exhausted from covering the vote all day. As I write this post, testosterone-charged Fateh hooligans have taken to celebrating in the streets, honking horns, flying their trademark yellow flags, and shooting into the air (one bullet just nicked our family room's window).

Initial exit polls show Fateh with a narrow lead in the national districts, but pollster Khalil Shikaki says it's very possible they will not form a majority. Either way, it's pertinent to remember the significance of all this—that Fateh and Hamas have nearly split the vote in half. I think both parties will be pleased, because Hamas doesn't want to be a majority and have to make the difficult decisions.

A little on the voting itself: My finger looks horribly bruised (according to Yousuf, who asks, "*Wa wa? Wa wa?*" meaning, "Is it hurt?" every time he sees it). I tried to convince the election worker to only put the tip of my finger in that dreadful indelible ink, but she dunked the whole thing in there. All tricks to make the ink removal easier failed to produce results (clear nail polish painted on before the voting, a buffer of Vaseline, etc.).

The election workers—more like election Nazis—were taking their jobs very seriously, which was good up to a point. Sometimes I felt they focused too much on procedure and too little on actually helping voters who may have been confused. At one point, I put my ballot into the box, didn't fold it, and got yelled at in front of everyone, "No no, you *must* fold it—stop." I felt like I was carrying a bomb all of a sudden and got very nervous. Finally, the man calmed me down, "It's OK, just go sloooowly, take your time."

Democracy 101[23]
Gaza City, Palestine, January 26, 2006

Just when you think you have things figured out here, they turn topsy-turvy on you.

In a matter of a few weeks, Sharon becomes comatose; the Palestinian streets go from chaos, hinging on anarchy, to an unsettling calm; and then the Islamic group Hamas, contesting elections for the first time and thought to be lagging behind Fateh by every measure, sweeps the first parliamentary elections in 10 years, shattering the ruling party's long grip on Palestinian politics.

Welcome to Gaza.

The latest events can only be described as a political earthquake, both locally and regionally. Not only are these the first truly democratic and hotly contested elections in the Arab Middle East; they also represent the first time an Islamic party has come to power through the system and the popular will of the people.

To say we are entering a new stage is an understatement. Everyone knew Hamas would do well in these elections and that it would constitute a significant challenge to the ruling party. But this well?

As one commentator on my *Guardian* blog put it, "Checkmate! Isn't democracy a wonderful thing?"

The Street Reacts, in More Ways Than One[24]
Gaza City, Palestine, January 27, 2006

Minutes after official results were announced last night, the street erupted in celebration, with Hamas supporters and others taking to the streets, honking horns, handing out sweets, and lighting fireworks in the downcast sky.

It was clear that no one—*no one*—expected Hamas to win. Strolling around the streets at night, it also became obvious, on a very basic level, why people voted for Hamas. Forget about the political horizon (or lack thereof) for a moment.

I was speaking to a storeowner about the results, when a friend of his burst in, beside himself, "Did you hear? Did you hear? I couldn't sleep all night. I can't believe it!" He was a municipality employee who barely made enough money to feed his family. His son had been injured in internal clashes six months ago, his groin muscles torn and disabled; he was sitting at home immobile. For six months, he has been chasing the PA for some medical compensation and hasn't received a penny, "while those nobodies travel around in their BMWs. Is that fair? Tell me?" Why did Hamas win? "Remember," said the man: "The feeling of oppression is a very powerful factor."

It's also about priorities. In Israel, security was a priority in 2001, and that is why the Israeli people, I think, voted in Sharon, the same Sharon they so fervently demonstrated against in 1982 in the streets of Tel Aviv. In Gaza, the priorities are security and survival. "A family with 10 children living under the poverty line is not going to think first about relations of the new parliament with Israel, or the United States, or the European Union. He is going to think about how he can feed those children," another man told me.[25]

. . . Fateh supporters were hardly celebrating. Their reactions ranged from shock, to denial, to bitterness, to arrogance, to humiliation, and, finally, lashing out against their own corrupt leaders tonight.

Yesterday, I spoke to Taha Nabil, a 25-year-old police officer in the bloated Palestinian security forces whose function is likely to be streamlined by the new Hamas government. He expressed his concern for the future and his shock that what he called a newcomer like Hamas could win so overwhelmingly. "I see all these celebrations, and, well . . . I just hope it's for the best," he said, fireworks blasting all around him.

"Since I'm a police officer and a Fatah supporter, I am not very happy by the results. I just hope the fruits of the victory will not be exclusively for one party or people. Who is Hamas anyway? We were the ones who began the revolution. Hamas have only been around for 10 years, and suddenly, out of nowhere, they changed Gaza." The question that Nabil and other Fatehawis are asking themselves tonight is, "How, and why?"

Gaza walls covered by electioneering posters.

Tonight, Fateh lashed out in a very different way. Young supporters, known as *shabeeba* here, or *shabeebit Fateh*, swarmed Mahmoud Abbas's house, calling for his resignation in three days and blaming the "old guard" of the Fateh leadership and their corruption for their crushing defeat. Then they swarmed the legislative council, where they created bonfires out of government vans, scaled the walls of the building, and ripped out air conditioners.

They were only slightly calmed down by a very emotional Mohammad Dahalan, who appealed for them to "make their voices heard" in a mass Fateh rally to be held Sunday (afraid to see how that turns out); Dahalan said Fateh will persevere despite what he referred to as "conspiracies" against it. They then marched throughout the city shooting wildly, reminding people via loudspeakers "FATEH IS NOT DEAD!" and asking them provocatively, "Do you really want to be ruled Hamas?"

Testosterone; crushing, humiliating defeat; and AK-47s: not a good combination. And if you're President Bush and company, be careful what you wish for.

Amid the Mayhem, Israel's Crimes Continue[26]
Gaza City, Palestine, January 28, 2006

This is a brief post whose purpose is to serve as a memorial for a little girl who has received scarce, if any, mention in the preoccupied media in recent days. Her name was Aya al-Astal. Aya was 13 years old. She was the second child killed by the Israeli army last week. Aya was carrying a basket and got lost on Thursday on her way back home to the al-Qarara area of south-central Gaza, not far from the border fence with Israel.

Israeli occupation forces shot her four times with live ammunition, two rounds at least hitting her in the neck, after suspecting she was a dangerous terrorist. (Their defense: "She got close to the fence.") But the media was too busy covering the "political earthquake that shook the region." Four bullets to the neck. This from arguably the most sophisticated army in the world. Apparently, the soldiers mistook her basket for a bomb. Binoculars anyone? Medics found her body, riddled with bullets, hours after she had been murdered. May you rest in peace, little Aya. May you rest in peace.

A Momentous Day (but Miles to Go)[27]
Gaza City, Palestine, January 31, 2006

In case you get the wrong idea, this post is about potty training, not elections. Not to digress from the theme of the past few posts, but yesterday was a momentous day in my household: Yousuf, whose morbid fear of sitting on our toilet I'm sure Freud would have a field day with, finally made his own little, um, you know what, in a potty of his own. . . .

Where the Sidewalk Ends[28]
Erez crossing, Gaza, Palestine, January 31, 2006

Yesterday, after a trip around Beit Hanoun with fellow journalists to speak to newly elected Hamas officials as well as people and gunmen on their thoughts, we headed to the Erez crossing. My colleagues needed to head back to Jerusalem, where they were based.

I hadn't been to Erez in a while, namely because there is no point. I am not allowed to travel to the West Bank, let alone Israel, based on some arbitrary—or maybe not so arbitrary—decision of some security official in the Israeli security matrix. The point is, as I got out of the taxi and looked down the long, turnstile-filled corridor modeled after a cattle shed, I realized that for me, this was, as Shel Silverstein puts it, "Where the Sidewalk Ends."

Going to Erez always serves as a stark reminder of what Gaza has become, because it is sometimes easy to forget when you are trapped inside the snow globe that a glass dome surrounds you; it starkly reminds me of the limits and the absolute control I am subject to, of the fact that I am a prisoner in my own land, that I am deprived of that most basic of human rights: freedom of movement.

In the distance, I could see the village of Siyafa, living under the terror of the newly formed no-go zone. Any movement can be deadly for these residents, who for five years lived sandwiched between settlements and captive to fear. Their movement is limited during the day, and they do not move at all in the dark. Meanwhile, construction continues on a concrete wall north of Beit Hanoun and Beit Lahia, where the borders are also being reinforced with the placement of new military bases and observation towers. The eastern part of Beit Hanoun was also declared a closed military zone last week, and the Israelis say anyone getting within 150m will be shot.

Welcome to the new, improved Gaza.

Sucks to Be You . . . [29]
Gaza City, Palestine, January 31, 2006

Poor Abu Mazen. I cast a sympathy vote for him this week, I really do.

Yesterday, farmers dumped truckloads of spoiling strawberries, tomatoes, cucumbers, and carnations near his home in protest of the ongoing unilateral closure of the Karni/al-Mintar commercial crossing by Israel and the impotence of the PA in doing anything about it. Dairy products and other food stocks, including baby formula, have dwindled in Gaza markets since the closure on January 15, with the only factory here in Gaza not able to meet the demands of all of the Strip's 1.5 million people. Farmers have been unable to export their two main products of this season—carnations and strawberries to Europe, tomatoes and cucumbers to the West Bank and Israel—and their produce has been left to rot or to serve as feed for the goats.

With disgruntled members of his own party shooting at his house, demanding his resignation after the party's crushing defeat in the elections, and calling him an "Israeli agent" on one hand, and farmers dumping piles of rotten tomatoes on his lawn in protest of the continued closure of Karni commercial crossing for three weeks and counting on the other hand (as one taxi driver put it, "This is what I call democracy—only in Gaza are people allowed to burn tires and dump tomatoes in front of the president's house"), Abu Mazen is all the while trying to appease Western governments so they will continue to speak to and fund his government.

To quote a popular blog award on AOL Instant Messenger, "It sucks to be you."

CHAPTER NOTES

1. For more information, see the United Nations Office for the Coordination of Humanitarian Affairs report on the one-year anniversary of the "Agreement of Movement and Access," archived at http://bit.ly/bQyLBG.
2. For details on the "no-go" zones, see "No-Go Zones Along the Perimeter Fence in the Gaza Strip," B'Tselem, May 30, 2010, archived at http://bit.ly/apmRTX.
3. The full original text of this post is archived at http://bit.ly/dtFmw9.
4. Archived at http://bit.ly/c10dAA.
5. Archived at http://bit.ly/dw0xdD.
6. Archived at http://bit.ly/aMm27r.
7. Archived at http://bit.ly/9XToYX.
8. Archived at http://bit.ly/9aPo4S.
9. Archived at http://bit.ly/bsHVv4.
10. For journalist Robert Fisk's take on Prime Minister Sharon, see his commentary in the *Independent*, "Ariel Sharon . . . ," archived at http://bit.ly/cDiFxb.
11. Archived at http://bit.ly/d8SUc3.
12. Archived at http://bit.ly/a6sfhj.
13. Archived at http://bit.ly/crEMLj.
14. Laila El-Haddad, "The Election Dance," *Guardian News Blog*, January 13, 2006, archived at http://bit.ly/9XDnhV.
15. Archived at http://bit.ly/daghdi.
16. Archived at http://bit.ly/cj0BFo.
17. Laila El-Haddad, "Fighting Talk," *Guardian News Blog*, January 18, 2006, archived at http://bit.ly/aNXfTe.
18. Archived at http://bit.ly/bML9Py.
19. Archived at http://bit.ly/cCwEq5.
20. Laila El-Haddad, "Countdown to Crunch Time," *Guardian News Blog*, January 18, 2006, archived at http://bit.ly/9zItg1.
21. Archived at http://bit.ly/dryBgc.
22. Archived at http://bit.ly/cQox4Q.
23. Archived at http://bit.ly/dC3E50.
24. Archived at http://bit.ly/9c7zor.
25. My *Al Jazeera English* story filed that day picked up on the same theme. See Laila El-Haddad, "Palestinian Street Voted for Change," *Al Jazeera English*, January 27, 2006, archived at http://bit.ly/deDBD3.
26. Archived at http://bit.ly/cg0utg.
27. Archived at http://bit.ly/bEm1Dw.
28. Archived at http://bit.ly/cN3dOo.
29. Archived at http://bit.ly/d1UkfO.

Chapter 8

The Counting Game

February–March 2006

*The months following the Palestinian parliamentary elections marked another turning point
for Palestinians. Following Israel's lead, the international community began to impose sanctions on the Gaza Strip—something that truly perplexed the overjoyed Gazans who had been
encouraged to participate in the elections by those same governments just a few months earlier. This Israeli-led siege, which continues to this day, was the brainchild of Dov Weisglass,
Ariel Sharon's policy adviser, who referred to the sanctions as a "diet" that would keep
Palestinians hungry but not starve them to death. The siege itself was merely an intensifica-
tion of a previous status quo, and the elections a pretext to embolden a longstanding closure
of the Gaza Strip and its people, in line with a gradual but systemic Israeli policy to destroy
the Palestinian political horizon.[1]*

*Gaza's economy was already suffering: The main commercial crossing, which Israel shut
down unilaterally for 21 days in January before Hamas came to power, was closed again
February 21. Still, ordinary Gazans with whom I spoke continued to harbor hope for the
future, saying they wanted first and foremost a resolution to the internal chaos that continued
to plague Gaza. Meanwhile, the Israeli Army's postdisengagement military tactics continued
unabated.*

How Might We Live?[2]
Gaza City, Palestine, February 14, 2006

The shells are falling again.

Interspersed with the occasional sonic boom, it's like a mix-and-match Monday
special. The army once compared it with a "hat of tricks." Let's see what we pull
out today: There's the sonic boom, which after a brief hiatus, is now making a

terrorizing comeback. Then there's the aimless but deadly tank shelling into empty fields in eastern and northern Gaza, so strong it can be heard and felt kilometers away, here in Gaza City.

And, of course, the ever-popular kill-a-Palestinian-herding-goats-or-a-child-who-got-lost-by-the-border-fence technique. That oughta really stop the rockets from flying.

They try different combinations each day—25 tank shells in a row; a gunship rocket attack; five more shells at eastern Gaza; drones whirring incessantly at varying speeds. Ten shells; 10 minutes of silence; sonic boom; 20 shells, with more firepower, in northern Gaza. Ten shells; one-hour intermission; shoot at someone near the fence. Stop to make sure there is no outcry and promise an investigation.

Then, it continues.

Yousuf is at a very sensitive stage, where he doesn't quite understand what's going on and looks to me for confirmation of whether he should be scared when the shelling starts. Following the advice of a friend, I continue to reassure and distract him.

Today, I tried a new technique. Yousuf loves to sing and dance, so, as the shelling started, we listened to some music my friend gave him as a gift—Suheil Khoury's *Bass Shwai*, a children's CD from the Edward Said National Conservatory of Music, in which four children ages 9 to 11 sing songs that Khoury composed, using lyrics that various Palestinian poets and writers created. Each song deals with a theme relating to children.

We listened to a song that imagines what the world might be like in different forms. I think it can be read in many ways. Needless to say, it was very therapeutic, perhaps more so for me than him. Sometimes, you need to take a step back and look through the eyes of children. Strange is what you make it, I guess.

> What if the world was made of wood
> Birds of wood
> Flowers of wood
>
> What if the world was made of paper
> Doors of paper
> Fences of paper
>
> What if the world was made of paper
> Walls of paper
>
> How might it be, I wonder?
> How strange . . . how strange
> How would it be, I wonder?
> How strange, how strange

The children then go on to invite us to imagine a world made of paper or of gold . . . and then ask:

> How might we live?
> How might we live?

The Parliament Convenes![3]
Gaza City, Palestine, February 18, 2006

The parliament convened its first session today, amid U.S. demands for the PA to return some $50 million in direct foreign aid and Israeli moves to bar Gaza workers, people, and goods from entering Israel completely, threatening to drive the final nail into the coffin of our already-crippled economy.

To quote the Israeli prime minister's adviser, Dov "Formaldehyde" Weisglass, on reaching an appropriate aid policy toward the Hamas-led government, "It's like a meeting with a dietitian. We have to make them much thinner but not enough to die."

The Israeli government also barred Gaza lawmakers, belonging mainly to the Hamas list, from traveling to the West Bank to attend the Palestinian Legislative Council session. It has divided the West Bank into three parts this morning to hinder the movement of Palestinian lawmakers from their respective cities to Ramallah.

A few Gaza lawmakers were given Israeli permission to travel to the West Bank, such as Independent Palestine member of Parliament Rawia Shawwa and Independent Christian candidate Hussam Taweel, who was backed by Hamas. They told me they chose to remain in Gaza anyway in "solidarity" with those forbidden from traveling.

Outside the building currently serving as a legislative council, the Rashad al-Shawwa Cultural Centre, representatives of different interest groups, such as disabled Palestinians and families of prisoners, had gathered to make their voices heard. Many forced their way into the crowded convention center, despite attempts by riot police to keep them outside.

Before the parliament officially convened, one man, holding a picture of his imprisoned son, walked toward the podium, shouting at security guards who attempted to escort him away. He was calmed down only by a composed Ismail Haniyeh, the Hamas leader heading the now-ruling party's victorious list and in line to be the new prime minister.

Some 7,500 Palestinian prisoners are currently serving sentences—most without charges—in Israeli prisons.

The commotion turned into a heated debate among onlookers as well, with some calling for more order and others saying this is just a small taste of what the parliament can expect to face in coming weeks.

The conference room was packed to the brim—not only by an army of journalists who had gathered to cover the historic day but also by outgoing legislators, civil society leaders, and ordinary Palestinians who wanted to get a glimpse of the members of Parliament they elected into power.

Despite the presession ruckus and initial technical difficulties with transmitting live coverage from the West Bank, the session went smoothly.

Palestinian National Council head Salim Za'anoun said in a speech to Parliament that despite the travel ban, the Palestinian Parliament would remain united, and he called for the inclusion of the several elected members of Parliament serving Israeli prison sentences via videoconference as well.[4]

Also, here is just one of the perspectives represented in the photostory I did for *Al Jazeera* on the views of nine Palestinians and their expectations from the new government:

Ahlan Imkhayer, 25, CAT scan technician:

"I didn't expect this result at all, but I hope our society made the right choice. I hope as much as possible for real, tangible change, and for a resolution to the problem of security—especially as it relates to the lives of young people.

"There is absolute lawlessness and chaos permeating college campuses here. It is in complete disarray, from attendance to lectures, nothing goes according to schedule, and there is a lot of institutional corruption and moral decay. Gunmen hijack the campuses and enforce their own rules. Honestly, we are sick of it. They also need to find jobs for the tens of thousands of young unemployed graduates."[5]

Please Check Your Guns and Chilies at the Door . . . [6]
Gaza City, Palestine, February 22, 2006

Yesterday, in between Yousuf highlighting our ceramic-tiled floor yellow and my chasing a cockroach around the kitchen to Yousuf's howling laughter, there was a slight "incident," to quote the Israeli Army, which I call the chili pepper incident.

Now before I continue, I should explain something. Gaza's famed green chilies are hot. And I don't mean eye-watering hot. I mean take-one-whiff-and-you'll-feel-nauseated hot.

. . . My mother inadvertently forgot one chili pepper on the kitchen counter that I was supposed to use that morning in an omelet—which I didn't, because the prospect of eating a nauseating omelet that likewise made me cry like a baby did not sound so appealing.

Instead, Yousuf got hold of the chili and—as is his habit with all things raw—began to poke and prod at it, rubbing it, tearing it apart, until he finally tired of the game. And then, slowly, the fiery vapors of capsicum began to make their way to his nostrils. Then came the inevitable eye rub. And the wails. Oh, the wails.

I was so hysterical! I thought the poor child had gone temporarily blind. His eyes looked crossed and extremely swollen and red, and he couldn't stop crying for 30 minutes straight. No amount of water flushing would soothe him—I don't care what the books say.

In the end, he was OK, but he developed a very mild case of what's known as a subconjunctival hemorrhage—basically a ruptured blood vessel in his eye, which heals in a matter of weeks.

. . . I always had a hunch those Gaza chilies were dangerous. But who knew?

Anything but Ordinary![7]
Gaza City, Palestine, February 24, 2006

"This agreement is intended to give the Palestinian people freedom to move, to trade, to live ordinary lives," said U.S. Secretary of State Condoleezza Rice confidently, of a border agreement she helped broker with much fanfare, following the now-comatose Ariel Sharon's disengagement from Gaza.

Now, maybe it's just me, but six months on, I wouldn't say my life is "ordinary" by any stretch of the imagination. In fact, I think it's quite outside the entire realm of the ordinary.

Just ask Yousuf. He often mistakes Israeli helicopter gunships for birds, dances to the revolutionary songs blasted during political rallies marching by our house, and has learned to distinguish between Israeli-tank shell fire and machine-gun banter.

When not making our own yogurt at home because of a shortage in the market, we scavenge Gaza City to find him Size 5 Pampers, because Israel has closed down the al-Mintar crossing, as it has done again this week, all while living in a disengaged-but-still-occupied territory whose parliament must convene via videoconference.

As one Palestinian woman, observing the new democratically elected Hamas-led Parliament convene last week, noted upon being asking about her thoughts of possible Israeli sanctions, "Our lives are incomprehensible."

To add insult to injury, I, along with most Gazans, cannot even travel to the other half of my nonstate entity.

But, I guess, I can see how I can be considered a security threat, what with Yousuf's chili incident.

And hey, we've always got Rafah crossing right? I mean after all, "The battle's done, and we kind of won." To quote the flag from the Chairman Arafat Shop down the street, we now have a "Free Gaza" and, of course, control of the only outlet for Gaza's 1.5 million Palestinians.

Unfortunately, control over the crossing, as brokered by Rice after the much-lauded unilateral disengagement and the end of Israel's occupation of Gaza, is completely fictitious.

My own friends and family can't even visit me here in my lonely little open-air prison.

Israel denied entry to Gaza to two American peace-activist friends of mine last week via the supposedly Palestinian-controlled Rafah crossing.

The reason cited: "affiliations with groups that are considered terrorist groups." Pat helped Palestinian villagers plant olive trees and nonviolently resist the encroachment of the Israeli wall on their land in the West Bank last year. He was coming to Gaza to volunteer with a local agricultural nongovernmental organization.

Two days earlier, two French aid workers coming to set up a sister city project in Beit Hanoun were likewise denied, for the same blanket reason. And the examples go on.

All this is leaving the case of my own husband aside, who, along with 50,000 other Palestinians, because he lacks an Israeli-issued identification card and family-reunion permit and is a refugee, cannot visit me in Gaza, except perhaps under extenuating circumstances that may render him "a humanitarian case," according to officials I spoke to. Even then, there is always the chance that he may be denied based on "security reasons"; after all, his son handled a chemical weapon.

Ordinary? Hardly, Ms. Rice.

As one Palestinian official put it to me, "It's all a grand illusion, and anyone who says or believes otherwise—from Abu Mazen down—is lying."

The Counting Game[8]
Gaza City, Palestine, February 27, 2006

It's 6:14 p.m. The shelling had been ongoing for some time; then, it suddenly occurred to me to begin to keep track, for no particular reason other than to actualize these episodes for myself.

It's 6:18 p.m. Thirteen shells. I lost count after that. But what I did remember about this particular bout was that Yousuf, for the first time, told me that he's "afraid."

Usually, he'll just say "*Yamma!*" in the rather animated way that children do (it means, "Oh, Mommy!"). But today, he associated fear with the earth-pounding noise—which he thought was coming from the kitchen, because that's where he was when he heard it ("*Khayif . . . hinak!*" ["Afraid . . . over there!"]). You can't explain such an incomprehensible existence to a 2-year-old. You just try and normalize his reality. That's why I love the film *Life Is Beautiful* so much.

He'll only get as scared as you do, sometimes. And sometimes no amount of reassurance can convince him that this loud and recurrent thud he hears every day is innocuous (so far). One Israeli friend who e-mailed to check on us even suggested I make a counting game out of it—how many shells can we count today? (Not a suggestion I'm likely to adopt anytime soon.) I sometimes think of Rafah's children and how their lives must have been during those nights under constant Israeli siege, how their lives will continue now, whether they can continue with any certainty at all. Being a mother puts a whole new spin on it.

One reader, Karin, portrayed her interaction with the siege on Rafah and how small individual actions can have a much wider ripple effect. She wrote:

> The story about little Yousuf reminds me of an incident that happened a couple of years ago.
>
> I was calling my friend in Rafah. My friend and a group of children were under siege!
>
> I heard children screaming and gunfire. "Help me, help me . . . oh, the children. We have no milk!" he screamed.
>
> [Then] the connection was cut.
>
> I was later informed that during this particular attack, no one was hurt, except for the trauma the children suffered.
>
> Needless to say I was shocked as well, and I wrote a report about the incident in our local newspaper. I mentioned the milk situation.
>
> A few days later, a milk-producing company in Indiana, one of the largest in the United States, offered to send dry milk to Rafah, but the milk was confiscated by Israeli authorities and not a [crumb] went to the children.
>
> This company's effort was in vain, and I was furious.
>
> I'm happy to report that this company did not give up and is sending the milk via a different route.
>
> Where there is a will, there is a way!

The Gaza "Diet" Begins[9]
Gaza City, Palestine, March 1, 2006

The ongoing closure of the al-Mintar (aka Karni) crossing, the main route for both commercial and humanitarian supplies into Gaza, has resulted in an estimated loss of some $10.5 million and the depletion of Gaza's main food staples, according to a report by the United Nations Office for the Coordination of Humanitarian Affairs (OCHA).

The crossing, considered to be Gaza's commercial lifeline, was shut down unilaterally by Israel for 21 days in January, before Hamas came to power, and again on February 21, despite promises not to do so in a border and access agreement that was brokered by U.S. Secretary of State Condoleezza Rice.

Wheat-grain stocks are dwindling as a result, and flour mills in Gaza have shut down, with residents having to rely on their home supplies. In the impoverished Strip, the overwhelming majority of residents bake their own bread.

In addition, the United Nations and the World Food Programme warned that sugar, which has increased in price at least 25 percent since the closure, as well as cooking oil will run out in two days.

Last week, Israeli prime ministerial adviser Dov Weisglass was quoted as saying at a meeting that the idea behind the closure policy was "to put the Palestinians on a diet but not make them die of hunger."

Defense Minister Shaul Mofaz has decided the crossing will remain closed on Thursday, despite earlier promises to open it indefinitely to "humanitarian aid" for Palestinian residents. In addition to serving as an export and import hub for merchandise, fruits, and vegetables—many of which are in peak season now and beginning to rot—medicines, vaccines, and kidney dialysis wash are also transported through al-Mintar.

The Israeli Army initially said the Gaza closure was due to "security threats" to the border, citing concerns regarding tunnels being dug under the crossing and the transfer of avian flu.

No such tunnels were ever found, and health officials have dismissed fears of the bird flu spreading, saying, "It knows no boundaries." Further, there has been no evidence yet of infections in Gaza, and Israel has prevented the entry of reagents to detect the virus.

Israel has been trying to pressure the PA to accept Kerem Shalom crossing as an alternative crossing, a proposal Mahmoud Abbas rejected today. According to a senior Palestinian official responsible for overseeing the implementation of the Access and Movement Agreement brokered by Condoleezza Rice, only four to eight cargo trucks would be allowed through the alternative crossing. The Rice agreement spoke about more than 160 trucks a day, though even before the closure, only 60 trucks were allowed to transport goods through Karni. The agreement also talked about Kerem Shalom as a parallel border, not a substitute, which would allow Israel to exercise complete control and the ability to shut down al-Mintar/Karni at its leisure.

The United Nations also reported that Israel remains responsible, as an occupying power, for ensuring public order and the health and welfare of the Palestinian population:

> International humanitarian agencies do not have the capacity to take over the running of PA services even if the security situation allowed. Humanitarian assistance from the international community does not relieve Israel of this responsibility.

OCHA Director David Shearer said that the humanitarian situation has already seen a sharp deterioration since last month's legislative elections because of tightened Israeli control, adding that the situation will only get worse if aid is withheld:

> We were concerned that the PA might not be able to pay salaries and that will have an enormous impact, the fact that approximately

1 million people will not have a breadwinner, and what the implications might be if around 70,000 armed security forces are not receiving any money in an area where 65 percent of the population is already under the poverty line.

The Things We Do (When Not Counting Artillery Shells) [10]
Gaza City, Palestine,
March 5, 2006

Yousuf enjoys a swing on our farm with one of his pet rabbits (still unnamed . . . suggestions welcome) and later "reads" a book in the newly opened and absolutely amazing Qattan Centre for the Child in Gaza (a few seconds later, the book nearly ended up inside the hard drive of one of the library's computers as Yousuf tried to shove it in the CD drive—maybe we'll opt for story time instead next time).

And a big happy birthday for Yousuf—he turns 2 years old today!

Taking It All In[11]
Gaza City, Palestine, March 6, 2006

I'm tired, and mad at how unproductive being tired can make me, among other things. But mainly, I'm just tired. Sometimes, it can get exhausting being here.

It's not so much one single event but rather the sum total of a series of everyday, seemingly insignificant incidents that make up the occupation in all its ugliness and brutality and take their insidious toll on you, that creep up on you while you may think yourself not susceptible somehow, sometimes. A border closure here. A milk or diaper shortage there. A travel ban. An aerial assault. Anger, and depression, and despondence. All of this, combined with the daily realization that your life is not yours to live. The air is not yours to breathe. It's suffocating and psychologically demanding.

And working in the news, covering the news that's all around you, makes it even harder. It can be all too easy to lose perspective. It also makes you realize how easy it is to become the news yourself.

I was dizzy most of the morning and slept most of the afternoon. And when I woke up, I learned that the explosion I heard was an attack by an unmanned Israeli drone in the teeming, poverty-stricken Shijaeeya neighborhood not far from my house. It killed the intended "targets"—two members of Islamic Jihad. But it also killed three others, including two children—brothers, 8-year-old Raed al-Batch and his 15-year-old brother, Ala. They were with their mother at the time. She lived, only to learn that she lost two boys—at once.

I'm just so tired.

CHAPTER NOTES

1. Israeli sociologist Baruch Kimmerling described the policy as politicide: "a gradual but systematic attempt to cause their annihilation as an independent political and social entity."

2. The full original text of this post is archived at http://www.gazamom. com/2006/02/how-might-we-live/, shortened to http://bit.ly/dB4dsV.

3. Archived at http://bit.ly/aPWJH8.

4. I wrote more extensively about this first meeting of the PLC for an *Al Jazeera* article. See Laila El-Haddad, "Palestinian Parliament Raises Hopes," *Al Jazeera English*, February 19, 2006, archived at http://bit.ly/das34R.

5. Laila El-Haddad, "Gaza Voices: Hopes and Fears for the Future," *Al Jazeera English*, February 18, 2006, archived at http://bit.ly/agJsrW.

6. Archived at http://bit.ly/a8wriB.

7. Archived at http://bit.ly/b5DpMl.

8. Archived at http://bit.ly/dwH8Dt.

9. Archived at http://bit.ly/cyo6nS.

10. Archived at http://bit.ly/afjBHx.

11. Archived at http://bit.ly/9ZHRcH.

Chapter 9

Living the Siege

March 2006

In March 2006, the newly elected Hamas government was sworn into power in the Palestinian Legislative Council (PLC). A Western boycott and Israeli freeze on aid and tax revenues immediately followed.

Israeli elections were held shortly thereafter, on March 28, 2006. They resulted in a strong victory for the recently formed Kadima party, which had been headed by Ehud Olmert since the near-fatal stroke of its founder, Ariel Sharon. Labour came in second and joined the ruling coalition under Kadima's leadership.

In the face of grim political prospects and ever-increasing physical and economic isolation, Palestinians in Gaza reacted to the Israeli elections with apathy—or indignation. There were unprecedented bread shortages after the two-month-plus closure of the Karni commercial crossing. Israel's freeze on transferring PA revenues to Gaza left the 70,000 members of Palestinian security forces without their salaries, causing great suffering for them and their numerous dependents. (Israel withheld the pay of these security-force people despite the fact that they continued to take their orders from Mahmoud Abbas and his Fateh Party rather than the now Hamas-run Prime Minister's Office.) Lawlessness and infighting were on the rise. Gaza was isolated—and simmering.

Lethal Ambiguity[1]
Gaza City, Palestine, March 8, 2006

The Israeli occupation army has long been known to have a book of unwritten rules concerning its open-fire regulations, and a "Code of Silence" among its soldiers, in order to be able to exonerate them from the killing of innocent and unarmed civilians in the occupied West Bank and Gaza Strip, the most glaring examples being that of Iman al-Hams and, just last week, Amer Basyouni of the al-Ain refugee camp.

In a new video, the Israeli human rights group B'Tselem provides testimonies of soldiers speaking about their open-fire regulations. The testimonies show that soldiers receive intentionally ambiguous orders about when and how they are to use their weapons, giving the soldiers flexibility, a high civilian death toll, and immunity from responsibility. It is a policy B'Tselem calls "lethal ambiguity."[2]

B'Tselem says that although in the past open-fire regulations only covered law enforcement, with the outbreak of the second Intifada, the Israeli government instituted significant changes in the regulations and made them more "ambiguous":

> The army no longer gave soldiers a printed copy of the regulations, and they greatly expanded the kinds of situations in which soldiers were allowed to use their weapons. Israeli security forces have killed at least 1,806 Palestinians who were not taking part in the hostilities at the time they were killed. The vagueness of the orders given to soldiers on when to open fire is one of the principal causes for the high number of casualties. [T]he general practice is of not investigating cases of the killing of civilians who were not taking part in the hostilities. This situation transmits a grave message to the soldiers of contempt for the most basic human right, the right to life.

According to an Israeli Army reservist I spoke with, even if soldiers are punished for torture or murder, it is symbolic at best. "If there is a trial, [it] will be only the [soldier] and the battalion commander. . . . It's what they call 'discipline.' . . . The soldier hears out [the commander] and says to him 'OK, sure,' then spends seven days in prison, and no one except the unit will know about it, including the press."

B'Tselem says such "offensive sentences," together with the Israeli Judge Advocate's Office's new policy of limiting the number of criminal investigations during this Intifada, contribute to a sense of immunity and transmit a message to officers and soldiers that "even if you violate the regulations and harm innocent persons, it is extremely unlikely that you will be punished."

The policy of ambiguity applies equally to Gaza's border "killing zone," where nine unarmed Palestinians, including five children and one 8-month-old child, have been killed since the disengagement.

Nine-year-old Aya al-Astal was killed by Israeli snipers stationed on Gaza's borders on her way back home to her village of Qarrara, in southeast Gaza. No investigation was ever made into her death.

B'Tselem says that according to its recent research, "The army made no attempt to warn the Palestinians to move farther away from the fence or to give them a chance to surrender."

Here is an excerpt from the testimony of the cousin of one of the victims (16-year-old Sayyed Abu Libdah), who was killed while in his family's orchard, 600m away from the border:

> Last Friday [December 2], my cousin Sayyed, who was 16 years old, and Zuhdi Abu Shahin, 17, a friend of mine, who both worked with me, finished working at 6:00 p.m., and we went straight to my family's land, while we were still in our work clothes. We got there at 7:00 and started to water the olive trees, finishing at 9:00. Then we made a fire and tea. [W]hen we got up to put out the fire and go, shots were fired at us from the towers along the border. The gunfire continued for 20 minutes nonstop. I was the first to be hit, in my right thigh. I fell to the ground, cried out, and couldn't get up. Zuhdi and Sayyed ran away, and the shooting continued. . . . The next day, one of the nurses told me that Sayyed had been killed and that Zuhdi had been wounded in the chest and leg.
>
> I know that the soldiers saw us there many times, because we go there to water the trees. They know this is our land and that we go there to take care of it. I don't understand why they fired at us.[3]

Meeting Ismail Haniyeh[4]
Gaza City, Palestine, March 10, 2006

In between planning Yousuf's birthday and dealing with a spell of constipation he got along with a nasty cold (all I'll say is that the miracles of olive oil never cease to amaze!), I was too preoccupied for any serious writing last week. But I did manage to meet with our prime minister designate, Ismail Haniyeh.

It happened sort of by coincidence. I met up with Helena Cobban, longtime journalist and writer, currently a columnist for the *Christian Science Monitor,* and also author of one of the first comprehensive books on the Palestine Liberation Organization (PLO). She e-mailed to tell me she was in Gaza for a few days.

It was a sort of weird convergence of threads in the Palestinian tapestry, or at least my budding family's own tapestry. You see, she covered the fall of the Tel-Zaatar camp to the Israeli-Syrian–backed Flangist forces in 1976. The camp happened to be where Yassine and his family lived before fleeing to Baalbeck's Wavel camp (and where his uncle went missing after the massacre and remains missing to this day).

So we met up, and we chatted and lunched it up in our house as if we were old friends or family. We also drove around with Ahmed al-Kurd, the Hamas-elected head of Dair al-Balah's municipality, to take a look at some of the institutions Hamas built there.

The next day, I went to meet up with members of Parliament during a break from their grueling and heated two-day session. It was convened by videoconference because of the Israeli-imposed travel ban—linking up to fellow legislators in the West Bank through a large screen wrought with technical difficulties. To quote my colleague Khalid Amayreh, "Because of Israel's complete control of nearly all aspects of Palestinian life, it is easier for most Palestinians, including public officials, to travel anywhere in the world than to commute the 20-minute drive between the Strip and the West Bank."

In the corridors, I met Helena again, this time about to interview Ismail Haniyeh informally. He had just slid away into his office from a swarm of television cameras. So I joined her to assist in translation.

My first impression of Haniyeh (besides his towering height) was his warmth and casual demeanor, which leaves you at ease when you talk to him. He doesn't speak much English. Helena just said she wanted to interview him for 10 minutes, and he said, jokingly, "OK, *ahham ishee inrakiz a'al* '10 minutes.'" ("OK, as long as we focus on the 10-minutes part.").

Nothing he said was particularly groundbreaking, which I expected. But it was interesting to get to know him a little bit better and compare him with some other Hamas leaders I've met in the past, such as Ismail Abu Shanab, Rantisi and Ahmed Yasin. He was markedly more pragmatic and soft-spoken. I'd compare him most to Ismail Abu Shanab. Some highlights:

When asked about whether he thought Hamas could get the job done, vis-à-vis internal reform and rebuilding, he said:

> Hamas has lived through all of Palestinian society's conditions. We have succeeded in the past in this respect, and we are confident we can succeed in this new challenge, in organizing the "Palestinian house." We have, in the past, been successful in reaching internal agreements with other factions despite the tense internal political climate. We held our fire when all other factions didn't. This does not mean there are no challenges—internal and external. The responsibility is huge and not a simple one. That is why we hope to form a national unity government that together can help realize the desires of the Palestinian people. Our people want internal security now.

He added that he considered the PLO one of the most important Palestinian accomplishments and that he considered Hamas was now a part of this achievement. He also said that "Hamas has relationships with many EU [European Union] countries" already but did not elaborate on which ones when pressed.

When the issue of borders and recognizing Israel came up, he said:

> Why are answers needed over and over again for questions that have been responded to? We ask that the international community demand that Israel recognize the rights of Palestinians for once and to recognize a Palestinian state. Then, for sure, we will have a response to this question. We cannot separate ourselves from the

reality of occupation. At the same time, we hope to become less and less dependent on them.

Gaza Scenes[5]

Gaza City, Palestine,
March 11, 2006

*A view of Gaza from above
(the 15th floor, to be precise).*

The Energy Circle: "Fueling" the Occupation in Gaza[6]

Gaza City, Palestine, March 12, 2006

Today, dozens of taxi drivers announced a strike in protest of the rising price of fuels in Gaza. They burned tires throughout the Strip, blocking roads and junctions and refusing to transport people to schools and jobs.

The price of gasoline has reached 5.45 shekels a liter, and diesel is 3.85 shekels a liter. A cylinder of cooking gas has reached a high of 47 shekels ($10 . . . my jaw nearly dropped when the gas people delivered it to our door today) compared with 4 Egyptian pounds (less than $1) in nearby Egypt—all this in a territory with an 84 percent poverty rate.

But who's to blame for the energy spike? Aren't the Israelis gone? Can't Gaza become its own state and produce its own energy?

The local rumor mill is abuzz with theories on the issue of the price rise itself. Some suggest that the outgoing Fateh Party, in collusion with Israel and the United States, is trying to put the pressure on Hamas from the get-go and decided to raise prices. Of course, the Palestinian Energy Authority produces only 5 percent of Palestinian electricity, limited to production of biomass, small private electricity generation, and solar energy.

The Palestinian energy sector relies almost fully on imported energy, either directly from Israel or under the supervision of the Israeli authorities for oil products. Under the Paris Protocols of 1994, Palestinians are forced to rely on Israel for their energy needs. About 95 percent of the Palestinian electricity is generated by the Israel Electricity Corporation.

The Gaza Strip has a rich natural gas reserve in its territorial waters, which could be converted to electricity, used locally, sold abroad, and even transferred for use in the West Bank, which currently relies completely on Israel for electricity and natural gas.

But because Israel continues to maintain control of the Palestinian coastline and borders, despite the much-lauded unilateral "disengagement" of late last year, the PA cannot capitalize on this resource or market it at the moment. To quote Jimmy Carter, "Circumscribed and isolated, without access to the air, sea, or the West Bank, Gaza is a nonviable economic and political entity."

Most Gaza families cannot afford gas ovens as a result of the outrageously high prices. They rely instead on small, single-burner electric stovetops. Of course, electricity is likewise expensive here—in fact, Palestinians are said to pay more for energy than anyone else in the world.

The only difference is that electricity is provided in advance, without having to pay for the service as one would gas by the cylinder. So the result is that in many parts of Gaza, entire neighborhoods haven't paid their electricity bills in months (and, in some cases, years), because they simply cannot afford to.

One man told me his bill today turned up at 6,000 shekels in overdue payments. The energy authority has no choice but to keep sending notices, without shutting off their electricity, and usually ends up relying on donor agencies or charitable individuals to absorb the costs (part of the recent EU aid package is going to pay off the Israel Electricity Corporation). Some call it freeloading; others call it poverty and desperation.

These people aren't living beyond their means—the means are just beyond them. I saw the home of the man who owes 6,000 shekels. His daughters bake bread for their eight-member family every other day on a small electric, locally made toaster oven with World Food Program flour. They have no phone line, a few light bulbs, and a fridge. That's all.

Of course, I can't help but think if we as Palestinians were given true sovereignty over our borders and were able to use and export our own gas and make our own electricity—or even if Israel reduced the prices of the electricity while this happens—all this could be avoided in the first place; millions of dollars could be saved, and millions of people could live better lives. This is just one small, if technical, example of how Israel continues to "fuel" the occupation in Gaza, following the equation of maximum control and minimum responsibility.

How to Win an Israeli Election[7]
Gaza City, Palestine, March 17, 2006, *Guardian Unlimited*

An 11-step guide to success in the polls:

1. Say there is no negotiating partner on the Palestinian side (you should say this even if the president was Gandhi).

2. Murmur, every once in a while, your willingness to make "painful concessions" for peace . . . if only you had a partner (which is—and emphasize this point by raising your voice and looking upward toward the heavens—unfortunately not the case).

3. Make a distinction between yourself, a peace-loving yet strong and courageous man and the "lunatic settlers," whose enterprise must eventually end (although do not spell this out and continue to support them blindly in any way possible).

4. Following through with point 3, declare illegal settlements in the heart of the West Bank as important to you as Tel Aviv and an eternal part of Israel.

5. Discreetly begin building police headquarters and "other facilities" extending from a future Palestinian capital to the largest Israeli colony in the West Bank, Ma'ale Adumim. Cite "natural growth" needs if pressed by allies, which is unlikely to happen.[8]

6. Repeat "terrorist attacks" and "security" several times in each sentence of a public speech.

7. Unpredictably close down Palestinian commercial crossings (while making sure to mention "security" and "terrorist attack"), despite promising not to do so in agreements brokered by the United States.[9]

8. Place hungry Palestinians on a forced "diet," and laugh about it.[10]

9. Escalate and provoke by assassinating Palestinians, making sure to refer to child casualities as unfortunate bystanders; firing an incessant barrage of artillery shells capriciously in a self-declared buffer zone; and detaining other Palestinians belonging to a group that has stuck to a cease-fire for more than 12 months.[11]

10. Get prodemocracy America to destabilize the democratic result of your next-door neighbor's elections.

11. And, for the grand finale, stage an *Apocalypse Now*–type raid on a Palestinian prison to defend the honor of a slain Israeli war criminal . . . er, minister . . . complete with helicopters, tanks, and armored bulldozers, and finish off with an Israeli general and newspapers crowing, "We got 'em!"

◁◁

Beware the Ides of March[12]
Gaza City, Palestine, March 16, 2006, *Guardian Unlimited*

It all seems so predictable in retrospect. It was, after all, only one day before the Ides of March and just 13 days before the Israeli elections.

Seemingly out of nowhere, Jericho, the oldest city in the world, and the Marxist-Leninist Popular Front for the Liberation of Palestine (PFLP), one of the oldest Palestinian national organizations, were dramatically thrust onto the world stage (in the PFLP's case, after a long period of absence and of being overshadowed by Hamas). And on both sides, national heroes were born all over again.

In an *Apocalypse Now*–type raid, with tanks and bulldozers and helicopter gunships, Israeli military forces laid siege to the Palestinian prison in the otherwise sleepy desert town. This came, conveniently, just 30 minutes after American and British observers left their posts (but then, with the British at least, that seems to have been the pattern of the last 60 years), citing concerns that prisoners were allowed to use cell phones, among other things.

Ultimately, Israel seized the men it was after, most prominent among them Ahmed Saadat, held in the Jericho prison for four years without ever standing trial in a deal that involved American and British observers.

Saadat was accused of overseeing the assassination of the Israeli tourism minister, Rehavam Ze'evi (in what tireless Israeli peace activist Uri Avneri referred to as an Israeli-style targeted killing) in retaliation for Israel's extrajudicial assassination of [PFLP] leader Abu Ali Mustafa (Mustafa al-Zibri) in August 2001.[13]

Ze'evi was a self-declared ethnic cleanser who referred to Palestinians as "lice" and "cancer." He was a founder of the Moledet Party, an extremist, ultranationalist party that openly called for the transfer of all Palestinians from the West Bank and Gaza and for the annexation of Jordan, even after its 1994 peace deal with Israel. Yet Ze'evi served as an Israeli cabinet minister nonetheless, without so much as a peep from either the United States or the EU.

The inherent hypocrisy speaks for itself and has resulted in a great deal of ire in an already simmering Gaza and West Bank.

Israel acts not just with absolute impunity but with the blind and active support of Western powers: That is the message that has been reinforced here.

The Israeli daily *Haaretz* cited government sources, saying that Israel has considered several times over the last year "intervening," as they did in Tuesday's showdown, to take Saadat into their own custody: "However, as long as the British and Americans were there, Israel refrained from acting, out of fear that they would be injured."

Fun and Games[14]

Gaza City, Palestine, March 17, 2006

A brother and sister play with an old tire they found lying around on Gaza's beach yesterday.

Bread Runs Out in Face of Israeli Closure[15]

Gaza City, Palestine, March 18, 2006

Walking around Gaza today, one would have thought there was a war looming (well, I guess we are in a perpetual state of low-intensity war, but still). Most bakeries throughout the city were closed by mid-afternoon. The only ones remaining open were jam-packed with customers, with lines extending out to the streets until late at night.

The reason: Flour stocks have officially run out in Gaza because of a 44-day, and still-going-strong, Israeli-imposed closure of the only commercial crossing for goods and humanitarian supplies. Palestinians in Gaza consume around 350 tons of flour per day. All flour mills have shut down because of the depletion of wheat stocks, and bakeries are working through their last bags of stored flour. As word of the shortage spread, residents flocked to bakeries.

In one bakery I went to, the scene was one of panic and fear, with Israeli war jets roaring overhead; men lined up for hours, with children taking their place sometimes. At one point, two men's nerves snapped, and a fight nearly broke out about whose turn it was. A group of armed men immediately came in to break it up (a police officer walked casually by, despite my pleas to get him to intervene).

Bags of bread were rationed—two per family—to make sure there was enough for all, as the final truckload of stored flour was delivered to the bakery.

Your Love Gives Me Such a Thrill, but Your Love Won't Pay My Bills . . . I Want Money![16]
Gaza City, Palestine. March 20, 2006

Six people were wounded today (two in a separate incident) in fighting in Gaza between Palestinian police and gunmen demanding jobs and unpaid wages.

The gunmen blocked off the main road leading to the Erez terminal—used mainly by Palestinian officials and VIPs—and exchanged fire with security forces in a two-hour-long battle. Palestinian President Mahmoud Abbas's motorcade was on its way to Tel Aviv at the time for a follow-up meeting with Americans, Egyptians, Europeans, and Israelis on the humanitarian situation in Gaza.

The gunmen then took the battle to Gaza City near where I live, shooting at a police station and in front of the Ministry of Foreign Affairs. Machine gun fire echoed throughout the city as police sirens wailed up and down the streets.

The gunmen belong mainly to Fatah's al-Aqsa Martyrs' Brigades, many of whom are demanding to be absorbed into an already bloated and unsustainable security apparatus (the PA was running training workshops for some of the Brigades members, according to two guys I overheard talking in an elevator last week. "But it will be a major problem. They just don't realize how many of us there are," one said). Some were part of a group hired into the security forces just before Hamas took power and have not yet received their wages, as I reported in a story for the *Guardian* today.[17]

The wage fears are not limited to security forces, which many argue do need to be streamlined anyway—municipality workers have been on strike for two days protesting late wages. Uncollected rubbish has piled up throughout the city, with many neighborhoods opting to burn it to prevent rats from nesting.

The cash-strapped authority is finding it increasingly difficult to pay the salaries of the approximately 130,000 people it employs as is—up to 70,000 of them security personnel—especially in the face of rising international pressure on the newly elected Hamas government.

All of this is happening at a time when Gaza faces an unprecedented food shortage. (Israel briefly reopened al-Mintar to allow trucks to deliver food today, only to close it again an hour later—in line with Dov Weisglass's "diet but don't kill" policy.) Gaza's economy is losing about $600,000 a day because of the closure, which has forced some farmers to feed their rotting vegetables to goats. Others are reduced to selling what remains of their marked-for-export produce in bulk on donkey carts in the city, charging only 1 pound for 20kg of tomatoes on the vine.

Security will suffer in the long term: James Wolfensohn, the international community's envoy, recently warned that the Palestinian Authority could face imminent collapse unless aid was continued, leading to more violence and chaos.

David Shearer, director of the United Nations Office for the Coordination of Humanitarian Affairs, told me last week that if the money for the security forces payroll runs out, there will be 70,000 men running around Gaza unable to feed their families—most of them armed—and approximately 1 million Palestinians without a breadwinner.

These men, along with the al-Aqsa Martyrs' Brigades members, will constitute one of the biggest challenges for the upcoming government—something I wrote about in a feature story for *Al Jazeera*. The brigades, along with Islamic Jihad and the Marxist PFLP, are responsible for the bulk of rocket attacks against Israel and for kidnappings of foreigners, not Hamas.[18]

These men are loose cannons, used to the days of quick and easy payoffs, and are now demanding to be absorbed into an already bloated and unsustainable security apparatus—"or else." Along with Israeli moves and Western aid cuts, their actions threaten to destabilize the nascent Palestinian government before it even gets started.

How Hamas will deal with such threats remains to be seen, especially in the face of increasing international pressure and isolation.

Child Killer Gets Compensation; Parents Get More Grief[19]
Gaza City, Palestine, March 23, 2006

I'm disgusted.

The infamous Captain "R" will receive 80,000 in the new Israeli shekel in compensation from the State of Israel after being cleared of all charges in relation to the killing of 13-year-old Iman al-Hams. According to *Haaretz*, the judges who acquitted Captain R accepted his version of the event: that the shots that he fired were not aimed directly at the girl's body, that he opened fire in order to create a deterrence, and that he believed that the young girl posed a serious threat.[20]

Perhaps it is a good time to review Chris McGreal's chilling detailing of the event in the *Guardian*:

> [I]t was broad daylight, 13-year-old Iman al-Hams was wearing her school uniform, and when she walked into the Israeli army's "forbidden zone" at the bottom of her street, she was carrying her satchel. A few minutes later the short, slight child was pumped with bullets. Doctors counted at least 17 wounds and said much of her head was destroyed.[21]

What more is there to say?

The Story of Saeed Abu Salah[22]
Beit Hanoun, Gaza, Palestine, March 24, 2006

Living in the Gaza buffer zone has taught Saeed Abu Salah a thing or two about patience and treading carefully.

He and his 21-member family live in the northernmost region of Gaza's recently declared "no-go zone," where surviving has become a delicate balance of dodging artillery fire and sheer luck.

Forty years old with graying hair and warm eyes the color of chestnuts, Abu Salah's home is in the farming town of Beit Hanoun, less than a kilometer away from the border with Israel—and the fence and wall that bulldozers, active even as we spoke and visible in plain distance, were building.

Directly across from his house, at the end of a dirt path that used to lead to his farm, was an Israeli watchtower. It was equipped with a camera that monitors the family's every move and a sniper, who fired "warning" shots at us throughout our conversation.

"He doesn't like you being here, as a journalist. It's normal. He shoots day and night but particularly when visitors come," explained Abu Salah of the unseen sniper, whom he talked about as though he were a close acquaintance.

Israel says armed Palestinian groups were using areas in northern Gaza to launch rocket attacks on southern Israel. Palestinian groups refer to retaliation for Israeli attacks on Gaza.

Mobile Israeli artillery batteries have fired several thousand shells into the area, killing dozens of Palestinians, damaging homes, and leaving Palestinian farmlands inaccessible to their owners.

Israeli forces are allowed to direct artillery fire to within 100m of civilian homes, greatly increasing the danger to residents in the area.

Many Palestinians have fled the buffer zone for safer pastures, but Abu Salah's family refuses to leave. And they have paid the price.

His 40-dunam (9.8-acre) orchards, as well as poultry, dairy, and fish farms, were all destroyed last year.

In addition to destroying the entire second story of his home and farm, shell shrapnel wounded his 21-year-old son Eid, who after 14 operations still requires surgery to dislodge fragments near his heart.

Still, Abu Salah has remained unflinching in his determination to stay put, asserting that he will only allow Israeli troops to drive him out, which he said they have tried to do so many times before, "over his dead body."[23] He added, "The Israelis are always firing at us, and when not firing, then shelling, and when not shelling, hovering over us with F-16s and drones, or dropping leaflets telling us to leave, mocking us, provoking us, trying to show us that we are surrounded from all sides and that we have to eventually leave."

The UN Development Program estimates the damage done to his farm, which once employed more than 30 Palestinians, is nearly $0.5 million. With the help of human-rights organizations, he filed a case against the Israeli Army demanding compensation, but to no avail.

Aid organizations stepped in and helped Abu Salah erect a zinc-sheeted shed on his land, which acts as a de facto "red line" demarcated by Israeli military authorities as a no-entry zone.

His three horses, one still bleeding from a bullet wound to the thigh, guide themselves to graze in the area that he is kept from entering. But even they know their limits.

"They don't get near the sniper or the border; they know when to stop," he said, laughing.

His horses fare better than his cattle: They have all been killed by artillery fire.

In photos he took as evidence, his dead cows lay alongside each other, their intestines spilling out of their bloated stomachs, ripped open with bullets.

"It's as if they wanted to say, 'This could be you,'" explained Abu Salah, with his young children peering through the iron-barred window in front of us. The youngest of the 20, with piercing blue eyes, was giggling beneath his arms. They have recently started to wet themselves from the panic.

"We just can't afford to buy any more cattle or plant any more trees. Why should we? The Israelis will just destroy them again," he said, staring at the ominous tower in the distance, now a fixture of the landscape.

There are no clinics where he lives. No grocery stores. Nothing is allowed in. His wife is expecting any day now, but Abu Salah is worried an ambulance may not reach them.

Despite his situation, or partly because of it, Abu Salah has immersed himself in a newfound hobby—collecting and decorating spent artillery shells.

Over sage tea and sweet, strong coffee, he displayed his "museum of Israeli war artifacts"—a room full of 55kg tank shells now converted into vases decorated with an arrangement of brightly colored plastic flowers. The vases have made him somewhat of a celebrity in this impoverished strip, and Abu Salah can barely keep up with the demand.

"I give them away as gifts. People like them for some reason. Maybe it's the contrast of making something beautiful out of something so ugly and destructive," explained Abu Salah as he walked under archways neatly trimmed with a belt of 7mm bullet casings and near shelves displaying spent flares and missile shrapnel in his home.

"I am not a Hamas supporter, but let me say that we've given enough concessions—a whole decade of concessions for free. The PLO decided to recognize Israel and what did recognition bring us? Have them recognize our rights first, our freedom to live, our right of return; then, surely, we will recognize their rights," he said.

After sunset, the family remained hemmed in the southernmost corner of the home and huddled together in one room for safety, far from any windows.

"This is our reality. This is our fate. And we will bear it out but never another exile—I will stay here till they bury me in my grave."

More of the Same: Palestinians See No Change in Israeli Elections[24]
Gaza City, Palestine, March 28, 2006

In the face of grim political prospects and ever-increasing physical and economic isolation, Palestinians in Gaza are reacting to the Israeli elections with indignant apathy.

Many see the outcome as a given and consider the front-running Israeli parties to be essentially two sides of the same coin. Even the surprising number of seats won by Avigdor Liberman's radical Yisrael Beytenu came as no surprise to most.

Abu Diyab Abu al-Awf, 72, lives in the al-Bureij refugee camp in eastern Gaza. "Each of the candidates is worse than the next as far as Palestinians are concerned," he said. "The only difference is, some are stronger and make certain pragmatic decisions, and some don't." But ultimately, Abu al-Awf believes, "none has the interests of the Palestinians, or of a just peace, in mind."

Rami al-Mugheiri, a 31-year-old editor, said, "Past experience has taught us not to expect much from Israeli elections. Whatever leader will come to power, the most we will get is tough lengthy negotiations that mainly concentrate on marginal issues."

By way of example, al-Mugheiri referred to the elections in 2000, when Israelis voted Ehud Barak's Labour party into power. Barak was "nevertheless intransigent regarding the Palestinians' right to return, Jerusalem, and continued settlement expansion" during the Camp David talks.

Palestinians believe that any new Israeli government, even a Kadima-Labour coalition, will inevitably continue the policy of unilateralism and imposed solutions established by Sharon. That would make a negotiated settlement and a Palestinian state impossible, they say.

As one political analyst explained, the elections are not irrelevant to Palestinians; instead, the loss of interest is attributable to the Palestinians' preoccupation with their "harsh realities and daily living," which have rendered the elections outlandish to them.

Palestinians "are convinced that there is no qualitative difference between Israeli political parties," which they see as vying with each other to torment Palestinians, deny them their rights, and steal their land. "So the bulk of the Palestinians do not think there is anything worthwhile that can be expected from the Israeli elections."

⊗

Israeli Army to Probe Murder
of Gaza Shepherdess by Occupation Soldier[25]
Gaza City, Palestine, March 30, 2006

According to *Haaretz*, the Israeli Army has launched a formal investigation into the death of a Palestinian shepherdess, 25-year-old Nayfa Abu Imsa'id, who was killed by Israeli sniper fire as she was herding her flock with her friend last month. I reported on the story, which got very little press at the time (surprise, surprise), for *Al Jazeera*.[26]

According to the article, "An investigation on the scene raised the suspicion that the soldier violated the army's rules of engagement." Ya think?

Nayfa was killed by a single, high-velocity bullet to the heart. It was broad daylight outside. And she was several hundred meters away from the fence. Yet time and again, such atrocious acts are completely dismissed by both the media and the Israeli military apparatus.

When I confronted an Israeli Army spokesperson about the incident at the time, I was told that after soldiers saw Nayfa and her friend near the border, they "fired two warning shots." They claim that it is difficult for them to "distinguish" between woman, child, or gunman, insisting there are "rules of engagement" to be followed in such circumstances.

As I mentioned when I wrote about the issue earlier, Gaza's border area has become an ostensible killing zone, where anyone—child, man, or shepherdess—will get killed if they enter within several hundred meters of the zone.

According to UN statistics, at least 30 unarmed Palestinians, including five children, have been killed or seriously injured by Israeli troops for being too close to the Gaza border since the Israeli disengagement.

B'Tselem says that since the start of the second Intifada, out of thousands of Palestinian deaths, 20 percent of whom were minors, the military police investigated only 131 cases involving shooting by soldiers. Eighteen of these investigations resulted in the filing of indictments.

Only one was convicted for shooting to death a Palestinian boy. His penalty was four months in jail and a reduction of rank.

When I confronted the Israeli Army about such figures (which were more or less confirmed) during an investigative piece I wrote in May 2004, around the time of the second Rafah incursion, the spokesperson insisted that the army does punish soldiers for their actions, even if such punishments are not "publicized."

When pressed, the spokesperson was unable to provide examples of how soldiers convicted of other crimes were punished.

⊗

Words We Learned Yesterday[27]
Gaza City, Palestine, March 30, 2006

Yousuf's vocabulary is increasing exponentially these days. My father calls him a "parrot." Things you don't think he'll remember, even words he overhears you saying, will inevitably stick. Of course, being in Gaza, a 2-year-old's vocabulary includes words that you may not otherwise expect.

Salta'one: Crab (a Gaza delicacy, which Yousuf attempted to eat by himself—I guess you have to learn the hard way sometimes)

Fijil: Radish

Hamas: Hamas (as in, "*Hih! Shoof! Hamas!*" ["Look—it's Hamas!"] after seeing celebratory rallies and music and a wave of green flags pass by our house after the new cabinet was voted in)

Thi'ib: Wolf (as in "Little Red Riding Hood"; in Arabic, *Laila wal thi'ib*).

Qassif: Shelling (as in "*Yamma! Qassif! Ma'alish—matkhafeesh!*" ["Oh Mommy! Shelling! It's OK—don't be afraid!"], after a night of earth-pounding shelling)

Gaza under Attack . . . [28]
Gaza City, Palestine, March 31, 2006

It's 1 a.m. Gaza City is under heavy aerial and navy bombardment, unlike anything the city has seen in recent years. As I write this, F-16 warplanes—not Apaches or tanks—are bombarding Gaza City just a few roads away from my house. The entire house is shaking, and the windows have cracked. The explosions are so powerful my ears are ringing. . . . They are like sonic booms, but they are real. There are several casualties reported by local radio, but other than that, we know little else. . . . I'm going to take cover now.

Update: We passed through the night safely, and for now, the F-16 attacks have stopped. This morning, navy gunships (which can be seen off Gaza's coast) have been pounding Jabaliya and other areas of northern Gaza. Internally, the security situation has calmed down as well—after a bloody day of factional infighting, the gunmen are now off the streets (and Mr. Dahalan is far away from the accusations being thrown at him, in the United Arab Emirates). More will follow on this matter later.

Just Another Day in Paradise[29]
Gaza City, Palestine, March 31, 2006

> You better duck when that awful sound goes
> (Boom, boom, boom)
> Yeah, that's what's happenin' in the parking lot
> (Boom, boom, boom)
>
> Yeah, that's what's happenin' on stage
>
> Bang bang, that awful sound
> Bang bang, my baby shot me down.

The Roots and Nancy Sinatra—what better way to describe another day in paradise . . . er, Gaza? I hear that word a lot, "paradise." From people describing their homes, their gardens, their razed orchards. They don't see the war, and the destruction, and the lawlessness, and all the ugliness of occupation and anarchy.

They see beauty.

Living here is always surreal, to put it mildly. But you learn to compartmentalize and move on with your life. Internalize, adapt, and survive. Sometimes, for a moment, I try and detach this adapted self from my body, to regain perspective.

Yesterday, as I was having mint tea and date cookies with my cousin, who is here visiting from the United Kingdom, where her husband is completing a Ph.D. (her daughter is the cutie pictured behind Yousuf in the photo). My cousin's father-in-law, a fiery little man of 80-something years, was debating with his son about the differences between the Palestinian educational system "then and now." Yousuf was trying to compete for Dalia's (my cousin's daughter) attention, playing with her dolls and baby stroller (yes, my son is in touch with his feminine side).

And swirling all around us, the entertainment for the evening was a "symphony" of war, as people like to describe it here. The distinct double-boom of tank artillery shells—"BOOM boom" every few seconds, along with the single explosions of what I would later learn were navy gunship attacks—interspersed with rapid machine-gun fire, a swarm of drones whirring incessantly overhead, and Apache helicopters attacking areas in northern and eastern Gaza. My cousin told her daughter they were just fireworks and not to be alarmed, so she (4 years old) casually ignored them.

The shelling ceased for a while after that, until around 3 a.m., when we were literally shocked awake by a tremendous explosion. Just two streets down from us, an F-16 warplane had dropped a bomb on a playing field that was the site of a large celebration attended by more than 100,000 Palestinians, including Ismail Haniyeh, and members of different factions commemorating Land Day.

The field was empty, but the explosion left a tremendous crater, and its sheer force scared us senseless. At first we thought it might be a sonic boom, but it did not have the distinct after-echo that accompanies that. This explosion was so loud I thought I might find the street in front of me taken out—that or doomsday was upon us. Sometimes I think when it comes, I might not know the difference. We weren't sure what was happening, and because of the drones overhead, all the television satellite signals were scrambled, so we panicked and held hands in bed until it passed.

It's quiet again this morning. The sun is out. Yousuf is taking his nap. Beit Lahiya wild berries are in season. Bees are pollinating with spring's explosion of color and fertility. And somewhere off Gaza's besieged coast, a fisherman is lamenting his luck at sea.

It's just another day in paradise.

CHAPTER NOTES

1. The full original text of this post is archived at http://www.gazamom.
   com/2006/03/lethal-ambiguity/, shortented to http://bit.ly/bO4JLS.
2. View B'Tselem's video, "Lethal Ambiguity: Israeli Soldiers Talk about the Rules
   of Engagement," archived at http://bit.ly/cbmusv. To read more about Israel's use
   of firearms, see B'Tselem's report archived at http://bit.ly/dcPMUM.
3. "IDF Soldiers Shoot and Kill Sayyed Abu Libdah, 16, When in His Family's
   Orchard, 600 Meters from the Gaza Perimeter Fence, December 2005," B'Tselem,
   December 5, 2005, archived at http://bit.ly/aiAJtX.
4. Archived at http://bit.ly/b1I31h.
5. Archived at http://bit.ly/9bwbqg.
6. Archived at http://bit.ly/cUUGWp.

7. Laila El-Haddad, "How to Win an Israeli Election," *Guardian Unlimited*, March 17, 2006, archived at http://bit.ly/9q9Qtc.

8. See *Al Jazeera*'s reporting on the continued development of the E-1 area, connecting East Jerusalem and the largest West Bank settlement of Ma'ale Adumim: Khalid Amayreh, "Israel Starts Work on New Settlement," *Al Jazeera English*, March 14, 2006, archived at http://bit.ly/8YZ8zq.

9. To find out more about Israeli policies on crossing closures, see my post, "The Gaza 'Diet' Begins," archived at http://bit.ly/cyo6nS.

10. See Gideon Levy, "As the Hamas Team Laughs," *ZNet.com*, February 22, 2006, archived at http://bit.ly/ab2rGs.

11. See *Electronic Intifada*'s special report on extrajudicial killings, archived at http://bit.ly/9nrep7.

12. Laila El-Haddad, "Beware the Ides of March," *Guardian Unlimited*, March 16, 2006, archived at http://bit.ly/cUbCWf.

13. See CNN's profile of Ze'evi: "Rehavam Ze'evi: A Controversial Figure," *CNN.com*, April 28, 2002, archived at http://bit.ly/drZkLn.

14. Archived at http://bit.ly/avMRjV.

15. Archived at http://bit.ly/cBSFte.

16. Archived at http://bit.ly/97pgwr.

17. Laila El-Haddad, "Gaza Gunfights Point to Fears over PA Salaries," *Guardian*, March 20, 2006, archived at http://bit.ly/bMQKYW.

18. For more on the security situation in Gaza following the 2006 election of Hamas, see Laila El-Haddad, "Hamas Faces Security Challenges," *Al Jazeera English*, February 22, 2006, archived at http://bit.ly/aWQ99j.

19. Archived at http://bit.ly/92TLqq.

20. Amos Harel, "IDF Officer Cleared in Death of Gaza Girl to Receive Compensation from State," *Haaretz*, March 22, 2006, archived at http://bit.ly/d1WIbt.

21. Chris McGreal, "A Schoolgirl Riddled with Bullets. And No One Is to Blame," *Guardian*, October 21, 2004, archived at http://bit.ly/9eqWBY.

22. Archived at http://bit.ly/btaqxa.

23. Abu Salah's house has since been completely demolished and his family driven from their home and land.

24. Archived at http://bit.ly/d0bR4d.

25. Archived at http://bit.ly/9jtWRc.

26. Amos Harel and Arnon Regular, "IDF to Probe Shooting of Palestinian by Soldier," *Haaretz*, March 30, 2006, archived at http://bit.ly/a1swdg; and Laila El-Haddad, "Israeli Soldiers Kill Palestinian Woman," *Al Jazeera English*, February 14, 2006, archived at http://bit.ly/bJvpqZ.

27. Archived at http://bit.ly/doDStC.

28. Archived at http://bit.ly/dtRcPU.

29. Archived at http://bit.ly/bGy88T.

Chapter 10

"The Earth Is Closing In on Us"

Early April 2006

As the year wore on, the Israeli military intensified its use of the same tactics it had used since the disengagement: perimeter artillery fire, which resulted in an ever-increasing number of deaths of innocents, physical isolation, collective punishment. The Israeli Air Force bombed numerous targets, including the residential compound belonging to Mahmoud Abbas and the Palestine National Football Stadium. And travel restrictions on Palestinians got ever tighter. In the end, veteran Israeli journalist Amira Hass explained, none of this was "news" because the asphyxiation of Palestinians—the rupture of everyday Palestinian life—had become so routine.

Springtime in Gaza[1]
Gaza City, Palestine, April 3, 2006

The mixture of bright colors such as lilac, fuchsia, and red that one sees during the spring are often reflected in traditional Palestinian embroidery, originating from Beer il-Sabi', Isdud, and other areas in and around the historical Gaza district.

Israeli Warplanes Attack Gaza Presidential Compound, as the Gaza "Diet" Continues[2]
Gaza City, Palestine, April 4, 2006

Israeli fighter jets have been roaring forebodingly, and with great intensity, over Gaza's skies all morning. So we figured it was only a matter of time before an aerial attack ensued. Predictably, we soon heard two consecutive, powerful explosions that rocked the city—and, again, we wondered: sonic boom or bomb attack? Because we could hear the jets roaring beforehand, we could assume it was only a real attack.

The local radio stations and Palestine television confirmed this: Mahmoud Abbas's presidential compound was under attack. Israeli F-16s bombarded Abbas's helicopter launch pad/runway, which is located near his office in the presidential compound in Gaza City, and another location in northern Gaza that security forces use to train.

Hospitals reported two injuries.

So the question becomes, why would they attack the presidential compound? Most certainly, there are no Qassam rockets being launched from there.

One explanation is simply because they can. It is a demonstration that no one is immune—not even the president or his security forces.

This attack represents a serious escalation on the part of Israel that can be likened to the attacks and eventual isolation and "irrelevantization" of Yasser Arafat and his *Muqataa* compound in Ramallah.

Because obviously that was a successful strategy, so why not repeat it? *Sigh*.

According to the World Bank, if there is no dramatic change, 75 percent of Palestinians will be below the poverty line within 2 years (that amount already is at or just above the poverty line). The current rate is 56 percent, compared with 22 percent in 2000.

Update: Following the aerial attack, Israel resumed pounding areas of northern Gaza with tank artillery shells, killing a Palestinian man and injuring several members of his family, including a mother and her 6-month-old baby, after Israeli tanks shelled civilian areas in northern Gaza.

Has Gaza now become the new Ramallah *Muqataa*? Is it perhaps the entire Strip, rather than just the compound, that is being confined to "irrelevancy"?

Fédération Internationale de Football Association (FIFA) on Gaza Air Strikes[3]
Gaza City, Palestine, April 7, 2006

Last week, I wrote about a series of powerful Israeli F-16 air strikes against Gaza City that shocked us awake, rattling our windows and leaving our ears ringing.[4] One of these attacks was against a soccer field in the middle of Gaza City, just two streets down from where I live. The bomb left an enormous crater in the middle of the stadium (one of Gaza's best and only stadiums), which is located in the middle of a densely populated residential neighborhood.

Now, FIFA, the world's football association, is effectively condemning the attack, saying it was "without reason."

"[T]he field was not being used by Palestinians as a missile launching pad, as Israel's ambassador to Switzerland had claimed," said Jerome Champagne, FIFA deputy general secretary in charge of political issues.

"FIFA has been fighting for more than a century to make this game universal. To hit a football field is really the wrong signal. . . . [F]ootball should remain outside of politics . . . "

Champagne has taken the matter up with FIFA President Sepp Blatter, and the two will announce a "decision" next week.

Not that it will have much consequence, but at least someone (FIFA of them all) is taking notice of an increasingly ignored situation in Gaza and the disproportionality and immorality of Israeli "reprisals" against the civilian population.

Well, at least this way, if we starve, we'll always have football.

Six Killed in New Israeli Strikes, Shelling Continues[5]
Gaza City, Palestine, April 7, 2006

At least six Palestinians are reported to have been killed in Israeli air strikes in the teeming southern Gaza refugee camp of Rafah, including a 5-year-old boy who was dismembered. The attack was targeting members of the Popular Resistance Committees. At least 15 injuries have been reported—two serious, according to medics, who are having a difficult time identifying the bodies, which they say are arriving in pieces.

Meanwhile, Israeli shelling continues in eastern and northern Gaza. At one point, I counted one shell every 10 seconds. *Haaretz* reported that the Israeli Army fired 300 shells within the past 24 hours.

Update: It's after 11 p.m. here in Gaza, and the shelling has increased dramatically. I can hear artillery being fired from two different locations at once, spaced about five seconds apart. The lights are shaking above me from the force of the explosions as I write this. I've moved Yousuf's bed away from the window in case the glass shatters. The shelling has been going nonstop for two days now. It's getting inside our heads. Several people I've spoken to today have complained of lack of sleep and irritability, because the shelling continues throughout the night.

Just Another Gaza Friday[6]
Gaza City, Palestine, April 8, 2006

I've always loved Fridays in Gaza. In the mornings, except for the lone garbage collector futilely sweeping the abandoned streets and municipality park that are littered with plastic cups, watermelon seeds, and mangled straws from the night before, the hustle and bustle of the city comes to a standstill.

It is a serene, if lethargic, time—an escape from the sea of chaos, uncertainty, and violence that grip our lives each waking day and night. For a few hours, things seem ordinary in a place where ordinary is an illusion. And it doesn't seem like anything can disrupt those moments, as if some force is saying to the madness that envelops us, "Come back another hour!"

Slowly, the streets come to life again as evening takes hold. This is Yousuf's favorite time. He likes to go out to the balcony, as we did yesterday, and "people watch"—just take in the incongruent sights and sounds of another Friday in Gaza.

In the park in front of us, children boisterously played football, women licked ice cream cones and chatted, and wedding motorcades (*zaffit sayyarat*)—which, no matter what the season or situation, you can always expect to hear on Thursday and Friday evenings like clockwork—made their way to beach-side hotels and lounges. They tirelessly honked their horns in sync with live wedding *dabke* music, blaring out from portable speakers or played by live for-hire bands seated in the back of rented pick-up trucks decorated with carnations.

Boys and relatives clamor for a standing space in the back of the trucks, dancing and clapping feverishly along with the music. Young children chase them down the street to join in the fun. If the wind is just right, the sky becomes a showcase of homemade kites, dancing and flirting with each other, challenging the physical bounds imposed upon this battered area's residents, reaching to places they can only dream about, allowing them to navigate freedom, no matter how purposeless, for just a little bit.

In the distance, the ubiquitous double thuds of artillery fire could be heard exploding a few kilometers away, increasing in number and intensity as the evening progressed, only to be drowned out ever so slightly by the cacophonous symphony of Friday blitheness, as if to say, "Not today! Today, you will not steal our moment."

The evening passes, the clock strikes midnight, and suddenly, the carriage transforms into a pumpkin again. The magic dissipates. The missiles strike. And six people are dead.

Just another Gaza Friday.

"The Earth Is Closing In on Us"[7]
Gaza City, Palestine, April 10, 2006

Palestinian poet and activist Mahmoud Darwish often wrote of his homeland and its occupation. His poem "The Earth Is Closing In on Us"[8] inspired some of the following thoughts:
The shells keep falling. They've gotten inside my head, so that it's not just my house shaking but my brain throbbing. It's like someone is banging a gong next to my ear every few minutes—sometimes five times a minute, like last night. And just when I savor a few moments of silence, it starts again, as if to say, "You're not going to get away that easily."

We went to sleep to the rattling of our windows and invasive pounding and after-echo of the shells. We sleep as they fall. We pray *fajir*, and they fall again. We wake, and they are still falling. When they are closer, when they fall in Shija'iya east of Gaza City, they make my stomach drop. And I want to hide, but I don't know where.

"The Earth Is Closing In on Us."

That's the thing about occupation—it invades even your most private of spaces. And while the shells were falling inside my head, they also killed little Hadil Ghabin today.

A shell landed on her home in Beit Lahiya, shattering her helpless body and injuring five members of her family, including Hadil's pregnant mother, Safia, and her 19-year-old sister.

My headaches seem inconsequential when I think of little Hadil. Sometimes people here say they prefer death to this existence; you'll frequently hear at funerals, "*Irtahat* . . . she's at peace, more comfortable now anyhow—what was there to live for here?"

The Earth is squeezing us. I wish we were its wheat so we could die and live again.
That has become our sad reality. Death provides relief.

Sometimes it feels like we are all in some collective torture room: Who is playing God with us this night? When I look up into the sky and hear the shells or see the faceless helicopter gunships cruising intently through the moonlit sky, I wonder, do they see me?

And when the shells start falling again, I can't help but imagine some beside-himself-with-boredom 18-year-old on the border, lighting a cig or using the Short Message Service to reach his girlfriend back in Tel Aviv—"Just a few more rounds to go, Hon. . . . Give it another whirl, Ron, it's been two minutes already."

Sometimes, when I'm on edge, I might just yell out and wave my arms at them.

Do they hear me?

We decided to escape this evening to my father's farm in central Gaza, where we roasted potatoes and warmed tea on a small *mangal*, as we listened to *thikr* about the Prophet on the occasion of his *mawlid* from a nearby mosque, under the ominous roars of fighter jets, patrolling the otherwise lonely skies above.

"Where are you heading off to?" asked Osama, the shopkeeper downstairs. "Off to the farm. We're suffocating," I replied, Yousuf tugging at my arm. . . . "Mama . . . *Yallah! Yallah!*"

"*Wallah*, Laila, we're not just suffocating . . . we're asphyxiating. I feel I can't breathe anymore. And my head is pounding and pounding. All I hear is BOOM boom now."

"The Earth is Closing In on Us."

And little Hadil is dead.

And Suddenly, the Seams of Childhood Disappeared[9]
Gaza City, Palestine, April 11, 2006

Hadil Ghabin, 9 years old, was killed last night after an Israeli shell struck her family's home. Thirteen other members of her family were injured, including her pregnant mother, several toddlers, and her 10-year-old brother Ahmed, who lost his eyesight.

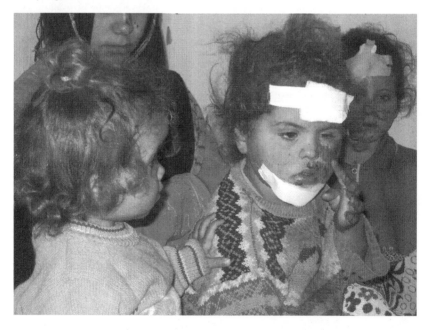

Hadil's mother was baking bread when the shells began to fall around them. She gathered her children, and they huddled inside the house for safety.

According to her aunts, Hadil loved reading, writing stories, and playing "make believe." "She would always gather all the neighborhood children and tell them all sorts of wild stories," her aunt told me.

And why not, for sometimes imagination is the only refuge we have here, the only realm that cannot be invaded. May she live the fairy tales she could only imagine during her short life.

> *And suddenly the seams of childhood disappeared*
> *Lightening and Thunder pounded the earth*
> *And the stories and games flew away like a kite*
> *The game flew away, and with it, the story*
> *And the children became, parts of the story*
> *The story written on the village terraces*
> *The timid village lit like a candle*
> *And the candle shone bright, and the scream reverberated*
>
> —Marcel Khalife, "The Child and the Kite"

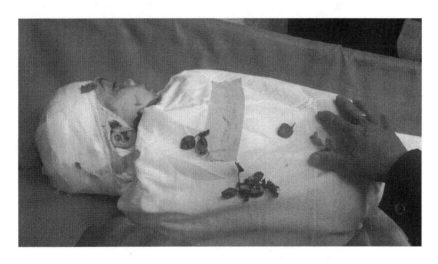

Israel's Über-wardens and the Story of My Friend B.[10]
Gaza City, Palestine, April 13, 2006

A friend and neighbor of mine, B., recently got accepted to get a master's in engineering at Bir Zeit University in Ramallah. She is around 30 years old. After numerous attempts, B. had to withdraw her standing (after paying one semester's tuition), because Israel kept denying her permit to travel to Ramallah based on—you guessed it—"security reasons."

B. has also not seen her sister who lives in Ramallah for five years now because of the travel ban. The most they can do is exchange photos through her personal family blog and talk on the phone—even though they are only one hour apart, the moon may as well be closer! This is the case for almost all Gazans.

B. came to Gaza with her family during the "Oslo Days" with many other Palestinians who lived outside, in her case, from Syria. After years and years of exile, they were able to obtain permits and eventually identification cards (issued by Israel) in a deal that allowed many Palestinians to return to Gaza. Now, says B., she went from being in one prison on the outside, unable to live in her homeland, to another internal prison, unable to move, study, or visit her family.

B. also had to drop all her dreams of higher education in one fell swoop because of Israel's "über-wardens":

"The soldier at the checkpoint or behind the Civil Administration counter . . . the Israeli über-warden . . . is the last, least important, link in the thicket of restrictions and limitations . . . implanting the jailor mentality in thousands of Israeli young people, soldiers, clerks, and policemen—an intoxicating mentality of those who treat those weaker than they with impunity," explains Amira Hass, in another gripping article where she describes ever so eloquently the matrix of Israeli control over Palestinians.[11]

"A thicket of physical, corporeal barriers of all types and sizes (checkpoints, roadblocks, blockades, fences, walls, steel gates, roads prohibited to traffic, dirt embankments, concrete cubes) and by way of a frequently updated assortment of bans and limitations."

Periodic bans supplement permanent ones; in the end, none of it is "news," Hass says, because the asphyxiation of Palestinians—the rupture of everyday Palestinian life—has become so routine.

Control without responsibility, the true formula of disengagement, the recipe for ultimate disaster.

Occupation? What occupation?

Sharon through Palestinian Eyes[12]
Gaza City, Palestine, April 14, 2006, *Al Jazeera English*

Here's a piece I wrote investigating a long-forgotten massacre in the central Gaza Strip, carried out by a young Ariel Sharon's "Unit 101" death squad. There has been little, if any, witness testimony from that grim day, and the attack was overshadowed by an even deadlier one in the village of Qibya two months later, using tactics honed at al-Bureij.

The announcement that Ariel Sharon is no longer prime minister has brought no solace to the refugees of Gaza's al-Bureij camp, who say they are still haunted by memories of his massacres and night-time raids.

Tucked away behind lush clementine groves, al-Bureij's crumbling shelters house three generations of expelled Palestinians.

Their homes are packed along winding alleys and overshadowed by unfinished three-story breeze-block houses. The smells of citrus and sewage intermingle.

It was to al-Bureij, 52 years ago, that Palestinian families fled after attacks on their homes in Ashdod and Yibna [in what became Israel]. And it was there that a 25-year-old Ariel "Arik" Sharon would make his debut.

Name calling

To many Israelis, Sharon was Bulldozer, a military maverick who saved their country from defeat numerous times in its wars with the Arabs.

Ehud Olmert, the former Israeli prime minister, called Sharon a man of "greatness," saying that for the Gaza withdrawal plan, "he came up with the initiative, took the responsibility, marked the goals, took the risks, and won thanks for all that."

George Bush, the U.S. president, has called him a man of peace, but to Palestinians in the refugee camps of Sabra and Shatila in Lebanon, he is the Butcher of Beirut.

In Gaza, he is the man who left a legacy of terror and destruction. To the people of al-Bureij, he is remembered as the man who carried out the massacre there when he was commander of the infamous Israeli Unit 101.

Deadly raids

Nicknamed "the Avengers," the unit was an elite squadron tasked with attacking so-called Arab infiltrators entering the newly declared State of Israel after the 1948 war.

According to Israeli historian Benny Morris's book *Israel's Border Wars, 1949–1956: Arab Infiltration, Israeli Retaliation and the Countdown to the Suez War*, Israelis mounted a violent campaign against Arab "infiltrators," labeling refugees and farmers trying to reclaim their lands as enemies of the state and terrorists.

Morris, a member of the New Historians, a group of scholars who have challenged much of the received wisdom of the origins of the Israeli-Palestinian conflict, also says Israel retaliated with great, sometimes unmerciful force against Arab civilians.

According to Zakariya al-Sinwar, a history lecturer at the Islamic University in Gaza, "When the war of 1948 happened, many people of Gaza began to return to get their money and belongings. They initially left their homes to seek refuge for what they thought was a few days, not forever, so they wanted to go back."

Salman Abu Sitta, a Palestinian researcher, said their attempts to return were used as grounds for attacks against the refugee camps and villages.

"The successful continued war against the returning Palestinians by ruthless expulsion and killing returnees on the spot gave rise to a well-planned policy justified in the media as retaliatory raids. Hence, Unit 101 was formed to undertake this task," Abu Sitta explained in an interview.

It was a unit that Sharon himself described as "spirited," as one that stood out among the "many outstanding units" of the Israeli army. In his autobiography, *Warrior*, Sharon wrote, "They [Unit 101] understood fully the stakes they were fighting for; they were imbued with the need to react."

During the next 3 years, Sharon and his men carried out a number of strikes against targets in the West Bank and the Gaza Strip. Mostly, these targets were villages or refugee camps, such as al-Bureij.

Deliberate mass murder?

On their way into al-Bureij on the night of August 28, 1953, Sharon's squad was spotted by Palestinian farmers.

According to the chief UN observer at the time, Vagn Bennike, rather than retreat, Unit 101 forced its way through the village and attacked refugees with explosives and automatic weapons.

"Bombs were thrown through the windows of huts in which refugees were sleeping and, as they fled, they were attacked by small arms and automatic weapons," said Bennike, in a report to the Security Council.

Mohammad Nabahini, 55, was 2 years old at the time and lived in the camp. He survived the attack in the arms of his slain mother.

"My father decided to stay behind when they attacked. He hid in a pile of firewood and pleaded with my mother to stay with him. She was too afraid and fled with hundreds of others, only to return to take me and a few of her belongings with her," he said.

"As she was escaping, her dress got caught in a fence around the camp, just over there," he gestured, near a field now covered with olive trees.

"And then they threw a bomb at her—Sharon and his men. She tossed me on the ground behind her before she died." Neighbors confirmed the account.

Forty-three Palestinian refugees, including seven women, were killed in the attack.

Deaths in Qibya

A few weeks later, Sharon's unit participated in the attack and expulsion of Bedouins of the Azazme tribe in the western Negev desert, killing an unknown number and expelling 6,000 to 7,000 of them into Egyptian territory, according to the United Nations.

Another 2,000 Palestinians were forced from El Majdal to the then-Egyptian-controlled Gaza Strip under Sharon's command, according to Major Bennike.

In October 1953, Bennike would report on another attack Sharon carried out in the village of Qibya, killing 69 Palestinians in their homes, half of them women and children.

"Bullet-riddled bodies near the doorways and multiple bullet hits on the doors of the demolished houses indicated that the inhabitants had been forced to remain inside until their homes were blown up over them," he said.

Uzi Benziman is an Israeli reporter and author of two books on Sharon. In a personal interview, Benzimann told me that Sharon never apologized for his actions and defended them till the end.

"He never admitted he made mistakes—not only with the military, but with the Arabs. He was quite arrogant—he never publicly stated that he regretted any of his actions, even when faced with military inquiries.

"He and his supporters continued to say that the Lebanon war was the most right and justified war he had fought."

Beware the Arabs

Benziman says Sharon's career was characterized by a fear of Arabs.

"The main theme was 'beware of the Arabs.' He talked about them in the generalizations reflected in his terms, 'All the Arabs are the same.' I think he believed up to his last days as a sober person that we cannot trust them and that we cannot come to terms with them because we cannot trust them.

"Sharon's childhood, growing up on his father's farm surrounded by Arab tribes, enforced the belief that the Arabs were trying to harm him and damage his property.

"His career as a military person was according to these themes. That we and all Israelis have to defend [ourselves] from Arab aggression."

In an interview by phone, Baruch Kimmerling, a sociologist at the Hebrew University currently on sabbatical in Canada, says Sharon implemented a strategy of inciting Arabs and Jews to fight one another, but that this inflicted suffering on both sides.

"The fact was that Sharon's expansive actions caused greater casualties, not only among the Arabs but among Israeli soldiers."

During Sharon's invasion of Lebanon in 1982 to remove the PLO, nearly 18,000 Lebanese and Palestinians, most noncombatants, and 675 Israeli soldiers were killed.

The killing of about 2,000 Palestinian refugees in the Sabra and Shatila camps by Phalange militia in an area controlled by Israeli forces caused an international outcry and embarrassed Israel.

Sharon was eventually forced to resign as minister of defense.

Bulldozer's comeback

In 2001, after holding several ministerial posts, Sharon was elected prime minister.

No longer an eschewed defense minister, and now embraced by a vulnerable Israeli population recoiling in anger and rebounding from the shock of a failed peace process, Sharon found an opportune reentry into politics and lived true to his nickname.

According to Israeli human rights group B'Tselem, under Sharon's tenure more than 3,360 Palestinians were killed between September 2000 and April 2006. Of those, 690—or one in five—were children.

Live ammunition, rubber-coated metal bullets, tear gas, and other Israeli military measures wounded nearly 30,000 Palestinians, with at least 6,000 of them permanently disabled, the Palestinian Red Crescent says.

In the same period, the Israeli Army says that 1,084 Israelis have been killed and another 7,633 wounded by Palestinian fighters and bombers.

Legacy

To much of the non-Arab world, Sharon's lasting legacy will probably be his much-heralded withdrawal of illegal settlers and troops from Gaza.

Israeli author Benziman says, "History will judge him as the first Israeli leader who started to withdraw from territories."

But was Sharon a peacemaker?

"He might have paid lip service to peace, but in his heart he still did not believe that peace was possible during his lifetime," Benziman said.

For Nabahini, who grew up without ever knowing his mother, Sharon was never a man of peace.

"Peace is not just with words," he says. "It's with real actions. And his actions are that of a blood-thirsty murderer."

CHAPTER NOTES

1. The full original text of this post is archived at http://www.gazamom. com/2006/04/springtime-in-gaza/, shortened to http://bit.ly/9iKbm3.
2. Archived at http://bit.ly/bYiKZQ.
3. Archived at http://bit.ly/cVf6xb.
4. See my post, "Just Another Day in Paradise," archived at http://bit.ly/bGy88T.
5. Archived at http://bit.ly/bpFO3i.
6. Archived at http://bit.ly/b4JwLA.
7. Archived at http://bit.ly/ckHn4n.
8. Mahmoud Darwish, "The Earth Is Closing In on Us," trans. Abdullah al-Udhari, in *Victims of a Map* (London: al-Saqi Books, 1984), p. 13.
9. Archived at http://bit.ly/9n6srN.
10. Archived at http://bit.ly/aGg787.
11. Amira Hass, "The Über-wardens," *Haaretz*, April 12, 2006, archived at http://bit.ly/9fEZRU.
12. Laila El-Haddad, "Sharon through Palestinian eyes," *Al Jazeera English*, April 14, 2006, archived at http://bit.ly/9utxes.

Chapter 11

I Complain, Therefore I Am

Mid-April through mid-May 2006

Tensions continued to escalate in Gaza between the newly elected Hamas government and its Fateh rivals. Leaders on both sides traded verbal jabs. Hamas Politburo Chief Khaled Meshaal, who has lived in Syria since Israel's then–Prime Minister Benjamin Netanyahu tried to have him assassinated in Jordan in 1997, accused Fateh of "following a carefully laid-out plan" that the United States had sponsored to bring them down.

Although Hamas was now heading the government, it was not in control of the security forces, who still answered ultimately to PA President Mahmoud Abbas. Meshaal reminded Fateh that it was not long ago when Abbas himself, who had then been prime minister, resigned after PA President Yasser Arafat would not cede his control over the most important security branches to him. Hamas's temporary answer to the chaos that was being sown in Gaza was the formation of a new all-volunteer armed "operational force," headed by an influential clan leader, Popular Resistance Committees' (PRC) Jamal Samhadana. (Israel later assassinated Samhadana.)

On a personal level, I reflected on finally weaning Yousuf and on the comfort and solace he provided for me during the most mentally taxing of times. We also, once again, departed Gaza for the United States to be with Yassine.

On Breastfeeding and Weaning under Occupation[1]
Gaza City, Palestine, April 15, 2006

I'm going out on a limb and assuming my audience is mature enough to stomach a breastfeeding post, so if I haven't already lost you, here goes:

It's official (OK, semi-official): Save for a minor postnursery, prenap, and postnap relapse, after two years, one month, and six days, I have officially weaned

Yousuf. For those who don't know, I am an ardent—some would say zealous—breastfeeding advocate. Simply put, it is one of the most amazing abilities God granted women, everything from the way it is produced to the way the content changes based on your child's nutritional needs (c'mon—can Nestle do *that*?). It is the perfect infant food.

I always planned to breastfeed Yousuf until he was around 2 years old, the age recommended for weaning in the Quran and because we both enjoyed it and benefited from it (hey, when you shed 500 calories a day producing breast milk, who needs a gym?).

Unfortunately, that plan turned out to be easier said than done. Every time I would get up and say to myself, "This is the day to reclaim my . . . ," I would grow weak in the face of his pathetic blubbering and heart-wrenching cries . . . "*Looolooooo!!*" (my nickname). It was as if I were depriving him from the one certainty in his life, the one constant. And now I was telling him that it would no longer be available for his use and abuse, whenever and however frequently he wanted. During the difficult times we live in, it was a step I was always afraid to take. It was his comfort zone, and I was taking it away.

For Yousuf and me, the past two years have been an interesting journey, to put it mildly, wrought with the obvious hurdles of living under occupation, and nursing him has helped us both get through it. It was our moment together—our special time that, although time-consuming and difficult at times, we both equally enjoyed. No one could interfere with this connection, no matter the time or circumstance (save for an hour when I was interrogated by the Shin Bet in Rafah crossing, and then-2-month-old Yousuf was howling in the other room with a female soldier because they forbade me from taking him in the interrogation room with me).

It was something no one else could provide him, something that I will always relish (though I have to admit at times in the early days, I began to feel biologically equivalent in life's purpose to a cow).

Further, my ability to breastfeed him—to be a portable milk machine when Israeli closures resulted in shortages of formula—has gotten us through some tough times, especially when traveling. I think back to those terrible moments and shiver, comforted by only the fact that the nursing sometimes got Yousuf past the hours-long waits in the painful heat of August or bone-numbing cold of winter at checkpoints or at Rafah crossing, waiting for the Israeli "über-wardens" to let us through, as they bellowed out orders to the thousands of desperate travelers, including us.

And knowing that our chances of making it through on any given day were contingent upon the mood of the soldier manning the checkpoint did not make it any easier. When a young, heat-exhausted Yousuf was on his final crying breath, hysterical, hungry, and confused, I would nurse him quietly in the taxi as we waited and waited and waited—and *bam*, like magic, he would calm down and sleep. And that meant so could I.

So now, here we are. It's difficult enough weaning my little babe and dealing with his mommy-milk withdrawal, but to attempt to do so under the continuous barrage of Israeli artillery shells . . . well. After a brief lull (and I use "lull" cautiously here . . . meaning a few hours), the shelling resumed last night full throttle following a Palestinian hand-made rocket that landed in an Ashkelon sports stadium (kind of ironic, given the Israeli F-16 attack on Gaza's stadium a few weeks ago).

The explosions were more frequent and powerful than before. At one point, I counted 10 shells falling per minute, some from different locations at once. We could literally feel the shock waves penetrating the house, rattling its windows and leaving the walls trembling.

Needless to say, we got minimal sleep between that and the constant ringing of my orange cell phone because of someone who turned out to be an Israeli caller looking for a "Tsedek" and then "Isabel." I futilely explained to him in broken Hebrew that it was the wrong number—while leaving out the minor detail that he had actually called a Palestinian in Gaza.

Usually if Yousuf wakes up, I can nurse him back to sleep, but now we no longer have that to fall back on. He is taking it all like a champ, especially after I "explained" to him that breastfeeding— "*azza*," as he calls it—is for babies and that he is now a big boy. After a few initial "Yeah right!" episodes, he seemed to understand. Sometimes he looks at me if he is tempted to lift my shirt and says, "*Lal baby?*" ("For baby?"), looking for confirmation.

Palestinians Commemorate Prisoners' Day, as All Hell Breaks Loose[2]
Gaza City, Palestine, April 17, 2006

I'm very tired, so instead of posting something on how all hell breaks loose between one second and the next, and how just when you say to yourself, "Well, how about that: only 20 shells today, and no gun battles between bickering gunmen, and no suicide bombings" . . . well, needless to say, things have a way of turning very bad very quickly here. Nine killed in Tel Aviv, another Palestinian boy killed in Beit Lahiya by Israeli shelling (that makes 16 since the start of the year) . . . and I just heard an explosion near my house.

So . . .

I'm going to talk about commemorations of Palestinian Prisoners' Day (yes, we have so many commemorative "days") and then go to sleep, because God knows we *all* need sleep.

Thousands of Palestinians—mothers, sisters, daughters, sons, from all different factions—filled the streets of Gaza City today to commemorate Palestinian Prisoners' Day on April 17.

Palestinians marched through the streets of Gaza to the Palestinian Legislative Council, carrying pictures of their imprisoned family members and in some cases symbolically tying their hands together with chains. They called on Palestinian Parliament members and ministers, human rights organizations, and the world community to make the release of the prisoners a top priority.

The parliament convened a special session to address the plight of the prisoners.

One of the demonstrators, 27-year-old Leila Dabbagh, had not seen her fiancé, who is being held in an Israeli jail, for five years. They were legally married but had not yet consummated the marriage at the time of his imprisonment.

Others are able to see their detained loved ones by means of the Red Cross, only through glass partitions. Extended family members cannot go, however. One woman wept as she told me she had not seen her only nephew in 18 years. Most are detained at a relatively young age. They leave behind children who grow up without ever really knowing their fathers.

The issue of the prisoners is a uniting factor, a common denominator among Palestinians.

Some 8,000 Palestinians are being held in Israeli prisons or detention centers by the Israeli Army, including 370 minors and 103 Palestinian women, according to the Palestinian prisoner's rights and support group, Addameer.[3]

More than 750 are held without charge or trial.

The overwhelming majority of Palestinian prisoners are regarded as political captives who have been arbitrarily imprisoned or detained under the broad banner of "security," according to the Israeli human rights group B'Tselem.

"If these same standards were applied inside Israel, half of the Likud party would be in administrative detention," noted the group in a report.

Palestinians have been subjected to the highest rate of incarceration in the world. Since the beginning of the Israeli occupation of Palestinian territories in 1967, more than 650,000 Palestinians have been detained by Israel, constituting some 20 percent of the total Palestinian population and 40 percent of all Palestinian men.

According to Amnesty International, Human Rights Watch, and B'Tselem, their conditions of detention are extremely poor, with many prisoners suffering from medical negligence, routine beatings, position torture, and strip searches.

I Complain, Therefore I Am[4]
Gaza City, Palestine, April 21, 2006

I'm fairly certain I exist.

Descartes tells me so and, before him, Ibn Sina. And when my son drags me out of bed to play with him in the predawn hours, I really know I do.

So you can imagine how distraught I was when my existence was cast into serious doubt by a major airline.

After booking a flight online with British Airways out of Cairo (the nearest accessible airport for Palestinians here, eight hours and a border crossing away from Gaza, because the Gaza airport is incapacitated—much like Sharon), I attempted to enter my "passenger details," including country of citizenship and residence.

Most people wouldn't give this a second thought. But being the owner of a PA passport (which one can acquire on only the basis of an Israeli-issued identification card), I have become accustomed to dealing with kafkaesque complications in routine matters.

And sure enough, in the drop-down menu of countries, I found the British Indian Ocean Territory, the Isle of Man, and even Tuvalu—but no Palestine.

Now, I understand "Palestine" does not exist on any Western maps. So I would have settled for Palestinian territories (though Palestinian Bantustans may be more appropriate), Gaza Strip, and West Bank, or even Palestinian Authority, as my "pursuant to the Oslo Accords"–issued passport states.

But none of these options existed. And neither, it seemed, did I.

I was confused. Where in the world is Laila El-Haddad if not in Palestine, I wondered? Certainly, not in Israel (as one of many customer relations representatives casually suggested).

I sent an e-mail of complaint to British Airways, humbly suggesting that it amend the omission. Several days later, the reply came: "We are unable to assist you with your query via e-mail. . . . Please call your general enquiries department on BA.com, then select your country from the drop-down list."

Now, I realize you don't need a Ph.D. to work in one of these posts, but I assumed it was fairly self-evident from my first e-mail that "my country is not listed" in the drop-down list. I explained this to "Diana" in a follow-up e-mail and was told to contact my "nearest general enquiries department" (if I were to take that literally, that would be Tel Aviv). Instead, I opted for customer relations in the United Kingdom, whose Web support told me there was no guarantee I would ever get a definite answer.

I relayed the tale to my friend, whose own status as an East Jerusalemite is even more precarious than mine as a postdisengagement Gazan. "Could it be," she posited, "that there is no definite answer because we aren't considered definite people?"

I'll leave that for British Airways to answer.[5]

The New Order: Hamas Forms New Security Branch[6]
Gaza City, Palestine, April 21, 2006

Something strange is happening in Gaza.

Municipality workers are actually working.

The streets seem a bit cleaner.

And for once, I actually saw a policeman arresting a criminal in a dramatic pick-up the other day, much to the chagrin of his gang, who stoned and shot at the police car (futilely), and the "oohs" and "aahs" of onlookers (including myself).

In Gaza, we have become accustomed to the rule of lawlessness. And people are sick of it—in fact 84 percent, according to a recent poll, place internal security as their number-one priority.

This is not to say that gangs and armed gunmen somehow roam the streets as in some low-budget Western. But for sure, it is brawn and bullets that win the day and decide everything from family disputes to basic criminal proceedings.

Last week, there was a "reverse honor crime" of sorts. A man was found murdered in Gaza City after being accused of molesting a young girl (reverse, I say, because presumably it usually works the other way around and the *woman is punished*). The crime was immediately decried by local human rights organizations and people alike.

But when there is no one around to enforce the law——or rather, no one *able* to enforce the law, other than verbal condemnations—there is little else that can be done. If the accused were jailed, his family would have inevitably intervened, hiring gunmen to break him out or taking it out against another member of his family. It's a vicious cycle. Citizens don't feel accountable, and law enforcers are impotent.

This is where Hamas's power of moral suasion comes into play. I've seen it at work in such areas as Dair al-Balah, which was spared the bloody clan disputes that such areas as Khan Yunis and Beit Lahiya suffered, when the Hamas-elected municipality leader intervened.

Of course, they have no magic wand, but they seem very effective at what they do—and their networks and ability to "talk" to people as "one of the people" resonates well.

The bigger problem is: What do you do when the law enforcers themselves are the ones breaking the law?

Last week, 50 masked gunmen belonging to the Preventive Security Forces (PSF), the official security apparatus of the PA, blockaded off the main street between northern and southern Gaza, demanding their wages, as they have been accustomed to doing over the past few years (though the mass media would have us assume otherwise, citing the incident as "the first sign" of frustration with the new government).

They are the same old group that has always made trouble, whether for Mahmoud Abbas or Ismail Haniyeh, and are effectively supported by Mohammad Dahlan, who fondly refers to them in his inner circles as his "little army." Hamas and others accuse them of being a "minority," stirring trouble to attempt to speed the downfall of the new government and "score political points."

Many of them also belong to the al-Aqsa Martyrs' Brigades (AMB), Fateh's rogue military offshoot.

As I've mentioned before, this group poses one of the biggest security challenges to Hamas. Members are loyal to Fateh but seemingly answerable to no one (except Dahlan), and very strong figures who want nothing else but to see this new government fail support a contingent of them.

So what is Hamas to do? For one, form its own security force.

Yesterday, new Minister of the Interior Saeed Siyam held a press conference in Gaza's Omari Mosque in the old city (an interesting choice—the oldest mosque in Gaza and a place for the "masses"). He announced the formation of a new armed "operational force," headed by PRC leader Jamal Samhadana—a brawny, bearded fellow with broad clan appeal who is constantly surrounded by a posse of heavily armed body guards and wanted by Israel for masterminding several of the highest-profile bombings of the second Intifada.

The all-volunteer force would also consist of a police arm, with thousands of members of armed groups, such as the AMB, PRC, and Izz-i-deen al-Qassam Brigades, directly subordinate to him. As if this weren't confusing enough, this move was meant to counter Mahmoud Abbas's recent presidential order appointing Rashid Abu Shbak, former chief of PSF in the Strip, as head of "Internal Security," which is a new entity that unites the interior ministry's security agencies and ensures they remain under Abbas's rule.

Have I lost you yet?

The Israeli press was quick to condemn the move, à la "wanted militant to head PA police."

However, this is probably one of the smartest moves Hamas could make during this stage.

Why? For one, the Samhadana family is one of the most powerful clans of southern Gaza. By appointing one of its own (who also happens, of course, to be the leader of the PRC) as director general of the police forces in the Interior Ministry and absorbing members of the PRC and AMB—who account for two of the most volatile factions in Gaza—into the new force, Hamas is effectively ensuring their allegiance and making them "keepers of the street" rather than "keepers of the clan." They all pledged to fight (the word was more like "crush") lawlessness and crime.

What about the money for wages? Well, simple. There *are* no wages. The new force is an all-volunteer one, so the members are working for status and ideals rather than money (of course, at some point, there will be mouths to feed).

Things could always backfire—and it's not difficult to see how, especially since Abbas does not recognize the new force, and factions have attempted to form similar forces unsuccessfully in the past. But I think for the time being, it is a very interesting "think outside the box" move by Hamas.

As usual, time will tell whether it will truly succeed in ensuring safety and security for Palestinian citizens.

Hamas v. Fateh: Round 1 (or As My Friend Says, "Beirut, Baby")[7]
Gaza City, Palestine, April 22, 2006

I'm writing this in almost pitch darkness. It is not because of artillery shells, from which we've been spared for a whole 24 hours. But the friendly folks of AMB (or, as I like to call them, my friendly neighborhood gunmen) shot our neighborhood's electricity cables accidentally this evening, after hoisting their flag on the now Hamas-dominated Legislative Council in front of our house in protest of recent Hamas statements. (Someone needs target practice. Then again, better the cable than me.)

Last night, they also decided to hold a predawn bash, smack-dab in the middle of the city (deciding to "avoid areas populated by Hamas"), which continued until the wee hours of the morning.

Of course, the protests were dumb, but even dumber perhaps were Khaled Mishal's statements—no matter how true they rang—to which the "protests" were a response.

The Hamas political head in Syria, known for his inflammatory rhetoric, made verbal jabs at Fateh and Mahmud Abbas, blaming them for the state of financial ruin that the PA is currently in, among other things, and said Hamas would not stand for Abbas's decisions to annul the new security branch created by the Ministry of Interior yesterday.

Meshal said, roughly, "We can understand Israel and America persecuting us and seeking ways to besiege and starve us, but not the sons of our people who are plotting against us, who are following a carefully laid-out plan to make us fail. Today is not the time to expose them, but the day will come soon when we will reveal to all the truth in detail about all they have done."

Meshal also noted that is was not long ago when Abbas himself resigned over this very issue—when Arafat would not cede his control over the most important security branches to then–Prime Minister Abbas.

As he was speaking on *Al Jazeera*, and as people cheered him on in the audience, senior Hamas leader Mahmud Zahar, who was in attendance, remained quiet, as if to say, "No, no, Meshal—not the time or place!"

Fateh, of course, wouldn't have it, immediately issuing a condemnatory statement through its revolutionary council accusing Meshal of "igniting a civil war" by calling Abbas a traitor. (Meshal never mentioned Abbas by name but made veiled references. He later apologized and said he was misunderstood, calling for dialogue.)

But it wasn't long before young Fateh cadres, *Fateh shabeeba* as they are called here—hard-core supporters of Mohammad Dahalan (who helped found the movements in 1981)—took to the streets in wild protest. Hooligans were also looking for "something to do," shooting belt after belt of automatic weapons and keeping me awake a good part of the night (not to mention disrupting a really good chapter in the book I was reading).

As my cousin noted, "Young people here are so bored. These are a bunch of young *shabab* with nothing better to do. They are a small contingent of Fateh looking for any opportunity to lash out at Hamas," which they hate, some have confessed to me, "more than the Israeli occupation itself."

Today, the clashes spilled over into the rival universities of al-Azhar (Fateh run) and al-Islamiya (Islamic University, run by Hamas). Apparently, the Fateh student council in al-Islamiya and, later, al-Azhar students plastered the pristine walls of al-Islamiya with condemnatory and accusatory flyers. Push came to shove (quite literally), and, though it did not get fatal and weapons were not involved, around 15 people were injured in fistfights, stone throwing, and firebombs.

Amid the madness, a lone vendor roamed around the angry crowds selling licorice juice to thirsty stone throwers (honestly, only in Palestine). All that was missing, joked my cousin, was a kiosk selling souvenirs—perhaps T-shirts and hats stating, "Anti-Hamas Protests 2006—I Was There!" I'm sure the local PLO flag shop could make some big bucks.

According to my cousin, it's not all bad. The university (she attends al-Azhar, the only university at the time of her enrollment that taught it) is now on strike for three days—which means time off to study for exams. "Catastrophes for some, benefit for others," she smiled.

We argued about where this could lead to, theoretically.

"They would never be able to plan a civil war; they aren't up to it," she says. We've gotten so accustomed to living without law and order that we don't like anyone to rule us, whether it's Israel, Mahmud Abbas, or Hamas: "People take it very personally. They just don't like anyone telling them what to do. Everybody wants to rule themselves." She thinks a third party needs to intervene to keep the order at this time, such as the Egyptians.

I tend to agree that this would not spill over into civil war for a variety of reasons (though sometimes it's not difficult to see how it could when there is as much negative energy as I saw today, with so much anger and emotion in such a confined space . . . think hamsters crowded in a cage). I think the one thing stopping this from happening is that, even when Hamas supporters do engage *Fateh shabeeba*, things usually are stopped from escalating by the higher echelons of Hamas—who instruct its supporters to stay quiet and indoors and not to fall prey to "Fateh provocations," as they have tonight. As they say, it takes two to tango.

For now, the streets are calm once again, Yousuf is sound asleep . . . and it looks like the electricity just came back on. So I think I'll continue reading my book while it's quiet. . . .

That Terrible Feeling Inside[8]
Gaza City, Palestine, April 27, 2006

OK, I admit, I've been a little lazy this week. Part of that has to do with the fact that, wrapped up in my pretravel anxiety as it were and my mad rush to tie up as many loose ends as possible and write as much as possible, I think I burned myself out.

That and being here can be overwhelming at times; this week has been one of those times. Sometimes I'm too caught up to notice, but then on a "down" week, it catches up with me. I feel powerless, even crushed, in the face of an ugly, foreboding, larger-than-life force that seems to grow and mutate with every passing day. It is everywhere and nowhere at once. And try as you might, you cannot hide from it.

It squeezes you tighter and tighter, instilling within you a feeling of helplessness and dejection and isolation, until you begin to feel you are alone, even among 1.5 million others. And there is nothing you can do about it.

Sometimes I don't want to do anything about it. I just want to run away, somewhere I hope it can't reach me. Sit on the beach, listen to the troubled stories that the Gaza's lonely Mediterranean is desperately trying to tell. "Take me to the beach at sunset, so I may listen what the beach says . . . when it returns to itself, calmly,

calmly."[9] Yousuf frolicked about in the sand, building and destroying his imaginary creations, pleased with his newfound prowess. He glanced over at me, sensed something of sadness in my eyes, and patted me on the shoulder, "Ma'lish, mama, ma'lish," he said ("It's OK") . . . and suddenly, just like that, everything was.

A Conversation in Jabaliya Souk[10]
Jabaliya, Palestine, April 30, 2006

Yesterday, Yousuf and I, along with my mother and her friend, went to the Jabaliya refugee camp's market to do some shopping and search for old Palestinian *thobes* (embroidered dresses), which I collect. Given the economic strangulation of Gaza, the souk was less lively than usual but as colorful as ever. Here is an excerpt of a conversation we had there:

MOM'S FRIEND: How much for the *mulukhiya*?

VENDOR: Three shekels a kilo.

MOM'S FRIEND: Three shekels! The man next to you sells *il arba'a bmiyya* . . . 4 kilos for 10 shekels!

VENDOR: Life is expensive these days, lady.

ME: *Wil bani adam rkhees* . . . (And human beings are cheap).
[Approving nods]

VENDOR: Besides, his *mulukhiya* tastes like grass. I know what I grow—none of those crap chemicals go into it. And it's first of the season. I challenge you to find any *mulukhiya* as tasty as this in all of Gaza!
[Shelling in the distance]
Shit! there they go again.
[Everyone briefly ducks for cover.]

MOM'S FRIEND: Fine, fine—bag it.

Farther along . . .

ME: Do you have any *askadinya baladiya* (local loquats)?

ANOTHER VENDOR: Forget the *baladiya*. . . . Try the Israeli ones, they are the best! But I'm all out today; Karni[11] is closed again.

ME: The Israeli ones taste like water. And they are unnaturally large. That's not how *askadinya* should look or taste. I'll stick to the *baladiya*, thank you.

VENDOR: Well the *baladiya* is still sour. You might as well go buy lemons. Here, want some lemons?

YOUSUF: *Khiyar! Khiyar!* (Cucumbers!)

VENDOR: No *khiyar*, but we have *fa'oos*,[12] come over here, sunglasses lady . . .
[A young boy shoves a bunch of mint in my face.]

YOUNG BOY: "*Na'na' baladi* . . . Want some?"
[More shelling, getting closer]

ME: I'll pass, thanks. [Yousuf helps himself to a *fa'oosa* as the entire pile plummets to the ground.]

Note: Seven Palestinians were injured in the shelling. Two of them were children.

Mulukhiya *stew with rabbits (the man was right, it was fabulous) eaten Gaza-style,* with dagga *salad and hot chilies.*

Days of Catastrophe[13]
Gaza City, Palestine, May 5, 2006

I'm in a final dash to pack up my things for my anticipated Monday travel to the United States via the Cairo and Rafah crossing to meet up with Yassine. And that means finishing up as many of the articles I have left to write as I can. . . . Someone was commenting yesterday that "Well, we have advanced so much, now at least we can cross Rafah without having to worry about Netzarim checkpoint and Abo Holi. . . ." Funny, it's all a matter of perspective I guess . . . one step forward . . . two steps back!

What in any other universe is completely in the realm of the absurd is all of a sudden an acceptable status quo . . . to have to travel eight hours simply to access an airport, while there is one sitting a half hour away from my house in perfect running order. Every country on earth has to deal with securing its borders and its airports—Israel is not unique in this regard. But all these other countries still manage to get planes off the ground and allow people (and goods) in and out freely on a daily basis, using state-of-the-art security screenings and checks. Every country except Israel, which closes borders and denies and blocks Palestinian people and goods movement and access all in the name of blanket security; not one person, not two people, who may be deemed "security threats," but more than 90 percent of the population—namely, anyone who is not a part of the Fateh collaborating elite with which they deal.

Tomorrow, I visit Gaza's "ghost" airport to shoot a photostory for *Al Jazeera*. After that, I must finish up an article[14] on the 55,000 Palestinians living in the West Bank and Gaza with no status, waiting for Israel to grant them family reunification permits and ID cards for going on 10 years.

In the meantime, Israeli shells continued to pound Gaza hard today. And the souks have lost their usual Thursday hubbub. People feel suffocated. Someone commented to me the other day how he thinks 90 percent of Gazans have some form of depression. And if the other 10 percent doesn't, there must be something *really* wrong with it. . . .

I digress from the topic of what was meant to be a short post, but I just cannot avoid the despair and hopelessness—it is everywhere I look. But so are the positive, uplifting acts. Sometimes we have to look a little harder to find them, but they are there.

I saw a man sweeping the street next to us the other night with his children, collecting stray rubbish in a wheelbarrow and disposing of it in a nearby garbage container. Curiosity got the better of me. After going upstairs, I headed back down to ask what he was doing—and he casually replied, "Just something my sons and I like to do every now and again. . . . We choose a different street each week and we clean it" . . . Say *what*?! That made me smile, along with a crudely written handmade sign in a public taxi that I took today that read, "Smoking is not allowed in my taxi!"

So, the point of all this is to remind everyone of the 58th anniversary of *al-Nakba* . . . as Israelis celebrate their "independence" this month, Palestinians commemorate their "days of catastrophe." Usually this is May 14, but "*filisteenyit il-dakhil*"—1948 Palestinians—mark it to parallel Israeli Independence Day, when they march to a different ethnically cleansed Palestinian village each year. Thus comes a moving article by my colleague Jonathan Cook. An excerpt:

> The Palestinian refugee families were joined by 150 Israeli Jews in an annual procession to commemorate the mirror event of Israel's independence called the Nakba (Catastrophe), that drew the

overwhelming majority of Palestinians from their homes and out of the new Jewish state.

This year, the families marched to Umm al-Zinat, a Palestinian farming village whose 1,500 inhabitants were forced out by advancing Israeli soldiers on May 15, 1948, a few hours after Israel issued its declaration of independence.[15]

Fifty-eight years . . . and waiting. A longer *Nakba* post later, *inshallah*.

On the Way . . .[16]
Cairo, Egypt, May 9, 2006

Well, this is just a quick post to say that Yousuf and I have made it safely out of Gaza—we are currently in Cairo after a pleasant and quick trip through Rafah crossing and Sinai (I can't believe I'm actually using "pleasant" and "Rafah crossing" in the same sentence). The new Egyptian terminal is running very smoothly, and on the Palestinian side we were impressed with its efficiency. Hey, Yousuf even got a toffee and a "How are you?" in what I think was Swedish from one of the European monitors. I couldn't help but think, though, of the thousands of Palestinian families who were split apart, unable to travel to Gaza because they lacked Israeli-issued identification cards—still required despite Israel's disengagement from Gaza last year.

Here's Yousuf on a bus out of Rafah crossing, waiting, always waiting, like the rest of us.

We stopped by al-Arish for a fish lunch before continuing our journey through Sinai.

We left so quickly that I hardly had time to think about leaving Gaza. I keep thinking I'll step outside and see the ice cream place, and when I hear planes from nearby Cairo airport overhead, my instinct is to take cover.

I feel lonely here. And yet, somehow, as a Palestinian, it seems lonely everywhere.

I hope to write more soon but I am still drowning in leftover work (brought my laptop with me) and, of course, the mandatory shopping here in Cairo . . . so more soon.

CHAPTER NOTES

1. The full original text of this post is archived at http://www.gazamom. com/2006/04/on-breastfeeding-and-weaning-under-occupation, shortened to http://bit.ly/9qNo05.
2. Archived at http://bit.ly/cymnj1.
3. To find out more about Palestinian prisoners held in Israeli jails, including conditions faced by those prisoners, how their arrests relate to international humanitarian law, and some of the advocacy efforts currently in effect, visit Addameer's website, archived at http://bit.ly/diYkf0.
4. Laila El-Haddad, "I Complain, Therefore I Am," *Guardian Unlimited*, April 21, 2006, archived at http://bit.ly/9qwSjE.
5. Since the time of publication, British Airways has in fact added "Occupied Palestinian Territory" to the drop-down menu of countries listed on its reservations website.
6. Archived at http://bit.ly/c6pYPK.
7. Archived at http://bit.ly/dsT3ZT.
8. Archived at http://bit.ly/bRKoWK.
9. Excerpt from Mahmoud Darwish's poetry.
10. Archived at http://bit.ly/8YlUR7.
11. Karni commercial crossing.
12. Known in English as Chinese cucumber or Chinese snake gourd.
13. Archived at http://bit.ly/9tpt37.
14. Laila El-Haddad, "A Life in Legal Limbo," *Al Jazeera English*, June 27, 2007, archived at http://bit.ly/9ufrcM.
15. Jonathan Cook, "Palestinians Recall Day of Catastrophe," *Al Jazeera English*, May 4, 2006, archived at http://bit.ly/c1ku6r.
16. Archived at http://bit.ly/cBXocY.

Chapter 12

Out of Palestine, Still in Pain

Mid-May through November 2006

This period saw me journeying back to the United States, this time for a longer stay than before, all the while reflecting painfully on Gaza from a distance. I took the opportunity to attend conferences as well as give many talks on the situation back home. Much happened in the Middle East during my absence, including the capture of Gilad Shalit; Israeli "retaliations" on the Gaza Strip, such as the destruction of its only power plant (the effects of which are still being felt to this day); and the July War that Israel waged against Lebanon, which displaced more than 1 million Lebanese residents. They included my husband's family, who are Palestinian refugees living in Lebanon.

Meanwhile, Yousuf made headlines of his own after finally being potty trained!

You're from Where?[1]
Columbia, Maryland, May 14, 2006

Well, I made it (one border crossing, an eight-hour taxi ride, two planes, and a broken engine generator–induced delay later). I must say I feel totally dislodged from my element. I have no sense of time, or space, or being, as odd as that sounds (and from the sleep-talking Yousuf has been doing, neither it seems does he). Our plane was late leaving Cairo by three hours because of a mysterious problem with the engine generators. . . .

So we missed our connecting flight in London's Heathrow, which wasn't all bad, given that British Airways put us up in a five-star hotel for the night, complete with a Jacuzzi tub (which Yousuf seemed to enjoy . . .). And yes, it took the ticket counter people a while to "place" us, à la, "You're from *where*?" [*click . . . click . . . click . . .* hushed whispers to colleagues . . . and finally typing in the correct code to "bypass" the system's oversight of my identity]. I must have been asked that question a dozen times during the course of our trip.

It took us a while to get through immigration in London, where we were put up for the night—and given our strange combination of passports, misspelled names, and travel history, I wasn't the least bit surprised. . . .

"Palestinian *what*?" asked the bare-headed man behind the counter. After lengthy consultation and questions about why we were carrying two passports, an expired Jordanian travel document (which we previously held and which the Jordanian government is phasing out for all PA passport holders), and our PA passports, and who received what passport and why—including various interventions from each of my parents and attempts to restrain Yousuf, who made a canvas out of the immigration hall's metal poles—we were finally allowed through, only to be stopped by an nameless intelligence officer for "further questioning," which included whether we thought the Middle East conflict would be resolved.

I hate all-encompassing questions like that. What the hell is "the Middle East conflict" anyway (I posited in a slightly more toned-down rhetorical)? And is the approval of my entry visa contingent upon my answer? Will a resounding "Hell no—not in our lifetime!" ensure I sleep in the airport, not the nice comfortable bed with four Belgian chocolates tucked under the pillow and shower with complimentary mint-sage shampoo? I thought for a few seconds and then replied to his raised eyebrows, "There is a famous Palestinian novel—a sort of absurdist tale with a comical, *Don Quixote*-esque hero—called *The Secret Life of Saeed the Pessoptimist*. You should read it. That sort of sums it up."

He gave us a cautious smile, called me "diplomatic," and then proceeded to ask me about the "new" government, about whether it wanted a place in the international community and how it would go about doing that, about what Palestinians thought about Olmert, and whether things would change under his rule. I babbled something about the reign of unilateralism as my father tried to shut me up with his glaring eyes. Obviously, the officer knew everything—at least I assumed as much. I had been exposed to this line of questioning before—by both Israeli and American intelligence: He was simply testing the waters, fishing for certain answers, and checking for consistency.

He then asked about our mysterious combination of passports and why we all had different names in them (complicating matters, our names aere spelled differently in each respective passport, no thanks to the incompetent passport officers who issued them and the Israeli law that requires a woman take her husband's name in her Palestinian passport . . . never mind your personal or religious preference or the fact that said authorities don't recognize my husband). . . . My father's name is Moussa El-Haddad in one, Mousa alHaddad in the other; mine Laila El-haddad in one, Laila Dawood in the other; while Yousuf's was Yousuf Daoud . . . you get the picture. So I had to take a few minutes to explain the history of the Palestinian-Israeli conflict, the issue of identity documents, refugees, 1948, 1967, and family reunification. . . .

We were finally let through and helped ourselves to the all-expenses-paid hotel buffet and a beautiful walk through London's parks.

The next day, we made it to the United States and received similar quizzical looks from a Chinese American immigration officer who barely spoke English—and, of course, no Arabic—and who I think was even more confused than his British colleagues. Luckily, we were not taken for further questioning, as I breathed a sigh of relief (given my past experiences with U.S. immigration, including my detention and the confiscation of my passport for 3.5 months allegedly for carrying a vile of *Barrad* essence and working for *Al Jazeera*—at the time recognized as Public Enemy #1). Customs checked our bags (all seven of them) and confiscated a single bag of green wheat—known as *freeka* in Palestine—that my mother insisted on bringing. They asked, once again, where exactly we were from (which prompted the comment, "Oh, how is the weather over there? I'll bet it's great all year-round!" Yeah, the weather . . . sure.

Then we were off and reunited.

Now, I'm trying to recover from the jet lag and still finish up the insane amount of work I have, including an interview I'm working on with the head of the Council of Unrecognized Palestinian Villages in the Negev to mark the ongoing *al-Nakba* tomorrow.

For now, I sign off . . . and get back to unpacking my bags!

Either Return . . . or Return[2]
Columbia, Maryland, May 15, 2006

This month, Palestinians mark the 58th year of their ongoing dispossession.

It is 58 years since Yousuf's grandparents were forced out of their villages of Wa'arat al-Sirris and al-Yajur, both of which were completely destroyed and ethnically cleansed.[3]

Now, this fourth generation carries on the torch of dispossession. Like his father and grandparents before him, Yousuf, too, is a refugee. And like it or not, he—and the millions like him—will not "disappear," much as the government of Israel would like them to: While trying its utmost to render their return unfeasible and their plight irrelevant, it lives on. And American passport or not, "Palestinian" is stamped on his forehead (and in my identity document, to which he is added and thus rendered "Palestinian," not "American," by Israeli forces, meaning he is not allowed to return or visit Haifa) . . . as the Palestinian Gazan poet Haroon Hashim Rasheed said, "*Filisteeni ana ismee Filisteeni . . . naqashtu ismee ala kulil mayadeeni, bikhatin barizin yasmoo ala al-anaweeni*" ("I am Palestinian, my name is Palestinian . . . and I have etched my name in every space and domain . . . in clear, bold writing that transcends all titles").

There is so much to write and say on the occasion of *al-Nakba* and what it means to each of us as Palestinians. I decided to search my archive for three pieces I wrote last year while visiting Yassine's refugee camp and others like it in Lebanon.

The first is an interview with Palestinian Nakba specialist Dr. Salman Abu Sitta. . . . [4] Dr. Abu Sitta's words echo stronger than mine could, at least right now. In the interview, he told me:

> There is nothing in international law or in our sense of morality that says racist or ethnic exclusive considerations should overrule principles of justice.
>
> By what scale or measure is it that the refugees in Gaza live only 5km away from their homes, to which they cannot return, and Israel is seeking out obscure tribes in India and Guatemala and bringing them over in a hurry to populate the land [that] belongs to the refugees?
>
> [W]e have found by looking at maps, both old and new, that 90 percent of [pre-1948 Palestinian] village sites are still vacant today.[5]

What Am I Doing?[6]
Columbia, Maryland, May 29, 2006

Well, for one—finding my way around "suburban hell." It's been quite a long stretch of nonblogging for me, and my fingers are starting to itch. But I'll make it up during the coming days, I promise! Between packing our things, getting ready to move down to North Carolina, finishing up some work, giving talks and interviews, and, well, just having fun with my family, I've had little time for anything else. We're currently staying with my brother in a Maryland suburb called Columbia.

It is a "planned community"—meaning it was built from the ground up with family suburban living in mind—and the picture perfection of it all can really get to you: Everyone has a manicured lawn, two kids, and a dog; there is a park on every street; and the "town villages" are named things like "King's Contrivance," "Harper's Glen," and "Hickory Ridge" . . . you get the picture! You begin to feel like you are living in this bubble where nothing else matters in the world. To me, as comfortable as it is to slip into that zone, it is also unsettling.

It's also a very stark contrast to everything in Gaza, of course (which I'll get to in another post), as BBC's Dan Damon suggested to me in an interview last week. But one needn't go that far to see the divide—journey 20 minutes to downtown Baltimore, and you'll see the contrasts in America itself between rich and poor are as vivid, if not more so, than perhaps anywhere else. In fact, according to the Census Bureau, some 13 percent of Americans are poor—in the richest country in the world. And, of course, Katrina gave us a taste of that. Mind-boggling.

Here, Yousuf stuffs his face at a local farm, hoping no one sees him. At the farm, we met a Palestinian woman from East Jerusalem who must renew her residency status every three years (where Jewish residents of the city do not) and continue living at her father's house there in order not to lose her right to return to her homeland. Her husband, who is from Ramallah, along with her kids have to sneak around checkpoints through the mountains to join her in Jerusalem because they lack East Jerusalem identification cards. Israel makes it nearly impossible to add spouses and family to East Jerusalemite identification cards in an attempt to push Palestinians out of the city.

Where There's *Toot* . . . [7]
Columbia, Maryland, June 24, 2006

. . . [T]here are Palestinians! It's true! The subtly sweet luscious, oblong mulberry is in prime season now. Few people here know they are even edible, I think. And because they drop to the ground when they are ripe for picking, even fewer bother to. But the trees are everywhere you go here (at least in Virginia and Maryland, and I remember seeing a few in Massachusetts some years ago), usually discreetly hidden among other trees, in parks, or forests; if you look closely, you'll find wild raspberry bushes of different varieties (we found yellow and black) lurking not far behind. We went berry picking (and eating) a few times, and Yousuf ate I think his weight in berries. We had a lot of curious passersby with kids asking their fathers, "What are they eating?"

And at almost every tree (or other berry farm) we'd go to, we'd find some Palestinians or Syrians picking, too. That's because the trees, known as *toot* trees back home, are very popular and considered somewhat of a delicacy because the berries are difficult to collect and are extremely perishable. Usually a small container sells for 10 shekels in Gaza fruit stores.

There is something of respect and heritage associated with the *toot* tree, because, like the olive and the nearly extinct jumayz tree (lesser-known cousin of the fig), they have deep roots, last for hundreds of years, and are a sign of steadfastness and resiliency. (Sadly, the jumayz is a dying breed. Many of the remaining trees in Gaza, including the one whose drooping branches we used to swing on at my grandfather's farm, were bulldozed in the early days of the second Intifada by Israeli troops.)

Watch the World Cup, Join the Army, Get a Green Card![8]
Columbia, Maryland, June 25, 2006

There is a lot going on and a lot to say and write, including how my talk on Capitol Hill went on Friday and recent happenings in Gaza. I'm going to digress for a moment for a World Cup post. Not to worry, it will weave its way inevitably into our conflict.

. . . It wasn't until yesterday that we realized we could watch the World Cup on Arab Radio and TV (ART) America, which you can subscribe to on the Dish Network. Up until then, we had been viewing it on the Spanish channel. . . . Of course, watching the World Cup in America and football in the United States—well, that's just another, very sad matter. It's almost as though there *is* no World Cup at the moment . . . with the cover of last week's *Sports Illustrated* about baseball and this week's about basketball.

There was one good column in *Sports Illustrated* about the matter by columnist Steve Rushin ("World's Right; We're Wrong"). An excerpt follows:

> The average American eats three hamburgers a week, 16 orders of French fries a month, 25 pounds of candy a year . . . and is profoundly uninterested in the World Cup. Soccer, it appears, is the only thing we don't want crammed down our throats. What does this attitude toward the World Cup say about the U.S.? It illuminates many of our least-flattering qualities as a nation, not least of which is a breathtaking incuriosity about the rest of the world.[9]

He goes on to say that a new Roper poll says two-thirds of Americans between 18 and 24 can't find Iraq on the map (you know, that country they're at war with) . . . and half can't find New York City!

. . . So, back to ART. Excitedly, we flip on the switch and learn during commercial breaks that "The 2006 World Cup is brought to you by the U.S. Army and the FBI" and are inundated with commercials telling us ("us" being Arabs) about the wonderful career opportunities available to us in the Army and FBI; how, if we join the Army, we could bring fresh water to thirsty Iraqi children (let's not mention that bombing part . . . too ugly for the cameras); how we can be "a bridge between two worlds," because we speak two languages; heck, how we can all out "change the world." And—as an added bonus if you act *now!*—$10,000 and a green card! Hoorah! Now I know what to do with my life! Also brings to mind the 1992 Israeli movie starring Palestinian actor Mohammad Bakri called *Cup Final* (*Gmar Gavi'a*).[10]

Bracing for the Worst—Electricity Cut Off, Bridges Bombed, Sonic-Boom Attacks Resume[11]
Columbia, Maryland, June 27, 2006

On June 25, 2006, Israeli soldier Gilad Shalit was captured in a cross-border raid outside southern Gaza in a joint operation between Hamas's armed wing, the PRC, and a small previously unknown group called the Army of Islam. The Palestinian gunmen infiltrated an Israeli army post on the Israeli side of the southern Gaza Strip border after crossing through an underground tunnel there. Israel responded by bombing Gaza's only power plant, destroying its 140-megawatt reactor, in addition to Gaza's main connector bridge in an operation code named "Summer

Rains." It was the first ground operation since the disengagement and was immediately followed by another operation named "Autumn Clouds."

In the process of packing and moving down to North Carolina on Thursday . . . and writing some columns and lengthier posts on the situation back home . . . but for now . . . just a brief post:

Friends and family in Gaza have told me they are bracing themselves for the worst, while praying for the best. In Rafah, the refugee camp that has not been spared the wrath of the Israeli Army on so many occasions in the past, where 16,000 Palestinians lost their homes to armored bulldozers, families have holed themselves up indoors, fearing for their lives.

Israel has taken control of the border area, including Rafah crossing and the airport. Colleague, friend, and activist Fida Qishta, with whom I toured the northeast United States, is on her way to Gaza in Egypt; she will have to remain there until she will be allowed to return home by Israeli forces, who have sealed off the Gaza Strip in its entirety. I was worried about her safety, because she is from Rafah, but I received a frantic telephone call from her in a London airport, where her flight was delayed and where she was making plans to remain exiled in Egypt. Meanwhile, journalist colleagues have told me that CNN and BBC crews from Jerusalem were also not allowed through the Erez crossing into Gaza yesterday.

Update: Israeli F-16s bombed Gaza's main bridge, right next to my father's farm, between northern and southern Gaza. They have also destroyed Gaza's *only* power plant, and electricity in most of Gaza has been cut off as a result. I've just spoken to my grandmother in Khan Yunis, who confirmed the entire Strip has plunged into darkness, with people stocking up on food and supplies. The electricity, of course, has also been cut off in hospitals and clinics, and I'm not sure how long the generators can last.

Friends in Gaza City also tell us that terrorizing sonic-boom attacks have resumed, stronger than before, full force, by low-flying jets breaking the sound barrier throughout the night over the civilian population—a tactic that is illegal in Israel, the United States, and most of the world.

Red Tape and Red Mist[12]
Durham, North Carolina, July 25, 2006

. . . Last August, Israel withdrew its troops and settlers from the Gaza Strip. The world rejoiced, rushing to declare that Gaza was now "free." So why are the Palestinians not satisfied? Why, almost a year on, would they capture an Israeli soldier and continue to fire homemade rockets into Israeli towns when they could have built a better life for themselves?

The reality is that Gaza has been under effective Israeli siege for more than a decade now, subject to the merciless grip of a complex Israeli matrix of administrative control that seeps into and affects every aspect of our lives.

Only several months on from the disengagement, Gaza resembles the largest, highest-security open-air prison on earth.

It soon became apparent—long before even Hamas was elected into power—that the Israeli occupation of Gaza had not ended. It had just become more sophisticated and entrenched: Gaza's skies and the Palestinian borders, air space, travel permit system, and population and birth registry all remained under Israeli control.

The intoxicating sense of freedom we felt during the days after the last of the Israeli settlers departed dissipated nearly as quickly as it had descended upon us. Though internal barriers and checkpoints were lifted, there existed a larger, seemingly impermeable barrier surrounding every aspect of our lives.

Israel continued to impose a blanket travel ban to the West Bank and Jerusalem on more than 90 percent of Palestinians in Gaza, particularly those between 16 and 35 years of age.

Even Palestinian control over the dreaded Rafah crossing—Gaza's only route to the outside world—turned out to be ultimately fictitious, with Israel effectively controlling who uses the crossing (only Palestinian identification-card holders have so far been allowed in, and now the crossing is closed altogether).

Israel also continued its freeze on issuing more than 50,000 Palestinian identification cards, or *hawiyas*, based on family reunification claims, which would have allowed Palestinian couples to join their spouses and travel freely in and out of Gaza.

My husband, a Palestinian refugee who grew up in Lebanon's refugee camps after his family was driven from Haifa in 1948, is still forbidden from visiting me and our son, Yousuf, when we are in Gaza, let alone returning to his native home in northern historic Palestine.

Yassine, now a physician in the United States, is still without any citizenship or country to claim as his own and is unable to live legally with his family in his own country.

These and other restrictive Israeli policies were in place well before Hamas's election victory and, in fact, may have contributed to it. They also help explain why Palestinians have not overwhelmingly demanded the release of the captured Israeli soldier, despite the consequences.

The feeling among Palestinians following the disengagement was that Gaza had been left to the wolves.

But Israel and the outside world were through with Gaza. It was behind them now, a done deal; Israel had "withdrawn," and, in the end, that was all that mattered. What more did Palestinians want?

Gaza was for Palestinians to deal with now, no matter that almost every aspect of it was still controlled by an outside force that no longer assumed responsibility for the welfare of the people whose land it still occupied. Never mind the lack of freedom, of sovereignty, of any semblance of statehood or territorial contiguity.

Gaza had become hell on earth, its inhabitants surrounded on all sides, deprived of their most basic freedoms, completely bereft of their rights and their sovereignty—and yet somehow expected to bow in submission and accept their fate.

There is, of course, another element to all this. We have been inundated with articles in the mainstream press about the fate of the Israeli soldier Gilad Shalit (though attention has shifted toward Lebanon at present), while the international community and mainstream press remains relatively silent in the face of Israel's illegal detention of Palestinians.

There are nearly 9,000 Palestinians in Israeli jails or detention centers. Most are being held without charges, under deplorable humanitarian conditions, including medical negligence, in unsanitary surroundings, subjected to routine beatings, position torture, and strip searches. Many were kidnapped while in the safety of their own homes and are detained in the absence of any law defining their status and rights.

Most Palestinian prisoners are political captives who have been arbitrarily imprisoned or detained under the broad banner of "security," according to the Israeli human rights group B'Tselem.

Also in Israeli jails, often imprisoned for charges such as "stone throwing"—or for no charges or without due process at all—according to Defense for Children International, are 388 children.

Thousands of other minors have been detained and subjected to violence, position torture, and brutal interrogation tactics in Israeli jails and detention centers over the course of the past six years. Often, they are abducted from the safety of their own homes or neighborhoods.

If we were to count the total number of Palestinians detained or imprisoned since 1967, it would amount to 20 percent of the population and 40 percent if one were to count only men—the highest rate of incarceration in the world. That is the rough equivalent of more than 12 million Britons.

Is it at all surprising, then, that a recent poll showed that most Palestinians were in favor of demanding something in return for the Israeli captive?

What many people would perhaps find surprising, though, is that, as of late July 2006, 65 percent of Palestinians, in varying degrees, were in favor of resuming the peace negotiations with Israel, given the opportunity.

The way Palestinians see it, instead of offering an olive branch, Israel has bombarded our cities, withheld our aid, and closed our borders, citing the lack of a negotiating partner on the Palestinian side, no matter who was in power.

In the end, the lesson to be taken when—if—this most recent "escalation" is over and done with is that the policy of unilateralism can never succeed in achieving a just and secure peace.

Israel's ongoing war against the Palestinians will not solve anything. It does not matter whether this is conducted through extrajudicial assassinations, grossly disproportionate artillery strikes against civilian populations in northern Gaza (in response to fewer than 400 homemade rockets fired into Israel since March, Israeli has launched more than 8,000 heavy-caliber artillery shells), or the continued asphyxiation of the economy and the people through economic and political blockades and border closures, all of which predate the democratic election of the current, Hamas-run government. Israel's actions will only spur further retaliations, resulting in more bloodshed, the loss of more innocent civilian lives, and the perpetuation of the conflict.

The only way to achieve lasting peace is by fully ending Israel's occupation of the West Bank and Gaza.

Meanwhile, in Palestine[13]
Durham, North Carolina, August 13, 2006

We went berry picking the other day, scavenging to find what little blueberries remained on the thinning bushes during the season's departure. "*Toot azra*'" my nephew calls them. Nearby, we noticed a crop of Muscadine grapes, the first time I had ever tried this particular variety.

Homesickness getting the best of us, my mother—who came to visit when I did and is now stuck, along with my father, here with us—decided to ask if we can pick the leaves to make *waraq inab* (stuffed grape leaves). So we did, nostalgically, remembering our little farm in central Gaza's *Zawayda* village, now bursting with unpicked, past-their-prime, plump seaside grapes.

Later at home, we boiled the leaves, and we boiled them some more—only to realize this particular variety was too fibrous for our *mahshi*. Durham is no Gaza, I suppose. . . .

Saddened, we stopped wrapping and called home. Our cousin gave us the latest: The electricity comes on, still a couple of hours a day; however, when it does, the municipality water does not. When the water does flow, about once every three to four days, there is usually no electricity to pump it to top-floor apartments in Gaza's plethora of high-rise towers.

So most residents have opted to rent lower-level housing or move. And so people can no longer use their kitchen-sink water filters[14] as a result of the unsynchronized water/electricity flow, so those who can afford it are opting for bottled water or drinking water sold by the gallon for a shekel in tank trucks, where most people survive, in the most "ordinary" of times, on less than 9 shekels a day.

Later, we made apricot jam, and my mother told me of the refugee family in Khan Yunis in 1948 whose daughter died because she ate bitter apricot seeds prematurely, which were soaking in water to become sweet.

And we learned that in July, the Israeli military killed 163 Palestinians in the Gaza Strip as "Summer Rain" continued. But the headlines here tell us that the days are "tragic" for Israel. Tragedy had a different meaning for us; children are not children; mother's tears are no tears at all; we are less human.

On the Lebanese front, Israel's assault continues. Yassine's sister moved with her children and husband from *Sour* (Tyre), which has been heavily bombed in recent days, to *Sayda* (Sidon). She is taking shelter in a place that has no doors or windows with 40 other people.

So we drift, from one news report to the next, from one phone call to the next . . . from one story to the next, and nothing quite makes sense anymore. Unaligned and displaced, we carry on with our lives, not knowing quite what to do with ourselves, until Yousuf inevitably asks me, distressed:

> *"Mama, aish fee?"* ("Mama, what's the matter?")
> *"Mama za'lana, habibi."* ("Mama's sad, sweetheart.")
> *"Bas laysh?"* ("But why?")
> *"Ana wawa habibi."* ("I'm hurting, sweetheart.")
> *"Tayib roo'i 'al duktor!"* ("OK, then go to the doctor!")

If only this *wawa* (hurt) had such a simple remedy.

Rest in Peace, Um Fuad[15]
Durham, North Carolina, August 13, 2006

Last year, while visiting Yassine's family in Baalbeck, I met Um Fuad.

Um Fuad was married the year of the Nakba. Then a young girl, in the chaos and attacks on her village, Yajur of Akka, she was separated from her husband. She fled to Jordan, and her husband to Lebanon. And for two years, they lived apart.

"People would see me hanging laundry in the refugee camp there and come ask for my hand. They didn't realize I was already married, and those who did thought I had given up hope," she told me.

Eventually, two years later, he came for her, making his way across the border from Lebanon into Palestine, "infiltrating," because he was not allowed back to his village as a refugee; from there to Jordan, he asked around until he found her. She had taken him for dead or at least having abandoned her. Together, they snuck back to Lebanon, where their families were.

Thirty-four years later, she was widowed. Abu Fuad and two of their sons were killed by an Israeli air strike against Baalbek in 1984.

And now, 22 years later, this second invasion had taken her. She sought refuge in Syria after Baalbek was targeted a couple of weeks ago, living with hundreds of other Palestinian refugees in a public school.

Um Fuad died today, away from all her remaining sons in Lebanon, a twice-over refugee, unable to return or be buried in her home in Yajur.

Another story, another statistic, another "inconvenient" refugee. Um Fuad, dead at 72.

May she rest in the peace she never found in her life.

Israeli Army Document: Rafah Closed as Collective Punishment[16]
Durham, North Carolina, August 30, 2006

The shock! The horror!

An internal military document, *Haaretz* revealed, has raised strong suspicions that—*gasp*—Israeli security officials are keeping Rafah crossing closed to apply "pressure" (see: torture) on the civilian population of Gaza.

Sari Bashi and the good folks at Gisha: Legal Center for Freedom of Movement filed an appeal with Amir Peretz based on the information, demanding that the crossing be opened (not that he's likely to listen, but still) and that he stop "the collective punishment against 1.4 million Palestinians who have been trapped in the Gaza Strip for 10 weeks," a situation that has become accepted as the status quo. (Does everyone out there realize that we are speaking about hermetically sealing a border and caging 1.4 million people, like animals in a zoo, which probably get better treatment?)

. . . According to the letter written by Attorney Sari Bashi, Gisha's executive director:

> Imprisoning 1.4 million Gaza residents to apply pressure on those who are holding the abducted soldier—despite how painful and important that subject is—constitutes collective punishment in violation of international law. Using the closure to apply pressure contradicts Israel statements to the European observers who monitor the crossing. Israel has claimed that the crossing must be closed because of security warnings.
>
> The Fourth Geneva Convention prohibits collective punishment of residents of an occupied territory.

Gaza's Darkness[17]
Durham, North Carolina, September 6, 2006

A few months ago, I spoke about the plight of 10 Gaza students of occupational therapy in Bethlehem University—except they've never been to Bethlehem. How, then, do they study, one might wonder? Try videoconference, remote control, and out-of-country lab work.

And, without electricity, well, you can bet there are no classes.

Like almost everything else for Gaza's besieged population, welcome to the Twilight Zone.

. . . Gisha, along with the Gaza Community Mental Health Program and Bitona for Community Development, continues to fight the students' legal battle, and *Haaretz* has published a detailed article about their case today, interviewing the occupational therapy students.[18]

As part of the public campaign, the organizations published a quarter-page ad in today's *Haaretz*, which 200 Israeli professors and lecturers signed, asking the defense minister to undo the ban.

Of course, the ban is in the context of the larger Israeli matrix of administrative control, also affecting the lives of such people as my dear friend Sam Bahour, a Palestinian American from Birah who has lived there for the past 15 years and is now being expelled from his own home; suddenly, the powers that be say his permit is no longer valid. Amira Hass wrote in *Haaretz* about the administrative tools being used and manipulated in such expulsions in the article, "The Slippery Slope of Expulsion." Sam tells me he's fighting it out in the courts until his final breath.[19]

My Potty-Training Miracle . . . and Other Things[20]
Durham, North Carolina, September 18, 2006

So much to blog about, so little time these days.

Of course, I could write about the unity government—which, as I told Pacifica Radio the other day, won't mean squat so far as the United States is concerned; in fact, nothing the government does will ever mean squat until the recognition of Palestinian rights becomes an equal precondition for the resumption of negotiations and advancement of peace.

It's so sad to think that the United States and Israel have done everything possible to undermine this government without really thinking of the consequences; then again, those consequences are irrelevant to them—to heck with financial mismanagement (of U.S. money) as long as they do what we say! Sooner or later, our government will collapse or resign or be forced to disband, and we will see a reign of anarchy and return to the cronyism and malfeasance of the past with the new, improved Fateh party—just what the United States wants and what Palestinians don't.

I was thinking the other day, imagine how the news broadcasts would read if the situation were reversed:

> Thousands of Jewish families are on the brink of starvation and the Israeli economy on the verge of collapse after the sixth month of a U.S.- and EU-imposed boycott, staunch blockade of any international aid, and hermetic sealing of all the borders. Officials say aid can only resume once the Israeli government, responsible for multiple terrorist attacks that have killed scores of Palestinian civilians, recognizes a Palestinian state, renounces violence against the Palestinians, and accepts and implements all previous peace agreements in their fullest.

Yeah right. But seriously, who out there can deny that they would find such news *more* appalling and skin curling than the same policies against Palestinians, reminiscent of the Holocaust?

But Palestinians, well, they are just less human, so it's OK.

But the *really* big news this week has nothing to do with politics at all. Forget the Pope's ill-advised comments, or the fate of Gilad Shalit. . . .

No, the really big news, which I'm sure will make no other headline than my own, is that I have, it seems, successfully potty trained Yousuf!

(Pause for cheers, applause.)

OK, I know this seems so trivial in the realm of things, but you have no idea what this seemingly insignificant advancement has meant for me: no more changing five diapers a day, which get nastier exponentially with age; or buying those diapers—which you never realize how much you shell out for until you are through with them; no more changing diapers in extremely uncomfortable settings, such as borders crossings with tanks pointed at you; and on and on.

How did it happen, you might ask?

How do these things ever happen? Frankly, I wish I knew, so I could have something in the way of more empirically sound advice to offer to people. The reality is, it just happened. . . . I had nearly given up. I had resigned myself to the fact that my son would go to kindergarten, dressed fashionably in plus-size Pampers.

And then one morning, as I was on my computer, Yousuf interrupted his play to announce that he needed to pee and was going to the bathroom. "Right, right," I thought to myself, "the bathroom." And then, I did a double-take, and sure enough, my little boy had gone to the bathroom, attempted to pull down his pants, and pee on his own.

What did I do to deserve such a moment? On the verge of tears, I thought it was too good to be true, so I decided not to blog about it immediately. I also decided to test that it was not a one-time thing by placing him in underwear the entire day;

time after time, he used the bathroom. When it came time for nap time, I hesitated at first but decided to throw away the diapers once and for all.

And, to my astonishment, it was indeed a modern-day miracle!

So far, my little boy has been diaper-free for two weeks and counting. Now I won't deny it's taken some additional training to make sure he understands how he needs to wait to reach the bathroom. But as of a few days ago, we have that down, too.

What I've Been Up to: Talks, Travel Guides, and Other Things[21]
Durham, North Carolina, October 3, 2006

I've been absurdly negligent of my blog lately. My poor blog—at one time, a daily visit would not even suffice. Now I'm lucky if I get around to it even once a week.

But I hope that will change soon: I'm happy to report I'll be returning to Gaza for a few months in November (assuming the border is open by then).

I've been busy—this time not with potty training but with making arrangements for various upcoming trips.

Last week, I traveled to Washington, D.C., to apply for my Norwegian visa, which I got in a record two days. (I figured the whole "this passport was issued pursuant to the Oslo Accords" line in it might help.)

I've also been working on updating the Gaza section of a (fabulous) travel guide, which the Bethlehem-based Alternative Tourism Group publishes. It's one of those kafkaesque experiences, an exercise in the absurd.

I write about all the wonderful experiences in Gaza, where to stay, what to do, and, of course, an update on the humanitarian and political situation. Yet as I write, I realize in the back of my mind no one can *get into* Gaza in the first place, unless they have a Gazan, Israeli-issued Palestinian identification or are UN staff or diplomats.

And if you try to get a permit through Israel, you are taken on a wild goose chase where, as in *Alice's Adventures in Wonderland*, no one can provide you with clear answers, and nothing is what it seems: "We aren't responsible for Gaza, and therefore don't issue permits to travel there; yet we still occupy it and control its borders—including what and who pass through there."

Yet I continue to write anyway, and with conviction at that; Yassine thinks it's an exercise in defiance of the occupation and an act of creative resistance, if you will. It's the same sort of experience I go through when I read about various restaurants or travel agents in the West Bank or East Jerusalem in the al-Quds daily paper: It's not physically possible, yet everyone likes to pretend it is. I think it's part of trying to imagine or create a reality other than the one imposed upon us.

So in a nutshell, that's what I've been up to. That and fasting during Ramadan, which is simply not the same as it was in Gaza, where stores fill up with Eid candies, dried fruits and nuts, and other Ramadan staples faster than you can say "*bismillah*." That, and *Atayif* stations on every corner. Mmmm.

But, of course, there is literally a black shadow cast over Gaza this Ramadan. My neighbor told me today they went 24 hours with no electricity in Gaza City, with backup generators greatly overburdened. And it's bound to continue like this for a while. I'm anxious to get back to tell you more firsthand.

The Pain Behind the Occupation[22]
Durham, North Carolina, October 13, 2006

Why are the Palestinians really fighting each other on the streets of Gaza?

It's a conundrum for most people, and a difficult issue to talk about, even between Palestinians. During a time when they are being bombarded by some 300 artillery shells a day, exposed to deafening sonic-boom attacks, and living under an increasingly brutal occupation without electricity and very little water, they are killing each other. Palestinian versus Palestinian.

"Why are the Palestinians doing this? If they don't fight Israel, they have to fight someone, so they fight each other!" I've heard time and again.

So why are the Palestinians killing each other? And why does it concern Israel?

The real question is: Why haven't they been killing each other sooner?

They are trapped in a cage that roughly provides 1 square kilometer of space per 4,000 human beings. Their freedom of movement is restricted, dividing brother and sister, husband and wife. Their borders are sealed off, preventing them from exporting goods or receiving medicines, foods, and vaccines and stopping them from paying their salaries. They have been bombed night and day, destroying their only electric plant. If people are treated in this way, you can rest assured that eventually they will attack each other.

It is useful to draw on an example that Palestinian psychiatrist Eyad Sarraj shared with me from his student days. An experiment is undertaken whereby two guinea pigs are placed in a cage and exposed to various stressors. For several days, they receive a continuous supply of food and ample space in their cage; the next, they do not. They are then shocked when they do approach the food, and so forth. Eventually, the guinea pigs exhibit signs of severe psychosis and attack each other.

That's the easy and most obvious explanation.

There is another element to this, of course. Who is really protesting against the government on the streets of Gaza? Is it the hungry and disenfranchised? The employed but unpaid? The disgruntled and dispossessed?

The reality is they are mostly none of these things: They are hooligans, members of the young Fateh guard and other members of security forces loyal to Mohammad Dahlan, the strongman who is now Fateh's second-in-command. And they are protesting despite the fact that everyone—including them—realizes that the inability of the government to pay the public sector's salaries is the result of Israeli policy.

As under the Arafat regime, protesters are dispatched in a kind of "organized anarchy" under the guise of disillusionment and hunger, taking advantage of the real concerns people in Gaza are suffering from for their own political ends. The Gaza street word has it that if you take part in an antigovernment protest, you can expect a handsome 200 shekels for your trouble.

So besides some spare change, what would the protesters, the security forces, and the other "disgruntled" elements get out of this? Namely, they want a return to the days of payoffs and patronage—when every hostage situation, work fallout, and disenchantment could be resolved through guns and dollars, and when there were plenty of dollars to spare.

It was in the U.S. and Western interest to ensure a "peace," no matter how unsustainable or unjust.

It is even not farfetched to suggest that the United States—and possibly the United Kingdom—is funding Dahlan, as it did before the Palestinian elections, in an $11-million (£6-million) bid to stave off a Hamas election victory.

This time, the aim would be to try to bring about an "organic" change of power, because starving the Palestinian people hasn't worked out too well.

So how—or why—is this an Israeli problem?

Israeli journalist Amira Hass explained it well in one of her columns:

> Because those who dispatched these militants have a shared inter-
> est with Israel in regressing to a situation in which the Palestinian
> leadership collaborates with the appearance of holding peace
> talks, while Israel continues its occupation and the international
> community sends hush money in the form of salaries for the
> Palestinian public sector.[23]

Following the Hamas victory in January, the United States was faced with a conundrum: how to get Hamas out of power without calling outright for a change of regime. Thus, the quartet preconditions were born. These preconditions were never demanded of Israel, and it was unforeseeable they would ever be met, thus forcing an internal Palestinian government collapse.[24]

And what is the alternative? Going back to a situation of subcontracted occupation, where the fat cats get fatter and the disenchanted get more disenchanted? This time around, they'll have had a taste of what to expect if they decide to disagree and vote for change.

To Mankato and Oslo[25]
Mankato, Minnesota, October 19, 2006

As usual, so much to blog about, like the United States financing Hamas opponents with a nice fat $42 million, a campaign projected "to bolster Hamas's political opponents ahead of possible early Palestinian elections" (i.e., Dahlan and Company).[26]

But speaking of better things, yesterday I arrived in Minnesota and delivered the Kessel Memorial Lecture at Minnesota (emphasis on "sota") State University in Mankato, where corn and empty fields abound.

The *Mankato Free Press* published a humbling article that said, "Never in the impressive history of the Kessel Institute has anyone come to campus with the perspective of Palestinian journalist Laila El-Haddad."[27]

It went well, except for the fact that I was ready to topple over by the Q&A session—too many connecting flights, too little sleep, and fasting during Ramadan.

Today, I head to Oslo, where I'll attend the Norwegian Social Forum and speak on blogging as activism (and, I think, writing tourist guides as activism!), and then on Tuesday, I go to Trondheim in northern Norway to speak with the Journalist's Association there.

I return to the United States on Thursday, *inshallah*. Two weeks later, it's off to Gaza, once again (well, first to Egypt; then, we play the waiting game at Rafah).

Flying While Muslim[28]
Oslo, Norway, October 21, 2006

Writing from a café in Oslo where, surprisingly, few places offer free wireless—you either have to pay for access or have the passport, a capitalist practice for a socialist country.

So far, I've had a wonderful, if chilly, time. My hosts have been incredibly warm and friendly and tried to stuff me full of all sorts of Norwegian goodies. (As my friend Amira asked—"What's your *suhoor* like? Let me guess—a combination of cold smelly fish and soft cheeses?" Fairly accurate, but delicious nonetheless.)

Today was the first day of the conference, which went very well and was an experience for me in Norwegian socialist leftist culture, which I'll talk more about when I have more time, as well as my impressions on Norwegian discourse on Palestine.

First, a little about the airport on the trip over, always an adventure:

Perhaps you've heard the expression "flying while Muslim"? Well, it never fails. I feel like it's a self-fulfilling prophecy: I'm always so nervous they'll stop me, and they always do.

So I'm checking into the airport for my flight to Chicago from Minneapolis, and I get stopped by one of the security officials, who casually asks me, "Ma'am, have you ever been 'SSSSed' before?"

"SSSSed? What does that even mean?" I wondered, but I didn't bother to ask, because I guessed it was probably something sinister. Something to do with stopping people who seemed to be suspicious and probably plotting a terrorist attack (that or they happen to wear hijab or "look" Muslim). Accordingly, I answered, "I'm not sure what that acronym means, but if I were to guess, I'd say pretty much every time—it's become a routine."

"We have a female SS here; someone help, please," the agent bellowed out in front of the long line of nervous onlookers.

"So now, it's only two Ss?" I thought. I waited and was escorted by another official for a check before being asked about what potentially lethal liquids or gels I had. In my possession was a 4-ounce strawberry Dannon Light & Fit yogurt.

"Ma'am, are you aware of our new security regulations?" he asked staunchly.

"Yes, yes, sure, just go ahead and toss it out," I said, contemplating the potentially lethal nature of strawberries, corn syrup, and bacteria.

"You can eat it if you want," he suggested.

"I'm fasting," I replied.

After this, my hand baggage was checked, and I was casually asked about what I do for a living. Then, I was torso searched by a female agent who explained, eruditely, "Do you know why you were stopped here today?"

"Maybe you can tell me," I offered. "I get stopped every time, so I've sort of become accustomed to not asking why."

"It's probably because of the way you booked your ticket, which set off a red light. Maybe it was booked in the last 24 hours, or it was booked one way, or you made changes to it at the last minute," she said.

"I booked it nearly a month ago, I've made no last-minute changes, and I'm flying round-trip," I retorted to her silent stares.

Why do I even bother? To make matters worse, there was a big orange sign indicating that today's terrorist threat level was "high"—probably people looking suspiciously, thinking they had caught the suspect: the strawberry yogurt–toting Gazan on her way to a social forum in Norway, because that all links back to the Oslo Accords, a good cause to sabotage, if there ever was one.

Sigh.

To Exist Is to Resist[29]
Durham, North Carolina, November 4, 2006

As I returned from Norway, I had to come to grips with more bad news from back home.

It appears Israeli and American attempts to cause an internal revolt against the Palestinian government have so far been unsuccessful. So they've gone ahead with the second, seasonal "operation" against Gaza (since "Summer Rain" brought no relief, they've decided to try to provide some shade through "Autumn Clouds").

In Norway, one of the panels I was invited to speak on was titled "Creative Resistance in Palestine." We discussed the various, alternative forms that resistance has taken in Palestine from the traditional armed resistance.

In the West Bank village of Biliin, that resistance takes the form of weekly, creative, nonviolent protests against the Wall that is swallowing the villagers' lands and livelihoods. On the Internet, that form can also take blogging. In Gaza, where any resistance is met with much more brutal responses and where we fight against an enemy we see only by way of F-16s, gunships, tanks, and distant snipers, creative resistance becomes much more difficult.

But last week in besieged Beit Hanoun, the women showed there is another way—and they paid for it with their lives.

After the death toll rose to nearly 20 in one day, they went to the defense of the men holed up in the local mosque, with no arms, risking their lives under the direct fire of Israeli armored vehicles.

Two died, and 16 were injured. A gripping BBC video report shows the women running defenseless, the army firing at them, and two of them falling down.[30]

The hail of fire did not deter them—they continued to march, over and beyond the barriers erected by the Israeli Army, directly in front of the tanks. Hail to people power—and specifically women power.

At times like these, I am reminded of the powerful slogan I saw in a picture of the Wall in the West Bank that read, "To exist is to resist."

To me, it really captures what it is like to be in Gaza in such times, or to be Palestinian—simply being able to keep your wits about you and survive under such conditions is in and of itself a form of resistance.

⌀

Massacre in Gaza: I Remained Silent, for I Was Not Palestinian[31]
Durham, North Carolina, November 8, 2006

"Withdrawing" implies, in whatever vague and euphemistic sense, an end—or at least a waning—of hostilities. But yesterday I woke to discover that the Israeli army has perpetrated a massacre on a scale unseen in Gaza for a long time: 18 dead, including children, women, and the countless faceless others.[32]

All members of the same family. Brushed aside as unfortunate mistakes, with a generous dollop of regret, from an otherwise morally superior, well-intentioned army.

Israeli human rights groups have said it (repeatedly), and it bears reminding once more: There can be no good intentions deriving from an army ordered to fire heavy-grade artillery shells within 100m of civilian areas. None.

And I am sick to my stomach. I am sick of hearing the "we regrets" and "sorries" and the empty promises of investigations that never materialize and whose only purpose is to exonerate the accused. I am sick of the well-intentioned "moral" army of "defense" routine, the army that only attempts to attack "militants," as if to imply the entire occupation is justified if sustained by this absurdist rhetoric. I'm just sick of it all.

We want an end to the occupation—period. To quote Peace Now: Instead of apologizing, stop the war against us. So much energy and enthusiasms devoted to death, and destruction, and debilitation, and asphyxiation, and occupation—so little devoted to ending it all.

When such a massacre occurs, in addition to the anger and frustration, I cannot help but feel lonely, and abandoned, and afraid.

It is the feeling we all have as Palestinians, the feeling that boils inside us, sometimes drowning us with its complexity, and force, and unrequitedness. To quote Mahmoud Darwish:

> We are alone. We are alone to the point
> of drunkenness with our own aloneness,
> with the occasional rainbow visiting.[33]

And don't think for one moment that this somehow does not affect you, whoever you are, as you recoil in your comfort zone, choosing consciously to look the other way. It affects all of us—Israelis, Palestinians, humankind—when humans become less human, when their blood becomes worth less than ours. Martin Niemöller's confession rings truer than ever:

> They came first for the Communists, and I didn't speak up because I
> was not a Communist. . . . Then they came for the Jews, and I did not

*speak up because I was not a Jew. When they came for me, there was
no one left to speak out.*

Let us add to the famous lines:

*Then, they came for the Palestinians, but I remained silent, for I was
not Palestinian.*

CHAPTER NOTES

1. The full original text of this post is archived at http://www.gazamom.
   com/2006/05/youre-from-where/, shortened to http://bit.ly/aQcnRt.
2. Archived at http://bit.ly/9pFAUz.
3. The website PalestineRemembered.com carries background information on the
   Nakba, including oral histories of the Palestinians' dispossession and dispersal
   from 1947 to 1948 and details of Israeli settlements and Palestinian refugee
   camps. To find out more about the history of the Haifa district towns that
   Yassine's family were driven from, see *Wa'arat al-Sarris*, archived at http://bit.ly/
   aIm5iu, and *al-Yajur*, archived at http://bit.ly/9Ntv53.
4. The other two articles referred to here are presented in Chapter 2: "Palestinians
   Keep Dream of Return Alive" and "Safeguarding Palestine's Past."
5. Laila El-Haddad, "Is Right of Return Feasible?" *Al Jazeera English*, May 31, 2005,
   archived at http://bit.ly/9vSajR.
6. Archived at http://bit.ly/cb0Vtm.
7. Archived at http://bit.ly/9XbsIy.
8. Archived at http://bit.ly/anXBX8.
9. Steve Rushin, "World's Right; We're Wrong," *Sports Illustrated*, June 5, 2006.
10. More information about this subtly antiwar movie is at http://bit.ly/dhsP8p. The
    capture mentioned in the post was that of Israeli Defense Forces corporal Gilad
    Shalit, captured by unknown Palestinians gunmen while on active duty on the
    Israel-Gaza border.

11. Archived at http://bit.ly/bGe9uY.
12. Laila El-Haddad, "Red Tape and Red Mist,"*Guardian Unlimited*, July 25, 2006, archived at http://bit.ly/bVUpZ7.
13. Archived at http://bit.ly/aEbiXf.
14. Gaza's drinking water contains dangerously high levels of saline and nitrates and is generally unfit for human consumption without filtering. This is the result of a combination of factors, including the contamination and overpumping of the coastal aquifer, the sole source of fresh water for Gaza's 1.6 million people.
15. Archived at http://bit.ly/auOS0T.
16. Archived at http://bit.ly/cYz6gR.
17. Archived at http://bit.ly/9V3SXn.
18. To read the *Haaretz* article about the experiences of the Gaza students of Bethlehem University, see Tamara Traubmann, "For Gaza Students, Classes by 'Remote Control,'" *Haaretz*, September 5, 2006, archived at http://bit.ly/c4Nwyt.
19. Sam finally received his Palestinian identity card (*hawiya*) in May 2009. In an e-mail correspondence on August 3, 2010, he said, "I am now am a 'proud' Palestinian locked in a Ramallah cage" in reference to the perverse system of Israeli administrative control and the Catch-22 nature of the *hawiya*.
20. Archived at http://bit.ly/974KV8.
21. Archived at http://bit.ly/9Vnp80.
22. Laila El-Haddad, "The Pain behind the Occupation," *Guardian Unlimited*, October 13, 2006, archived at http://bit.ly/dsjsVO.
23. Amira Hass, "Not an Internal Palestinian Matter," *Haaretz*, October 4, 2006, archived at http://bit.ly/9FXx3J.
24. To find out more about the preconditions established by the Quartet, see Ewen MacAskill and Simon Tisdall, "Bush and Powell in Public Split over Israel," *Guardian Unlimited*, June 13, 2002, archived at http://bit.ly/duC1N4.
25. Archived at http://bit.ly/d3gdfk.
26. Reuters, "US Launches Plan to Help Hamas Opponents," *YnetNews.com*, October 13, 2006, archived at http://bit.ly/arNmMb.
27. Robb Murray, "Mothering in a War Zone," *Mankato Free Press*, October 16, 2006, archived at http://bit.ly/duZpM3.
28. Archived at http://bit.ly/95rwyE.
29. Archived at http://bit.ly/a7271Q.
30. BBC video of the women outside the mosque in Beit Hanoun, archived at http://bbc.in/9hx8rn. Read the BBC article on the incident, "Gaza Women Killed in Mosque Siege," archived at http://bbc.in/c7rUZd.
31. Laila El-Haddad, "I Remained Silent," *YnetNews.com*, November 9, 2006, archived at http://bit.ly/9tYQsA.
32. On November 8, 2006, Israeli army shells hit a row of houses in Beit Hanoun, killing 19 Palestinians and wounding more than 40; 13 of the dead were from the same family.
33. The lines immediately preceding the ones quoted are: "*The siege is lying in wait. / It is lying in wait on a tilted stairway / in the midst of a storm.*"

Chapter 13

We Are Alone

Mid-November through early December 2006

After an extended stay in the United States, Yousuf and I again returned to Gaza. And once again, we found ourselves waiting in Egypt in the face of an extended closure of Rafah crossing. It had been one year since the U.S.-brokered Agreement on Movement and Access (AMA) had been concluded between Israel and the PA, shortly after Israel's "disengagement" from Gaza. Under the AMA, Israel had agreed to operate the Rafah crossing and Gaza's other, separate freight crossings—which go into only Israel—continuously and to not close any of the crossings because of security concerns unrelated to that particular crossing. During our wait, the UN issued a report noting that Israel had broken every single provision in the agreement.[1]

The AMA had also promised that the Palestinians could control Rafah crossing by November 2006, after a transitional year in which EU monitors would supervise the Palestinian side of the border while Israeli security forces would also monitor their performance remotely by video. The transition to Palestinian control never happened. Instead, Israel maintained its effective control over our borders and, by extension, over our lives. As we remained mired in the uncertainty of this situation, Yousuf, who was just a few months short of 3 years old, began for the first time to ask the difficult but inevitable questions that I had always dreaded: Who was closing the border, and why? When could he return home? In essence, he was learning what it meant to be Palestinian.

Gaza or Bust[2]
Durham, North Carolina, November 11, 2006

We're beginning our journey back to Gaza tonight, but first we have to fly to Cairo; from there, I will make a brief detour to Doha, where I will be attending the—hold your breath—launch of *Al Jazeera International*[3] on November 15 (yes, finally!).

Welcome to the Neighborhood, Heba![4]
Cairo, Egypt, November 13, 2006

We're in Egypt now, after a very long transatlantic flight, where we'll wait for the border to open and then take off to Gaza, God willing.

But I'd like to introduce you all to a new Gaza blog (drum roll please . . .): My friend and neighbor (and reader!) in Gaza City, Heba, has finally acted on my advice to put her thoughts as a Gazan simply trying to survive into words. She has started a new blog, "Contemplating from Gaza,"[5] and I would like to take this opportunity to welcome her to the Palestinian (and global) blogging neighborhood! I hope it is long and fruitful—and do not let the naysayers deter you.

Heba's first few entries are gripping and poetic—she has a saliently melancholic way of capturing that feeling we all have inside us as Gazans—the one that eats away at our very existence. Here's a taste:

> How can Gazans deal with the negative stress they face on a daily basis while their problems trespassed, long ago, coping with continuous stress to coping with changes in their personalities, tolerance, and manners to the worse as a result of being exposed to negative stress? It is not about not being able to perform your duties. It is rather about a legacy of fear and anxiety transported to our children and the next generation. . . .

Aah, the Power of Citizenship!
(aka Born Palestinian, Born Cursed)[6]
Doha, Qatar, November 14, 2006

Some people are just more trustworthy than others—more amenable. You know what I'm talking about, right? The friendly happy-go-lucky ones who cause no problems. To the Gulf states, this means rich *ajanib* that they just *love* to let into their countries' fancy resorts so they can spend spend spend and tan their future skins away. Others, however, well—are not so trustworthy.

Take Palestinians, for example. The moment you see someone holding that ominous, forest green Palestinian passport[7] or Palestinian refugee travel document, you know there's trouble on the horizon; you know to be afraid—very afraid.

Because Palestinians are stateless, and by extension, squatters; whoever they are, wherever they go, they will seek jobs and eventually citizenship if they can find a way. And if they don't, they'll simply become beggars or a huge burden on the economy. Whether they live in the United States, Europe, or Mars, this notion still applies. Whether they are brain surgeons or bricklayers, it doesn't matter—they have Palestinian written *all* over them, and it reeks from miles away.

Such is the case with most Arab countries and their treatment of Palestinians and my all-too-familiar experience trying to get to Doha today for the launch of *Al Jazeera International*. It's difficult enough finding a flight or hotel reservation now with the Asian Games being hosted there, but I was almost laughed out of the airport when—upon being prompted to present my visa—I told them that my editors suggested I obtain one in the airport upon arrival, and this would be no problem.

I know what all Palestinians with travel documents out there are asking: "*What were you thinking??*" Well, I wasn't, I guess. I was told repeatedly, "You are Palestinian!" So when I attempted to switch my ticket from Egypt Air to Qatari Airways—with whom I was told I stood a better chance—I was literally told, "Maybe . . . if you had any nationality *except* Palestinian."

And that exception does not include Israelis—who can obtain a tourist visa in the Qatari airport with proper coordination or, of course, Americans, such as Yousuf. That's right: My rambunctious little 2.5-year-old can go to Doha, no questions asked. But me? Or his father—a Harvard-educated ophthalmologist in training? Keep dreaming.

Silly me. I should have thought of the consequences of being Palestinian when I was a little embryo in my mother's womb. To quote her, 25 years ago, when she was likewise stopped in Cairo Airport and denied entry because she was Palestinian (and pregnant with my younger brother):

"How is it my fault that I was born Palestinian?"

Update: In the end, I managed to make it to Doha two days after the launch. It was a minor miracle that involved a bit of networking and a lot of unforeseen *wasta* (connections).

The Border of Dispossession[8]
Al-Arish, Egypt, November 21, 2006

After returning from Doha on Sunday, my family[9] and I drove off to the Egyptian border town of al-Arish yesterday—a five-hour drive from Cairo and a 30-minute drive from the Rafah crossing. Al-Arish is the closet (and largest) Egyptian town to the border.

During times of extended closure, like this summer and last year, it becomes a makeshift Palestinian slum. Thousands of penniless Palestinians, having depleted their savings and never anticipating the length of the closure, end up on the streets. Shopkeepers and taxi drivers relayed story after story to us from this summer.

In response, the Egyptian police no longer allow Palestinians driving up from Cairo past the Egyptian port city of al-Qantara if the border is closed and al-Arish becomes too crowded. "They turn it into a ghetto. That, and the Israelis didn't want them blowing up holes in the border again to get through," explained Ayman, a local broker.

Last night, we carried false hopes, transmitted down the taxi drivers' grapevine—the ones who run the Cairo-Rafah route—that the border would open early this morning. So we kept our bags packed and awoke early to the crashing waves of the Mediterranean—the same ones that just a few kilometers down were crashing down on Gaza's besieged shores.

But it is 4, then 5, then 6 a.m., and the border does not open. And my heart begins to twinge, as I recall the last time I tried to cross Rafah; how I could not, for 55 days of aloneness and displacement—during which Yousuf learned to lift himself up into the world and took his first fleeting steps in a land that was not ours.

The shopkeeper down the street tells us he hears the border may open Thursday, "but you know how it is—all rumors." No one can be certain. Some say tomorrow, some say Thursday—but in the end, no one ever knows. Even the Egyptian border officials admit that ultimately, the orders come from the Israeli side. It's as though they take pleasure as we languish in the uncertainty. The perpetual never knowing. As though they intend for us to sit and think and drive ourselves crazy with thought.

Even the Palestinian soccer team has been unable to leave Gaza to attend the Asian Games because of the Rafah closure. No one is exempt. Peasant or pro football player, we are equally vulnerable.

So, as always, we wait. We wait our entire lives, as Palestinians—if not for a border to open, for a permit to be issued, for an incursion to end, for a time when we do not have to wait any longer.

What is so frightening about borders—and particularly Rafah—that drives chills down my spine? They are, after all, crossings like any other crossing, I tell myself. What differentiates one meter of sand from the next, beyond that border? They are exactly the same. It is history, and life, and identity, and occupation, and isolation that changes them.

For Palestinians, borders are a reminder—of our vulnerability and nonbelonging, of our displacement and dispossession. It is a reminder—a painful one—of homeland lost and of what could happen if what remains is lost again. When we are lost again, we lose a little bit of ourselves every time we wait to cross and then cross.

So it is here, 50km from Rafah's border, that I am reminded, once again, of displacement. I have become that "displaced stranger," to quote Palestinian poet Mourid Barghouti.[10] Displacement is meant to be something that happens to someone else, he says, to refugees the world cares to forget; when the border closes, we are one day closer to becoming those forgotten refugees.

Yassine cannot even get as far as I have—to Egypt—to feel alone. He feels alone every day and is rejected every day, finding belonging in other, nonstatic things: family, love, and work.

But the Palestinian never forgets his aloneness. He is always reminded of it on borders. That, above all, is why I hate Rafah crossing. That is why I hate borders. They remind me that I, like all Palestinians, belong everywhere and nowhere at once. They are the Borders of Dispossession.

The Waiting Game[11]
Al-Arish, Egypt, November 22, 2006

We've been in al-Arish 48 hours now. Our journey, not including the days spent in Doha, has spanned more than five days.

We've rented a small beachside flat here. They are cheaper than in Cairo and certainly cheaper than hotels and are usually rented out to Palestinians like us who are waiting for the border to open. It's low season now, and the going rate is a mere $12 per night. In the summer, rates jump to a minimum of $35 per night. We can afford it. But for many Palestinians who come to Egypt for medical treatment and without large amounts of savings, even this meager rental fee can begin to add up.

We went downtown today to buy some more food. We are buying in small rations, "just in case the border opens tomorrow." I feel like we've repeated that refrain a hundred times already. I go and check my e-mail. I feel very alone; no one cares, no one knows, no one bothers to know. This is how Palestinian refugees must feel every day of their lives.

I read the news, skimming every headline and searching for anything about Rafah. Nothing. One piece is about the Palestinian football team; another is about the European Union border monitors renewing their posts for another six months. We do not exist.

. . . So now we are back in the flat. We sleep, and wake up, and wait for the phone to ring with some news. Every time we receive a knock on the door, we rush to see if the messenger brings good tidings. Today? Tomorrow? A week from now?

No, it's only the local deaf man. He remembers us from last time, offers to take out our trash for some money and food.

We sit and watch the sunset. What does it know of waiting and anticipation and disappointment—a million times in one day?

The Politics of Uncertainty[12]
Al-Arish, Egypt, November 23, 2006

It's our third day in al-Arish and still no word about the border. Everyone is suddenly a credible source on when it will open, and anxious ears listen.

One local jeweler insisted it would open at 4 p.m. yesterday—a suggestion that the taxi drivers laughed off (they placed their bets on Thursday)—but Thursday has come and gone and still no sign of the border opening. The woman staying in the flat next to us, a Syrian Palestinian businesswoman also waiting to enter Gaza, says she has "credible information" it will open in a matter of "days." Atiya, our taxi driver, says *he* heard it wouldn't open until the Muslim pilgrimage (*Hajj*), a few weeks from now. A border official we call every morning at 5 a.m. says only the Israelis know for sure.

How is it that when waiting for passage through borders, time is suspended—yet somehow, the rest of the world goes on uninterrupted? How is it that all sense of time and belonging and life come to a standstill?

... As an Israeli friend put it, "uncertainty" is used as part of the almost endless repertoire of occupation.

In the end, security is all that matters and all that ever will. As Palestinians, we've come to despise that word: security. It has become a deity more sacred than life itself.

... Our identity has come to be defined by restrictions, and borders, and permits, and limits. That is the nature of the occupation. If you are from Gaza, you cannot travel to the West Bank; you cannot travel to Jerusalem; you cannot use Allenby, il-Jisr, or Erez, or any of the airports. You cannot obtain travel permits for you or your spouse—nor family reunification. They cannot obtain identity cards. You cannot fly, you cannot fish, you cannot move, you cannot breathe, you cannot live. If you meet all these "cannots," then you know you are from Gaza.

What Yousuf's Been Up To . . . [13]
Al-Arish, Egypt, November 26, 2006

As we continue our wait, Yousuf waits along with us. Kids are remarkably adaptable, more than we give them credit for. Of course, for Yousuf, this is the second time in his young life he's had to wait for such a long time for the border to open (the last time, he was a tender 8 months). That doesn't mean he doesn't notice what's happening around him. He's remarkably intuitive that way.

Now he's taken to the habit of asking us regularly, "When will the border open? I want to go to *Lazza*." (Yes, "Lazza" . . . he still has trouble pronouncing the *ghayn*.)

He provides my parents and me with a bit of comic relief when out of the blue, or when he has just woken up, he stammers, "You know, I think today is the day. I think they will open the crossing today," when, of course, he has no idea what he's going on about.

In the meantime, we've tried to make the experience as enjoyable as possible for him—walks on the beach and playing in the sand with my father, taking him on tacky manually run amusement park rides, and his favorite of all, the one that gets him jumping up and down, riding the jam-packed public bus to "downtown" Arish.

We've also finally chopped off that mane of his—people were beginning to confuse him with a sheep!

Good Tidings . . .[14]
Al-Arish, Egypt, November 27, 2006

We've given up trying to call the "*ma'bar* hotline"—a direct line to some bored-stiff Egyptian border official for the latest news. Inevitably, the answer is always "no instructions from the other side yet."

But today finally came the call we were waiting for—my cousin from Gaza phoned to tell us the border is opening tomorrow—for three days only, in both directions! My neighbor in Gaza City confirmed it by MSN Messenger.

My mother says it's because she finally cooked a meal yesterday. We always eat out in case the border is opened.

Of course, they are still all rumors until we hear for certain from the border. . . .

We bid farewell to al-Arish tomorrow morning. . . .

False Alarm!!![15]
Al-Arish, Egypt, November 27, 2006

Just when we were getting excited. . . .

We turned on Palestine television this evening to read some breaking news out of Gaza, reporting that the Rafah crossing will in fact *not* be opening tomorrow, Tuesday, despite earlier reports to the contrary.

A friend who contacted the EU representatives stationed in Rafah confirmed the bad news and thinks it might be because of reports in *Haaretz* that Ismail Haniyeh was due to leave tomorrow for a three-week tour to different countries and that the Israelis may have "intervened" to stop him.

Makes *perfect* sense . . . as usual. . . .

According to Palestinian wires, more than 3,200 people are waiting to cross, many directly in the border itself. . . .

Our wait continues.

Humanity Lost[16]
Al-Arish, Egypt, November 29, 2006

We stood, and we waited, and we cried, and we returned back to Egypt yesterday and again today—along with thousands of others.

It was anguish, misery, and desperation personified in every woman, man, and child.

One hour turned into two, then three, then five, as we stood shielding our eyes from the piercing midday sun on Wednesday, when we were told the crossing would be opening for a few hours, despite a late-night about-face to the contrary.

Some wailed in exhaustion, others fainted, still others cracked dry humor trying to pass the time. We stood, thousands of us, packed together elbow to elbow like cattle, penned in between steel barriers on one end and riot-geared Egyptian security guards on the perimeter. They were given orders not to allow anyone through until they heard otherwise from the Israelis—and to respond with force if anyone dared. Gaza was visible less than a kilometer away.

Many of the people had been waiting for more than two weeks to cross back into Gaza, sometimes making the trip to the crossing several times a day upon receiving word of its imminent opening.

"We have been waiting for 15 days now. Only God knows when it will open—today, tomorrow, the day after?" said 57-year-old Abu Yousuf Barghut, his shrapnel-riddled arm trembling by his side.

His tearful wife, Aisha, added, "God knows, we only want to seek treatment for him and to come right back. And now we are stuck and waiting for us in Gaza are my four children. This is the most basic of rights—to be able to return to our homes, and we are even denied that."

"The only way anyone will actually pay attention to our plight is if one of us dies here, and even then, I'm not sure the world will care," stammered one young man, Isam Shaksu, his eye heavily bandaged after having received a corneal implantation in Jordan.

In July, seven Palestinians waiting to be let into Gaza from Egypt died waiting to cross Rafah.

After the hours and the sun, one would have thought the black steel gates ahead of us were the gates to heaven. In fact, they led to only more masses, more waiting, more hell.

There is something you feel as you stand there, and sometimes squatted, for hours at a time, waiting to be let through the Egyptian side of Rafah crossing. It is something of your humanity slowing drifting away. It is gradual, but unmistakable.

And you are never quite the same again.

There were mixed Israeli orders—first to open the crossing for three days, starting Wednesday, yesterday; then, breaking news at 11 p.m. retracted that order, and by Wednesday

morning, another about-face, saying that the border would, in fact, be opened. By the time we arrived, it was 11 a.m., and already somewhere around 2,000 people had amassed in front of the gates. And no one was budging.

Yousuf waited along with us, asking incessantly, "When would the crossing open?" and begging me to pose the same question to the Egyptian officers manning it. Every time, he'd see the gate budge open he would get excited and yell, "It's open! It's open!" And everyone would heave a heavy sigh.

When we finally did make it inside the "second sector" of the Egyptian side, the relief was overwhelming—we had moved 50m! And we could wait another four hours if it meant we'd finally be allowed through. But instead, we faced yet another uncertain wait; it was like some sadistic game with no certain ending.

As we waited, we saw members of the Palestinian athletic teams heading to the Asian Games after a two-week delay.

We also saw Ismail Haniyeh on his way out to his Arab tour. He stopped to mingle with the desperate crowds, some hailing him, some complaining about how long they had waited.

We finally learned that the crossing had been closed this entire time, and the Egyptians were only allowing people through to give them some hope to cling to—and to prevent the masses from rioting, which has happened before.

We thought once Haniyeh had passed, we'd be allowed through. But it was then we learned that Mahmoud Zahar had crossed into Gaza earlier that morning—carrying suitcases full of $20 million.

The European Monitors were not pleased. How could he not declare the money, and how could he have the audacity to try to bring in money to feed his people in the first place?

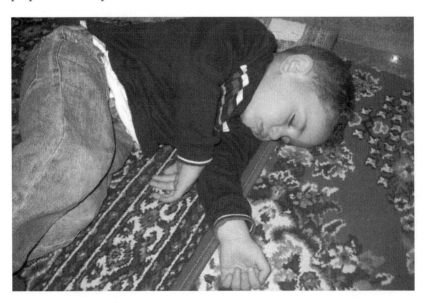

They filed a "complaint" with the Israelis, who immediately told them to shut down the crossing, without giving a reason, leaving thousands—including Yousuf, my parents, and me—stranded.

My mother and Yousuf had gone ahead of my father and me—and our bags— into the terminal, and Yousuf fell asleep in the mosque. It was then that the officers had informed us the crossing was no longer operational—and everyone who was inside, even those who had already made it as far as the Palestinian side, would have to go back.

We pleaded with an Egyptian officer: "It took us six hours to get this far inside the terminal; please let us through."

"Big deal—it took me 10 hours to get here from Cairo," he retorted, as I reminded myself they get paid a measly 180 Egyptian pounds a month and couldn't care less.

"What you have to understand is that no one gives a damn what happens to you—you could sit here and suffocate for all they care. You are simply not human enough for them to care," another officer said.

When is it that we lost our humanity, I wondered? And when is it that the humanity and desperation of a people, waiting desperately to be let through to their homes, was less important than the call of duty? And that a government was made to choose between feeding its own people or giving them passage to their homes?

Inside the terminal, the scenes were dizzying. Already disoriented from lack of sleep and little food, I looked around in awe. It was nothing short of an internment camp, and I lost myself somewhere between the silent anguish of old men; aching, teary-eyed women on the verge of collapse; and children, some strewn across the floor in exhaustion, others who were sick, in wheelchairs, wailing. . . .

We returned to Arish, exhausted and sleep deprived, only to find that all the apartments were occupied by returning passengers. The only flat we found was one without hot water and leaky ceiling pipes, but we couldn't care less. By 9 p.m., we were all out.

The next morning, we left again for the border—where we had left our suitcases—despite word from taxi drivers that the crossing would not open. We waited again, this time for only five hours, until we decided it was an exercise in futility.

Everyone was looking for answers—some answers, any answers. When would the crossing open? Was there hope it would open today? If so, what time? Should we wait, should we return to Arish? Nobody knew.

Every now and then, someone would make a call to some secondary source they knew in Gaza or on the border, and rumors would spread like wildfire across the masses. "At noon—they say at noon there is a possibility it will open! Patience, patience!"

And then we would wait some more.

One man, frustrated, took his bags and began to push them back on a trolley and out through the throngs of exhausted passengers.

"Where the hell do you think you're going?" bellowed one of the Egyptian officers.

"To Jerusalem! Where do you think?" he snapped.

It was nearing the end of our long day. Overcome by exhaustion, we didn't know whether to laugh or cry.

A friend in the United Nations told me the Europeans had left their posts after yesterday's "incidents," and thus the Palestinian side of the crossing has shut down indefinitely now.

And so now, we return to square one. Back in Arish, waiting, as ever, for the border to open.

Make Some Noise![17]
Al-Arish, Egypt, December 2, 2006

With the border still closed, I've been trying to keep busy—and take some action in any way I know how. For me, that means writing and networking to inform as much media as possible. I'm working now on getting some television crews out to film the border—though with the tight Egyptian security bans, that might be difficult.

So for now, I've been writing: two articles for *Al Jazeera*; one on the UN OCHA report, which finds that Israel has broken every provision of the year-old U.S.-brokered AMA; and another short feature on people who are caught at the crossing.

I've also written a commentary for the *Guardian Comment Is Free* blog and have continued doing audio postcards for the BBC's *World Update* program as well as a report for Pacifica's Free Speech Radio News. My thanks and thoughts with all of those who have sent e-mails of support and solidarity.[18]

No Way Home[19]
Al-Arish, Egypt, December 1, 2006

My son Yousuf and I, along with my parents, left the United States, where we were visiting family, to return to Gaza nearly three weeks ago.

But we are not in Gaza.

For the past two weeks, we have been stuck on the Egyptian side of the Rafah crossing, in the face of an ongoing Israeli-imposed closure of the Gaza passage.

The crossing—which is the only passage in and out of Gaza for 1.4 million Palestinians there— was shut down by Israel in late June of this year, after Palestinian fighters attacked an Israeli military base, killing two soldiers and capturing another.

According to the UN OCHA in Gaza, it has been open for just 20 days since that time, less than 14 percent of the scheduled operating days.

The problem is, of course, that the Rafah crossing is Gaza's gateway to the world—and the only passageway in and out of the area for 1.4 million Palestinians. Without it, Palestinians cannot seek medical treatment unavailable in Gaza and cannot reunite with family members or attend universities or jobs abroad.

And those on the outside, such as my son and I, cannot return home.

. . . The closure continues despite this week's joint Palestinian-Israeli truce—a Palestinian commitment to cease firing rockets into Israel from Gaza and an Israeli vow to stop aggression against the Palestinians.

The ongoing closure also coincides with a visit by U.S. Secretary of State Condoleezza Rice for talks with Palestinian President Mahmoud Abbas and Israel on Thursday. They will discuss extending the "truce" to the West Bank and reimplementing the year-old AMA, which she brokered following Israel's disengagement from Gaza.

The AMA was supposed to hand over control of Rafah, among other crossings, to Palestinians, within a year of implementation. The year has come and gone; all our crossings, our air, our water, and our lives remain under Israeli control.

Among other things, Israel had agreed in the AMA to operate this and other Gaza commercial crossings continuously and to not close a passage because of security incidents unrelated to the crossing itself.

For example, rocket fire into Israel—though it has now ceased—does not constitute a valid reason for closing Rafah and thus shutting in and out all of Gaza's occupants. Neither does an attack against a military base a few kilometers away—six months ago.

According to a UN report issued yesterday, Israel has broken every single provision in the agreement, including this one.

Yet the Rafah story continues to go largely underreported in the mainstream press. Opening Rafah and providing Palestinians with their most basic rights—the right to move freely in and out of their own land—is critical to furthering peace and ensuring and a viable Palestinian state.

What Do I Tell a 2-Year-Old?[20]
Al-Arish, Egypt, December 3, 2006

He keeps asking me about the border. Yousuf, I mean. He overhears things, *ma'bar* this and *ma'bar* that . . . and so, naturally inquisitive, he asks what we are doing and why are we still here, and each question is followed by another and another.

YOUSUF: Mama, can I ask you something?

ME: Anything, my love.

YOUSUF: Why are we still here, in Arish?

ME: Because we are waiting to enter Gaza, dear.

YOUSUF: But then why don't we go to Gaza?

ME: Because the *ma'bar* is closed, my love.

YOUSUF: Why is it still closed?

ME: [Silence.]

YOUSUF: Mommy, why is it still closed?

ME: I don't know. [I know, my dear, but do you really want to know? Do you really need to know?]

YOUSUF: Well, who's closing it, Mommy?

ME: [What do I tell him?] Some bad people.

YOUSUF: You mean like in the stories, like Shere Khan in *The Jungle Book*?

ME: Yes, sure, like Shere Khan.

YOUSUF: But who are they? Who are these bad people? Is it the *yahood*? [mimicking what he's heard on the border]

ME: [What do I say? I hesitate.] Look, they are just some people; some of them are good, some are bad, just like people everywhere. And the bad ones are closing the border.

YOUSUF: But why? What did we do?

ME: [I wish I knew, my dear. I wish I had all the answers, my love, so I could answer all your questions. I wish I didn't have to answer such questions. But now I do, and what can I say to you?]

YOUSUF: Mommy, please tell them to open it.

ME: I tried, *habibi*.

Yousuf: Try harder. Try again. Tell them again. Please, tell them, "Yousuf wants to enter Gaza."

And so here goes:

> Dear Mr. Peretz:
> My son Yousuf, 2 years and 9 months, would like me to inform you that he wants to enter Gaza. He has asked me to tell whoever it is who is keeping it closed to open the border for him immediately. In fact, he asks me every day. And now, asking is no longer sufficient: He wants answers, too. Why is the border still closed? And who is keeping it closed, and why? So, in addition to asking you to open the border, I am also writing to ask you what I can tell a 2-year-old to satisfy his insatiable curiosity. What can I tell him of borders and occupation and oppression and collective punishment?
> What would *you* tell him? Lying doesn't work. Two-year-olds are like natural-born lie detectors. And so he figures it's "the bad guy"—like in the stories that we all read growing up. And now, he demands to know who the bad guy is. What do I tell a 2-year-old, Mr. Peretz, about the bad guy who won't let him return home?
> A Palestinian mother

The Only Thing That's Certain[21]
Al-Arish, Egypt, December 5, 2006

My mother saw a group of men collecting some wood off the beach the other day. She assumed they were custodial workers and thanked them for their work, asking why the municipality didn't send people out to clean up the beach more often.

Yousuf Abu Safiya

It was then that she realized they were actually not trash collectors but Palestinians searching for driftwood to light a small campfire. Not only that, but as she would learn, it was the Palestinian Minister of the Environment Yousuf Abu Safiya (who has a permanent post that predates this January's elections) and two of his co-workers. It appears they are also stuck in Egypt and staying a few flats down from us. They came over later at night as we discussed everything from politics to the adverse affects of the water's nitrate content on children in Khan Yunis.

Apparently he tried calling Mahmoud Abbas's office today to ask whether they knew when the border might open. Their answer: "Well, we heard maybe today. But if not today, for sure tomorrow, or the day after . . . or Friday. . . . "

As a cousin in Gaza joked, "There's only one thing for certain: Nobody knows when it will open!" The only certainty is uncertainty.

Is Tomorrow the Day?[22]
Al-Arish, Egypt, December 5, 2006

More rumors—everything beeped and rang at once. Our cell phones, instant messaging programs. . . .

Even the phones of our guests from the Ministry of Environment, who were over, began ringing . . . news from Gaza, from so and so source at the border, from a local radio station, from an Internet news site, that the border would open tomorrow for one day, from 8 a.m. to 5 p.m., during which time thousands will try to return home and thousands of others to go out—including pilgrims on their way to Mecca.

The news seemed to confirm itself one phone call after another; then, Palestine television and more and more Internet sites brought the breaking news.

So, once more, we are packing up our belongings, just when our neighbor was contemplating buying a frying pan, and we'll head to the border tomorrow at 7 a.m.

From there, as ever, we will wait and see what happens.

Home Sweet Home[23]
Gaza City, Palestine, December 6, 2006

At last—we've made it through. We left at 6 a.m. and by late afternoon were in Gaza City. But we were only a handful of thousands—I estimated 5,000—still stranded and unable to get through to Gaza or out of Gaza. All of Rafah's roads have been blocked off by the sheer number of people trying to get out. More will follow tomorrow, plus some pictures.

There Is Method in This Madness . . . [24]
Gaza City, Palestine, December 10, 2006

So we're back, and I think I'm only now beginning to recover from what I call the "Rafah Crossing Hangover." You feel fine at first, and once you finally get home and set your bags down you think, "Hey that wasn't so bad!" Then, around 6 p.m., it hits you like a sack of rice. First your back gives way, and it feels like a truck ran it over. Then you begin to lose sensation in your legs as they go numb. Disorientation . . . and soon, collapse!

By 8 p.m., we were all out cold, and I woke up the next day not knowing where I was and with a headache no amount of coffee could fix. Yousuf woke up and walked to the door leading to our balcony instead of the house—not realizing where he was either. It took us a few days to regain consciousness finally.

The border itself was a picture of agony. Because of the sheer numbers of people waiting to cross, the Egyptians had sectioned off the crowds via several roadblocks. Our final goal of making it into Gaza seemed formidable at 7 a.m., as we arrived and saw thousands upon thousands of passengers trying to get through in any way possible.

When my parents realized they wouldn't be crossing anytime soon—with a donkey cart full of luggage behind them—Yousuf and I went ahead with only our passports and my backpack, only to find about 5,000 people amassed in front of the Egyptian gate awaiting entry.

Only a few were being allowed in at a time, because ultimately the buses that were sent off into the Palestinian side could accommodate about 80 people—procedure passed down from the Israelis.

As we reached the outside of the gate, all I saw in front of me was people climbing on top of each other, looping their bags around and through the crowds to try to make it to the front. Simply making it *to* that gate was a task. It was every person for himself. In the chaos, one woman forgot her daughter, about Yousuf's age, and I picked her up lest she be crushed under the thousands of legs.

A few hours later, I made contact with my parents—they had miraculously made their way to the front, while I remained in the back. With a lot of yelling and jostling, I managed to wind my way through the crowds to join them, and, of course, there was more waiting ahead. By the time we finally made it to the Palestinian side, it was about 1 p.m. We waited in the infamous "bus" for the Israelis to give the approval for us to pass—apparently the video monitoring extends to the outside of the terminal as well.

Blue-bereted EU monitors watched intently. I looked around at the faces of each of the people on our bus, including a man who had metal rods in his leg after his fifth leg operation in three years. I couldn't help but think how no one will realize what all of these people have been through . . . just to return to their homes.

The crossings closed shortly after we made it across, and thousands remain stranded behind us. I looked back, feeling for one second I had abandoned them, not knowing what more I could do.

I keep getting asked how it feels to be back. My first impression was feeling as if I were sucked into a black hole or vacuum. Very eerie going into a place that has methodically been turned into one of the world's most isolated. You feel sort of distant and displaced and unsettled. And, of course, there is a mixture of exhilaration and relief and uncertainty.

But you also feel accomplished, as though by merely being able to cross you have exercised an act of awesome proportions—defying the far-reaching grip of the occupation in even the remotest and most seemingly insignificant of ways.

I think the most disturbing and overwhelming feeling of all is having to come to grips with the realization that your life and how you live that life continue to be controlled wholly and absolutely by an Occupier and that its ability to deny you entry to your own home so abruptly, so arbitrarily, and yet so methodically—largely because of the acquiescence and complicity of the world—has become so accepted.

Gideon Levy on Rafah Crossing[25]

Gaza City, Palestine, December 10, 2006

Check out *Haaretz*'s Gideon Levy on the story of Rafah crossing (hey, Yousuf gets an honorable mention!) in today's paper:

> These people want to return home. Israel does not even allow them this. They are human beings with families, plans and commitments, longings and dignity, but who cares.
>
> ... Without anyone paying attention, the Gaza Strip has become the most closed-off strip of land in the world—after North Korea. But while North Korea is globally known to be a closed and isolated country, how many people know that the same description applies to a place just an hour away from hedonist Tel Aviv?
>
> ... What memories will the toddler harbor from the three weeks of waiting in a crowded line with his mother on the border, humiliated and sad on the way home, to incarcerated Gaza, withering in its poverty? And who will be brought to account for this in the end?[26]

CHAPTER NOTES

1. Laila El-Haddad, "UN: Israel Breaks Border Agreement," in *Al Jazeera English*, December 1, 2006, archived at http://bit.ly/9Q5Xx9.
2. Archived at http://bit.ly/8YFJhe.
3. The channel's name was later changed to *Al Jazeera English*, because "one of the Qatar-based channel's backers decided that the broadcaster already had an international scope with its original Arabic outlet." Leigh Holmwood, "Al-Jazeera Renames English-Language Channel," Guardian, London, November 14, 2006, archived at http://bit.ly/bhVXwg.

4. Archived at http://bit.ly/9b5JmL.
5. Heba stopped blogging in 2008. In an e-mail correspondence on May 21, 2010, that is emblematic of why more Palestinians don't blog, she explained her position: "I stopped the blog because of pure personal frustration. Although I believe in the importance of raising awareness of the Other on the situation of Gaza people, I felt that what I was doing was hollow and pointless in a world that simply does not care. I felt besieged within and unable to share my mind with other people!"
6. Archived at http://bit.ly/aEMVHh.
7. I am happy to report the new passports are navy blue (perhaps as a tactical move intended to make the passports more credible, with forest green being the color of choice for much of the developing world).
8. Archived at http://bit.ly/adZWrz.
9. My parents, who were visiting the United States, were traveling.
10. *I Saw Ramallah*, Mourid Barghouti.
11. Archived at http://bit.ly/cHSk6o.
12. Archived at http://bit.ly/djeDih.
13. See also Laila El-Haddad, "Politics of Uncertainty," *YnetNews.com*, November 27, 2006, archived at http://bit.ly/d4mMFu.
14. Archived at http://bit.ly/9SBSpz.
15. Archived at http://bit.ly/dw52sQ.
16. Archived at http://bit.ly/cNtdaG.
17. Archived at http://bit.ly/clrvh2.
18. Archived at http://bit.ly/buoqtA.
19. For more of Laila's coverage of the closed Rafah closing and its legality and effects, see Laila El-Haddad, "UN: Israel Breaks Border Agreement," *Al Jazeera English*, December 1, 2006, archived at http://bit.ly/cMEcvo. See also Laila El-Haddad, "Caught at the Crossing," *Al Jazeera English*, December 1, 2006, archived at http://bit.ly/bXLLyy.
20. Laila El-Haddad, "No Way Home," *Guardian Comment Is Free*, December 1, 2006, archived at http://bit.ly/c17qO9.
21. Archived at http://bit.ly/cvCIfW.
22. Archived at http://bit.ly/dg5Xko.
23. Archived at http://bit.ly/bGGN1H.
24. Archived at http://bit.ly/aLcqeL.
25. Archived at http://bit.ly/9m34qp.
26. Archived at http://bit.ly/b6TaEc.
    Gideon Levy, "Elbow to Elbow, Like Cattle," *Haaretz*, December 10, 2006, archived at http://bit.ly/9qC7Xz. See also Laila El-Haddad, "Meanwhile: Gaza, My Home and My Prison," *New York Times*, December 13, 2006, archived at http://nyti.ms/dtB0iL.

Chapter 14

Gaza on the Brink

December 2006

Gaza spiraled ever closer to all-out anarchy this month, as not so random acts of violence became a fixture of our daily lives. From the wanton murder of young children (whose father was a high-ranking security chief) to the killing of two judges and the attempted assassination of Hamas ministers, Gaza was truly on the brink of implosion. Control over the Palestinian security forces continued to be the main point of contention. Residents had no sense of security or stability anymore, as fear and uncertainty gripped the city. Any periods of "calm" were fleeting, as the worst was yet to come.

Hamas Prime Minister Ismail Haniya gave a speech to reassure the people that all was well, while Fateh President Mahmoud Abbas called for new, early elections. The rhetoric was often heated, and the vitriol and incitement were rising on both sides. Meanwhile, in Washington, D.C., Congress voted to send massive quantities of assistance to Abbas's presidential guard. In Israel, the High Court voted to legalize the practice of extrajudicial murder. And the Rafah crossing remained sealed to Palestinians.

Gaza Mourns Victims of Unknown Assailants[1]
Gaza City, Palestine, December 11, 2006

It began at about 7 a.m.: continuous machine gun banter, dozens of rounds in a row, and only one street down from our house. More infighting, we assumed, or maybe disgruntled security forces. But it didn't stop. We turned on the local radio station and learned that three children had been killed—children belonging to Colonel Baha Balousha, a senior intelligence official loyal to Mahmoud Abbas's Fateh party.

They were shot dead in a car outside their school in Gaza on Monday, spilling pools of blood along the street.

Balousha, along with Mohammad Dahalan, was infamous for his involvement in a then-Fateh-run government crackdown against and torture of Hamas members a decade ago and has been at odds with Hamas for some time. Hamas denied responsibility for today's killings and called the crime gruesome.

Fateh supporters blocked off the main roads in the city with burning tires. Others called for a general strike, shooting at stores that refused to close.

Fateh gunmen also stormed the Parliament and called for the Hamas-run government's immediate resignation.

Everybody wanted someone to blame, and, for Fateh, that someone was Hamas.

Hamas withdrew its forces to avoid confrontation. Later at night in a show of solidarity, representatives of all the factions, including Hamas, joined forces with Fateh in a candlelight vigil against "violence and criminality" in front of the father's house.

. . . Today's sad events have triggered widespread fear and uncertainty. The tension is palpable in the air and threatens to boil over at any time. As the florist down the street told me, "I used to say before I was afraid of what is coming. But now, I am *really* afraid. Nobody knows what's going to happen next."

Who Done It?[2]
Gaza City, Palestine, December 12, 2006

Twenty-four hours after yesterday's shocking attack, rowdy Fateh protests have continued unabated throughout Gaza.

Fateh supporters continued to run amok in the streets, spraying bullets into the air during charged demonstrations, blocking off major city roads with burning tires, and pitching protest tents in front of Mahmoud Abbas's Gaza City home.

The incident continued to dominate conversations almost everywhere around Gaza—in barbershops and taxis, in schools and homes. Mostly, people are trying to solve the mystery of who was behind the attacks, having largely dismissed initial theories that it was Hamas gunmen.

According to some inside sources, the act was actually a Fateh-on-Fateh attack.

Balousha allegedly had some incriminating information on another high-profile figure within Fateh that somebody thought should die with him. Except, of course, that somebody missed the target.

Others say Balousha had documented CIA money transfers to senior figures within Fateh as well as such details as who was getting paid. He also allegedly had

evidence about local drug dealers. I guess if you are an intelligence chief, people would want you dead for an unlimited number of reasons.

Fateh supporters have been blaming Hamas for being slow to respond, saying they were able to catch those who fired upon Hamas Interior Minister Saeed Siyam's car within hours. Hamas's response: If its security forces were given the chance, then they could do their job. Apparently, Hamas's executive force is not allowed to deploy everywhere or operate fully—Abbas's orders.

Regardless, it appears Balousha and his people have some idea who was responsible—or so he hinted during an interview on Palestinian television today.

It seems the perpetrators of yesterday's heinous crime are now in the custody of the preventive security forces (who remain under the president, not the prime minister's, authority . . . confused yet?), though the alleged head honcho, Atif Bakr, is still at large.

Second Judge in One Week Murdered[3]
Gaza City, Palestine, December 13, 2006

For the second time in a week, a judge was murdered today in broad daylight by unknown assailants in the southern Gaza Strip town of Khan Yunis. Bassem el-Farra happens to be a relative of ours on my mother's side of the family. He was on his way to the Shari'a Court, where he works, when four gunmen pumped him full of bullets, only two days after the gruesome killing of the three children of a senior Fateh intelligence chief.

Hamas has accused the so-called death squads of Fateh for the attack against el-Farra, who is also a senior leader within Hamas's Izz-e-din al-Qassam Brigades.

Fateh supporters have blamed Hamas for the surge in lawlessness in recent days, an accusation that Hamas flatly rejects.

"It's strange that the situation intensified after Fateh announced that unity government talks are at a standstill," remarked Hamas Palestinian Interior Minister Said Siyam in Palestinian newspapers.

According to Siyam, internal security is the responsibility of not only the interior minister and the government but also of Abbas, who is considered the commander-in-chief of the Palestinian security forces.

"The recent kidnapping of journalists and many of the recent violent incidents were actually carried out by Fateh. We [Hamas], on the other hand, fired operatives who were involved in aberrant incidents," Siyam explained.

"Fateh-affiliated security forces rejected our request to detain the operatives responsible for the kidnappings, and Fateh continues to support them," he added.

Three days ago, another judge, Jamal Abu Salim, was killed in the same area.

Amid the chaos, both sides have noted the absence and silence of Palestinian president Mahmoud Abbas, demanding that he make his voice heard and come to Gaza to quell rising fears of civil unrest.

Israel Legalizes Assassinations[4]
Gaza City, Palestine, December 15, 2006

Overshadowed by the bloody aftermath of Prime Minister Ismail Haniyeh's return to Gaza was his eight-hour delay by the Israelis because of the money he brought back with him for the Palestinian people. Later, in an attempt on Haniyeh's life by Fateh gunmen, his bodyguard was killed and 20 others injured, including his son. Israel's High Court of "Justice" ruled unanimously to legalize assassinations by Israeli forces against Palestinians.

A three-judge panel ruled that they could not prohibit in advance every Israeli "targeted killing," a now-popular euphemism for assassination of Palestinian figures.

The ruling gives legitimacy to a practice that, though illegal under international law, Israeli forces routinely uses against members of the Palestinian factions. According to the Israeli human rights organization B'Tselem, 339 Palestinians have been extrajudicially killed over the past six years, almost half of them bystanders. . . .

Gazans Speak Out on Early Elections[5]

Gaza City, Palestine, December 15, 2006

Tension was palpable in the air today in Gaza, as Hamas's executive forces deployed alongside the presidential guard hours after an attempt on Prime Minister Ismail Haniyeh's life. Luckily, the tension has so far not spilled over into violence in Gaza, as in the West Bank, and both forces have shown admirable restraint.

Haniyeh gave his speech, which many people I spoke with viewed as "reassuring" given the volatile climate of recent days and weeks. Still, many questions remain: How will the money he was able to raise make its way into Gaza? Is a unity government still realistic? What is the alternative?

Tomorrow, Mahmoud Abbas is scheduled to give a nationwide talk in which he will hint at—but not overtly call for—early elections, something that Hamas and even Fateh's Farouq al-Qaddoumi reject. It is a suggestion that the (Fateh-dominated) PLO Executive Council recommended last week, however.

Al-Quds al-Arabi editor and prominent Palestinian journalist Abdelbarry Utwan, who participated by phone with me last week on Gaza's *Nightdrive* English radio program, said that a call for early elections is a call for civil war, "and we all know who is behind that."

He said it would be a grave mistake for Abbas to call for early elections and compared Gaza with Algeria of the early 1990s, while noting the contradiction of U.S. support of the Sinora government and opposition to Hamas.

I went around and talked to people about their thoughts on early elections last week in the following photostory for *Al Jazeera*. Do bear in mind that it was written before Haniyeh's speech, which seems to have had a good deal of influence in people's confidence level, according to many local analysts.

Most people seem confused and uncertain and just want a way out of the current crisis. At the same time, opinions are extremely polarized.

Gazans Speak Out on Early Poll[6]
Gaza City, Palestine, December 18, 2006

Before the Palestinian president made his announcement on December 16 that he would call for early elections, *Al Jazeera* asked ordinary Gazans what they thought about such a proposal.

Laila El-Haddad asked residents if their allegiances had changed during the events since Hamas trounced Fateh at elections in January. This is what they said:

Mervet Naim, 34, English teacher (government schools)

"I am completely against the idea of early elections. President Abbas and Fateh in general must give Hamas a chance and let them serve the full four years. Even if we are not being paid, we are still behind our government 100 percent.

"They are fair individuals and they feel with the suffering of our society, because they are from the people. We cannot just judge them from the first nine months.

"The whole world is against them—so the least we can do is support them in these dire times. I voted for Hamas before, and I would vote for Hamas again."

Yousef AlHelou, 27, radio producer/translator

"I am with any solution which can lead us away from this crisis. Even if there is no law that allows for early elections to be called, one must be created.

"We have to do something for the sake of the people, not for the sake of the factions. Hamas says its popularity will increase if early elections are called—but they are also opposed to the idea, so there is a contradiction there.

"At the same time, Fateh should not impose its opinions on Hamas since it is, after all, in the minority now.

"I oppose the idea that the government is somehow responsible for the situation we're in—it's clearly collective punishment by the West.

"At the same time, Hamas should be flexible. The ministries of the interior and finance should be run independent of any faction. I voted for Hamas in January's elections to punish Fateh because of its corruption, but I'm not sure how I would vote again."

Salim Sbayta, 30, waiter

"I am for early elections. Our living conditions are unbearable, and, God willing, early elections will solve the crisis, because I think every citizen knows what it is we need in a government now.

"We need a government that can deal with foreign and Arab governments and understand our reality. We are a society that survives on foreign aid.

"There has to be a pragmatic solution to the problem. I didn't vote in the previous elections, but if new elections are held, I will certainly vote for Fateh."

Reem Akram, 20, university student

"Even though I'm a Fateh supporter, I'm against new elections. They will only lead to more chaos and infighting and instability. If Hamas is voted out, it will return to fighting and resistance.

"At the same time, Fateh and the PLO need drastic reform in their ranks, and this has not yet happened.

"We need both players in the government. I'm still hopeful a unity government can be formed. I voted for Fateh in the previous election and would vote for them again. But I think this government should be allowed to serve out its term."

To see the other seven interviews in this series, go to http://bit.ly/cT3YFI.

Abbas Calls for Early Elections[7]
Gaza City, Palestine, December 16, 2006

In a fiery and lengthy speech broadcast nationwide that was at sharp contrast with Haniyeh's more conciliatory talk last night, Mahmoud Abbas has called for early presidential and parliamentary elections in Gaza, the West Bank, and East Jerusalem.

Abbas spoke for more than 1.5 hours, hurling verbal insult after insult at Hamas and its leaders.

But throughout the speech, it was not clear that Abbas would come outright and call for new elections. . . . The whammy of the announcement came as the final sentence of his speech, at which point those in attendance jumped to their feet amid thunderous applause. Outside, Fateh supporters shot gunfire in celebration and honked their horns.

. . . Abbas's talk was riddled with contradictions. He condemned the actions (firing rockets and attacking Israel) of the very people he later praised as heroes languishing in Israeli jails—Marwan Barghouthi, Ahmed Saadat, and others. He also made no mention of the fact that the ones who continue to fire rockets are his own AMB.

Abbas went on to accuse the [Haniyeh] government of prolonging the siege and blamed the capture of the Israeli soldier Gilad Shalit for the death of some 500 Palestinians and injury of more than 5,000 at the hands of the Israeli Army since this summer.

He also categorically denied any "conspiracy" to assassinate Ismail Haniyeh, saying the same people Hamas accused of being "conspirators" in the attempt on his life are the ones who helped facilitate his arrival and departure through Rafah.

Abbas also criticized the throngs of Hamas supporters who welcomed Haniyeh "with machine guns and RPGs" instead of with "bouquets of roses."

He said the Rafah crossing was operating smoothly, "and people could get through within minutes." It was the Hamas supporters who destroyed it two days ago.

OK, I don't know what crossing Abbas has been using, but the one I just crossed over *did not take* a few minutes. It certainly was not under Palestinian control and never has been.

Abbas focused his energy on attacking and tearing apart Hamas and its government, blaming it for everything from the state of siege and hunger we are in to the death of hundreds of Palestinians in Israeli attacks this summer to the closure of the Rafah crossing. He ignored completely the fact that Gaza's imprisonment and isolation began *long* before Hamas was elected into power, something verified by the UN OCHA itself.

Abbas also had few kind words for the Hamas political leadership. In a verbal jab aimed at exiled Hamas chief Khaled Meshal, Abbas said, "He who talks about the illegitimacy of the executive power of the PLO is the very one who is protected by it on the outside. He talks from afar, in comfort, without dirtying his shoes in the soil of our land."

Many people, including independents like Mustapha Barghouthi, consider the PLO an aging, defunct body that needs to be either dissolved or reformed. So I don't really see Hamas's objections as entirely outrageous.

. . . It seems Abbas has assumed the role that he once condemned in Arafat: The entire reason the role of prime minister was created in the first place in early 2000 (at the prodding of the United States) was to serve as a counterbalance to the absolute authority of Arafat. Abu Mazen served as prime minister for a while before resigning in protest, because he felt he could not properly carry out his job and the president continued to exercise ultimate authority. Interesting how the tide turns. . . .

The Streets of Gaza[8]
Gaza City, Palestine, December 18, 2006

Things are grim here in Gaza City. During the day, few shops opt to stay open anymore; at night, the city is transformed into a ghost town. And then the shooting begins. Tonight, in addition to the usual machine gun banter, we also heard a large unexplained explosion—it appears to have been a mortar attack in northern Gaza near the *Mukhabarat* (intelligence) building.

Yesterday, a Fateh-linked security officer was kidnapped and killed, and clashes ensued in front of the Ministry of Foreign Affairs after unknown assailants fired on the convoy of Mahmoud Zahar. Later, Fateh gunmen took over the Ministries of Agriculture and Education in what Zahar has described as an attempted military coup; and in Jabaliya, in the north of the Gaza Strip, clashes continued today despite a tenuous "ceasefire" (people are now trying to keep track of which ceasefire is which).

Every hour, new blood is spilled, and every hour, we hear new condemnations and regret at the fact that brethren are doing this to each other. How does a society actually slip into civil war? Is it gradual or abrupt? When is that red line finally crossed, the point of no return, when all precedents are broken and wrong can suddenly be right?

And why are we in the media so anxious to call this a civil war, almost as though we want to will it into existence, while the civil war in Iraq has been raging for years and no one knows how to characterize it yet?

Today, we saw members of the presidential guard, who were deployed last night, cautiously manning every corner of Gaza City. They were stopping cars on the city streets, asking us to turn on our lights inside our vehicles as we drove (perhaps so as to avoid becoming unintended targets?). For a change, we actually felt a little safe, though also a little more vulnerable.

I can't help but think of Amira Hass's article of this past summer. Her words reverberate in my mind repeatedly:

> The experiment was a success: The Palestinians are killing each other. They are behaving as expected at the end of the extended experiment called "what happens when you imprison 1.3 million human beings in an enclosed space like battery hens.

The average person doesn't know what to think anymore. People are confused, exhausted, and mostly very afraid.

As a friend of my mother's put it today, "We don't know any more who's right and who's wrong and who's at fault and who isn't. And we just want it to end."

A Tense Calm, but Who's to Blame?[9]
Gaza City, Palestine, December 22, 2006

There is a tense calm holding in Gaza. But tense or not, people couldn't care less, so long as they feel safe walking the streets now.

During the past week, street battles were waged with automatic weapons, rocket-propelled grenades, and even mortars among members supportive of both factions and often plainclothes residents with a score to settle, such as the Dogmosh family, leaving most residents holed inside their homes or fleeing for safety. Even making it to the corner convenience store has become a challenge.

Universities canceled their classes, and most stores closed shop. Many parents have even stopped sending their children to school.

But almost overnight, all this changed as members of the Hamas Executive Force and Abbas's countless security forces that were previously deployed throughout the city were withdrawn.

The question most people on the outside keep asking is: Who is fighting whom, and why? It's a question whose answer even locals are unsure of. Often the "cards" as it were are mixed, and those actually doing the fighting are embedded in gang/mafia/clan warfare, with members operating under factional cover, as with the most recent spate of violence.

And in the absence of rule of law, sovereignty, security, and, most importantly, authority, it devolves into a cycle of revenge that is characterized as "factional."

But there is also another element to all this. With the enthusiastic help of the Central Intelligence Agency, Abbas has recruited, equipped, and trained a new presidential force expected to number 3,000 men, whose salaries are paid in full.

And this week, the U.S. Congress is expected to pass a bill sanctioning $90 million in "special" aid to the presidential guard.

. . . None of this surprises me. We are a failed state, before we can even become a state. Can anything else be expected given the severe conditions under which the society has been placed? The answer may seem obvious to some, but I am always surprised there is not *more* internal fighting, given the situation. I guess, at the very least, we have to be thankful for that.

Gaza Voices: 11 Months under Hamas[10]
Gaza City, Palestine, January 12, 2007

In February last year, shortly after Hamas's surprise election victory, I spoke to nine Palestinians about their hopes and fears for the future.

Since that time, rigorous economic sanctions have been imposed on the Hamas-led Palestinian government and the Palestinian people. The economy has been devastated, which has resulted in unprecedented levels of poverty and left nearly a quarter of the population without salaries. Israel has withheld hundreds of millions of dollars in tax revenues owed to the PA. Gaza's border crossings have been all but shut, sealing in Gaza's 1.5 million residents and isolating them from the West Bank, Jerusalem, and the outside world.

I tracked down four of the original group and asked them about the current situation and whether they have shifted allegiances.

Riyad Ni'mami Jabin, 36, farmer

"You want the truth? The situation is the same. We haven't benefited anything from anyone— whether from the new government or the old. You came and spoke to me last season when I was unable to export my strawberries due to a continuous Israeli-imposed closure of the Karni crossing. Most of my harvest spoiled. And now 11 months on, I'm in the same situation. Only last year, no one compensated us for our losses, and as a result I couldn't prepare for this year's harvest. There is no support, and no one looks out for the farmers.

"If new elections were held, I'd most likely vote for the PFLP again. But in the end, it's really a vote for the sake of voting. Before it was Fateh, now it's Hamas. And where have we come?

"I blame the situation. There's nothing to be done except to stay quiet and accept it. From here to 800 years, it won't change."

Mohammad Hinbawi, 58, confectioner

"We were hoping for a government that could help create a lively economy. But the results were not what we expected.

"This started with countries shutting their doors to our government representatives and was followed by the international boycott and Israeli closures to prevent us from even our daily bread, in addition to the withholding of our tax revenues. We've endured heavy losses.

"But despite this all, I still support Hamas and would vote for them again— everyone does. Hundreds of thousands show up at their rallies knowing full well the reality we face—hunger, murder, lawlessness. Yes, we want change, but we are in the middle of a war of convictions, and, unfortunately, many people lack faith and patience. Hamas truly wants change—that's why they were elected—but they have simply have not been given an opportunity."

Khamees Akeela, 37, restaurateur

"The situation has worsened, and work is very bad. I didn't vote last time—partly because I was too busy at work and partly because I assumed the outcome [a Fateh victory] was a given. But if new elections are held, I will definitely go out and vote, and I will vote for Fateh. Everything is worse than it was before Hamas came into power, and I blame the government for not adapting to the reality surrounding it.

"Still, I say a unity government is best, and this is what we are holding out our hopes for. But every one seems to be rejecting it on the political level."

Leila Dabba, 58, handicrafts shopkeeper

"My opinion is the same as it was 11 months ago: There is no stability, there is only fear, and the situation is worse than ever. The only difference is we are fighting each other, and Israel is happy to see us do so. We only have ourselves to blame. While some people are wreaking havoc, others are just staying quiet about it. People need to speak out against what's happening!

"I didn't vote last time—I didn't really think it would make a difference. But for sure, I will cast a ballot next time and bring a hundred others with me in order to make sure Hamas does not win again. Despite everything that was wrong with Fateh, at least things were moving along—no matter how small a movement that was, we were not going backward. We don't want to eat or drink, we want stability. We want to sleep at night without having to hear constant shooting."

Gaza Prepares for Eid al-Adha[11]
Gaza City, Palestine, December 28, 2006

With Eid al-Adha just a few days away, Palestinians in Gaza have begun preparations for the Muslim holiday amid bleak economic conditions, an ongoing Israeli siege, and a tenuous truce between Hamas and Fateh.

On Eid al-Adha, Muslims commemorate Prophet Ibrahim's willingness to sacrifice his son for God. People slaughter an animal, share the meat, give charity, and buy new clothes and toys for children.

Vendors spread out their wares along the otherwise jam-packed streets of Gaza City's old market on Wednesday ahead of the Eid despite inclement weather.

They were busy selling traditional Eid fare: brightly packaged chocolates, date biscuits and other sweets, children's clothing, toys, meat, and salted fish, known as *fseekh.*

Many merchants say they hope that business this Eid will be brisker since the government recently paid about 70,000 civil servants, ranging in amounts from $200 to $400.

One shopkeeper said, "If you asked me one week ago, I would have said forget it, I might as well close shop. But now, people have some money to spend, and what better time to spend it than Eid?

"At the same time, with the ongoing closures, everything is more expensive now for us, the sellers, and for the consumer, so people will not be buying in as large amounts as before."

The Ministry of Finance began to distribute public-sector salaries in full on December 25 to those employees who had not received the funds via a deal brokered with the European Union.

Tens of thousands of Palestinian civil servants have received only part of their salaries since Hamas took office in March because of a Western aid boycott and Israel's refusal to transfer tax revenues owed to the PA, amounting to about $52 million monthly.

According to the UN OCHA, Israel has allowed, on average, 12 out of a promised 400 trucks a day to pass through Gaza's major commercial crossing, Karni/al-Mintar, since the beginning of the year.

As a result, the price of goods in Gaza has risen because of a scarcity in supply.

Abu Mustafa, a taxi driver, keeps his checked headdress wrapped around his face to ward off the winter chill as he maneuvers around Gaza's busy city center souks.

"This Eid is not really an Eid," he says.

"It might have the look and showiness of Eid, but it certainly does not have the feel of Eid.

"There isn't a household that's not affected by the situation in one way or another, whether that situation is the international siege or the infighting.

"Sure there is a calm now, but it's fleeting. Believe me, things could explode again at any moment, both internally and with Israel."

One of his passengers added, "The word optimism no longer exists in our vocabulary."

Mohammad Hinbawi, a street vendor who has been selling homemade sweets for more than 20 years, disagrees.

"As long as we have this to eat, we're OK," said Hinbawi, waiving a sesame sweet decisively with his hand.

"Sure, the situation is hard, but we continue to have faith and patience in God and in our government. They have not been given a chance, so we cannot blame them."

Nearby, women farmers sat on the ground behind a spread of their day's harvest of mint, arugula, and dill.

"God willing, it will be a pleasant Eid. Our life is difficult, but the calm is reassuring. Let's hope it stays that way."

Mariam Abo Odeh, 42, added, "No matter what's happening, Eid is at the very least a welcome break from our tortuous routine.

"The market comes alive, and some excitement and happiness fills the air. That in and of itself is enough."

Meanwhile, thousands of Palestinian men, women, and children stood waiting in poor weather for entry into Gaza on the Egyptian side of the Rafah crossing, the only passage in and out of Gaza.

The crossing has been closed by Israel since late June 2006, opening only erratically since—and for just nine hours during the past three weeks.

The Story of the Year[12]
Gaza City, Palestine, December 18 2006

The Middle East has made its fair share of headlines this year—from the stunning victory of Hamas in January's Palestinian elections to the sudden death of Ariel "the butcher" Sharon to Israel's blitzkrieg of Lebanon.

But perhaps the most harrowing—and sidelined—story of the year has been the story of Gaza and its gradual abandonment.

During the past nine months, Israel, backed by the United States and Europe, has methodically laid waste to a society of 1.5 million people, hermetically sealing in its residents, impoverishing it to unprecedented levels on par with Africa, besieging its land and people like never before— punishing them where no crime existed.

It is the first time in history, according to John Dugard at the United Nations, that an occupied people have been subject to international sanctions, especially sanctions of this magnitude and rigor.

Before our very eyes, global powers have colluded together to create a strip of land more isolated than North Korea itself, sentencing Gaza's residents to a living death in the world's largest internment camp, largely to the acquiescence of global powers.

The result has been Gaza's gradual decline into anarchy and the unraveling of its entire social, political, and economic fabric.

The moral of the story is: Beware of whom you vote for.

And it will serve as potent reminder from here on in of the consequences of electing the wrong party.

And that, to me, is the story of the year.

CHAPTER NOTES

1. The full original text of this post is archived at http://www.gazamom.
   com/2006/12/gaza-mourns-victims-of-unknown-assailants/, shortened to
   http://bit.ly/9rYyug.
2. Archived at http://bit.ly/dqrgrV.
3. Archived at http://bit.ly/bqtgIb.
4. Archived at http://bit.ly/a37zVO.
5. Archived at http://bit.ly/a9mqbL.
6. Laila El-Haddad, "Gazans Speak Out on Early Poll," *Al Jazeera English*,
   December 18, 2006, archived at http://bit.ly/cT3YFI. Originally reported some
   days earlier.
7. Archived at http://bit.ly/cEPVf7.
8. Archived at http://bit.ly/9XpT9D.
9. Archived at http://bit.ly/buigpV.
10. Laila El-Haddad, "Gaza Voices: 11 Months under Hamas," *Al Jazeera English*,
    January 12, 2007, archived at http://bit.ly/dCbXUn. Originally reported
    December 2006.
11. Laila El-Haddad, "Gaza Prepares for Eid al-Adha," *Al Jazeera English*,
    December 29, 2006, archived at http://bit.ly/95c9Wm. The Eid occurred on
    December 31, 2006.
12. Laila El-Haddad, "The Story of the Year," Listening Post, *Al Jazeera English*,
    December 18, 2006, archived at http://bit.ly/casq46.

PART III

Palestinian Democracy
and Unity under Assault

January 2007–December 2009

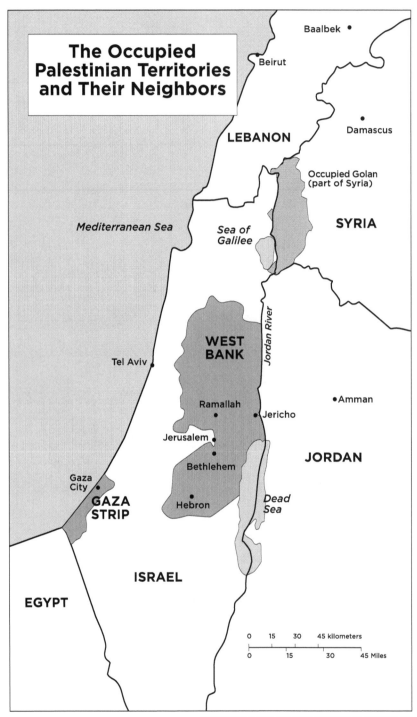

The Occupied Palestinian Territories and Their Neighbors

Baalbek

Beirut

LEBANON

Damascus

Occupied Golan
(part of Syria)

Mediterranean Sea

Sea of
Galilee

SYRIA

Jordan River

WEST
BANK

Tel Aviv

Ramallah

•Amman

Jericho

Jerusalem

JORDAN

Bethlehem

Gaza
City

GAZA
STRIP

Hebron

Dead
Sea

ISRAEL

EGYPT

| 0 | 15 | 30 | 45 kilometers |

| 0 | | 15 | 30 | 45 Miles |

Chapter 15

Gaza: From Conflict to Unity?

January–February 2007

In fall 2006, I planned a two-month trip with Yousuf back to Gaza; however, we spent half that time in Arish waiting for the border to open, so our time in Gaza was fairly short. Then, starting in 2007, I began to spend more time with Yassine in the United States and less time in Gaza.

In February 2007, after another spate of clashes, it finally seemed that—just maybe—the Palestinian factions had finally reached a political agreement in Mecca, Saudi Arabia. The residents of Gaza, whose lives and livelihoods had been crippled by the internal fighting and chaos, greeted the Mecca Agreement—signed by Khaled Meshaal and Mahmoud Abbas— with resounding approval. A national unity government was formed in the wake of that agreement: 83 PLC members voted in favor and only three against. But many Palestinians still feared that the agreement carried false hopes and was merely a temporary fix for a more chronic and intractable problem.

Meanwhile, Israel designated the Erez border crossing, which leads from northern Gaza into Israel, an "official border" in an attempt to absolve itself of responsibility for Gaza while it still maintained control over it. (The move was doubly bizarre, given that Erez was already inaccessible to Palestinians anyway; so it made little difference to us.) And at home, Yousuf was beginning to question the fighting.

My Recent Blogging Hiatus[1]
Durham, North Carolina, January 11, 2007

Yousuf and I left Gaza at the end of December to join Yassine for the holidays. As with my arrival, it was extremely abrupt. My bags were packed, and we just waited for a phone call from the taxi driver, which he said could come at any moment.

It came at 1:30 a.m. two weeks ago, not at all unexpected when the Israelis inform the Palestinian side of Rafah's opening only a few hours ahead of time. So a very sleepy Yousuf and I took our bags and drudged off to the border, where we waited in the taxi in a very chilly Rafah from 2:30 a.m. until 10 a.m., when the Europeans arrived two hours late and the border officially opened for business. Only two busloads were allowed through before the border closed again, and we barely made it out (very barely—we were nearly left out of our bus but for the heroics of one passenger, who whisked Yousuf away from my arms through the bus window as I jostled my way in amid a few hundred others).

I then took it upon myself to take a holiday not only from work but from blogging as well (that, and I was busy with Yousuf and his two cousins, ages 5 and 2).

Coming back, as usual, was very surreal, as if I had just dropped into some alternate universe, which, like Gaza, is in its own vacuum but in an entirely different way.

There is so much to blog on, and I will continue to do that and update you on my latest articles, of which there are a few.

Our Story on NPR²
Durham, North Carolina, January 18, 2007

Dick Gordon interviewed me for his daily program, *The Story*, on NPR this week. It was a very lengthy and intense interview, which of course had to be cut down, but what aired is available on *The Story* website under the title "A Home in Palestine."³ The segment is described as follows:

> Laila El-Haddad is a Palestinian journalist who divides her time between Gaza and Durham, N.C. She was in Gaza City this December when violence broke out between the two factions. Dick talks with Laila about the prospect of civil war in Gaza. He also hears what it's like to raise a child under occupation. Laila has a son, 2.5-year-old Yousuf, who is just now beginning to question what the fighting is all about.

We talked a lot about the big questions of identity and existence and homeland—and how and why one develops an attachment to the land and whether it is even a choice sometimes, especially for Palestinians.

Of course, we also discussed raising a child under occupation and then recent events and what I make of it all. A lot was cut out, namely a lengthy discussion we had about how to characterize the Hamas-Fateh fighting. In the end, I think it is a fight for legitimacy and for the national historical narrative of the Palestinian struggle—will it be a secular nationalist narrative, one that Fateh considers itself the "founding father" of, and which eventually degenerates into the story of a bunch of corrupt old men who are trying to desperately revive that vision? Or is it a more recent and quicker Islamic nationalist narrative that, whether or not one agrees with it, threatens to unravel the entire "history" of the Palestinian struggle and recent "peace-making" efforts?

Update from Gaza[4]
Durham, North Carolina, February 5, 2007

No, I'm still in Durham but keeping up to date, with much concern, with the latest happenings in Gaza via my parents and their vantage point in Gaza City. They passed through a terrifying few days last week—street battles swirled all around them. My mother got stuck (again!) on her way back from Khan Yunis in southern Gaza, where she was visiting my grandmother.

She heard gunshots, and then people began to talk about another "clash," so she stopped at my aunt's house for a while. But then, for fear my father might be foolish enough to drive out to get her, as he's done before (and subsequently found himself in the middle of a gun battle), she decided to take it by foot! Of course, she didn't tell us of her (reckless?) heroics until later.

Halfway there, when it became too dangerous ("I heard gunshots and saw masked gunmen and just said 'Salaam' to them, but I couldn't really see where the gunshots were coming from"), she called my father, who came to pick her up from near the Islamic University, which was up in flames after Fateh forces had attacked it ("It was the saddest thing I've ever seen—a university burning"). That's emblematic, perhaps, of the entire situation in Gaza.

To make matters worse, the electricity had cut off for a straight 40 hours, leaving them amid the incessant ricochet of bullets in the dark.

My father says things are once again "calm" now, as yet another ceasefire goes into effect and hostages from either side have been released. No one knows what tomorrow will hold. They struggle to pass each day and live as normal lives as they know how.

Before I left Gaza, I conducted a series of interviews with fighters representing or affiliated with either side of the fighting from Fateh and Hamas—the result can be seen in "An Eye for an Eye in Gaza."

An Eye for an Eye in Gaza[5]
Durham, North Carolina, February 1, 2007

On January 26, 2007, Mahmoud Abbas, the Palestinian president and leader of Fateh, told a press conference at the World Economic Forum in Davos that talks with Hamas, the ruling party, on the formation of a national unity government ought to conclude within three weeks.

He reiterated his call for presidential and parliamentary elections if the talks failed.

Hamas has refused to endorse another election. It suspended unity government talks on the same day as Abbas's address in Davos after more than a dozen people were killed in Palestinian factional fighting.

Since mid-December, more than 40 Palestinians have been killed and scores injured in what has been described as a power struggle between supporters of Hamas and those of Fateh. The fighting has also encompassed clan feuds and vigilante groups.

[I] spoke to four of those involved in the fighting, asking why they had participated and what they thought the future may hold.[6]

My head is full of slogans and propaganda. It is the end of a very long day. But what scared me the most about it was not the guns and the tough talking, or even the very real prospect of getting caught up in a sudden flare up of the fighting, but rather that I have reached a point where I can understand how and why a Palestinian civil war is possible—and why it is nearly impossible to extract a nation from its grips once its people are deeply and loyally entrenched.

It is a monster that feeds on itself and on the equally believable narratives by which both sides live and die.

As I walk into the Gaza City offices of the Hamas Executive Force, I am greeted by Islam Shahwan, its exuberant and mild-mannered spokesman. He enthusiastically briefs me on a recent operation—cracking a bizarre local drug ring that had been operating out of a cemetery in the southern Gaza town of Khan Yunis—before introducing me to Isam Aqaylan.

Aqaylan, 22, is a stocky young man with a baby face. By day, he is a student of Geography in the Islamic University of Gaza. By night, he is a foot soldier in the Executive Force.

He was stationed near Shifa Hospital in Gaza City when clashes erupted between members of Fateh and the Executive Force a few days after Abbas called for new elections in a speech last month.

AL JAZEERA: How does a "clash" actually start? How did this one start?

AQAYLAN: We were stationed near the hospital to protect the staff there, and to prevent crimes, and the doctors there attest to this. There was a group of Fateh loyalists—members of the *mukhabarat* [intelligence service] moving in an ambulance, trying to track the movements of the members of the Executive Force.

We stopped them once, then let them go. When they didn't leave, we stopped them again, but to avoid trouble, we proceeded to call the head of their unit in the area. We then coordinated with the *mukhabarat* themselves so they would come and get them.

Suddenly, as if from nowhere, we came under direct fire.

There was no pretext for it—and the shots were obviously fired with the intention to injure or kill us. In fact, several of us were injured, and one—Ismail Abu Khair—was killed with a [rocket-propelled grenade].

Members of the *mukhabarat* took position on the rooftops surrounding the hospital and fired at him. His body was torn into pieces. After this, we were very careful. . . .

AL JAZEERA: But why were you personally involved in the clashes?

AQAYLAN: I was there doing my job, which is to provide security for the people of Gaza and safeguard them, as a member of the Executive Force. I never targeted anyone.

Generally what happens is that we would be stationed somewhere to protect ordinary people, and then we would get fired at out of nowhere, and word spreads around that we are targeting them [Fateh]. It's all obscure talk meant to distort the truth.

And then—only after we were targeted—did we begin firing back. . . . [He picks up where he left off about the incident at Shifa Hospital.]

We never fired without justification. Many times we were fired at and didn't fire back because there were civilians around.

There is a clear plan in place to distort the truth and the credibility of this government.

Heavy-grade advanced weaponry was being used by the other side—weapons we'd never seen on the Palestinian front before. And they were being used to attack the Executive Force, not to protect the people. One has to wonder where the funding for these weapons came from.[7]

AL JAZEERA: What about reports that mortars were fired at Fateh strongholds in Gaza, and specifically the claim that Fateh households are being targeted and sometimes surrounded?

AQAYLAN: We condemn the use of mortars and anything that leads to this chaos—it's clearly an independent entity with a score to settle who's doing this.

We have no enemies. We were created to help and support the police force, to provide security and safety for the society, and to coordinate and complement the Presidential Guard. But this has all been reflected very badly, especially since some people are organizing this chaos.

I later interviewed Ahmed Madhoon, a 22-year-old member of a Fateh unit with allegiance to Mohammad Dahlan that he himself was not afraid to call by its commonly known name, the Fateh "death squads." He gave me his version of some of the events that Aqaylan described. While I was interviewing him, he took a phone call from someone he described as "the most important member of the death squads—one who happened to play a very significant role in the clashes that took place last week. And you're about to meet him."

This was Sameeh al-Madhoon, a member of the (pro-Fateh) Preventive Security Forces and also the northern regional commander of the [AMB]. I was driven to his home in northern Gaza in a newly imported white Toyota—the kind you often see in a hundred pieces after an Israeli assassination. We stopped halfway there to pick up an additional bodyguard.

Ahmed described the elder Madhoon as the "orchestrator" of the clashes in December, a ringmaster of sorts.[8]

The man I met in the heart of the Jabaliya refugee camp, allegedly one of those most wanted by Hamas, had a stature strikingly at odds with his larger-than-life public image. With drawn somber eyes and a shapely [trimmed] beard, al-Madhoon greeted us wearing a tracksuit and slippers, and initially we mistook him for a member of his household.

His living room was a showcase of low-grade weaponry—everything from a rocket-propelled grenade launcher to a basic Kalashnikov and, the pride of his collection, an M-16. He talked about all his weapons with the gusto of a proud father, insisting that they were bought with his own savings, not "tainted American money."

"Look, we didn't start this thing with Hamas," he begins abruptly. "It's escalated since elections last January.

"We accepted the situation and then, as part of the presidential Force 17, waited for our salaries to arrive so life can go on as normal. We could have taken over the ministries by force, but we didn't. And slowly, Hamas began to drown in its own mistakes—and resorted to things like murdering and kidnapping Fateh officials.

"Hamas men, members of the Izz-e-Din al-Qassam Brigades, fired at me without precedent. It all started after the Israeli disengagement.

"Abo Fadi [Mohammad Dahlan] gave us Jeeps as a small token of his appreciation, a reward for all of our efforts. Now that's not too much is it? Is it, men?"

He looks around the room for confirmation. He receives quick and enthusiastic nods of approval.

"So anyway, Hamas began to view these Jeeps with contempt, as vehicles of murder—which they were transformed into because of their provocations. I taught some of the Fateh *shabab* [youths] how to fire weapons. I mean, just basic training—again, nothing over the edge, right men?

"I taught them how to fire weapons, and Hamas interpreted this as us training what have come to be known as 'death squads.' No such group exists, as we all know."

He says this steely eyed, and the denial is contrary to claims by the young Madhoon.

"They tried to assassinate me. I even overheard them on this walkie-talkie of theirs, which I confiscated during an interrogation of one of their members."

He opens a small wooden drawer near his bed. It is packed full of amphetamines, sleeping pills, hand grenades, and a large black walkie-talkie.

"There are still negotiations over the hand grenades. If they return ours, we'll return theirs."

He clicks on the walkie-talkie to prove his claim and, through some static, we over-hear what appears to be Hamas operatives giving each other warnings and locations of approaching Israeli unmanned drones monitoring them overhead.

"So that's when my problem with Hamas started. The next day, we shot two members of the Qassam Brigades in retaliation, and things began to escalate. Members of the Qassam Brigades surrounded my house.

"After the elections, Hamas went out in a rally in Jabaliya, and a broadcast car stopped in front of my house and said, 'Here we are in front of the house of the despicable Sameeh Madhoon.'

"Then they shot at a Fateh car.

"The next day, with no shame whatsoever, they shot at a Fateh rally and even hurt some children. They didn't let us express our opinion in the rally. I personally would feel stupid shooting at a rally where people are expressing their political opinions, wouldn't you? But that's Hamas for you.

"I'm just wondering. . . . "

He breaks midsentence to puff at his bedside sheesha and then asks rhetorically:

"Where [is] Hamas leading us?

"I am ready to bring to account anyone who [transgressed against] Hamas. The question is: Are they willing to do the same?

"Look, if they fire at one of us, we'll shoot one of them. If they stop, we stop. It's that simple. If Hamas has a problem with Fateh, then let Haniyeh and Abbas go box it out somewhere, but don't get the street involved.

"We are waiting to see what Hamas's next move is—if things go smoothly, we'll be quiet. But if they are not quiet, then we won't be quiet.

"The whole situation has been reduced to one of family feuds and retaliations, and it's a losing game.

"If they say it's not us and we say it's not us, then we should work together on finding who it actually is."

He says this last statement in a tone that is at once conciliatory and sarcastic. Then he declares:

"As the commander of the northern legion of al-Aqsa Martyrs, I tell you, it is not us who started it, and I deny third-party involvement in the matter.

"Our actions are purely defensive, not offensive. We are also pragmatists—we know they are stronger than us and so are not so stupid as to make the first move."

AL JAZEERA: Who do you ultimately get your orders from?

MADHOON: There is a joint committee that gives us our orders.

AL JAZEERA: And Dahlan?

MADHOON: Look, everyone in the brigades and the security forces receives orders, and we follow those orders. That's all I'm going to say.

AL JAZEERA: What are those orders?

MADHOON: If you are shot, shoot back. If someone from Fateh is abducted, then abduct someone from Hamas. And if they withdraw, we withdraw.

AL JAZEERA: And your weapons? You must have heard recent reports about the [United States] funding Fateh and providing them with training and weapons?

MADHOON: I refuse weapons from the U.S. Our weapons have been purchased at our own expense.

Every action has been started by Hamas. Our kidnapping is a response to their kidnapping. They burnt a shop of my brother's, so I [burned] their brother's place. An eye for an eye.

AL JAZEERA: Are we headed toward civil war?

MADHOON: I blame any renewed escalation on Hamas. But as for civil war, we will be careful to ensure that it doesn't get to this.

We call for unity firstly and lastly, but I will say this much: Our patience is running out, and if Hamas calls us out to the streets for fighting once again, we will gladly oblige—and this time, it won't be defensively, and we won't hold anything back. We cannot stay on the defense forever.

Everyone, including me, has a certain threshold. And once that threshold is passed, I can't guarantee anything.

Right now, it's in the hands of the political leadership.

Hamas is creating provocations. Fateh is really innocent in all of this. Hamas is the one who is trying to instill hate in people [toward] Fateh. Hamas says that fissures are not between two truths, but between a truth and a nontruth—that's how they deal with us. And that is the essence of the problem—they do not consider us to be legitimate.

Palestinian Factions Agree on Unity Government[9]
Durham, North Carolina, February 8, 2007

Well, that's what the press is saying. I've just finished watching the press conference live on *Al Jazeera*.

It's obvious the agreement was more to please the outside world than each other. It is also clear that the international community won't have it either way, so it seems futile in that regard: They've said—in no uncertain terms—they will not accept a government with Hamas members in it, particularly one that does not meet its ridiculous demands. Ultimately, the demands remain hypocritical and unjust. What borders are they agreeing to when Israel itself does not have internationally recognized borders, and why should anyone be forced to accept unconditionally peace deals that are almost unanimously considered flawed or give up their right to self-defense, when they are still occupied? The whole thing is too bizarre for words, too kafkaesque for even Kafka himself.

Anyhow, Abbas was solemnly scratching his hair as the announcement was being made. Haniyeh looked on unceremoniously. Everyone seemed really tense, exhausted, not particularly enthused about anything that had been agreed on apparently.

Which brings us to the meat of the agreement. . . .

Personally speaking, I couldn't figure it out, and I listened to the whole thing. I just heard a bunch of old promises about dialogue and something about "overcoming egos." The most I got was: "They agreed to ban Palestinian bloodshed."

But nothing about the exact points of agreement. Just that it would be "agreeable" to the international community.

Nevertheless, the moment the announcement-less announcement was made, the streets of Gaza—according to my father who relayed the news by phone— erupted in celebration. "Do you hear that? Gunshots!" "What else is new?" I replied, not amused. "No, it's celebratory gunfire! And fireworks!" he said. "I don't think we'll sleep tonight! People are celebrating the agreement!"

Whether it will really be news to celebrate remains to be seen. Recent months haven't provided much to be optimistic about, but I suppose we must try. We have no other choice.

Rumors Abound on Unity Government Makeup[10]
Durham, North Carolina, February 12, 2007

It's semi-official: The individuals have been chosen; the dates have been set. But no official word yet from either the Quartet or Israel.

Everyone in Gaza is waiting anxiously for this miracle plan-of-all-plans, which is supposed to save Gaza from its ultimate spiral toward self-destruction.

According to my father, there is a lot of nail biting in anticipation of the official unveiling. Haniyeh is meant to give a nationwide talk tomorrow (Tuesday) evening upon his return from Mecca. (Incidentally, Amira Hass published a great article in *Haaretz* a few days ago on how Fateh officials were given the VIP treatment out of the West Bank en route to Mecca, while Hamas officials were purposefully delayed and harassed, and how this is official state policy to "ease burdens" on Fateh VIPs . . . hmm.)

Anyway, rumors abound about who will fill which ministerial slot. My father says he's heard that Fateh thug . . . er, strongman, Mohammad Dahlan, will fill the post of "deputy prime minister" to give him a taste of the power he worships but sort of "keep him in check."

"But isn't that just giving him what he wants?" I asked.

"At this point, it's not as important who is in what position as it is that they actually get a unity government done so people can live their lives. . . . We've seen some very black days in Gaza over the past weeks. . . . Did you see Iraq today? Three bombings. You want us to be like that?"

Apparently, the makeup of the new cabinet will include four independents (al-Mubadara's Mustapha Barghouthi is a likely contender here), five from other parties (PFLP, Democratic Front for the Liberation of Palestine [DFLP], etc.), nine Hamas, six Fateh.

Possible contenders include the following:

Minister of Finance: The Third Way's Salam Fayyad

Minister of Interior: Not sure about the name, but someone to replace Saeed Siyam, also from Hamas

Foreign Affairs: Ziad Abu Amr

Deputy Prime Minister: Dahlan

It should be interesting to see if they can make this work. God knows, we need something to work for us right now.

Gaza, Jerusalem, North Carolina[11]
Durham, North Carolina, February 16, 2007

Sahar is a Palestinian from East Jerusalem. I am a Palestinian from Gaza. Our cities are about an hour away (without interruption). But now, because of Israeli closure policies banning Palestinians on either side of the divide from traveling to each other's locales, the only place we could meet was Durham, North Carolina—not Gaza, East Jerusalem, or even Ramallah.

Sahar is a field officer with the Red Cross, here for a few months on a program at Duke University. We had lunch the other day with a mutual Israeli friend who's a Rotary Fellow at the University of North Carolina, Chapel Hill.

Sahar carries an East Jerusalem identification card. I carry a Gaza identification card. This means I am not allowed to cross Erez to visit Sahar in Jerusalem or the West Bank, and she cannot cross over to visit me in Gaza.

The Jerusalem identification card is particularly precarious, because the Israeli government makes it extremely difficult for Palestinian residents of East Jerusalem to maintain their residency there—and thus their status through a series of draconian laws that are not applicable to the city's Jewish residents.

It is part of a decades-old policy of maintaining the Jewish majority in Jerusalem at a ratio of 73.5 to 26.5 percent—and to reduce the Palestinian presence in the city. These measures included the controlling and revoking of identity-card holders inside the city for not paying such things as "television taxes" on time or

not being present at the residency address on a consistent basis (made more difficult by the wall and other restrictions that residents face).

Students who continued to study long years abroad have also had their identification cards revoked. Palestinians who married and stayed abroad lost their right
to be residents of the city. One Palestinian from Jerusalem I met last year who is
married to a Ramallah resident lost her Jerusalem residency and now has to sneak
in and out of the city to visit her parents.

The director of the Centre for Jerusalem Studies at al-Quds University, Huda
al-Imam, explained it well in an interview I did with her a few years back:

> "Our occupation is of a different kind than in the West Bank or
> Gaza," said al-Imam.
> "It has a clear strategy of annexing the land of East Jerusalem
> while not annexing the people, but transferring them," she added.
> "I have a difficult time explaining my legal status to people,
> even Israelis. I am not a citizen of Israel and at the same time I do
> not carry a Palestinian Authority passport [all signs of Palestinian
> nationhood are banned in Jerusalem, including flags]. I carry an
> Israeli 'travel document,' but this does not entitle us to any of the
> rights or services that citizens get."

The idea is, Israel wants East Jerusalem but does not want its people—bad for
its economy and for its demography.

That is one of the reasons Israel made sure its vicious Wall last year cut through
neighborhoods of East Jerusalem, cutting off nearly 150,000 Jerusalemites from
their schools, hospitals, and work in Jerusalem. Eventually, the journey across the
checkpoints and through the Wall may become too arduous, it is hoped, and they
will move out of Jerusalem altogether into the West Bank.

"It's like a force of habit—people reach for cigarettes, I reach for my *hawiya*
(identification card), even here in the United States," joked Sahar.

Jerusalem is the main exit for the north-south link in Palestine, from Bethlehem
to Ramallah, and from northern West Bank to southern West Bank. . . .

Ensure the Survival of Israel—from New Jersey![12]
Durham, North Carolina, February 20, 2007

תהיה אמון...
When things look the most problematic
Is exactly when *emunah* must be the wind beneath our wings
AMANA The YESHA Settlement Organization
Invites you to buy a house in Yesha
Come learn how you, a group of friends or even a community
Can own a home and strengthen the Zionist dream
Amana will reliably manage and rent your home.
Your investment is **insured, protected and 100% legal.**
Congregation Bnai Yeshurun   9:30   Sunday February 25th
641 W. Englewood Avenue   Teaneck, New Jersey

alonf@amana.org.il   nurit@amana.org.il

Amana Settlement Movement

Well, our foul-mouthed friends are at it again. Twelve settlers have reached a new low by attempting to market properties in illegal West Bank settlements, such as Shilo, Kiryat Arba, and Ofra, on the outskirts of Ramallah, to American Jewish congregations.

The convenient transaction, laid out in this flyer, would allow prospective buyers to "ensure Israel's survival" (and our destruction) without ever setting foot there and subsequently having their newly purchased illegal property rented out to illegal settlers at the expense of Palestinians in surrounding villages and towns.

According to the *Jerusalem Post*:

> The project is being billed as an opportunity for American Jews to have a say in Israel's future. The Amana campaign reminds US Jews that they could leave their "thumbprint" on Israel's destiny.
> "We are trying to help the settlements grow and prosper, and we see it as an investment in Israel's future," said Rabbi Pruzansky of Congregation Bnai Yeshurun [whose Teaneck, N.J., synagogue is hosting the event].

The article goes on to say that this new venture will enable young settler families to continue to "repopulate" (read "occupy") the settlements.

In Karnei Shomron, for example, said Amrusi, 100 couples married last year. In her home settlement of Talmon, one-third of the residents live in caravans or rented basements because there is no housing.

I'm devastated inside, really I am. If only it weren't for that whole occupation thing. . . .

If you're interested in buying—or protesting—the informational meeting is being held at Congregation Bnei Yeshurun on February 25.

And not to worry—according to the flyer, your investment is "insured, protected, and 100 percent legal."

The "Ghetto-ization" of Gaza[13]
Durham, North Carolina, February 26, 2007

Things seem quiet on the Eastern front. So says my father, who reports that the two-week truce negotiated at Mecca seems to be holding and that the members of the new Unity Government will be announced in days.

Meanwhile, the ghetto-ization of Gaza continues, with the Erez border crossing (already inaccessible to Palestinians—and Israelis) being designated an "official border" by Israel.

The few Israelis or foreigners who do cross over must have their passports stamped and are listed as having departed the country (to where?).

Amira Hass sums it up nicely in her article "What a Strange Abroad":

> Only Palestinians registered as residents in the Israeli computer system can cross at the Rafah terminal, when it is open. Israel has the authority to ban Gazans from traveling to the West Bank or living there, and has been doing so with increasing fervor since 1991, when it began implementing the closure policy. This is the "abroad" that Israelis require a passport to enter. This is the "abroad" for which Israel argues that it has no responsibility. And this is the greatness of the Israeli occupation: It manages to present itself as nonexistent, while its authority reaches all the way to the bedroom.[14]

What Is Gaza?[15]
Durham, North Carolina, February 26, 2007

It's been nearly two months since we've returned from our most recent visit to Gaza.

So you can imagine how surprised I was when, on a routine trip back from the grocery store last week, my nearly 3-year-old son, Yousuf, unexpectedly asked:

"Mama, what is Gaza?"

What is Gaza? I thought to myself, taking a moment to ponder what was most likely not intended to be a very profound inquiry.

"Is Gaza the *ma'bar* [the border crossing]?" he prodded with uncertainty.

"Well . . . not really. That is part of it. But Gaza is a place. It is home. It is where *Seedo* and *Tete* are," I responded.

"Then, why is it so hard to go there?"

And why do you ask so many questions, I *wanted* to say.

And what an absolutely absurd question it was.

Or was it?

In the mind of my 3-year-old son, Gaza has been reduced to his experiences awaiting entry on borders, under the mercy of an unseen, unknown occupier that all the while claims it is not responsible for this same border.

Leaving aside this peculiar fact, it is perhaps worth pondering Yousuf's question for a moment:

What *is* Gaza? Or rather, what has Gaza become?

The largest open-air prison, say some. An internment camp. A wasteland.

Earlier this month, in yet another step toward isolating Gaza completely, Israel officially designated the Erez crossing between Gaza and Israel as an "international border."

At first glance, this may seem insignificant. After all, this crossing is already inaccessible to most Palestinians and, more recently, Israelis. But the few Israelis who do cross into Gaza must now have their passports "stamped" and are registered as having "departed the country."

It is this paradox that is most exasperating of all. Israel continues to claim it is no longer responsible for Gaza. Gaza is a cesspool of misery and decay and the source of much of its angst it would much like to forget. But all the while, Israel continues to close its borders, control its population registry, control every last mundane detail of life and how we live it as Palestinians.

So it should come as no surprise that a report by John Dugard, a South African law professor and the UN's special rapporteur on human rights in the Palestinian territories, likened the situation in Gaza to Apartheid South Africa in a report issued Tuesday.

It is also no wonder that more and more people are beginning to speak about a future resolution in terms of a one-state, not a two-state, solution, now rendered all but impossible and probably undesirable to many.

So what is Gaza? How *do* I answer Yousuf?

Gaza is that strange faraway place that takes days and sometimes weeks to get to. The place no one wants to talk about anymore, that no one wants to hear about anymore. The place that is at once occupied and free. That is neither this nor that. The place Israel has disengaged itself from—and the place it is now trying to erase. And most of all, the place that no one can provide answers about, least of all to a curious and confused little 3-year-old.

Kiss Me! I'm Turning 3![16]
Durham, North Carolina, March 5, 2007

It's Yousuf's birthday today—and my little boy, the star of my blog, is turning 3!

Where did the months go? Seems like just yesterday that I was nursing him to sleep to the rhythmic battery of artillery fire . . . but that's another story.

We celebrated his big day last week with some friends and family. A little too much sugar was involved, though that is to be expected, I suppose. I figured that he had enough when his cheeks turned bright red by the end of the day.

Who needs cake when you have frosting?

CHAPTER NOTES

1. The full original text of this post is archived at http://www.gazamom. com/2007/01/the-hiatus-explained/, shortened to http://bit.ly/dfByuu.
2. Archived at http://bit.ly/95uecK.
3. Archived at http://bit.ly/b20rYC.
4. Archived at http://bit.ly/cXK6Xd.
5. Laila El-Haddad, "An Eye for an Eye in Gaza," *Al Jazeera English*, February 1, 2007, archived at http://bit.ly/bJtrtb. Reported in Gaza, late December 2006.
6. The whole article, including all four interviews, can be found at ibid.
7. His fears were not unfounded. In a groundbreaking investigative piece by *Vanity Fair*, it was revealed that in fact the Central Intelligence Agency armed and financed Dahlan's forces in an effort to overthrow Hamas following its stunning election sweep. The budget was $1.27 billion over five years. Further, Unity Government talks that Saudi Arabia brokered were sabotaged. David Rose, "The Gaza Bombshell," *Vanity Fair*, April 2008, archived at http://bit.ly/cNLLMr.
8. Sameeh Madhoun would go on to spearhead Fateh's fight against Hamas. He bragged in an interview on a pro-Fateh radio station that he had tortured and killed several Hamas fighters execution-style and torched the homes of others. He then broadcast a pledge to kill all members of the Islamist movement Madhoon was killed on June 14, 2007, during "the Battle of Gaza," in the Nusseirat refugee camp in central Gaza, allegedly by Hamas. Hamas denies the claim, saying it was the angry surviving family members of individuals Madhoon had tortured and killed who executed him.
9. Archived at http://bit.ly/ds9Z70.
10. Archived at http://bit.ly/bqwM0B.
11. Archived at http://bit.ly/bwT8dZ.
12. Archived at http://bit.ly/bOvqEO.
13. Archived at http://bit.ly/dsssva.
14. Amira Hass, "What a Strange 'Abroad,'" *Haaretz*, February 14, 2007, archived at http://bit.ly/bjXUgK.
15. Archived at http://bit.ly/dsssva.
16. Archived at http://bit.ly/aADVfR.

Chapter 16

"You Are Not Here"

Late March through early May 2007

The Mecca Agreement went into effect during the early spring 2007, and with it came the formation of a Palestinian unity government. However, the agreement did little to change the security situation on the ground: Kidnappings, in particular, rose at a dramatic rate. My friend, BBC Gaza correspondent Alan Johnston, was perhaps the most well-known victim. (He was freed four months later after Hamas consolidated its control over the Gaza Strip.)

To make matters worse, by the end of March, as an indirect consequence of the siege, Gaza's northern sewage treatment facility flooded and collapsed, killing five people. Human rights consultant Darryl Li had this to say of the disaster: "This is life in a 'disengaged' Gaza: It is not enough to be locked into an open-air prison by Israel—nor to be turned into a beggar by the international community for voting in a democratic election, nor to be torn apart by internal feuding. Now, Palestinians have to drown in their own shit?"

On a more personal level, I began to focus on some new projects, including directing two short films and narrating a meta-tourism project of Gaza City called You Are Not Here. *By the start of May, I was on my way back to Gaza to shoot* Tunnel Trade. *It would be my last journey before the final division between Hamas and Fateh and the dissolution of the unity government.*

A Hostage to Misfortune[1]
Durham, North Carolina, March 23, 2007

It's been more than a week since Alan Johnston, the BBC's correspondent in Gaza and a friend and colleague of mine, was kidnapped.

Alan and I crossed paths many times while reporting from Gaza. We often bounced story ideas off each other, particularly during the Israeli disengagement of 2005 and the historic Palestinian elections last January. In fact, both his office and home are a few short blocks from my own.

Alan is one of those well-seasoned reporters with a real sense for the human element to the story, the one that matters most. He has such a comforting voice that I could hardly imagine him getting angry at anyone, least of all a kidnapper.

And to his credit, he is also one of the few—if not only—foreign reporters living in Gaza, because most opt to remain in Jerusalem and parachute in when the occasion (or editor) calls for it.

This isn't the first time they've tried to come for him, of course, but it's the first time they've been successful. As a precaution, his office removed the BBC sign by their multilock door in Gaza.

In better times, we used to joke about the day he would finally get kidnapped: what kind of biscuits his captors would serve him and how he would take his tea—a reference to the experiences of former captives, conversations that seem ominous and not so funny in hindsight.

I say "finally," because catch-and-release kidnappings have become so frequent in Gaza in recent years as to become banal. The pattern is predictable: A foreign-aid worker or journalist (or someone mistaken for a foreigner) is abducted; certain, often juvenile, demands are made; and the captive is released unharmed—though shaken up—a few days (and often hours) later. Alan's abduction is only unusual in its length. Aside from Gilad Shalit, the longest incident of captivity in Gaza was that of two Fox News reporters, held for nearly two weeks.

According to the Gaza-based Palestinian Human Rights Centre, 28 kidnappings, with a total of 55 foreigners, including journalists and international workers, have taken place in Gaza during the past three years. Every hostage has been released unharmed.

During the same period, nobody has ever claimed responsibility for the kidnappings.

Though kidnappings have waned as a phenomenon in Gaza, they still happen; when they do, they elicit widespread disapproval and resentment in Palestinian society. Alan's kidnapping is no exception; in many ways, it is the proverbial last straw.

The last thing Gazans want to do is to drive away the few remaining foreigners—often aid workers—from the lonely open-air prison they call home. Or to further tarnish their image abroad, they say.

But their more immediate concern is their feeling that the Palestinian government and accompanying security forces have been too soft on kidnappers. . . . Critics, mainly local human-rights groups and nongovernmental organizations but also many civic groups and unions, say they are rewarding the kidnappers instead of punishing them, while providing an incentive for anyone with a grievance, real or imagined, to kidnap again in the future.

One can at least take solace in the fact that not a single act of kidnapping has ever turned bloody, as in Iraq.

All the major Palestinian groups—Hamas, Fateh, even the more combative AMB—have condemned the kidnapping, though recycled press releases are of little comfort, I am certain, to someone in captivity, and of little concern to a kidnapper who knows he will get what he wants anyway.

People in Gaza also seem to think press releases are no longer sufficient. The security forces need to be more proactive and take a stronger role in quashing the kidnapping phenomenon and bringing the perpetrators to justice, they say.

On the other hand, if the security forces can't seem to stop killing each other, who's to say they can stop criminal gangs committing wanton acts of kidnap?

. . . Certainly, a large element of all this is the hesitancy of any single armed group, or security force, to act on its own lest a new round of factional fighting erupt. Although Hamas has its own security force, only those under President Mahmoud Abbas's authority are authorized to act in such circumstances.

More than anything, Alan's abduction is yet another unfortunate manifestation of Gaza's lawlessness, another symptom of a society with no state, and no future.

And ordinary Palestinians in Gaza are certainly not reacting with complacency to his abduction.

"People are sick of such behavior," one friend in Gaza City remarked. "They blame the absence of law and order and also see this as a symptom of this absence, and they are pointing the finger at both the government and the president for not being able to impose it.

"So far no one has moved to take action against them, though they know who is behind the abduction, and that is what bothers people most. And they can't take any action unless they both [Hamas and Fateh] unite together to impose the law. . . ."

Gaza's Dogmosh clan is being blamed for the kidnapping, though it is now denying this. It is a gang responsible for a spate of kidnappings and criminal acts in recent years in Gaza. And this may be the latest in a series of its attempts to pressure police to release detained clan members.

The timing of the kidnapping is not accidental either—Alan was kidnapped only days before the new Palestinian government was to be announced last week.

. . . [I]n the murky world of Gaza lawlessness, Alan's kidnapping could have been perpetrated by pretty much any group with a small militia to back them up (increasingly easy to hire in Gaza these days) and a laundry list of motives to choose from.

As a neighbor put it, "I don't know who—or what—to believe any more."

The Death Swamps[2]
Durham, North Carolina, March 27, 2007

It was bound to happen. All the major humanitarian organizations issued endless reports and warnings about its imminent flooding. But even if the funding were available, the permission to expand and renovate the facility was not granted by the necessary "authorities" who built it (on a major aquifer) in the first place.

I'm referring to the collapse and flooding of Gaza's northern sewage treatment facility, known locally as the "Death Swamps."

Five people—including two toddlers and two elderly women—died when the cesspool that has been created as a result of the facility working at almost four times its normal capacity flooded today.

Darryl Li

"This was not only foretold; it happened twice before, in 1988 and 1993," said human rights consultant and friend Darryl Li, who has worked for Israeli, Palestinian, and international human-rights groups. Darryl's last trip was in August, to this very facility.

According to Darryl, the sewage facility is a collection of seven human-made lagoons at the edge of the former settlement bloc. "When working properly, the facility cleans waste water and then redeposits it into the aquifer. It has long been described as a major environmental problem: It is overtaxed, and untreated sewage has long been polluting the groundwater in the area; and the facility has flooded at least twice."

The facility stopped functioning entirely in the weeks after the power cutoff last year (when Israel bombed Gaza's power plant) and later functioned at very low efficiency levels with generators. Water levels consequently rose dangerously high.

The embankments of the cesspool have also been the target of frequent Israeli shelling, threatening their integrity, said Li.

Donor funding has been pledged for years, but the facility now falls in the border "security zone," and no guarantees have been forthcoming about construction or allowing the water to be transferred from Bayt Lahiya to the new site.

The only emergency solution is basically to pump the raw sewage out onto Gaza's seacoast. This would pollute Gaza's seacoast and the big desalinization plant in Israel's port city of Ashdod immensely.

According to a UN OCHA report issued in 2004, 110 acres were already flooded by waste from the plant by that year, and the area was growing. Fifty percent of the children in neighboring villages had digestive problems related to the overflowing sewage and contamination of drinking water in the area.

"In November 2003, an international donor withdrew support from an earlier agreement to fund a new treatment plant through a concessional credit. The donor was concerned by continuing political uncertainty and by anticipated delays in project implementation. The donor also feared that international technical consultants might not gain access into Gaza," read the report, in reference to Israeli restrictions (then and now even more) on the entry of foreigners into Gaza.

OCHA recommended the construction of an additional basin that would reduce the volume in the lake and, eventually, the construction of a new treatment plant.

New donors expressed interest later that year, but local officials say Israel has threatened to disrupt (by way of bombings) any construction effort. And now, with all major funding stopped and barely enough money to pay government workers—let alone renovate a major sewage treatment plant—there is little hope that anyone will take on this project.

"This is life in a 'disengaged' Gaza: It is not enough to be locked into an open-air prison by Israel—nor to be turned into a beggar by the international community for voting in a democratic election, nor to be torn apart by internal feuding. Now, Palestinians have to drown in their own shit? I can't wait to hear the latest excuse about how this, too, is their own fault," Li said.

You Are Not Here![3]
Rotterdam, Netherlands, April 12, 2007

I'm writing this as I coast across the Dutch countryside by train to the city of Rotterdam. What, you might ask, am I doing in the Netherlands? Well, besides stopping to smell the flowers and admire the windmills and sample the Gouda and whatnot, I am here to attend the biannual Dutch Electronic Art Festival (DEAF) conference.

Specifically, I am here to present a project/game/simulation that a few good folks and I have been working on together for a few months. (OK, they worked on it, I am just helping out.)

It's called *You Are Not Here* (YANH) and it is basically an urban tourism mash-up, fusing locations from one map, often in a conflict zone or isolated area, onto another urban area. Case one: Baghdad in New York.

The one I was graciously asked to help develop was Gaza in Tel Aviv. I know you must be thinking—Gaza in Tel Aviv? Gaza isn't Tel Aviv, make no mistake about it, nor does the game propose that it can be (thus, the name YANH).

What it does do is allow participants to become "meta-tourists" of sorts, to experience a tour of Gaza in the streets of Tel Aviv. As they do so, they can dial in site-specific audio codes to hear none other than yours truly narrating what they are seeing, as if they were in Gaza at this precise location.

We chose around 15 locations in Gaza worthy of sightseeing (ranging from the gastronomical to the political . . . for example, Gaza's bombed-out Palestine Stadium and Kathem's ice-cream parlor—a landmark, and the most famous ice-cream shop there).

YouAreNotHere.org

The idea is to bridge the psychological and political divide and challenge the conventional ideas about space and borders, says co-creator Mushon Zer-Aviv.

"We are trying to take terms like 'Palestinian' and 'Gaza' back to scale . . . terms that have been overblown or taken out of the human proportion by the media. We are trying to redefine the branding that has been imposed on Gaza by the mass media and years of conflict and reclaim the mediated perception of the city."

Says Mushon:

> While the disengagement of Israel from the Gaza Strip in the summer of 2005 was thought to open a new hope for Gazan civilians, it has practically turned Gaza to the biggest jail in the world. You see most Israelis are tired of the 40-years-long occupation and want to see it end. Yet in Tel Aviv, the general mind-frame is that after

the disengagement we are not *in* Gaza any more and therefore are not longer responsible for it. This is something we want to address through YANH.

My job has been to write out the descriptions of the locations our tourists are visiting and narrate them for the audio tour—easier said than done. It's been a real challenge immersing myself into the simulation and speaking through my voice to the participants as if they were actually seeing and living in the location I am describing to them ("Notice up ahead" . . . "If you look to your left" . . . etc.).

It's not all rosy, as I mentioned (notice the broken beach umbrella icon in the map . . . as well as the broken palm tree icons in the Baghdad map). Although we have chosen locations like Gaza's most famous ice-cream shop or historic stops like the Samara baths, we also guide them through the national football stadium, which was bombed by fighter jets last year, and Gaza's "Beach" refugee camp, and we even try to simulate sonic-boom attacks and electricity blackouts in the middle of the audio tour.

The project is due to launch in mid-May, when participants in Tel Aviv can obtain the finished, double-sided map (Gaza on one side, corresponding streets and locations in Tel Aviv on the other in English, Hebrew, and Arabic) from BLOCK magazine, which is collaborating with us. They also can download it for free from the Web.[4]

Out of Amsterdam[5]
Durham, North Carolina, April 19, 2007

I hate airports, I really do. I get so nervous when I travel that Yassine says I begin to look suspicious. When that dreadful message about the threat level increasing to orange or whatever blares out on the intercom system as I casually walk through the seating area, I feel that the collective glances of the entire waiting area are on me, as if they were thinking, "What if it's her?"

The same, of course, goes for the airplane. As I try to find my seat, consciously attempting to act just like anyone else, I can sense passengers' anxiety-filled eyes jolting up in fear that I might be "the one" and, heaven forbid, the one who is seated next to "them."

It gets really bad when I'm going through security, especially in busy airports.

Passengers, many in a rush, frantically remove their shoes, bag their liquids, and throw away their water bottles, some with grunts of annoyance. And every now and then I'll notice someone briefly staring me down, as if to say, "This is all your fault. Your people. Your kind. They are responsible for making our airport experiences so miserable. Because of *you*, I have to toss out my Snapple iced tea and my Lancôme toner."

Then another, more sympathetic glance, as if in my defense, "You are a victim too," all said in silence.

But I don't want either of them. By that point I just want to disappear, become totally invisible. I just want to pass through that airport and get to my gate like anyone else, without the accusatory, uncertain, or sympathetic glances.

More often than not, my airport experiences go something like that. I am sometimes pleasantly surprised, and don't get questioned or screened in front of a swarm of passengers.

But on Sunday, I left Amsterdam after the conclusion of the DEAF conference. I reach my gate out of breath after a mad dash to make my flight on time. Not surprisingly, I was stopped by security personnel for further questioning. The questioning was only unusual in that it happened on my way *out* of Amsterdam, not in, and involved detailed questions about what I was doing in the Netherlands, not why I was headed to the United States.

As is often the case with these routine questions, everything and anything you say suddenly takes on new meaning and can seem absurdly incriminating.

It went something like this:

> AIRPORT GUY: Step over here please.
> [I step beyond the podium accidentally.]
>
> AIRPORT GUY: I said *here*, not there. So . . . what were you doing in the Netherlands?
>
> ME: Attending a conference. In Rotterdam. [DEAF.]
>
> AIRPORT GUY: Aha. . . .
>
> ME: No, really.
>
> AIRPORT GUY: Do you have an invitation?
>
> ME: Don't you usually ask for that on the way in?
> [Stern stare]
>
> ME [nervously]: Ah, you're in luck, I still have it. . . .
>
> AIRPORT GUY: And what exactly were you presenting?
> [Why the hell does that matter?]
>
> ME [now sounding ridiculous and completely unconvincing]: Um . . . a project I am working with some friends . . . an urban tourism mash-up of Tel Aviv and Gaza.
> [Blank stare]
> Do you want me to show you the maps?
>
> AIRPORT GUY: Please.
> [He looks at maps confused and walks over to show them to his supervisor.]
> And where were your team members from?
> [What the hell does that have to do with anything?]
>
> ME: Um . . . Israel, France, and New York. . . .

[I decide not to mention the fact that Thomas, the Frenchman, was mistakenly arrested in John F. Kennedy Airport after being confused for an Algerian terrorist or that Kati's apartment is tapped.]

AIRPORT GUY: Why were you in Qatar and Oslo last year?

ME: What?

AIRPORT GUY: "You have visas here . . . . "

ME [stammering]: Oh right . . . um . . . because . . . I was visiting *Al Jazeera,* one of my employers."

AIRPORT GUY: Do you have something to verify that? A press card?

ME: What? No. I freelance.

AIRPORT GUY: Of course you do.

ME: Excuse me?

AIRPORT GUY: Nothing. And Oslo?

ME: [I was making contact with the local members of the YANH cell there you moron, what do you think I was doing?] Attending a conference on globalization and media activism.

AIRPORT GUY: Aha. Let me run this by my supervisor again.

After an animated briefing that includes the maps and the invitation, I am allowed to move onto the plane.

Terrorism, the Media, and Virginia Tech[6]
Durham, North Carolina, April 19, 2007

"Thanks to you, I die like Jesus Christ, to inspire generations of the weak and the defenseless people."

These are the words uttered by the name now known across America—and much of the world; the name plastered on every newspaper headline, Internet magazine, radio and television station.

But very few networks or newspapers chose to emphasize this statement, or even publish it. It was relegated to the end of the text in almost every article I read on the incident.

Why then is there no media frenzy to uncover and parse to death every possible "Christian fundamentalist" connection that Cho might have had, even seemingly benign ones ("You belonged to the Christian fellowship you say? You attended a local church? The church once hosted a controversial right-wing leader? Your high school roommate's estranged cousin attended anti-East rallies?"). You get my drift.

There is no question that Tuesday's attack was horrific and very sad.

What I am interested in though is, as is often the case, how is the media covering it?

The coverage initially started out by mentioning—between the lines—that this "did not seem to be an act of terrorism." OK, I might be picking at straws here, but if this isn't terrorism, what is? Not politically motivated, you say? Is that the standard common definition of terrorism anyway these days?

The attacker, as in the Baruch Goldstein case,[7] is being described as a mentally unstable wacko, one screw loose too many, and the attack as an unfortunate case where a gun found its way to the wrong hands—an exception to the rule, despite the fact that a special justice found his insight and judgment to be normal.

The methodical nature of his killing rampage and his pre-rampage preparations seems to add credence to this.

The question I'd like to pose is, given his preceding statement, which was extracted from his so-called manifesto and aired on NBC: Couldn't this, too, be classified as an act of religious terrorism (by the same standards employed by this media in categorizing "Islamic terrorism" or "jihadism" or whatever)?

Or more precisely, to make a fair analogy, couldn't one say that Cho derived "his inspiration" from Christian doctrine or the "Christian culture of martyrdom"?

I dread to think how the mass media would even begin to speculate and evaluate this if those same words were uttered by an attacker who happened to be of Muslim descent (exchanging Jesus Christ with some other Muslim figure). . . .

Gaza Bound[8]
London, England, May 1, 2007

We're off to Gaza again, Yousuf and I. Just a heads-up. We're currently en route (in Heathrow Airport to be exact) and will arrive in Cairo tonight, *inshallah*. From there, we drive directly to the Rafah border, across Sinai with our ever-reliable taxi driver, Atiyah (who works the Cairo-Rafah circuit and who himself is a refugee from Beer il Sabi'), in hopes the border is open. If not, we will return and spend the night in Arish.

CHAPTER NOTES

1. The full original text of this post is archived at Laila El-Haddad, "A Hostage to Misfortune," *Guardian Comment Is Free*, March 23, 2007, http://www.guardian.co.uk/commentisfree/2007/mar/23/itsbeenoveraweek, shortened to http://bit.ly/dhyOyM.
2. Archived at http://bit.ly/bDDsyb.
3. Archived at http://bit.ly/8XWVMf.
4. Find out more about YANH at http://youarenothere.org/.
5. Archived at http://bit.ly/cy8t7G.
6. Archived at http://bit.ly/94yiK2.
7. Baruch Goldstein was a Jewish Israeli-American physician who perpetuated the Ibrahimi Mosque massacre in Hebron in 1994, killing 29 Palestinian Muslims in prayer and wounding another 150 during the holy month of Ramadan with an automatic rifle and hand grenades. See http://bbc.in/bskwSR and http://en.wikipedia.org/wiki/Baruch_Goldstein.
8. Archived at http://bit.ly/bmuXwi.

Chapter 17

Gaza: Gloom, Impermanence, Dread

Early May through early June 2007

The month preceding June's "Battle of Gaza," and the collapse of the unity government that it signaled, was the worst I had witnessed in years. It was a dreadful combination of street-to-street infighting at its absolute peak, rampant criminality, and Israeli attacks. Gone completely were the days of postelection optimism or the relief and joy that overcame the public after the announcement of the Mecca Agreement. The first piece of advice I got upon my return: "Don't go out after evening prayers. Don't keep any valuables—particularly cell phones—in your car. And whatever you do, don't keep a lot of cash on hand. You'll do well to just stay alive."

The "Dayton Plan"[1] to sabotage the unity government was also in full swing. The U.S.-created coalition of Israel, Egypt, and Jordan had been training and equipping Fateh to defeat Hamas. Israel briefly opened the Rafah crossing, which it had otherwise shut down 50 percent of the year, to allow U.S.-funded, Jordanian-trained, Fateh fighters to enter Gaza from Egypt.

Meanwhile, the ethnic cleansing of occupied East Jerusalem continued. The Israeli government approved the construction of 20,000 new settler housing units there, raising the number of settlers living illegally on Palestinian land to 570,000 and creating an uninterrupted stretch of Jewish-only housing and amenities in an area ("E-1") that historically accounts for 30 to 40 percent of the Palestinian economy combined.

Gaza Gloom²
Gaza City, Palestine, May 4, 2007

Well, we made it safe and arguably sound, after another exhaustive battle through the nightmare that is Rafah crossing, or, as Gazans like to call it, "Rafah Resort."

The good news is we made it through after spending just one night in Arish—and just before the crossing was closed again. Of course, this was not without jostling through hundreds of tired, heat-exhausted, and dusty passengers. The *Khamaseeni* winds were fierce, dry, and merciless.

Because the crossing had been closed for a week before Thursday, there was a backlog of passengers, and the flow was excruciatingly slow. . . . I literally had to jam my way through the arms of Egyptian security guards, *à la* "Try and stop me," Yousuf in tow; together with another woman and her children, we steamrolled our way through a crack in the opening of one of the doors leading to the Egyptian side of the passage.

This move, in combination with a snide remark I made to the head Egyptian security guy about how they run the border on bribes, almost got me arrested. I was "asked" to apologize publicly for this accusation, which I refused to do. So my passport was relegated to the back of the pile until the "investigator" showed up, and then one officer "took pity" on me and let me through.

Because the crossing operates only a limited number of hours when it *does* open (on Thursday, only five hours), everyone is desperate to get through. Who knows when it will open again?

. . . Upon arrival, my first impression of Gaza after a few months of absence can be summarized in one word: gloom. The garbage-strewn streets were covered in a thin layer of dust, of course, from the winds, but it was not only that. It was the people. They were altogether absent from the streets—on a Thursday night.

"People are scared," offered my friend, as we went to grab some ice cream. "They are scared of the situation, of the absolute lapse of order and law, of where we are headed. And they are depressed and despondent—there's no hope anymore for anything. Not even with this unity government. The world has abandoned them. And the result is a foregone conclusion."

Forget about light at the end of the tunnel. The tunnel itself, as far as Gaza is concerned, has been destroyed.

The Honey's Just Better over There[3]
Gaza City, Palestine, May 6, 2007

We went to my father's farm on Friday. Spring is here. The flowers are in full bloom.

Gaza has a little more color to it, and, for just a few weeks, the gritty, gray horizon of unfinished cinderblocks is disrupted. Purple Jacaranda flowers burst into full blossom on the city streets, and the Jundi Park's hibiscus bushes are enflamed in vibrant reds.

It's also the best time to get some local honey—the good stuff, not the ones where the bees' diet is supplemented with sugar. As things go here, honey is expensive—at least 50 to 70 shekels per kilo ($12 to $17 per pound), depending on quality.

So my mother's friend and I strike up a conversation about honey. She tells me about her friend who lost everything and is now in debt after her bees gathered pollen from their neighbor's farm, newly treated with pesticides for the spring.

They dropped like, well, bees, and half her hive was gone, just like that. "The poor thing was crying on the phone. It was a project she'd started with a microloan from the Ministry of Agriculture.

"But anyway, the honey is better near the border," she adds.

"Near the border?" I inquire.

"Yes, you know, the Imsaddar household. Their farms are near the border with Israel in eastern Gaza. . . . Their bees fly across the border and gather pollen from the eucalyptus trees and orange groves in their farms. So the honey is just better."

How is it that honey from bees gathering pollen from trees across the border is better? Is it because the flowers are freer? Less empty, or trapped, or sad? Less occupied, perhaps?

"I think they just have more trees and flowers there. After all, most of our groves were razed during the Intifada," another friend explained.

Crime and Chaos[4]
Gaza City, Palestine, May 10, 2007

On Wednesday, a shadowy group calling itself the Army of Islam took official responsibility for the first time in a yet-to-be-aired video for the kidnapping of BBC correspondent Alan Johnston.

The group is the second in a month to claim responsibility for Johnston's kidnapping, but this is the first time demands have been made, including the release of Abu Qatada and other Muslim prisoners in Britain.

That has prompted discussion of whether al-Qaeda has made inroads into Gaza. Hamas leaders themselves, as well as others, have warned that its continued isolation and marginalization from the decision-making process will inevitably result in the growth of Salafi and al-Qaeda–type organizations in Gaza "who will make Hamas look like cupcakes."

But the question remains whether this is truly an al-Qaeda–type act or—as many here believe—merely one disguised as such in an attempt to gain moral and financial support from the organization or simply to gain more attention and secure a more lucrative financial deal for Johnston's return. After all, nothing in Gaza is ever quite what it seems.·

Many here say . . . that Johnston's capture should be read in the broader context of Gaza's continued lapse into chaos. And in the murky world of Gaza's lawlessness, anything goes. It is simply one more symptom of a society methodically cast into the abyss. Decaying, debilitated, and on the verge of implosion.

The perpetrators are still thought to be members of Gaza's infamous Dogmush clan, who ally themselves wherever the money is. . . .

The minister of information, Mustapha Barghouti, cast doubt on the authenticity of the video. Hamas continues to distance itself from the group. And ordinary Palestinians don't know what to think any more. One told me, "I'm convinced it's just an act of senseless, purposeful destruction . . . someone taking advantage of the situation. . . . I'm scared we're turning into Iraq. I just never expected it to get this bad."

All people *do* know here is how to be careful. Very careful.

"Don't go out after evening prayers. Don't keep any valuables—particularly cell phones—in your car. And whatever you do, don't keep a lot of cash on hand," suggested my father's friend upon my arrival last week. You can't even shop for groceries any more without worrying you'll be robbed—an elderly man's car was stolen a few days ago in Gaza city as he was buying fruit. All the car thief had to do was ask him for his keys—and cell phone. "That's how bad it's gotten," lamented a neighbor.

Indeed, during just a few months, Gaza has turned into something reminiscent of America's Wild West. The streets are now all but empty by sunset—just replace the tumbleweeds with plastic bags. Residents are more afraid than they've ever been.

"We just live to wait," says my friend Fares. "We wait for the border to open again. We wait for the salaries. We wait for the law to be restored."

This has happened despite an overabundance of security forces—some 70,000 loyal to Fateh and another 6,000 loyal to Hamas. Fueled by competing loyalties and foreign monies with vested interests, they are too busy fighting each other to stop crime. . . .

Gaza's Protectors Are Its Thieves[5]
Gaza City, Palestine, May 11, 2007

"*Ilee hameeha, haremeeha.*" That is how my friend Taghreed describes the situation in Gaza now. In other words, its protectors are its thieves.

Yesterday, new security deployments began—yet again—as part of the unity government's new "security plan," which will, in three separate stages, see security reinforcements comprising both Hamas and Fateh members fan out across Gaza.

But the plan was not made public, and it was unclear to everyone, including the security forces themselves, what exactly the purpose of the new deployment was and whether it was truly a mixed police force.

Two members of the newly deployed security force patrol a street in Gaza City.

As I was walking down the street yesterday, I stopped to chat with two policemen who had been deployed as part of the new plan. Before taking off, they asked me in hushed whispers, "Tell me, have you actually seen any Hamas members deployed? We heard rumors that they were supposed to be."

That evening, we had a sleepless night as Hamas members and newly deployed police guards went at it; apparently, some in Fateh were not thrilled at the prospect of guarding the streets alongside their rivals. Some in Hamas, in turn, were not pleased that they were not yet offered this opportunity and had not been deployed.

People in general have mixed feelings about the deployment. Some are holding out hope that it can resolve, or at least stabilize, the situation. Others consider it too little too late and just like deployments before it, which never managed to secure the Strip.

I personally believe in the continued absence of a strong, central, and sovereign authority; without the dissolution of both the global and Israeli siege, Gaza can never be truly secure. The two go hand in hand.

To quote Alvaro de Soto, the UN special coordinator for the Middle East Peace Process who just resigned today:

> The only way to impose law and order in the territories and to bring about a cease-fire is by strengthening the Palestinian security

mechanisms and creating conditions that will enable them to operate under a single command. . . . [T]his is possible only under the
Palestinian unity government. I find it hard to understand how
polarization in Palestinian society, sabotaging the unity government, and attempting to prevent it from fulfilling its responsibility
serves Israel's interests.[6]

The Ethnic Cleansing of Jerusalem Continues[7]
Gaza City, Palestine, May 12, 2007

I wrote about this yesterday for *Al Jazeera*'s website, but I'm still disappointed
(should I even be surprised anymore?) that is has not gained as much media
attention as, say, a certain Mickey Mouse–like show in Gaza. But I guess that's
because we're heartless, violent thugs who only want Israel's destruction. Israel,
on the other hand, builds things on Palestinian land, for, well, its security and
livelihood.

Who's destroying?

I'm referring to the plan that the Israeli government approved on Thursday for
20,000 new settler housing units, enough for roughly 70,000 to 90,000 new illegal
settlers, in occupied East Jerusalem, raising the number of settlers living illegally
on Palestinian land in the occupied West Bank to 570,000. That's 10 percent of the
Israeli population, folks.

To put things in perspective, these settlements will create an uninterrupted
stretch of Jewish-only housing and amenities between the eastern sector of the city
and two West Bank settlement blocs, in an area (the "E-1" area) that historically
accounts for 30 to 40 percent of the Palestinian economy combined. This is, of
course, despite continued (empty) promises by Israeli governments not to build
or expand there.

In typical Israeli government fashion, the announcement came just one day
after the World Bank issued a scathing report of Israel's West Bank closure policies, which also happened to coincide with the demolition of a special-needs home
in East Jerusalem (despite the fact that the report found most building violations
took place in West Jerusalem).

Israeli Border Police forcibly evicted the caregivers and children at dawn,
according to the Israeli Committee Against House Demolitions. A prayer vigil was
held before the center was completely demolished.

"Currently, freedom of movement and access for Palestinians within the West
Bank is the exception rather than the norm, contrary to the commitments undertaken in a number of Agreements," stated the report, which also said Israel had
purposefully fragmented the West Bank into cantons completely disconnected
from one another.

But as a legal adviser to the PA told me, the report offered nothing new as far as Palestinians were concerned: "We've been saying this for years. We just wish the world would wake up and not just listen but actually do something. We have a situation where every European state is currently violating its own laws by trading with Israeli settlements.

"If they are serious about the two-state solution, it's time for them to live up to their own rhetoric and do something about it."

Now, who exactly believes that a two-state solution is still viable?

Popcorn?[8]
Gaza City, Palestine, May 16, 2007

Things have been crazy in Gaza over the past two days. Very crazy. In between working and actually trying to keep our wits about us as we've been holed up indoors for two days now, I've had little time to blog.

Things are tenuously calm at the moment, with on-again-off-again gunfire, which is better than it was only a few hours ago. But things in Gaza have a way of changing very quickly—for better or for worse. Volatility is its defining characteristic.

We happen to sort of be in the eye of the storm, as it were. Fierce battles employing mortars, rocket-propelled grenades (RPGs), and heavy machine-gun fire were raging all around our house today, at times only a block away, interspersed with the thuds of Israeli gunships bombing areas of eastern and northern Gaza.

Yousuf, of course, became more and more concerned as the day passed, until I finally told him they were not firing, but rather making an enormous pot of popcorn outside that would fill the streets once it was done. At first he wasn't convinced; then, he later remarked, "Mama, I don't really like this kind of popcorn!" When the firing died down, he ran into my room excitedly shouting, "Mama, Mama! I think the popcorn is done!!"

The city was literally transformed into a ghost town, and civilian life was all but paralyzed.

. . . Impromptu checkpoints were set up along the major roads, cutting off access from Gaza City to the north and south of the strip.

Unidentified snipers took positions on high-rise towers through the city, as both factions vied for strategic control of various locations.

The victims, of course, in all of this were the residents, particularly those who lived in the towers. Many residents complained of having spent the past two days holed up in their kitchens without electricity and of ambulances not being given access to the injured in the buildings.

One woman told me gunmen searched apartments for armed men and set several flats on fire.

The most troubling part is how this is unfolding with such purpose, and yet with so little protest. There is something far more sinister behind it all—namely, the unambiguous plot of the United States to undermine the unity government by arming, training, and "strengthening" Abbas, Dahalan, and their respective security forces. The latest plan was uncovered in a Jordanian newspaper last week before being whisked off the presses.

. . . For now, we wait, and see what tomorrow brings.

Fanning the Flames in Gaza[9]
Gaza City, Palestine, May 16, 2007

The United States is arming Fateh in the hope of defeating Hamas. Meanwhile, everyone suffers.

No one ever seems quite sure how or why the spates of violence begin in Gaza, but a few days on, it becomes irrelevant anyway.

Firefights including heavy arms and mortars continued to rage all around Gaza City, all while Israeli gunships pounded east and north of the city, which has been transformed to a ghost town. Even the most foolhardy opted to stay indoors, and all but a lone convenience store closed. Masked Fateh and Hamas gunmen patrolled every street corner and took positions on every major high-rise tower, keeping residents, schoolchildren, and university students penned indoors as battles swirled around them.

Fateh called for a general strike and has taken to shooting into the air to scare people off the streets, stopping cars at self-imposed checkpoints, and detaining men with beards in response to what they say was a deadly Hamas ambush of the presidential guard (Hamas has denied involvement). Israel has claimed responsibility for the deaths of at least two of the Fateh guards. But by that point, it didn't matter anymore. The revenge machine was already in high gear. In some locations, angry Palestinians reportedly pelted rocks at jeeps belonging to the presidential guard.

Many here are referring to the on-again-off-again battles as a new *Nakba*, one that has coincided with the day Palestinians mark as their original "catastrophe"—when the state of Israel was declared on 78 percent of historic Palestine.

Tuesday marked the 59th anniversary. "Our *Nakba* has become two *Nakbas*," young protestors chanted in unison on the city streets this morning.

Palestinians are not pleased about the ever-worsening violence, which is threatening to unravel the recently negotiated unity government; however, there is little they can do about it besides watching things unfold to their inescapably grim conclusion, they say.

But the news that really upset many here was word of the Israeli government briefly opening the Rafah crossing with Egypt, which it has shut down 50 percent of the year to average residents here, to allow U.S.-funded, Jordanian-trained, Fateh reinforcements (450 members of the elite Badr Brigade) inside.

The fact is Gaza is not combusting spontaneously.

. . . [J]ust over a week ago, a 16-page secret American document was leaked to a Jordanian newspaper outlining an action plan for undermining and replacing the Palestinian national-unity government. The document outlines steps for building up Abbas and his security forces, leading to the dissolution of the Parliament and a strengthening of U.S. allies in Fateh in the lead-up to new elections.

Events have unfolded according to plan, with not so much as a peep or word of protest from the major world governments.

. . . The United States has allocated as much as $84 million to this end, directly funding President Mahmoud Abbas and Fateh strongman Mohammad Dahlan and their security forces, which are often one and the same, as the Fateh militias engaged in bitter battles with Hamas and even fired missiles at Israel.

That doesn't change the resentment in the streets over what has unfolded—and the utter cynicism associated with it.

"I'm just saying, what are they fighting over—the trash burning in the streets?" said one shopkeeper, referring to the piles of accumulated rubbish gathering as a result of a weeklong municipality protest.

"We all know what's going to happen next," he continued. "Government officials will convene with the military commanders and ask them to show restraint. The gunmen will withdraw from the streets. And for a few more weeks, things will be calm again. We're in a maelstrom, and I can't really see a way out. Gaza is burning. And the world is watching."

The Ghostly Streets, the Ghostly Skies[10]
Gaza City, Palestine, May 17, 2007

We're used to things going from bad to worse very quickly here. But we never expected the situation to get as bad as it has during the past few days.

After a terrifying 24 hours, we awoke this morning to sporadic gunfire and ghostly streets.

It was a welcome change. Sleep-deprived and anxious, my colleague Saeed, on his first visit to Gaza, and I headed to Rafah in the southern part of the Strip to continue shooting a series of documentaries.

Though the gunfire had subsided, the gunmen were still patrolling the streets, each this time casually manning his own turf, masked and fully armed.

Impromptu checkpoints were still set up along the main Gaza-Rafah road, and we were stopped for identification and affiliation checks.

As we approached Rafah, we received word that clashes had broken out there, too, following the funeral of four Hamas men killed in an Israeli air strike the night before.

We decided to avoid the town center, and headed instead to film near the border area along Rafah's edge. Young children blissfully flew handmade kites above the iron wall separating them from the Egyptian Rafah. Their *atbaq* flirted in the infinite sky above, with kites flying their way from the Egyptian side. "We play a game with the Egyptian kids," one boy explained of his unseen counterparts. "We meet here, through our kites, and see who can catch the others' kites quicker by entangling. So far we're winning—we've got 14 Egyptian kites," he announced proudly.

The children are small enough that they can wiggle their way through the cracks of the large iron gates along the wall—where once Merkava tanks made their unwelcome entrance to battered camps here. And so they can call out to their Egyptian friends and learn their names and new kite-flying techniques.

Even then, we could hear the fearsome roar of Israeli fighter jets overhead, interspersed with the banter of machine guns from feuding factions.

I then received a call from my father back in Gaza City—a tremendous explosion, which was the result of an F-16 jet bombing a nearby Hamas compound—had just sent intense shockwaves through our house. It was so powerful that it blasted off the windows from my cousin's home in the neighborhood behind us. This attack was followed by another, then another, and then another.

Hamas's Qassam Brigades have sent a barrage of rockets into Israel over the past two days. It has been in an attempt to redirect the battle toward the occupation, they say.

There have been six Israeli aerial strikes since this morning. The latest one happened just as we departed Rafah back to Gaza City. The victims this time were two young brothers, standing near a municipality garbage truck that was obliterated.

Even as I record this from back at home in Gaza City, we were shaken by another large explosion. Israeli tanks are amassing at Gaza's northern border, and unmanned Israeli drones are whirring menacingly, incessantly, overhead in great numbers, patrolling the ghostly skies that only the kites can reach—preparing, perhaps, for yet another strike against an already bleeding, burning, and battered Gaza.

A Wanted Man on Campus[11]
Gaza City, Palestine, May 19, 2007

To say that Dan Halutz's recent tenure as head of the Israeli military was rife with controversy would be a grand understatement.

After resigning his post in January, Halutz took some time off to better himself and has been attending an elite two-month advanced management program at the Harvard Business School (HBS) in the United States. Ironic though it may be, the Israeli Army has sponsored his training, according to a press statement that HBS issued.

But some Harvard University students are trying to make sure his crimes are not forgotten, while also castigating Harvard for admitting him—and others accused of human-rights abuses and war crimes—in the first place.

The Alliance for Justice in the Middle East has plastered the campus of Harvard University and its business school with mock "Wanted" posters.

The group launched its weeklong mock *Dragnet* last Tuesday to expose what it says is Harvard University's "pattern of admitting and hiring individuals with a credible and public record of war crimes and human-rights abuses." In addition to the "Wanted" posters, it is employing missing-person milk cartons, helium balloons, and the Internet to make its case.

The posters say Halutz is "wanted for war crimes" for ordering the indiscriminate bombing of Lebanon last summer, killing more than 1,000 civilians. The jets he commanded bombed houses and hospitals, ambulances and airports, refineries and roads. "The atrocities committed under his command were condemned worldwide as war crimes. Now he's hiding out and padding his resume in an executive education program at [HBS]," they read.

They say he is still "at large" and then ask people to contact the International Criminal Court if they spot him.

. . . The campaign organizers say the idea for their *Dragnet* came once the group recognized a pattern of admitting high-ranking army officers with command responsibility into Harvard-affiliated programs.

"We searched for as many war criminals and/or human-rights abusers that fit our profile, using recognized international law and credible media reports, without regard for nationality. We drafted dossiers for those for whom we did find a match," Maryam Gharavi said.

Their site also profiles the case of former Guatemalan Defense Minister Hector Gramajo, who was a Mason Fellow at Harvard's Kennedy School of Government in 1991. . . .

"What they want to know is: Why is the university rewarding known war criminals, and what will it take to stop this?" Ms. Gharavi said.

War Games[12]
Gaza City, Palestine, May 23, 2007

Just to reassure my readers, we are alive and well. I've just been busy reporting and filming and simply trying to go on with my life. The situation has a way of getting in your head, but you have to put it aside, compartmentalize, and move on.

I was down in Rafah again this week. While inspecting the site of a future park project my friend Fida is working on (and which we are making a film about), we were disrupted every few minutes by the voracious sound of multiple F-16 fighter jets flying overhead in unison. Sometimes, one or two; then, four or five.

Children scurried about playing football with a deflated basketball on the sand lot.

"Do you think I will be assassinated one day?" one child asked another solemnly.

I can't sleep. I get up maybe once every two hours. Go to the bathroom, walk around a little, and then doze off again—only to be awakened by the drones, followed by the manic hovering of helicopter gunships.

This time, they were directly over our apartment building. I would have been afraid, except this happened once before, maybe two years ago. Panicked and fearful at the time, I called my cousin, who reassured me that when an Apache is directly overhead, it means its intended target is about 500m to 1km away. It is information I wish I did not know.

So this time, I didn't flinch. I just waited for the dreadful conclusion. The intensity of the propeller's sound waned and intensified at various intervals, until finally two missiles were fired. I could hear them hissing and then exploding.

My friend Saeed, who is staying in a hotel next to us, said he saw flashes of light outside—apparently the drones taking pictures of the resulting explosions for keepsakes (and, of course, to show off to the media how "precise" their attacks are).

Former Israeli prime minister and current leader of the opposition Benyamin Netanyahu has called for Israel to cut water and electricity to Gaza, because that will do a great deal of good. We are still feeling the effects of last summer's attack on Gaza's power plants—especially as summer nears. Electricity is beginning to be rationed, and power outages are becoming more frequent now. The United Nations says there are solutions—but the energy authority, like every other institution in Gaza, is simply too financially strapped.

Electricity for about 50,000 people was cut off two days ago.

Meanwhile, Rafah crossing is still closed. It has only been open four days over the past month, less than 40 percent of the time over the past year. An estimated 5,000 people are waiting to cross on either side. . . .

And We Sleep[13]
Gaza City, Palestine, May 24, 2007

We go to sleep now waiting for the next round of Israeli attacks against "Hamas targets." That is what they are calling them now. Last night, I couldn't sleep again. The drones were waxing and waning in intensity overhead—and then, of course, the Apaches and the explosions.

But this time, the "target" wasn't some distant building or family gathering hall in Shija'iya or Jabaliya. It was a money changer on my very street, Omar al-Mukhtar, in Gaza's Remal neighborhood—and the supermarket next door.

After things calmed down, I dozed off, only to be shocked out of bed around 3 a.m. by a thunderous explosion, another attack. It shook us from our insides. My mother became hysterical, flailing her arms and screaming uncontrollably. We hugged each other, and I tried to calm her down. "It's OK; it's nothing, maybe an F-16. . . . It's OK."

But it was not OK. This explosion was closer than ever before. At first, we thought maybe the "target" was a store in our building. It turned out to be another money changer only a few shops down from our house, no more than 50m. The store was leveled.

And then there was nothing left to do but sleep. But there was a horrible, sinking feeling in my stomach, the result of panic and fear and the ugly certainty of it all. It took a few hours for the knots in my stomach to unwind and settle slowly. I felt nauseous.

What exactly the Israeli Army is "targeting" is a mystery. But, of course, the media machine spins it as "Hamas targets." This is how it read the next morning in *Haaretz*—including a note on how the attacks resulted in "no damage or casualties." I thought, maybe the author should come to Gaza.

The popular thinking seems to hold that Israel has simply run out of "legitimate" targets—whatever the hell that is anyway (members of Parliament? homes?)—and so has now resorted to bombing things like money changers and supermarkets. This is according to an Israeli Army general himself on the radio, who said his army really did not know what else to strike.

And there is nothing left to do but sleep.

Israel, United States to Train Fateh Forces[14]

Gaza City, Palestine, May 24, 2007

Of course, this is nothing new. But, for some reason, people seem to think it's a big conspiracy when it's not.

U.S. and Israeli loyalties to either side change quicker than a teenager's hormone-afflicted crushes. Remember how once, they were funding Hamas? And then Fateh. And then Fateh and Arafat were bad bad bad. That was in 2000. Now they are the good guys again.

So anyway, according to today's *Haaretz*, Israel has agreed to "extensive training of members of the Presidential Guard of [PA] Chairman Mahmoud Abbas in areas near Jericho, in the Jordan Valley."

The article goes on to state that this request was made through the Americans and that Israel agreed to the transfer of thousands of rifles and ammunition to Abbas's Presidential Guard.

So yes, there is something far more sinister occurring.

Temporary Life, Temporary Security[15]

Gaza City, Palestine, June 2, 2007

The streets are alive again. The Jundi park was humming with boisterous children and families, makeshift sheesha cafes, and peanut and corn vendors Thursday.

The fruit vendors, too, have resumed marketing their produce on donkey carts via megaphone along the city streets.

But overshadowing it all is an uncertain feeling that this sense of security, like everything else here, is temporary. The "interim" agreement is temporary. The

refugee issue is "temporary." Our legal status is "temporary."

You can sense it in people's tones: the fear of the unknown, of abandonment, of complete and total catastrophe and implosion. Even the head of Rafah's Preventive Security branch reflects it. "How can I serve and protect our society if I can't even protect myself?" he confided.

"Forget about a two-state solution. Forget about everything. We'd do well to just stay alive now."

Meanwhile, Israeli executions and attacks continue unabated. OCHA reports that a total of 53 Palestinians—including 5 children—have been killed and 185 injured from May 16 to June 1.

This does not include two young brothers, ages 11 and 12, searching for scrap metal to sell this week, when they were gunned down by Israeli snipers positioned near the border. The soldiers said they thought they were planting a bomb. The reality is—soldiers are authorized to shoot at any moving object that comes within 700m of the border.

During the same period, two Israeli soldiers were injured in Gaza, and two Israeli civilians killed.

A Life in Legal Limbo[16]
Gaza City, Palestine, June 27, 2007

In 1996, after 36 years in exile, Um Nael returned to Gaza along with her husband and two sons.

It was a momentous occasion, reuniting her with her parents and siblings and bringing her back home.

But the euphoria of those days is long gone, replaced instead with anger and disillusionment as she finds herself without legal status in her own country after nearly 11 years in Gaza.

System of control

Um Nael is one of more than 50,000 Palestinians, according to the Palestinian Ministry of Civil Affairs, who await a family reunion identification card, or *hawiya*.

The *hawiya* is issued by the Israeli military to residents of the occupied territories.

It enables Palestinians to move in and out of either Gaza or the West Bank and entitles them to residency there and to a PA travel document.

The Israeli authorities first began issuing them as part of a system of control imposed on the population following the 1967 war.

The Palestinian borders were sealed immediately after the war, and a door-to-door population census was conducted.

Cards were issued to only those Palestinians who were in residence and added to the population registry.

Millions of others who were abroad—studying, working, or visiting family—were immediately excluded.

Over the years, Palestinians who had direct family in the territories could apply for an identification card through a process known as family reunification.

But less than one-fifth of the applications were approved by Israel, subject to biannual renewal from within the occupied territories.

Failure to renew resulted in immediate cancellation.

It was only in the mid-1990s, under the terms of the Oslo Accords, that Israel established a quota for both temporary visitors' permits and permanent family reunion identification cards to Palestinians awaiting the *hawiya*.

Many, like Um Nael, jumped at the chance to finally return home—even if it meant she had to do so as a "visitor" to her own land.

Once she arrived, she immediately applied for the family reunification identification card.

"I expected I [would come back] to my land and would face no difficulty; now, I curse the day I came back. I don't exist as far as Israel is concerned," said Um Nael.

Since 2000, Israel has frozen all requests for family reunification identification cards and visitors' permits and has not permitted additions to the Palestinian Population Registry, leaving tens of thousands of Palestinians, like Um Nael, stranded.

"If you are born in the United States and get a citizenship, how is it that I was born in Gaza, and I can't get residency rights here? I have land and property here," said Um Nael.

The freeze has also affected Palestinians in the West Bank.

Amal Souf lives in the town of Qalqiliya, where she has been waiting for her identification card for more than 10 years.

Souf came to the West Bank on a visitor's permit to join her new husband there in 1997.

She renewed her permit three times; however, after that, the Israeli authorities told her she was not allowed to renew any more. If she left the West Bank, she could never return.

"I was pregnant and newly married. What was I supposed to do? I decided to stay here, not tear my family apart, but this also meant I would not be able to move."

Risking detention

Four years ago her father in Jordan became seriously ill.

"I began crying and saying I wanted to leave Qalqiliya to see my father . . . but I knew that if I left, I would never be able to return to my husband or my children. Imagine having to make such a choice."

Her father died shortly thereafter.

"Now, they are telling me my mother is sick, and I don't know what to do," she said tearfully.

Souf has trouble far closer to home, too.

Because she resides "illegally" in the West Bank, she risks detention even when crossing from Qalqiliya to neighboring Palestinian towns across Israeli checkpoints.

"I never leave Qalqiliya. I feel like I'm locked inside my own home," she said.

"Not Palestinians"

Shlomo Dror, the Israeli spokesperson for the coordinator of government activities in the territories, insists the onus lies on Palestinians, such as Souf and Um Nael, who "overstayed their visitors' permits."

"This is something they should have thought about from the beginning.

"There are many Israelis that have problems in the United States. For example, they overstayed their visas.

"It's the same story here. These people came here, asked for visitors' permits, and then decided to stay permanently.

"So when you are working against the law, you should expect that there will be a problem in the future," Dror told *Al Jazeera*.

"And from our point of view they are not exactly Palestinians. . . . [T]hey came on a permit to visit family inside and decided to stay even though they didn't have [identification] cards," said Dror.

Ameen Siyam, deputy Palestinian minister of civil affairs, argues that family reunification is a Palestinian's most basic right.

"So what are they, then, if not Palestinians? Tourists? Do you think they came to take in the views of shelling and destruction? Of course they came back to stay— it is their home after all," Siyam said.

He handles the family-reunification applications on the Palestinian side, but there is little he can do except send the files to the Israelis for approval and wait like everyone else.

He says each week he receives dozens of new applications.

"Choose a file at random, and it will be the same: a mother separated from her children, a husband from his wife. Most are humanitarian cases, but who will have sympathy to deal with them? No one."

Until the problem is resolved, Palestinians, such as Um Nael and Amal Souf, are trapped in legal limbo in their own towns.

"Sometimes, I dream I was actually allowed to travel . . . and then I suddenly get up and start crying when I realize it isn't true," says Um Nael.

"I wish I can go to get treated for my heart condition in Egypt or Jordan, that I can visit my daughters who live abroad, that I can go to Mecca to perform the *hajj*.

"But I can't do any of these things. I can only watch people go and cry and dream. I am trapped in a prison inside my own home."

CHAPTER NOTES

1. The full original text of this article about this plan is archived at "The Gaza
    Bombshell," http://www.vanityfair.com/politics/features/2008/04/gaza200804,
    shortened to http://bit.ly/cNLLMr.
2. Archived at http://bit.ly/dcBItQ.
3. Archived at http://bit.ly/9rNolr.
4. Laila El-Haddad, "Crime and Chaos," *Guardian*, May 10, 2007,
    archived at http://bit.ly/d5IGq3.
5. Archived at http://bit.ly/dCJbG8.
6. Alvaro de Soto, "End of Mission Report," May 2007, archived
    at http://bit.ly/avM1ZE.
7. Archived at http://bit.ly/aXFEOY.
8. Archived at http://bit.ly/bdcnjv.
9. Laila El-Haddad, "Fanning the Flames in Gaza," *Guardian Comment Is Free*,
    May 16, 2007, archived at http://bit.ly/d2cQNh.
10. Archived at http://bit.ly/b2pcWU.
11. Laila El-Haddad, "A Wanted Man on Campus," *Guardian Comment Is Free*,
    May 19, 2007, archived at http://bit.ly/aDa460.
12. Archived at http://bit.ly/cZtWrJ.
13. Archived at http://bit.ly/bkyCmG.
14. Archived at http://bit.ly/bvcrll.
15. Archived at http://bit.ly/8XNZol.
16. Archived at http://bit.ly/a3a59O. Reported in early June 2007.

Chapter 18

Gaza: From Prison to Zoo

Late July 2007 through March 1, 2008

July 2007 marked the beginning of a new period, both for our family and for Gaza. Though I never guessed it at the time, June 8 was the last time I would be able to set foot in Gaza for the next three years. (As it happened, I left Gaza with Yousuf just days before the fighting that marked the collapse of the Palestinian unity government.)

My life changed in other ways too: In January 2008, there was a new addition to our family—my darling daughter, Noor, was born. Unlike Yousuf, she would spend the first few years of her life outside Gaza.

During the months this chapter covers, Israel started to employ new strategies toward Gaza. Chief among them was labeling Gaza a "hostile territory," a move by which Israel sought to exonerate itself from bearing any responsibility for what happened inside the Strip (which it nevertheless continued to control, with deadly effectiveness). The Israeli government also adopted an approach referred to as "essential humanitarianism,"[1] treating Gaza less like a prison and more like a zoo—where the animals require "careful regulation of leash and diet" but where "the question of freedom is never raised," to quote my friend Darryl Li.[2] Gaza's Palestinians meanwhile adopted some new techniques of their own to defy the siege, even if only symbolically. In early 2008, they managed to fell the wall dividing them from Egypt successfully (though only temporarily).

The Closed Gates of Gaza[3]
Durham, North Carolina, July 25, 2007

I'm not sure how to begin blogging again after such a long absence.
. . . So much has happened since we left Gaza, and in such a short period. If it was mentally exhausting being there, it is even more overwhelming being away—and processing it all.

I was in Gaza during the months of May and part of June, shooting two films with my friend and colleague Saeed Farouky: one about the tunnels along Rafah's border and another about the remarkable story of young Palestinian photojournalist Fida Qishta and her attempt to establish Rafah's only true recreation center amid everything that is going on there. It was exhausting—but rewarding—work. We were traveling to Rafah from Gaza City almost every day, for the entire day, in the middle of internal clashes that gripped the city where we live.

We had planned to leave Gaza around the beginning of June, with tickets booked out of Cairo June 7. My parents were to come along with us for a visit. As is often the case in Gaza, things don't always go according to plan.

Rafah was open erratically during the month of May and closed entirely in the week before our departure. We received word that the crossing would open around midnight on June 6. Wonderful, we thought; at least we could make our flight, if only barely.

We spent 14 grueling hours on the crossing, along with thousands of other Palestinians, desperate to either leave or enter the Strip. Busload after busload, entire families and their children and spouses were clinging to the ceilings, crushed inside, or piled on top of the luggage in back. Some fainted. Others erupted in

hysterics. Everyone had a reason to travel. There were mothers separated from their spouses. Students ready to return to college. The ill. The elderly. And those with nothing particularly remarkable to preface their reason for traveling other than it was their right, after all.

In the early hours, there was a chill, and we warmed up with sugary mint tea and bitter coffee. But by noon, the midday sun was fierce over our heads, with no place to take shade. And so we waited. And we waited. And every time a bus would heave forward a few inches, our spirits would lift a tiny bit, everyone would cheer. . . .

At one point, hundreds of anxious passengers, each following the advice passed down along the Rafah-crossing grapevine from those who had successfully made the journey across, began to pour across the fence into the Palestinian terminal—throwing their bags over first, and then climbing across themselves. "It's the only way you'll get through today. . . . In a place where there is no order or sense or logic to why and how this damn place operates, you have to find your own way across." I thought of the

tunnels, how one tunnel lord told us some people pay him $5,000 just to get into Gaza via a tunnel when the crossing is closed.

The European monitors "suspended" their operations as a result of the "chaos" for several hours. They eventually returned, but by the time the crossing closed at 2:30 p.m., we were left stranded on the Palestinian side of the crossing, departure stamps in our passports, with the Egyptian side only meters ahead.

It is difficult to put into terms what it means when a territory of 1.5 million people's only passage to the outside world is closed for most of the time and open for only a few meaningless, infuriatingly slow hours when it is open at all.

We returned to our home in Gaza City exhausted, demoralized, dehumanized. We received word the crossing would open again the next day. We debated whether to attempt to cross after the day's events. We had already missed our flights out of Cairo, and attempting to explain Rafah to distant airline customer service representatives was never a simple task.

A few hours later, we were on the road again. We clung to the hope that, at the very least, the crossing might be less crowded the next day. We were sorely mistaken. Perhaps double the amount of people we saw the previous day was there. This time, the packed buses extended way beyond the crossing. We waited until the afternoon. It was only then that we began to hear—through the taxi drivers—that some skirmish had broken out between Fateh and Hamas in Rafah, that the Fateh-led Preventive Security building there was surrounded. But we made nothing of it. "Same old cycle," we thought to ourselves.

Never could we have imagined what would happen in subsequent days—that the on-again off-again street battles we'd witnessed over the course of the past few weeks (and years) would boil over into all-out civil war, eventually seeing Fateh fleeing to the West Bank and Hamas taking complete control of Gaza.[4]

We waited until the late afternoon. The prospect of our crossing became grimmer with each passing minute and each bus that didn't pass. We felt like we were going backward, not moving forward. Demoralized, my father decided he wanted to go back to Gaza City. "Let's just wait until next week; maybe it will be less crowded. We already missed our flight," he said. "No, wait, let me try one more thing," I suggested, remembering the advice of the passenger from the day before. "You have to find your own way across."

I had refused to give in to rule of the jungle. But today, I realized if I didn't do something quick, we would never get out.

We talked to a taxi driver who took us to the crossing the first time we tried to cross—a sly, strong-headed type you don't want to get into an argument with, from the Abu Eid clan in Rafah (the "Dogmushes" of the south). He owned a beat-up Peugeot that had seen better days. He mentioned he knew a way around the crossing—a path reserved for vehicles belonging to the security forces. Desperate, I asked if there was any chance he could take us through that way.

There were no guarantees we would be allowed through, but he could try. And so in a last-ditch effort, he drove us to a security gate. We were met with staunch refusals and hysterical laughter. "Are you crazy? Do you know what they will do to us if we let you through?" ... We pleaded with them, told them how we had waited 14 hours the day before, but still no pity.

Then, an empty bus on its way back from the crossing drove through. Our driver negotiated with him. He, too, refused, until he heard our story, saw Yousuf, and finally said, "What the heck, come on, I'll see what I can do. . . . "

And so we crossed, albeit backward. We drove into the Palestinian side of the crossing, passports already stamped from the day before. An officer saw us, remembered us from the previous day, and let us through hurriedly. As we were getting ready to depart, a European monitor greeted me. "Hello! How was your day?"

How was my day? Was this guy for real?

"Difficult. The crossing is very difficult."

"Oh, but at least, it's better than yesterday, at least people are crossing." It was then I realized these monitors were completely detached from the reality beyond the few square meters they . . . well . . . monitored in the sanitary confines of the terminal, and back again, 1km, to their headquarters in Kerem Shalom in Israel.

And so by evening, we were in Cairo. And slowly, within the coming days, news began to filter through about what was happening in the Gaza we had only just left behind, the Gaza whose gates were closed shut just after we had left it and whose gates remain shut to more than 6,000 people, 19 of whom have died so far.

So maybe you can begin to understand what I mean by mentally exhausting, having left a place where I desperately long to be—even in the worst of circumstances—and yet where I would have been stuck against my will, away from Yassine.

My parents are with me. It is a mixed blessing. My grandmother passed away last week, and my mother couldn't be there to grieve with her family or wait by her bed before she passed. Some Palestinians with foreign passports have been allowed through Erez into Gaza, but for those with PA passports (which we carry and which Abbas has decreed null and void unless issued from his new dominion in the West Bank. . .), there is no alternative other than Rafah. I've had so many thoughts about what's happening. But it's all been so overwhelming, so unbelievable—that there can be such collusion, both regional and global, with so little protest. . . .

And, of course, the icing on the cake is the recent *Haaretz* report that Palestinian sources said PA Chairman Mahmoud Abbas asked Israel (and Egypt) to keep the crossing closed to prevent the movement of people from Egypt to the Gaza Strip for fear that "thousands of people without supervision" could enter Gaza and strengthen Hamas—something, not surprisingly, that chief Palestinian negotiator Saeb Erekat and company deny.

Rafah crossing has been closed for 45 days now. There are food-supply and electricity shortages. Yet the internal situation remains calm, say family and friends—calmer than it has been in years.

When, I wonder, will the global conscience finally awaken?

The Law of the Land[5]
Durham, North Carolina, August 16, 2007

I've been following the situation closely back home. The past few months have really gotten me down—maybe it's journalist fatigue.

I get tired of having to explain the "situation back home" every time someone finds out I'm from Gaza and have recently been there. This might sound odd for someone with such a public Internet persona. But with many people I've come in contact with, I have to start from scratch . . . forget about identification cards, border crossings, and a nonfunctional, nonsovereign authority split between two still-occupied territories divided by borders, air, and water they don't control.

I suppose part of it is realizing my existence is at stake somehow in all this. I have to renew my Palestinian "passport" soon (I have that in quotations, because the "passport" is, as stated on the first page, issued pursuant to the sham of the Oslo Accords), but I can't go back to Gaza. I have nowhere to go to, nowhere to return to—at least not now. Permanence is transient. Transience is permanent.

I've taken to doing some senseless things lately, trying to clear my mind, regain some perspective. I watched a little bit of *Escape from Alcatraz* the other day. Funny, but it looked like paradise compared with Gaza now.

I'm not sure what it will take anymore for people to realize the absurdity of it all. I mean, sanctioning an occupied people for God's sake? Demanding an end to "violence" by those occupied people all while the United States shells out another $30 billion in military aid to the world's third-strongest army?

And I'm not talking about only the United States here. I'm talking about our very own Arab governments who, from Day 1, bowed in submission to U.S. commands to freeze financial transactions to Hamas. Yes, the world, including the Arab world, has been complicit in the methodical destruction of an entire society.

And now we have Abbas, the degenerate, thinking he's actually running the show in the West Bank. Suddenly, the money starts coming in, some prisoners scheduled for release anyway are released, leaving thousands of others languishing, and Abbas and his cronies are the new "moderates." Was it worth it? A few weeks ago, a friend working with a respected human-rights organization asked Saeb Erekat whether there had been any talks or negotiations with Israel regarding reopening Rafah crossing. Plain and simple, he answered "no."

. . . Amazing how just a few years ago, Sharon flew to Washington to convince Bush that Abbas was not a partner for peace.

And now, there are calls for early elections that will exclude parties who "don't obey the law." And what law might that be exactly?

You Are Now Entering Hostile Territory[6]
Durham, North Carolina, September 19, 2007

First, a blessed and joyous Ramadan to everyone. I only wish it were so joyous an occasion for my friends and family in Gaza.

Today, Israel officially declared Gaza a "hostile entity" (although that sort of had me confused—is this to say they were of "friendly-entity" status before?). My friend Darryl congratulated me on what he called a "status upgrade." "It's like getting bumped up to first class," he said. So now I am both hostile and stateless. Is that some kind of new record?

The new classification is, of course, an attempt by the Israeli government to grant itself a legal green light to do whatever the hell it wants in Gaza without being bound by the restrictions of an "Occupier." In the words of the al-Haq human-rights organization, it is "a deliberate attempt by Israel to obscure its continued Occupation of the Gaza Strip"—not that the law has stopped it before.

But fear not, country folk. U.S. Secretary of State Condoleezza Rice confirmed reassuringly that the United States "would not abandon the innocent Palestinians." Foreign Minister Tzipi Livni also said that Israel will continue to supply Gaza's humanitarian needs . . . just not "all the needs that are more than the humanitarian."

. . . Like fuel, for example, and electricity. So don't worry, people of Gaza, you won't starve (remember, you are on a diet). You will get to eat your (cold) Ramadan *iftars*—only in the dark and, of course, with no water to wash down that meal (or your clothes, for that matter), because the pumps are driven by electricity.

And no gas to heat your food or houses with come winter. And you'll have to consume what you get quickly, because the refrigerators (both yours and the supermarket's) won't work without power. And don't even *think* about getting sick—prevention is your best insurance policy now. Hospital intensive care units will have to be powered by generators. Kidney dialysis? Start writing a will. Baby formula? Breastfeed. Vaccinations? Stay home from school.

"Civilian levers" is what the Israeli cabinet has mockingly decided to call these "measures" of collective punishment. No doubt, this sick euphemism was the brain-child of the ever-reliable Dov Weisglass, of "the Gaza diet" fame.

And remember, you are the "innocent Palestinians" stuck in the middle of all this.

Now how about some thank-you notes to Condi? It's Ramadan, after all, the month of mercy, forgiveness, and thanks.

Raising Yousuf *and* . . . [7]
Durham, North Carolina, October 11, 2007

OK, I figure it's about time I make an announcement about this. But you know how it is when you forget to tell someone something, until the announcement, or phone call, or whatever becomes obscenely, inappropriately overdue?

Well, the big news is: Soon, *inshallah*, Yousuf will have a sibling! That's right—we are expecting our second child around the new year, which makes me seven months' pregnant.

Yousuf has already taken to his new role as older sibling like a fish to water and has promised to help me change diapers (a proposition I'm not likely to take him up on, unless perhaps I am in a state of sleep-deprivation-induced delirium). His curiosity is also peaking, as he endlessly asks, "How will they get the baby out?" ("Do they rip you open?") "When will it be time to bring her home?"

The doctor says it's a little girl, so we are looking forward to some degree of relative quiet, but then again you never know with these things! Please feel free to submit your name suggestions too! Maybe I should hold a competition—most original girl's name?

Preparing for the Dawn[8]
Durham, North Carolina, November 27, 2007

Even in the worst of times, there's one thing we're never short of in our troubled part of the world: another conference, meeting, declaration, summit, agreement.

Something to save the day, to "steer" us back to whatever predetermined path it is we are or were meant to be on—and to help us navigate that path.

Never mind the arguable shortcomings of this path, or the discontent it may have generated, for we all know what happens to people who question that. The important thing is to move forward, full steam ahead.

Enter Annapolis. I've been there a couple of times—beautiful port city; great crabs; quaint antique shops; and, of course, the U.S. Navy.

So what exactly is different this time around? Well, if you believe some of the newspaper headlines, lots. Like the fact that Ehud Olmert has promised not to build new settlements or expropriate land.

And yet, as recently as September, Israel expropriated 1,100 dunams (272 acres) of Palestinian land in the West Bank to facilitate the development of E-1, a 5-square-mile area in the West Bank, east of Jerusalem, where Israel plans to build 3,500 houses, a hotel, and an industrial park—completing the encirclement of Jerusalem with Jewish colonies and cutting it off from the rest of the West Bank.

The conference simply generates new and ever-more-superfluous and intricate promises, which Israeli leaders can commit to and yet somehow evade. An exercise in legal obfuscation at its best: We won't build new settlements, we'll just expropriate more land and expand to account for their "natural growth," until they resemble towns, not colonies, and we'll have them legitimized by a U.S. administration looking for some way to save face. And then we'll promise to raze outposts.

Each step in the evolution of Israel's occupation—together with the efforts to sustain it and the language to describe it—has become ever more sophisticated, strategic, and euphemistic.

Israel has also promised the release of 450 Palestinian prisoners (who have, by Israel's own admission, nearly completed their sentences) on Sunday ahead of the conference, while dozens of others are detained, and thousands of others remain in custody without charges or trial—making theirs the highest rate of incarceration in the world.

Still, Annapolis is being hailed as the site of the most serious "peace effort" in eight years. According to the U.S. State Department's spokesperson, the conference "will signal broad international support for the Israeli and Palestinian leaders' courageous efforts and will be a launching point for negotiations leading to the establishment of a Palestinian state and the realization of Israeli-Palestinian peace."

Support, I gather, that will also entail arms and money to help Abbas rid Gaza of Hamas once and for all.

So then, what are people's expectations in Gaza from all of this?

In short, not much. But then, if history has taught them anything, it's that they never have much of a say in anything that involves their destiny, be it Madrid or Oslo or the Road Map. And the moment they do attempt to take control, the repercussions are to "teach" them never to attempt to do so again.

To quote Palestinian national poet Mahmoud Darwish, "The siege will last in order to convince us we must choose an enslavement that does no harm, in fullest liberty!"

The stage has been set, the roles are the same, but the actors have been switched. That is the feeling of many in Gaza.

"The Annapolis meeting will not bring anything new for the Palestinians; it is a repetition of many other conferences which sought to reinforce the principle of making concession on the Palestinian national rights," says Yousef Diab, a 35-year-old government employee.

For Fares Akram, a young Gaza-based journalist, the conference will result in little more than token concessions aimed at further isolating Hamas-run Gaza and bolstering support for Abbas: "The Israeli government is weak this time. President Abbas may get some support in the conference, but the support will be for his struggle against Hamas. Gaza will remain forgotten, and the improvements that may come out from the meeting will only apply to the West Bank, while nothing will be done here in Gaza."

Fida Qishta, a videographer and community activist in Gaza's troubled town of Rafah, can't even be bothered with thinking of things as abstract and distant and—ultimately—irrelevant as Annapolis when life in Gaza as she sees it has all but come to a standstill:

"I wish you were here to see how life is: It is really like a body that died. I still can't imagine we are living through this, and I try not to think about it a lot."

Aliya Moor, a mother of eight, adds, "We're already dead, the only thing we need is to be buried, to be pushed into the grave and buried. It's already been dug up for us."

They are prisoners, others have told me, constantly waiting and helplessly hoping for decisions to be made that determine whether they live or die—both figuratively and literally.

Except there is a certain set of rules in prisons, and prisoners are guaranteed certain things, like food and water and access to medical care. Gazans are guaranteed none of these things. Instead, they are setting the bar as the first occupied people in history to be embargoed and declared "hostile." People are no longer waiting for Godot, they are simply waiting for the next awful thing to be imposed on them. "People just want out," explained another friend. "It doesn't matter whether it's Fateh or Hamas anymore."

We have become a people, to quote Darwish again, "constantly preparing for dawn, in the darkness of cellars lit by our enemies."

Who's Afraid of the One-State Solution?[9]
Durham, North Carolina, December 2, 2007

Olmert, for starters. A day after the theatrical display at Annapolis, the Israeli prime minister gave *Haaretz* a telling interview, in which he acknowledged in no uncertain terms Israel's apartheid-like nature:

"If the day comes when the two-state solution collapses, and we face a South African–style struggle for equal voting rights (also for the Palestinians in the territories), then, as soon as that happens, the State of Israel is finished."

Because heaven forbid Israel should have to face *that* struggle. Equal voting rights? Phshh. Why face a fight for equal voting rights when you can fight with Merkavas and F-16s; when you can sustain a decades-long occupation of land, people, and resources and mask it with an empty and unrealistic call for two states (see also his comments today: no firm timetable for peace talks, despite Annapolis)?

His statement—similar to one he made in 2003, when he "shudder[ed] to think that liberal Jewish organizations that shouldered the burden of the struggle against apartheid in South Africa will lead the struggle against [Israel]"—is essentially an acknowledgment not only of the untenability and the inequity of the so-called two-state solution and everything it entails (including sustaining a Jewish majority at the expense of the Palestinian population, no matter what the cost [i.e., ethnic cleansing]) but also of the inevitability of a one-state solution.

It's just *not* clear to me why more media have not caught on to this stunning declaration. Maybe it's easier to suspend reality for a while—a long while—in favor of an easier-to-digest fiction. Well, easier for some people. That's one mushy piece of fiction.

How about Some Hanukkah Paper for That Eid Gift?[10]
Durham, North Carolina, December 25, 2007

Eid al-Adha was last week (or, as we refer to it in Gaza, the meat Eid), and this time it happened to coincide with the holiday season here in the United States. So in shopping for an Eid gift for Yousuf, I had to deal with puzzled looks down south when I explained that we don't celebrate Christmas, but taken a step further, when I explained that actually it was also the Muslim Eid. I'm not trying to be facetious here, really. I'm just relaying conversations as they happened, and you be the judge.

Example:

> WOMAN AT CHECKOUT COUNTER IN TOY STORE: Oh what a lovely choice! Now is that a Christmas present for your son, or a birthday present . . . what kind of wrapping paper would you like?
>
> ME: Actually, it's a Eid present. Eid is a Muslim holiday. It happens to coincide with Christmas this year.
>
> WOMAN: I see. Well, we have Hanukkah paper right here!

You get my drift.

I had an equally enlightening conversation with our neighbor's grandson, who was in the process of showing off his new bike to Yousuf.

> JACOB: What did you get for Christmas, Yousuf?
>
> ME: Actually, Yousuf doesn't celebrate Christmas, Jacob. He celebrates Eid.
>
> JACOB: Well, we celebrate Christmas. And I got a cool new bike.
>
> ME: Yes, I know that, Merry Christmas. Our holiday is called Eid.
>
> JACOB: I thought you speak Spanish.
>
> ME: We speak Arabic, but that's not the point. . . .
>
> JACOB: Well, I got a bike for Christmas. What did Yousuf get?

I rest my case. I'm not asking for much here, am I? Is a simple "Oh, what's Eid?" too much to expect?

I'm not sure if I should blame the schools in this case, the media, the people themselves, or even the Muslim community. Maybe a little bit of each, coupled with the fact that it is just easier to ignore anything having to do with Islam here. Either way it's a little startling that so few people actually have any clue about what Eid is—compared with, say, Boston, where we used to live. I even took the initiative myself in one case and attempted to e-mail a supermarket chain I'm very fond of (Trader Joe's), explaining that it was also Eid and suggesting they add an "Eid Mubarak!" to their flyers along with "Happy Hanukkah and Merry Christmas."

The response: Thank you for contacting us. We will forward your comments to Marketing and get back to you." Needless to say, they never got back to me. But I'm still holding out hope.

Caroling against Conflict Diamonds[11]
Durham, North Carolina, December 27, 2007

And by conflict, I mean *the* conflict.

Such is the latest initiative of the conscientious Adalah-NY (the Coalition for Justice in the Middle East), which adopted one of the campaigns of the Campaign for Boycott, Divestment, and Sanctions against Israel in New York City. For weeks now, it has been organizing regular protests against Israeli diamond and real estate mogul–cum–settlement financier Lev Leviev in front of his newest jewelry store in New York City.

The group is organizing an encore performance on December 29.

Leviev, one of Israel's wealthiest businessmen, is helping build the Mattityahu East settlement on the lands of the village of Bil'in with partner Shaya Boymelgreen, the Zufim settlement on the lands of the village of Jayyous, and the strategic West Bank settlements of Har Homa and Maale Adumim around Jerusalem, which divide the northern West Bank from the southern West Bank.

Smother until Surrender[12]
Durham, North Carolina, December 28, 2007

How have things in Gaza changed during the past 12 months? Sadly, there are no rosy reflections to be found here. Things were bad in Gaza this year—very bad. Whether looked at from a political or purely humanitarian perspective, it's difficult to see the upside where there is such an orchestrated global drive to maintain the status quo: Smother until surrender.

The health indicators are telling: About a quarter of essential drugs and a third of essential medical supplies were unavailable in the Gaza Strip in October 2007. Less than half of Gaza's food-import needs are currently being met. Fuel reserves are almost at zero after punitive cuts by the Israeli government began last month. And with diesel-run water pumps unable to function, tens of thousands of Gazans are without access to fresh drinking water. Everything considered "nonessential" has disappeared from supermarket shelves (including chocolates, as one friend half-jokingly lamented).

It is as though depriving a nation of medicines, and fuel, and freedom of movement, and sanity will somehow make it turn against its rulers. And as though providing it with a trickle of "essential" supplies every few weeks is going to exonerate those people imposing and supporting the siege. Or sustain the besieged just enough so that they don't wither and die; because somehow, the onus is on them to undo all of this, and they need all the energy they can get.

Gaza's isolation has also come full circle this year. Traveling in and out of the occupied coastal territory has always been an exercise in the impossible, but now it's no longer an option that can even be exercised, in whatever degree of difficulty.

We Gazans stuck on the outside cannot return to our homes. The noose continues to tighten, even when we thought there was no more room to tighten it.

I was in Gaza through June. My son was with me. When I finished my work there, I left after a grueling 48-hour journey across Rafah crossing along with my family, who were coming to the United States to visit my brothers. That was the last day Rafah opened this year.

In fact, both my family and I have been unable to return to Gaza since that time. No, we don't carry foreign passports (and even if we did, there is no way in unless you are affiliated with a humanitarian organization). We carry PA "passports." (Passport to where? What good is a passport that can't even get you back home?) We are residents of Gaza. And we have nowhere to return to now.

What do rockets, or tunnels, or elections have to do with letting people return to their homes? Or with allowing students and the ill and even the average human being with no pressing concern to live their lives?

If one can say anything definitive about this year, it is that people's attitudes in Gaza (and the West Bank and East Jerusalem, for that matter) about the future have changed. They no longer believe in the myth of two states and, very likely, the West's call for democracy. This is not to say they don't want peace. They just no longer believe "peace," as defined and promoted by, well, virtually all the major powers that have a stake in it, is possible. Is peace living in two states, three territories, fragmented and divided by Israeli colonies and encircled by an enormous barrier, all of whose borders are still ultimately controlled by Israel and for whose security you, the occupied, are responsible? Is it not being able to pray, think, move, live freely?

According to a poll by Near East Consulting, more Palestinians than ever before think not. In fact, 70 percent of Palestinians in the Gaza Strip, West Bank, and East Jerusalem now support a one-state solution in historic Palestine, where Muslims, Christians, and Jews live together with equal rights and responsibilities.

This is not a state that prefers and attempts to sustain its Jewish population at the expense of its Palestinian one.

What has also changed is the Israeli government's recognition of this reality and its frank discourse surrounding it. Only two days after the theatrics of Annapolis, Israeli Prime Minister Ehud Olmert warned ominously in an interview with *Haaretz* about the consequences of facing a struggle for one state: "If the day comes when the two-state solution collapses, and we face a South African–style struggle for equal voting rights (also for the Palestinians in the territories), then, as soon as that happens, the state of Israel is finished."

It doesn't matter, then, how this Palestinian state will be fashioned, or what it will look like, so long as it is fashioned for the sake of demographics alone.

His statement—similar to one he made in 2003—complemented by his call for Palestinian President Mahmoud Abbas to recognize Israel as a purely Jewish state, as though the Muslims and Christians living there were aliens, is essentially an acknowledgment not only of the untenable nature and the inequity of the so-called two-state solution and everything it entails but also of the increasing inevitability of a one-state solution. As some commentators have noted, it is no longer an option up for debate; it is the new reality.

Israel in 2007 continued with its attempts to create its own realities on the ground to counter this phenomenon. (It also ironically continues to render a two-state solution a practical impossibility as it impedes any future plans to divide the city.) Earlier this month, its housing ministry gave the go-ahead for a new illegal settlement to be built in occupied East Jerusalem, with the deputy mayor affirming that he sees "no problem in building all-Jewish neighborhoods" (the housing minister has since backtracked, but plans have not been totally scrapped).

So if anything has changed in 2007, perhaps it is the global complacency and indifference toward Gaza and what is being done to its people with such purpose. And perhaps this is the most troubling aspect of it all—not that it is happening, nor even that it is happening so methodically, but rather that we, the collective world governments, mainstream media, and Mahmoud Abbas, no longer seem to find it so morally troubling. After all, Gaza is now a "hostile territory." So anything goes.

Down Goes the Wall[13]
Durham, North Carolina, January 23, 2008

Last night, I received a text message from my dear friend Fida. "It's coming down—it's coming down!" she declared ecstatically. "Laila, the Palestinians destroyed Rafah wall, all of it. All of it, not part of it! Your sister, Fida."

More texts followed, as I received periodic updates on the situation in Rafah, where it was 3 a.m.

Fida Qishta

Palestinians stock up on fuel in Egypt's Arish.

"Two hours ago, people were praising God everywhere. The metal wall was cut and destroyed. So was the cement one. It is great Laila, it is great," she declared.

For the first time in months, I sensed a degree of enthusiasm, hope . . . relief even, emanating from thousands of miles away, via digitized words, from Gaza. Words that have been all but absent from the Palestinian vocabulary. Buried. Methodically and gradually destroyed.

Of course, the border opening will only provide temporary relief, and the ecstasy it generates will be fleeting, as it was in 2005 when, shortly after Israel's disengagement, the once-impervious and deadly sniper-lined border became

The Rafah Wall dividing Gaza from Eqypt, as seen from the Palestinian side.

completely porous. It was an incredible time. I will never forget the feeling of standing in the middle of the Philadelphi corridor, as it was known, with hundreds of thousands of other Gazans, savoring the moment of uninterrupted freedom— in this case, freedom of movement. Goats were being lobbed over the secondary fence, mattresses, cigarettes, cheeses. Egyptians took back bags of apples from northern Gaza and comforters. For two weeks, it was the free market at work.

Once a nesting ground for Israeli tanks, armored bulldozers, and the like— all the war metal, the face of the occupation—that became synonymous with destructions and death for us in Gaza, and particularly for the residents of Rafah, Philadelphi had so suddenly become nothing but a kilometer of wasteland, of sand granules marking the end of one battered, besieged land and the beginning of the rest of the world.

But traveling this short distance had previously been so unthinkable that the minute it took to walk across it by foot was akin to being in the Twilight Zone. You couldn't help but feel that, at any moment, a helicopter gunship would hover by overhead and take aim.

It was then that I met a pair of young boys, ages 9 and 10, who curiously peered over the fence beyond the wall into Egypt. In hushed whispers and innocent giggles, they pondered what life was like outside Gaza and then asked me: "Have you ever seen an Egyptian? What do they look like?" They had never left Rafah in their lives.

And so once again, this monstrosity that is a source of so much agony in our lives, that cripples our movement and severs our ties to each other and to our world, to our families and our homes, our universities and places of work, hospitals and airports, has fallen through the will of the people; sadly, once again, it will go up. Of course, Egyptian President Hosni Mubarak has tried to take credit for this, blabbering something about how his country let them open it because Gazans were starving, while arresting 500 demonstrators in Cairo for speaking their mind against the siege.

The border opening also will not provide Gazans with an opportunity to travel abroad, because their passports will not have been stamped leaving Gaza; however, it will, at the very least, give them some temporary respite from the siege. I emphasize "temporary," because this, too, just like Israel's on-again off-again fuel stoppages, is not going to resolve the situation. Allowing in enough supplies to prevent a humanitarian catastrophe, in the words of the Israeli security establishment, somehow makes sense in the logic of the occupation, as does escalation and cutting off the fuel in response to rocket attacks. And Israelis can all learn to forget Gaza, at least long enough to feel comfortable.

People often ask me why such things—meaning people-powered civil protests that can overcome even the strongest occupation—don't happen sooner, or more often, or at all for that matter. We underestimate the power of occupation to destroy people's will to live, let alone resist and attempt to change the situation. This is the worst thing about occupation, whether a military occupation like

Israel's or a political one like Hosni Mubarak's in his own country. And it is only when you can overcome the psychological occupation, the occupation of the mind, that the military occupation in all its manifestations can be defeated.

Noor's First Protest![14]
Durham, North Carolina, January 29, 2008

I know I have to post more (newer) pictures of Noor. . . . Most of my days and nights are consumed with either nursing or attempting to sleep (or in some cases, both at the same time!), and yet somehow I have found myself committing to a variety of talks, interviews, and articles when I should be on "maternity leave" (right!).

Last weekend, my family and I participated in a small vigil/protest to end the siege on Gaza. Noor attended too—though she slept through it! Yousuf insisted on placing a sign on her car seat.

Gaza: From Prison to Zoo[15]
Durham, North Carolina, February 1, 2008

My good friend Darryl Li, a consultant with Human Rights Watch, has written this excellent article following his most recent visit to Gaza. In it, he describes the inhumane new Israeli policy of "essential humanitarianism." An excerpt follows:

> In place of any legal framework the state has proposed—and the court has now endorsed—a seemingly simple standard for policy: Once "essential humanitarian needs" are met, all other deprivation is permissible.
> This logic reflects the radical transformation of Israel's policy of blockade since the summer of 2007: from frequent and crippling closure to indefinite blockage of all but "essential humanitarian items." Israel has shifted from trying to punish the Gazan economy to deciding that the economy is a dispensable luxury.
> The policy shift is akin to treating Gazans not as prisoners but rather as animals; the Occupier as zoo-keeper, rather than prison warden.
> The metaphor of the Gaza Strip as the world's largest prison is unfortunately outdated. Israel now treats the Strip more like a zoo. For running a prison is about constraining or repressing freedom; in a zoo, the question is rather how to keep those held inside alive, with an eye to how outsiders might see them. The question of freedom is never raised.

The Rafah Border "Breach" and the Media[16]
Durham, North Carolina, February 12, 2008

A couple of weeks ago, I was asked to comment on the felling of the Rafah wall and the media's coverage of it for *Al Jazeera's Listening Post*, which I contribute to on a semi-regular basis.[17]

In short, my point was that the Western media tended to view the felling of the wall as something of a "jail break" and the Palestinians filing across as swarming insects and, at best, a deprived people out on a shopping spree. The tone of coverage tended to shift more toward the negative as days progressed. I even received a series of interview questions from an Italian journalist in which she said many journalists were commenting on how the "poor and hungry" Palestinians were returning from Egypt "charged with televisions and computers and mobile phones."

Suddenly, attention shifted from the event's proper historical and political context . . . of decades of isolation and occupation; of continued Israeli control over

Gaza and its borders; of a deliberate and sustained siege, ongoing for not one year, but more than a decade now in varying degrees . . . to Palestinian shopping habits and auditing their degree of need.

Of course, underlying all this is the fact that you cannot resolve a situation by simply providing Gaza's population with humanitarian supplies, enough to sustain them for a few weeks at a time, enough to prevent an international outcry, enough to prevent death and starvation, without addressing the continued occupation.

The same way you cannot resolve Israel's security dilemmas by simply demanding an end to rocket attacks and keeping the borders closed, while the occupation is ongoing at the same time; as though that status quo—of simply not attacking Gaza in response, but continuing the siege and the occupation—is acceptable to Palestinians.

And, of course, while the "border breach" brought temporary respite, it certainly did not resolve the deeper-seated Gaza crisis. Beyond the dramatic images of the border pilgrimage, the mass media are no longer interested in this issue. As far as they are concerned now, the situation has been resolved—Gaza's found a way out, so why the fuss?

Breaching the Other Border:
On Nonviolent Resistance and Mass Mobilizing in Gaza[18]
Durham, North Carolina, February 23, 2008

As gas ran out over the weekend in Gaza again, *Haaretz* reported "fears" among the Israeli military establishment of a mass civil protest toward Gaza's border with Israel.

The army apparently "beefed up troops along the border with Gaza, fearing thousands of Palestinians may march on the border to protest Israel's economic sanctions."

Many people have been calling for such a mass march, seeing it as the most effective way to break the blockade and draw global attention to the plight of Gaza.

Apparently, so does Hamas now.

Some 40,000 Palestinians are expected to march along the Gaza Strip's border beginning at 10 a.m. on Monday, including women and children.

The felling of the Rafah wall was powerful, but just a temporary respite and ultimately a distraction from the underlying issue; Gaza cannot continue to hover just above the brink of disaster, surviving from truckload to truckload of aid, from trickle to trickle of fuel; even if it does, it does not change the fact that the occupation is still in place, that the "status quo" of "accepting a harmless slavery, in fullest liberty!" (to quote Mahmoud Darwish) is no longer acceptable.

And unless it can be followed through with international action and a change in government policies of major powers, so too will a mass march toward Erez. However, I still feel such a march has enormous symbolic power. I think perhaps the Israeli Army would fear such an act of massive civil resistance more than anything, because it is not something it can easily "retaliate" against without drawing global criticism (though the world has largely been OK with the blockade Gaza is being subject to so far).

I often get asked why there is not more "nonviolent resistance" in Gaza. It's a tricky question to answer, but essentially, the thinking has been that the world isn't necessarily listening—or reacting—anyway, so why fight "fire with flowers" when you can fight "fire with fire"? At least, I think this was the common notion when the second Intifada started, during which Israel was using far more militarized and deadly force.

Another perspective on this is that I don't think one can necessarily place the burden of what kind of resistance to choose on a population that is being subject to the military force of the world's fourth-largest army (meaning, strategy and effectiveness aside, it comes across as almost self-righteous to dictate what and how an occupied people should resist).

This is not to say that nonviolent resistance has been wholly absent from the Palestinian struggle. The first Intifada was a prime example, but so, too, was the second Intifada in many cases—despite the fact that it was notably much more militarized.

An excerpt from an October 2007 article by Ben White in the *Electronic Intifada* notes:

> It is not just contentment (for the few) or sheer fatigue (for the many) that makes mass mobilization a challenge. Palestinians also fear that two critical elements for the success of nonviolent popular struggle are missing in their case: international coverage and limited repression on the part of the oppressor. As previously mentioned, "popular struggle" has always been a part of Palestinian resistance to occupation and colonization—but receives only a fraction of the press coverage afforded to violent resistance.

I have noticed that the tide's a-changing though. Hamas seems to be making a more concerted effort at such mass mobilization in Gaza, while making it clear that it will not relinquish its "legal right to other forms of resistance" (to quote from an interview with Khaled Meshaal that I will post soon).

A prime example was the felling of the Rafah wall—initiated by a group of women and children. So too was the effort of dozens of unarmed women of the Islamic movement (including member of Parliament Jamila Shanty) to shield and help rescue several fighters under siege in a Beit Lahiya mosque one and a half years ago.

Two of the women were killed by Israel.

And notably—Hamas was the first Palestinian group to initiate a "no-arms" policy in its public protests.

A Palestinian Birthday[19]
Durham, North Carolina, March 1, 2008

We celebrated my son Yousuf's 4th birthday two weeks ago last Saturday. We sang happy birthday. And we counted the bodies as the death toll in Gaza steadily rose. We ate cake. And my mother, stuck here with us in North Carolina and prevented by Israel from returning to Gaza, sobbed. We watched the fighter jets roar over Gaza on our television screen, pounding its narrow streets, and we shuddered. Yousuf tore open his presents and then asked my mother if the plane he saw overhead was a drone, an awful memory from his days spent living in Gaza. And we were torn open from the inside, engulfed by feelings of helplessness and anger and fear.

CHAPTER NOTES

1. The full original text of this article is archived at "Disengagement and the Frontiers of Zionism," by Darryl Li, Middle East Report Online, February 16, 2009, http://www.merip.org/mero/mero021608.html, shortened to http://bit.ly/ceyIjd.
2. Darryl Li, "From Prison to Zoo: Israel's 'Humanitarian'" Control over Gaza," Adalah Newsletter, Volume 44, January 2008, archived at http://bit.ly/btB271.
3. Archived at http://bit.ly/aVRrNX.
4. Hamas saw the takeover as a preemptive strike that aimed to stop an imminent U.S.-financed Fateh coup to overthrow it. This version of events has been corroborated by leaked Central Intelligence Agency documents, famously uncovered by journalist David Rose in his *Vanity Fair* article "Gaza Bombshell" in April 2008, archived at http://bit.ly/cNLLMr.
5. Archived at http://bit.ly/a7ZqZH.
6. Archived at http://bit.ly/b56i0M.
7. Archived at http://bit.ly/91aOPn.
8. Archived at http://bit.ly/c4guM3.
9. Archived at http://bit.ly/9EvvwL.
10. Archived at http://bit.ly/dgFQGb.
11. Archived at http://bit.ly/d0OAdy.
12. Laila El-Haddad, "Smother until Surrender," *Guardian*, December 28, 2007, archived at http://bit.ly/d1RcBZ.
13. Archived at http://bit.ly/bQxP2F.
14. Archived at http://bit.ly/c8NN66.
15. Archived at http://bit.ly/dcntXo.
17. The video of this episode of *Al Jazeera's Listening Post* with Richard Gizbert is archived at http://bit.ly/do4S8Q.
18. Archived at http://bit.ly/drlOl0.
19. Archived at http://bit.ly/aG0hAr.

Chapter 19

Belonging

March 2008–December 24, 2008

The noose around Gaza grew ever tighter during 2008. There were punitive power cuts and fuel restrictions, along with a continued hermetic closure of all of Gaza's crossings. I felt helpless and frustrated, at times, that I could not visit Gaza and that I could not share Gaza's stories with the world—even as a group of foreign activists successfully sent the first international boats to Gaza since 1967. Every little detail seemed to remind me of home.

And so I tried to find other ways to make a difference. Together with the still-nursing Noor, I attended protests, spoke at conferences, presented at film festivals. . . . I even participated in a confidential meeting with Palestinian and Israeli representatives from across the social and political spectrum (during which time I interviewed former Mossad Chief Danny Yatom). But nothing seemed to help in the face of a concerted global effort to suffocate Gaza and keep its people locked up.

In June 2008, Hamas and Israel agreed to a six-month truce. As they did so, Israeli commanders, under the direct order of Israeli Defense Minister Ehud Barak, were already planning for an attack that they would launch once the six months were up. To this end, on November 4 (and in clear violation of the cease-fire), they launched a military incursion into the southern Gaza town of Rafah, entering 250m into Gazan territory for the first time since the June truce took effect. A subsequent airstrike killed six Hamas fighters, prompting a volley of rockets in response. It was Israel's Gulf of Tonkin. The gears were put in motion for "Operation Cast Lead."[1]

Slowly Strangled[2]
Durham, North Carolina, March 1, 2008

Respected Israeli professor Ilan Pappe has said that genocide "is the only appropriate way to describe what the Israeli army is doing in the Gaza Strip." Genocide is not a word most people use lightly. But words laden with meaning have been used often, where Gaza is concerned, of late. Israel's deputy defense minister Matan Vilnai warned that a *shoah*, the Hebrew word most commonly used for the Holocaust, will come to Gaza if the rocket fire does not stop.

Many complained that Vilnai's use of the term cheapened the concept and the memory of the Nazi Holocaust. During its latest five-day onslaught, Israel killed 123 Palestinians, including 55 unarmed civilians. Twenty-seven children were among them, nearly a quarter of the total killed. Five Israelis were killed in the same period, four of them soldiers and one a civilian killed by a rocket landing in Israel.

And just last week, Israeli defense minister Ehud Barak sought legal opinions on the possibility of expelling Palestinian civilians from northern Gaza. Such attempts to drive Palestinians out of their homes and homeland began in earnest 60 years ago this year and continue today.

These numbers, of course, do not approach the magnitude of the Nazis' crimes. But should this make the deliberate and sustained siege of Gaza, and the mounting civilian death toll, acceptable?[3]

The real genocide in Gaza will not be assessed through sheer numbers. It is not a massacre involving gas chambers. Rather, it is a gradual, modern-day genocide—a genocide through more calibrated, long-term means.

It is cloaked in state-sanctioned legitimacy and "security concerns" and, as a result, tends to be overlooked. All is OK in Gaza, the wasteland, the "hostile territory" that is accustomed to slaughter and survival. Gaza, whose people are somehow less human, need not cause the world alarm, at least not until a mass killing or starvation is carried out. So the donors keep the trickle of humanitarian supplies coming, just enough to stave off disaster.

. . . Today, Gaza is being subjected to a slow, purposeful killing: a mass strangulation.

"We are living in dark and desperate times," my cousin Zuhair, a Gaza City lawyer and father of four, said solemnly on the phone to us from Gaza Sunday morning. His description was both figurative and literal. Israel continues to enforce court-sanctioned power cuts on Gaza's civilian population. This has meant living without reliable refrigeration for Gaza's residents. No power for pharmacies, restaurants, hospitals, hotels, morgues, dialysis, and neonatal units. And with diesel-run pumps unable to function with fuel reserves almost at zero, many Gazans are without access to fresh drinking water.

Minutes before we spoke with Zuhair, F-16 fighter jets leveled his neighbor's home, burying the entire family beneath the rubble. With continuous closures, even cement has run out, leaving no building materials to erect gravestones for the dead.

John Dugard, the UN special rapporteur on human rights in the Occupied Palestinian Territories, said, "Gaza is a prison, and Israel seems to have thrown away the key."[4] But even in a prison, inmates have certain rights, and the wardens have certain obligations they must fulfill toward them. They receive water, food, electricity.

In Gaza, Palestinians are guaranteed none of these things. And Israel, though obligated by international law to provide for the welfare of the population it is occupying, has declared the territory "hostile" in an attempt to evade its legal responsibilities.

Yet a recent poll in the Israeli newspaper *Haaretz* found that a majority of Israelis are in favor of their government engaging, rather than isolating, Hamas. They are calling for direct talks with the Islamic movement rather than punishing the entire population of Gaza because many of them voted Hamas into office. It is high time Israel and the United States began to listen. The consequences of not doing so are too high for both peoples.

In the Big Easy[5]
New Orleans, Louisiana, April 12, 2008

I'm in New Orleans with Noor this weekend to present "Tunnel Trade" at the New Orleans International Human Rights Film Festival.[6]

Several other Palestinian films being screened include *Bilin My Love*, *Driving to Zigzigland*, *Digital Resistance*, and *The Truth from Palestine*.

I am staying with a Lebanese family who live in—yes, it's true—West Bank (suburban New Orleans, west of the Mississippi).

Hana is an oncologist, and Mustapha is a pediatrician. They have three children, ages 13, 14, and 17. They graduated from American Uuniversity of Beirut and came to specialize in the United States in the late 1980s. Hana's house in Beirut just overlooked the camps of Sabra and Shatila, where she used to volunteer. "I remember carrying corpses of mutilated children—of children—in my arms," she says.

Waiting for the Rainfall[7]
Durham, North Carolina, April 18, 2008

I have a small garden behind the townhouse I rent, nothing terribly impressive. In fact, the soil is so acidic that it is inhospitable to most plants. It's mainly red clay, not unlike Gaza. Good for cucumbers and the like. But mainly, just mint grows in my garden. Lots and lots of mint interspersed with some thyme.

And a small Loquat tree.

Last year, my sister-in-law's Syrian father gave me the Loquat sapling from a larger tree that he smuggled in from Syria more than 20 years ago as a seedling and transplanted in Baton Rouge, Louisiana. Now, two decades on, I transplanted it in this small, acidic mint garden of mine.

The insects ate of the leaves what the tired soil did not. But it is spring, and somehow, new life has been breathed into it, and new leaves are coming out. It has survived.

But today, as North Carolina faces a continued drought, I contemplated for a moment whether I should even be watering this sad little garden of mine, or the brave little Loquat tree.

My mind travels. In Gaza, because of the Israeli-imposed power shortages, nearly 20 percent of Palestinians there receive water sparingly, for only three to five hours every four days.

The fuel shortages have cut the energy supply by 31 percent and have caused the suspension of garbage collection in Gaza City for the past two weeks.

And last week, 21 more dead. Five children, a farmer, a young cameraman, hit by Flechette shells . . . but who cares.

I decided not to water my mint or the Loquat. They can make do with the occasional rainfall.

Last week, my parents left for Egypt to try to return to Gaza. They were stuck here for nine months. They grew tired. So they figured they'd change pace and grow tired somewhere else—and wait, and wait some more, for the border to open, so they can return home, as if borders open on their own.

And if, after a month of waiting, or maybe two, there is no hope in waiting, they will return here to wait again.

And contemplate the ethical dilemmas of watering a mint garden during a drought.

Interview with Mossad's Danny Yatom[8]
Durham, North Carolina, April 25, 2008

This is an interview I did with former Mossad spy chief–cum–Labor politician Danny Yatom—in person. It was published on *Al Jazeera English* in two sections (parts one and two). I had the "opportunity" to meet Mr. Yatom at a confidential meeting of Palestinians and Israelis from across the spectrum—politicians, intellectuals, and journalists—who represented no one but themselves, hosted by the Swiss Foreign Ministry. Needless to say, nothing much came out of the meetings (except perhaps this interview!).

Here are the two parts of the *Al Jazeera* piece, each with some of its introduction:

> *Danny Yatom has held key military, security, and political posts during major junctures in Israel's history.*
>
> *But he is perhaps best known for his stint as the director of Mossad, Israel's intelligence agency, and the organization's botched assassination attempt on Khaled Meshaal, Hamas's political leader.*
>
> *In the first of a two-part interview with Al Jazeera conducted in April 2008, Yatom staunchly defends the assassination of Palestinians deemed "terrorists" by Israel.*
>
> *But he says his country is ready to negotiate with Hamas—albeit indirectly—to secure a cease-fire in the Gaza Strip and the release of Gilad Shalit, the Israeli soldier captured by Palestinian fighters in June 2006.*
>
> AL JAZEERA: In 1997, during your tenure as director, Mossad tried and failed to assassinate Khaled Meshaal, the Hamas political bureau chief. In retrospect, was the attempt to assassinate Meshaal a mistake?
>
> YATOM: I don't think so because he was and still is the head of Hamas, and he was situated in Amman. Now he is situated in Damascus, but all the links between the Gaza Strip and the West Bank regarding Hamas and the terror attacks during those days . . . were to Khaled Meshaal.
>
> The late Yitzhak Rabin [Israel's former prime minister] requested that King Hussein shut Hamas headquarters in Amman down.
>
> King Hussein refused. He said that his people can monitor Khaled Meshaal and his people better in Amman than if they were somewhere else. But the *Mukhabarat* [Jordan's security agency] did nothing.
>
> AL JAZEERA: How so?

YATOM: We had all the information. And Khaled Meshaal was the mastermind behind many attacks that claimed many lives.

After terror attacks in Jerusalem, Benjamin Netanyahu, the prime minister at the time, asked security chiefs to offer suggestions on how to fight Hamas—in addition to what Israel was then doing in the territories.

My suggestion was not Khaled Meshaal and was not Jordan.

AL JAZEERA: What was your suggestion?

YATOM: Something else. Not in an Arab country.

AL JAZEERA: Someone or something?

YATOM: Something.

Netanyahu decided that my suggestion was not tough enough on Hamas. He asked me to go after one of the heads—one of the four. They were Meshaal and three others: Ibrahim Ghosheh, Musa Abu Marzouk, and a fourth one.

And when the option came, when the plan became real, due to many reasons, it was Khaled Meshaal.

We very much understood the sensitivity of doing something in Jordan, so we decided to do it in a silent way. But there was a failure. The agents were caught by the Jordanian police.[9]

Immediately, when I got the information, I took a plane and went to see King Hussein and told him the entire story and that we had an antidote [to prevent Meshaal from dying].

We offered him—I offered him—the antidote, because I understood that if Meshaal was going to die after our people were caught, it was only likely to make the situation more complicated. The Jordanians refused to use it, because they thought it was [another] plot.

Meanwhile, Khaled Meshaal was dying, so the Jordanians demanded that we give them more information about the antidote. We gave it to them, and they were convinced. They gave him a shot, and since then he started to recover.

AL JAZEERA: . . . Would Israel assassinate Meshaal today?

YATOM: The Israeli policy is that as long as there is terror, the terrorist must understand that anyone who executes terror will not enjoy immunity.

AL JAZEERA: So Mossad carries out extrajudicial assassinations?

YATOM: The way I will refer to it is that whoever deals with terror should not enjoy any immunity.

AL JAZEERA: Without regard to international law?

YATOM: With regard to what [former president] Bill Clinton said:
There should be zero tolerance for terror.

AL JAZEERA: What do you think Israel should do now?

YATOM: I am against a large-scale ground operation, because I don't think that it will help—neither us, nor the Palestinians. It will only cause destruction and bloodshed and suffering.

But as long as Hamas fires rockets at our cities, we will fight back, and what is being done today is the way we should operate.

I think we have to support and to develop dialogue, via the good services of the Egyptians, with Hamas—not directly.

I am ready to negotiate a cease-fire that will cease all hostilities on both sides—one that will also seal the border and the Philadelphia corridor [the narrow stretch of land on the Egyptian-Gaza border] so that the Hamas will stop smuggling.

But only a cease-fire in Gaza, not the West Bank.

AL JAZEERA: Why?

YATOM: Because they don't control the West Bank. If there is an attempt to carry out terror in the West Bank, I don't want them to say "Israel violates its agreement" if Israel strikes there. I cannot agree to that.

AL JAZEERA: Hamas declared a unilateral cease-fire twice before, and Israel did not honor it.

YATOM: This is not true. What happened was that after a few days, rockets were fired at us by other [Palestinian groups].

A fully fledged cease-fire means everything.

AL JAZEERA: Do you think there is a military option in Gaza?

YATOM: I am against it.

AL JAZEERA: A recent poll by the *Haaretz* newspaper found that a majority of Israelis support talks with Hamas. Are you ready to engage Hamas, and, if not, why did Israel allow them to participate in the elections?

YATOM: We were forced by the Americans to allow Hamas to participate in elections, and it was a dramatic mistake because it was against what was written in Oslo—that only parties, not organizations, that accept our right to exist will participate in elections.

But, it was the pressure of George Bush, the U.S. president, and Condoleezza Rice, the U.S. secretary of state, that Ariel Sharon, the former Israeli prime minister, accept it. The common understanding in Israel and the United States was that Fateh would win. It was a surprise to all of us.

Second, as I told you, I am ready to talk to Hamas. But I am ready to talk to Hamas only on two issues in and in an indirect way: One is a ceasefire [in Gaza], and the second is the exchange of prisoners in order to get back Gilad Shalit. . . .

In the second part of an exclusive interview with Al Jazeera, Yatom, who remains close to Barak, says the [Labor] party would immediately start negotiations with Damascus if it returns to power.

AL JAZEERA: Is Israel ready to start negotiations with Syria?

YATOM: I support the idea that Israel should resume immediately talks with Syria, because I assess there is good chance to achieve full-fledged peace with Syria. This is not the position of my government.

AL JAZEERA: . . . Would Israel give up the Golan Heights in full?

YATOM: Rabin was ready, conditionally. He said that if all our needs are met, he will be ready to withdraw to the Fourth of June [the pre-1967 Arab-Israeli War] border. Barak suggested that he was ready also to withdraw from the Golan Heights; even Netanyahu . . . said to the Syrians that he was ready then to withdraw from the Golan Heights.

If it will be a full-fledged peace, and we will be able to secure our interests, there will be immediate normalization and exchange of ambassadors, open borders, trade—the answer is that we are ready.

AL JAZEERA: What has been the main stumbling block to this so far?

YATOM: The border.

Last time, during the summit in March 2000 in Geneva between [then–U.S. President Bill] Clinton and [then–Syrian President] Hafez al-Assad, Clinton proposed to the Syrians a plan that mistakenly said Israel would "give back to the Syrians *almost* the entire Golan Heights," and the word "almost" made Hafez furious, and so he stopped the meetings.

Other disputes include timetables, the nature of normalization, and when exactly to exchange ambassadors. But all of them are solvable.

AL JAZEERA: Are there back-channel negotiations going on now?

YATOM: The Syrian attitude since the time of Hafez al-Assad has been that of total objection to any back channel. Nothing is happening. If the [Labor] party becomes the ruling party, we will immediately start talks with Syria.

AL JAZEERA: . . . Yesterday, it was Palestinians in Gaza and the West Bank. Today, it is the Jerusalemites. Will the 1948 Palestinians—citizens of your own state—be next?

YATOM: Contrary to thought, they are loyal to the State of Israel. There were only some that executed terror attacks. I think the Israeli government should integrate them more into Israeli society. I think they should enjoy full rights and equality.

I don't think we will ever face a situation where the majority of them or a large part of them will try to execute terror attacks against Israel.

I am a great believer in two states: an independent, neighboring Palestinian state [where Palestinians] can enjoy all the rights in their homeland—the state of Palestine.

AL JAZEERA: But is such a state even feasible any more?

YATOM: Of course: In Camp David in 2000, we were very close to striking a deal, and I was highly disappointed that we accepted the American proposal as the basis for further negotiations and Arafat rejected it. We were ready to dismantle all the settlements that would be under the sovereignty of a Palestinian state.

Israel was ready to annex 9 percent of the West Bank in exchange for sovereignty over parts of Israel proper, equivalent to one-ninth of the annexed land.

We were ready to uproot all the settlements and to evacuate approximately 80,000 settlers.

AL JAZEERA: Were the constituents ready?

YATOM: We thought, with all those concessions—first, no right of return for [Palestinian refugees] to Israel . . . and second, that it would end the conflict between Israel and the Palestinians, the majority of the Israelis would accept it. Barak intended to go to referendum with the issue.

AL JAZEERA: But there is no referendum in Israeli society.

YATOM: We could pass a law for referendum.

AL JAZEERA: You are head of the West Bank Wall lobby. Why do you need a lobby?

YATOM: To put pressure on the [Israeli] government. It drags its legs. In the beginning of building in 2003, the plan was to finish it by 2005. Now there is only one half of it completed.

AL JAZEERA: The International Court of Justice ruled the wall illegal.

YATOM: I accept only the High Court of Israel's ruling.

AL JAZEERA: But not the ICJ ruling?

YATOM: No. No. No. The Hague rulings have no legal meaning.

AL JAZEERA: Is Israel more or less secure today than it was 20 years ago?

YATOM: Israel today faces only one existential threat: Iran. Meaning once Iran becomes nuclear, then it will be a threat to the state of Israel. I think Israel is safer, but if Iran gains, Israel will be less safe.

AL JAZEERA: Will Israel attack Iran?

YATOM: I hope the world will understand that Iran is cheating and concealing military activities.

Even today, there is evidence that Iran continues its military program and long-range missiles.

It is a problem for the entire world, not just Israel. And if the world does not take action, Israel will not sit idle.

Nakba at 60 and My "Blogger" Suspension[10]
Durham, North Carolina, May 11, 2008

. . . The reason for my absence of the past few days (besides the obvious preoccupation of motherhood!) is that Blogger suspended my blog, and I had to request a review to get it unlocked! I received an e-mail telling me that "Your blog, at http://a-mother-from-gaza.blogspot.com/, has been identified as a potential spam blog" and that though this was likely an error, I had to request a review. Eventually, it was unlocked.

However, I was curious and obviously upset, and upon further investigation, I found that several Palestinian and pro-Palestinian blogs have suffered a similar fate—their blogs being targeted as "potential spam blogs." Some took months to get unlocked.

. . . Cyber terrorism, perhaps, to mark the 60th anniversary of the *Nakba*? If so, shame on Google, shame on Blogger.

In other news, my parents remain in Egypt. They are making their way tonight to the border to attempt to get in on the single day of three days (the first in almost a year) that the crossing will be open for passage into Gaza.

Meanwhile, with Gaza's only power plant forced to shut down for lack of fuel, Gaza is suffering blackouts once again. The dead are being carried to morgues and cemeteries on donkey carts now. Cars are no longer in use. Light—and hope—are being shut out of people's lives. A bag of flour is now 160 shekels, with many bakeries threatening to shut down. Meats have doubled in price. Fida tells me that in Rafah, people are seen going door to door begging for morsels of food. . . .

Obama for Israel![11]
Durham, North Carolina, June 4, 2008

I shouldn't be surprised or anything, but really . . . did Obama's transition from clinching the Democratic nomination to all out American Israeli Public Affairs Committee prostitution have to be so stark? Maybe because I am not an American citizen and don't vote, I'm looking at this from a different perspective (as in, a national of that place you think should remain under siege).

I know it's one of those situations people keep hoping will turn out better than it really is or a lesser-of-two-evils type of thing: "He has to say that, but when he's in office. . . . "

But does he? Polls of past years showed that, in fact, most Americans were in support of a new U.S. Middle East policy: one where Israel was not allowed to get away with every damned thing, where it did not get blind support, where American pressure should be used to achieve a just and lasting peace. Yet presidential candidate after candidate continues to think otherwise. I mean, c'mon, Jerusalem, the undivided capital of Israel? That's very . . . how shall we say . . . Bush-esque? Billy Graham? Yesterday? What was that about peace in 2008?

I've said it once, and I will say it again: American politicians are stauncher Zionists than Israelis. As Sharon once said, Bush can be a mouthpiece for Israel. Or something like that. And now, we have Barak . . . er . . . Barack.

Pain at the Pump? Think of Gaza.[12]
Durham, North Carolina, June 17, 2008

. . . I was talking to my father today in Gaza. "How's the car doing? Did you fix that loud noise it was making?" he asked, ever the concerned parent.

"Yes, it's purring like a kitten now, and I'm $400 poorer," I said. "Lucky car. But the gas is $4 a gallon now."

"Yeah, well, we don't have gas; don't complain."

In fact, he was quick to point out that gas is in such short supply now in Gaza that it's selling on the black market for 600 shekels per 20 liters, the equivalent of $35 per gallon. Yes, you read that correctly: 1 gallon = $35.

Of course, the real problem is not for the average "consumer," because Gazans are not really "gas guzzlers"; it is for the things that fuel powers—everything from water pumps to hospital generators.

A brief e-mail from my dad and a picture he took:

> Dear Laila:
> I attached some pictures of Gaza today. Almost no cars in the streets as there is no gas (my car is parked), little diesel by ration to taxis. People started using biodiesel (cooking oil instead of diesel), which causes irritation to the skin, eyes, and breathing. People use masks when they walk to minimize the smell. Streets are clean, as you can see—100 times cleaner than Cairo. Food supplies are twice as expensive.
> Taxis are scarce now. But if you find one, it costs double or triple what it used to be. Public taxis run on biodiesel now because of shortage of fuel: 2 [new Israeli shekel] NIS per person. Private taxi costs 20 NIS in town. People walk a lot more now.
> I attached a photo of empty streets of Gaza because of the fuel shortage and people standing in long lines to receive coupons to get gas by ration, just like what happened in Europe during [World War II].
> Baba.

Moussa El-Haddad

The sign reads: "Travel... Education... Medical treatment... Hajj... Humanitarian needs...why have we been prevented from them?"

Land of the Cursed[13]
Asheville, North Carolina, July 11, 2008

A few weeks ago, a colleague of mine sent me a story he had received by e-mail, asking if I could publish it. It was the firsthand account of a Palestinian man, his Gaza-born wife, and their family, all of whom were born and raised in the West Bank. It was the story of their attempt to cross the Allenby Bridge into Jordan for a much-needed break and to visit with some relatives in Amman.

They soon learned that the curse of being Gazan—or in this case, even being related to someone born in Gaza—followed them even to the West Bank.[14]

Last year, I reported on the issue of the 50,000-some Palestinians living lives of legal limbo in the West Bank and Gaza (and abroad) because one of their family members lacks a *hawiya*—the Israeli-issued identification card used to maintain control over the Palestinian population registry. In my own case, Yassine has not yet been granted a *hawiya*, even though I applied for him in 2004. This is nothing compared with the tens of thousands who have been waiting since the mid-1990s.

Similarly, because Israel continues to control the Palestinian population registry (yes, even after disengagement), it controls Palestinian movement and life. It tears that movement and life and the families that would want to enjoy them apart.

Rest in Peace, Mahmoud Darwish[15]
Asheville, North Carolina, August 10, 2008

Palestine lost one of its greatest sons yesterday, and it is not just Palestinians who mourn the loss of the iconic Mahmoud Darwish. His words touched the consciousness of Palestinians and non-Palestinians alike, the world over. He was imbued with the ability to stir our emotions, evoking tears and smiles, hope and fear, belonging and displacement, all at once—putting to words what every Palestinian felt, defining us at different moments as a nation. In so doing, he transcended the status of a mere "poet," or artist, or even activist. Below is one of my favorite and most oft-quoted of his poems. Rest in peace, poet of a nation and our struggle.

> The Earth is closing on us
> pushing us through the last passage
> and we tear off our limbs to pass through.
> The Earth is squeezing us.
> I wish we were its wheat
> so we could die and live again.
> I wish the Earth was our mother
> so she'd be kind to us.
>
> I wish we were pictures on the rocks
> for our dreams to carry as mirrors.
> We saw the faces of those who will throw
> our children out of the window of this last space.
> Our star will hang up mirrors.
> Where should we go after the last frontiers?
> Where should the birds fly after the last sky?
> Where should the plants sleep after the last breath of air?
> We will write our names with scarlet steam.
> We will cut off the hand of the song to be finished by our flesh.
> We will die here, here in the last passage.
> Here and here our blood will plant its olive tree.[16]

—Mahmoud Darwish

Out Fishing in Gaza![17]
Asheville, North Carolina, August 25, 2008

Moussa El-Haddad

After a long and hard trip, a group of activists who sailed to Gaza from Cyprus in the first such event in 41 years plan to return and take with them a few stranded Palestinian Fulbright scholars. While in Gaza, the Free Gaza human rights group delivered hearing aids to a charity—Atfaluna Society for Deaf Children (whose handicrafts, made by deaf men and women, I absolutely adore).

But before doing so, they accompanied Palestinian fisherman yesterday morning to help them break the maritime siege on their fishing boats. The Oslo Accords were supposed to "grant them" (a natural right, but they decided it should be bestowed nonetheless) the right to fish 20 nautical miles out to sea. In reality, this has translated to no more than 12 nautical miles in the best of times; 4 nautical miles at the height of the second Intifada, based on my interviews with fishermen; and 6 nautical miles in the past few years.[18]

Their fishing vessels are frequently shot at by the Israeli Navy, the fishermen themselves harassed; thrown into the water; beaten, detained; and, in many cases, killed, rendering their once-bustling profession and mainstay of the Gazan economy one of its most dangerous jobs.

The hope was that, accompanied by international activists and a swarm of media alongside them, the Israeli Naval boats would lay off; and despite circling them from afar with their enormous guns pointing toward them, they did.

My father and mother accompanied one of the fishing vessels to aid in translation and protection. Initially, the fishermen were afraid to leave for fear of being shot at by the Israelis. Slowly, they decided to attempt to surpass the nautical-mile limit imposed on them.

And they did.

The fishermen told him it was their most successful catch in four years!

⟨⟩

Bigotry in Virginia, Alive and Well[19]

Fairfax, Virginia, September 22, 2008

So, I had a run-in with a bigot yesterday. It's one of those scenarios that is almost so generic, you might think it is destined for made-for-television films (and it's also very likely that's where the bigot in question got his lines from).

I was visiting my older brother and his family this weekend in northern Virginia—Fairfax, to be exact. Incidentally, he's a cardiologist. We were toting our small army of children and babies to a local state park and made a pit stop at a Walmart for some trout worms and juice (an odd grocery list, I confess).

I'll also confess that my brother's driving can be a bit frantic at times. I was trying to keep up as he sped into the parking lot, and next thing I knew, I was at the receiving end of a voracious honk from a car to my right in a four-way intersection. The car was a good distance away and hadn't moved, but I suppose he wanted to make a point.

That was that, and we parked, waiting for my brother to retrieve the necessary items and come back. Just then, a stout white man of, oh, 45 years, walked by my car, giving me a very prominent middle finger and a very articulate "F*&* you" (and I thought the joke was you wouldn't make it far in Boston without a middle finger!).

"OK—fine, he's clearly upset, not yet making any connection, and I'm fasting, so I need to control my temper," I thought, and I let it go.

I stood outside the car with an antsy Noor, while Yousuf took a nap in his car seat. Soon, my brother emerged from the Walmart, and, lo and behold, behind him was the same man. He came up to me.

"Is there something bothering you with me, sir?" I beckoned.

"Yes, your driving—you nearly ran into my vehicle!! You . . . you. . . . "

"I'm sorry—I was actually quite far away from your vehicle, and it was my right of way."

"Free Palestine? Palestine's already free!" he raged, gesturing to a bumper sticker on the back of my windshield as he began to walk away.

Clearly, my driving wasn't the only thing bothering him.

"I'm sorry?"

He then turned around and bellowed out, "Why don't you go back to your country!?"

"We live here, and I'll have you know our values are probably more American than yours will ever be."

"Yeah, right," he muttered, continuing on his way.

At this point, my brother, an American citizen, went up to confront him. The man came up within an inch of his face, pointing and yelling something about his tax dollars, and how there was no occupation, and how we should all go back home. His blood began to boil, and he looked about ready to swat my brother, who was explaining to him where his tax dollars were really going.

"I dare you to lay one finger on him," I said. "Go ahead. We'll press charges. It's called a hate crime, and you'll end up where you belong. You, sir, are a bigot. Go ahead and say what you just said on a loudspeaker to everyone in this parking lot, if you weren't such a coward."

Mind you, we are in northern Virginia. During the 10 minutes I stood in the parking lot alone, we were passed by Indians, Mexicans, Chinese, Arabs, and African Americans. I wonder what he would have had to say about all of them.

A few people took a moment to glance at what was happening. But for the most part, they kept on their way. And that was what was really frightening—bringing to mind a social experiment that was conducted and filmed for the ABC News *What Would You Do?* series about a racist cafe owner refusing to serve a Muslim woman (the incident was staged and repeated dozens of times on tape) on its February 26, 2008, show.

Several people vocally supported the man in denying her service and telling her the same things he did ("Go back to where you came from" . . . "If you were really American, you wouldn't wear a towel on your head" . . . "Take your jihad out to the parking lot," etc., etc.), even giving him a thumbs up and saying they would do the same. Many opposed him, saying they were deeply offended and that he was disgusting. But the overwhelming majority stood by and did nothing.

And that is the scary part—you realize that maybe for every person angry and stupid enough actually to verbalize his racist thoughts, there must be five others who are thinking them.

Back to my story. Several other Muslims going shopping with their families emerged from their cars, asking if we needed help, calling him a racist and telling him to leave us alone. He soon backed off and was on his own cowardly way.

As I said, it's sort of one of those incidents you anticipate (at least as a veiled Muslim woman or even as a person of color and minority) your entire life. Shortly after September 11, I was once called a terrorist by an elderly man in a CVS pharmacy in Cape Cod; his daughter insisted that he was suffering from dementia. But, for the most part, I usually expect (and receive) the good in people—people accusing airport personnel of profiling me, for example, or asking if I need help, or just saying hello.

But when something like this does happen, I suppose the shock value is still so high that you never quite know how to respond. And you sit there stewing for a while, wondering how human beings can be so unabashedly vile—especially in this day and age—to one another.

Someone suggested I should have told him to crawl back to the rat hole he emerged from, in response to his asking me to go back home (I also imagined that if everyone in this country was asked to go back "to where they came from," there wouldn't be anyone left, except maybe the Native Americans).

That might have been satisfying. Another part of me wished I had just told him that it was Ramadan and that I would pray extra hard for God to bless him with a kinder spirit and a more tolerant soul, so his next victim would be spared a similar, if not worse, fate. Amen to that.

Belonging[20]
Durham, North Carolina, November 3, 2008

Every day, I sit down in front of my laptop during that single hour of time that I own but that somehow seems to own me, after my children fall asleep (sometimes on the couch . . . but who's counting?). I sit down, and I say, "OK, time to write a new post." But it doesn't happen; instead, I begin to go off on tangents until I wonder how my precious hour passed. So today, I decided simply to let my words spill out without worrying about excessive editing and beautification. Today, my tangent was thinking about a time in my childhood when I actually had time to feel "bored."

I've also been distracted by other thoughts—thoughts of homeland, of absence, of belonging, suspension of time, and place, and space.

And the elections, of course, and all that jazz . . . counting the visit to my brother's this weekend, we've have five house visits from Obama campaigners, "Change" buttons plastered to their vests, clipboards in hand. I applauded their efforts but stopped them short to save them the trouble. We aren't citizens, I told them, and I'm not sure how I got on their list (their answer: The lists don't specify citizenship). I also suggested they work on my blue-collar neighbors; with a house full of at least five—hold your breath for this one—undecided voters, they had their work cut out. You may have heard, North Carolina has been thrust into the limelight as a swing state all of a sudden—and so forth. As though it mattered, as though I belonged, somehow, to this season, to this cycle, to this time, to this place.

I keep up to date with all the Free Gaza news of the ships traveling to and from Cyprus and Gaza. And I think how lucky they are, to have the luxury of choosing to sail voluntarily to Gaza to prove a point. I think how in this day and age, in this time of ours, where borders and all they signify seem to dissolve, they have actually never mattered more; citizenship has never mattered more—the paradox of my existence.

My father provides his daily updates on Skype: collection of the olives from his farm during the fall harvest; pressing them for oil today; they had a surplus. Persimmons are finally in season, but still expensive. They'll get cheaper though, he assures me, as though it will matter. As though I belong to that season, that cycle, that time, that place.

It's chilly outside. My fig tree stands upright and green, branching out near the rosemary and Loquat, as though snubbing its nose at the weather. It is estranged, too. And who, in my lonely little garden, really belongs to this place or this season. Some thrive, and others make do with the reality before them: They predict a harsh winter this year. Conserve your energy, like the dormant mint, until the season passes.

Gaza's Darkness[21]
Durham, North Carolina, November 15, 2008

Last night, I dreamed I was in Gaza. I woke up to Noor's crying and shot out of bed.

It takes a while for my faucet to switch from cold to hot. But the hot water feels better in the winter. Every time I take a warm shower, I think of Gaza. Of the days we had no warm water. Or any water for that matter. Every single time I take a shower, I think of Gaza.

I haven't heard from my parents in two days—unusual considering we are usually on Skype daily.

So I call my father, and, as I suspected, the electricity has been out for 48 hours now.

"We'll make do, we always do. Just like everyone else," he says matter-of-factly. They are lucky. They are not hungry.

Others have no such faith to fall back on.

UN food distribution centers, on which nearly half of Gaza's population relies—20,000 at any given time—have also shut down, their supplies depleted as a result of Israel's recent tightening of the blockade on Gaza.

Soon, there will be more pressure to get the wheels running again. People must be fed, after all; even prisoners are fed. But no matter if they lose all hope. After all, the civilized world does not invest in hope. It only invests in destroying it. Bullets are more tangible than hope. Hunger is an easier statisical indicator than disillusionment and depression and broken dreams.

Yousuf Gets Creative—Again[22]
Durham, North Carolina,
November 24, 2008

I honestly don't know what to make of this. . . .
On the face of it, it appears to be some sort of
structure constructed out of plastic forks and a
traditional Japanese swan vase (and which he
later forbade me from taking apart, saying it
was his masterpiece).

Should I:

1. Be upset that Yousuf destroyed $10 worth
of plastic cutlery (including the many "trial
runs")?

2. Be delighted that his creativity is budding
and that he can entertain himself with common
household items—and to hell with the plastic?

3. Be worried that he can entertain himself
for hours with plastic and toothpicks?

Hmm.

It's in the Details[23]
Durham, North Carolina, December 24, 2008

We celebrated Eid al-Adha last week with my brother. We made a seven-layer
chocolate cake and decorated it to look like the *Kaaba*—around which the kids
circulated seven times as though performing the *tawaf* in *Hajj*. The children got a
kick out of this gastronomical pilgrimage. I was tempted to make little marzipan
pilgrims, but I thought it might be a bit gruesome eating their heads.

As usual, I Skyped my father to wish him glad tidings and to hear of the death
of his cousin, "the one who always sat on the street in front of Khamees's store,
sipping a bottle of sparkling water, in the green bottles, from Egypt."

The funeral coincided with Eid, so my father's scraggly, awkward stubble of a
beard, which he was growing in anticipation of the holiday following the prophetic
tradition (though he has never before grown it as long as I can remember) could
have easily been mistaken as a sign of respect in the incidence of a close family
member's death: two in one.

The news seemed to get darker by the day. At first they were happy with losing
electricity for only four hours a day, and then eight, 12, and 15 hours. And now,

they are going for 18 to 20 hours of outages at a time. They have a generator—purchased from the tunnel gray markets in Rafah, says my mother. It's giving them some problems, and so they have sent it to be fixed by a local mechanic. The local mechanics fix anything—old microwaves, broken toasters, laptops, digital cameras, blenders. Most learned during their days as day laborers in Israel.

In addition to the generator, they also share a line with our neighbors, the ones who own a famous Gaza boutique and who are originally from Nablus—five brothers. They are on a different grid, and so the outages are at different times and vice versa.

We're Skyping less and less these days. When the electricity is on, my father takes the opportunity to log on immediately or call me to let me know he can talk. Sometimes, he logs on with the generator, but then we can only use audio and for a limited time.

"How are things?" I ask, nonfacetiously.

"Well, we got a bird."

"What?"

"A *hasoon*. You know, they are quite rare these days."

"Doesn't he get cold?"

"You're just like your mom. She asked the same question. Birds don't get cold—how do you think he survives in the wild? But anyway, I cover him at night and put him out on the balcony during the day."

"But he's not in the wild. Anyway, where did you get him?"

"The guy who takes care of your mom's land in Mawasi. . . . He likes to catch quails, and he caught this *hasoon*, and so I bought it from him. . . . "

"He gave us cauliflower and cabbage from the land. . . , " chimed in my mother. She rambled on about the land, and the man who is taking care of it, and the condition it's in, and what's growing there, and what the plans are for it, or lack thereof—details that now escape me. The land used to be my grandfather's, and it is very sentimental to my mother.

The details seem boring. But they are what keep them going. What keep us all going. You see, trying to find a way to keep up with the boring details, to manage them, also keeps alive the illusion of normalcy. It is some kind of anesthetic I suppose. It keeps the hope afloat that the dawn is near—even if "near" is actually not so near at all.

CHAPTER NOTES

1. Read *Haaretz*'s "Disinformation, Secrecy, and Lies: How the Gaza Offensive Came About," by Barak Ravid and *Haaretz* correspondent, December 27, 2008. The full original text of this post is archived at http://www.haaretz.com/news/ disinformation-secrecy-and-lies-how-the-gaza-offensive-came-about-1.260347, shortened to http://bit.ly/aCtWN8. See also the Israeli National Security Council's assessments for 2009: "If the current Hamas-Israel truce in Gaza breaks down, the NSC recommends that Israel launch a wide-ranging operation to topple Hamas in Gaza."
2. Laila El-Haddad, "Slowly Strangled", *Guardian*, March 13, 2008, archived at http://bit.ly/annR0g.
3. Read the *Guardian*'s Jonathan Steele on the European response to the Gaza siege, archived at http://bit.ly/bxZMBi.
4. Reuters, "UN Human Rights Envoy Says Gaza a Prison for Palestinians," *Haaretz*, September 26, 2006, archived at http://bit.ly/98Uy76.
5. Archived at http://bit.ly/cxeggj.
6. Find out more about *Tunnel Trade*, archived at http://bit.ly/anN2Mu.
7. Archived at http://bit.ly/df8EdU.
8. Archived at http://bit.ly/cEeuWK. Also published in two parts on *Al Jazeera English*. See "Part 1: Ex-Mossad Head Defends Meshaal Plot," *Al Jazeera English*, April 25, 2008, archived at http://bit.ly/c1RMAS; "Part 2: Yatom: Peace with Syria Is Possible," *Al Jazeera English*, April 26, 2008, archived at http://bit.ly/d3XTn4.
9. Paul McGeough, *Kill Khalid: The Failed Mossad Assassination of Khalid Mishal and the Rise of Hamas* (New York: New Press, 2009).
10. Archived at http://bit.ly/dliHFU.
11. Archived at http://bit.ly/9IrXVc.
12. Archived at http://bit.ly/9CW6XK.
13. Archived at http://bit.ly/9WBwQZ.
14. You can read the family's whole story at ibid.
15. Archived at http://bit.ly/ccpYrg.
16. Mahmoud Darwish, "The Earth Is Closing on Us," trans. Abdullah al-Udhari, in *Victims of a Map* (London: Al-Saqi Books, 1984), 13.
17. Archived at http://bit.ly/9JzyMp.
18. The mileage fishing limit has most recently been reduced to 3 nautical miles.
19. Archived at http://bit.ly/atD0xT.
20. Archived at http://bit.ly/9IYX1n.
21. Archived at http://bit.ly/9Myazs.
22. Archived at http://bit.ly/bjdp5d.
23. Archived at http://bit.ly/cSh8Rd.

Chapter 20

The Lead Is Cast

December 27, 2008–January 18, 2009

On December 27, 2008, Israel launched the long-planned onslaught against Gaza, code-named Operation Cast Lead—and otherwise known as the Gaza War or the Gaza Massacre. Israeli officials said that it was designed to stop the rocket fire that some Palestinian groups had been sending into Israel (just as Israel had been sending heavy artillery fire into Gaza, assassinating Palestinians and keeping Gaza's crossings completely closed) since a six-month cease-fire came to its end in mid-December. But Israeli officials and commentators made clear that their aims were also political: to "restore the credibility of Israel's deterrent power" throughout the region, while in Gaza they hoped to inflict such punishment on the population that it would rise up and overthrow Hamas.

The initial wave of fierce air and artillery attacks took Gaza by surprise. On the first day alone, nearly 200 people were killed, many of them newly minted police officers attending their graduation at the police academy. A week into the assault, the Israelis escalated the conflict to include an invasion of ground troops from land and sea. But 22 days into the war, they had still not conquered Gaza, and they failed to turn Gaza's people against Hamas. The assault ended on January 18, just a few days before the inauguration of President Barack Obama.

Israel's war effort saw the summary execution of civilians and the systematic targeting of private homes, farms and agricultural infrastructure, civilian police stations, universities, places of worship, medical facilities, fishing boats, and factories. It intentionally targeted the security infrastructure first, as it had done following the eruption of the second Intifada, when Yasser Arafat was in power. Some 1,400 Palestinians and 13 Israelis were killed. It was a terrifying and dark time for my parents, who were right there in central Gaza City with no electricity, no water, and nowhere to flee to. It was challenging for me as well, as I tried to maintain contact with them, not knowing if they would live to see us again from one day to the next, while I also tried to convey what they were seeing and experiencing to the wider world.

The Rains of Death in Gaza[1]
Durham, North Carolina, December 27, 2008

We woke up this morning to the news in Gaza. It seems we always wake up to news there, so it's become a matter of perspective how bad the news is each time; how remote it seems each time; how real or not; how severe—and whether the severity warrants an "international outcry" or whether the "animals" in the zoo that all of Gaza has become can continue to fester in their cages for a while longer.

We received a call from my in-laws in Lebanon's Baalbek refugee camp at an early hour, checking in on my family in Gaza, because they cannot call them directly. We call my parents. My father does not answer. We call his mobile—we reach him. He has just returned from Shifa hospital—we hold our breaths.

"We are OK. We went to donate blood and to see if they needed any help," says my father, a retired surgeon.

"I was out in the souk when the strikes began—I saw the missiles falling and prayed; the earth shook; the smoke rose; the ambulances screamed," he said, sirens audible in the background. He was on Talateeni Street at the time of the attacks, just a few blocks down from the site of one of the first attacks against a police-academy graduation ceremony.

My mother was in the Red Crescent Society clinic near the universities at the time of the initial wave of attacks, where she works part-time as a pediatrician. Behind the clinic was one police center that was leveled. She broke down at first, the sheer proximity of the attacks having shaken her from the inside out. After she got hold of herself, they took to treating injured victims of the attack before transferring them to Shifa hospital.

There, she said, medical supplies were in short supply: face masks, surgical gloves, gowns. . . .

My parents live in the city center, and the Israeli war planes attacked people and locations all around them. More than 50 "targets" by 60 warplanes, read the headlines in *Haaretz*. And more than 220 killed—in broad daylight, in the after-school rush.

Like a movie tagline. Or a game. If you say it enough times, it does not sound real anymore: 50 targets, 60 warplanes, 200 people, 1 day: the War on Gaza.

All very sanitary. Very sleek. Neatly packaged: war in a gift box.

"There is a funeral passing every minute. The bodies are piling up," my dad continued. Gaza's air is saturated with the smell of burning human flesh. There is panic, as one would imagine dogs would panic in an overcrowded cell when several of their own are violently, abruptly killed. But dead dogs—in a cage, no less—would create an outcry.

The rains of death continue to fall in Gaza. And silently, we watch. And silently, governments plotted: How shall we make the thunder and clouds rain death onto Gaza, Egypt, the United States, Israel?

And it will all be made to seem, in the end of the day, that this was somehow a response to something. As though the situation were not only acceptable but normal, stable, in the period before whatever this is a response to. As though settlements did not continue to expand; walls did not continue to extend and choke lands and lives; families and friends were not dislocated; life were not paralyzed; people were not exterminated; borders were not sealed; and food, light, and fuel were in fair supply.

Update: Gaza[2]
Durham, North Carolina, December 28, 2008

Gaza's punishment continues today. Communication has been intermittent, but we have managed to keep the lines open. My father just called to inform me he was OK after warplanes bombed the Islamic University, considered to be the Strip's premiere academic institution.

A little later, I called my mother, only to hear her crying on the phone. "The planes are overhead," she wailed. "The planes are overhead." I tried to calm her down—planes overhead mean the "target" is farther away. But in such moments of intense fear, there is no room for rationality and logic.

There is only you, and there are war planes; and nothing in between, besides military orders and a video-game screen.

Her panic subsided slightly. . . . "OK, OK, your father says it was the navy gunships. . . . They hit the pier. . . . The poor fishermen, it's not like it's even a real pier . . . it's just the pier, just the pier. . . . "

She tried to convince my father not to go out to the mosque today. But he did. Most people stayed indoors.

So far, the death toll has surpassed 300, with nearly 1,000 injured, many critically.

OCHA reports that search operations for dead bodies trapped under the rubble are still ongoing. Piles of bodies were placed in front of Shifa hospital for identification—some too charred or dismembered to identify.

Most fatalities were civilian police; others included at least 20 children, nine women, and 60 other unarmed civilians.

The plotters have plotted; the pawns were in place; and the living dead continue to be massacred without a protest.

Bloodied in Gaza[3]
Durham, North Carolina, December 30, 2008

"There is a complete blackout in Gaza now. The streets are as still as death."

I am speaking to my father, Moussa El-Haddad, a retired physician who lives in Gaza City, on Skype, from Durham, North Carolina, where I have been since mid-2007—the month Gaza's borders were hermetically sealed by Israel, and the blockade of the occupied territory further enforced.

He is out on his balcony. It is 2 a.m.

"I can only see gray plumes of smoke slowly rising all over the city, everywhere I look," he says, as though they were some beautiful, comforting by-product of some hideous, malicious event.

My father was out walking when the initial strikes began. "I saw the missiles falling and prayed; the earth shook; the smoke rose; the ambulances screamed," he told me.

My mother was working her shift in the Red Crescent Society when one of the police stations behind the clinic was leveled.

Now, three days later, they are trapped in their own home.

My father takes a deep restorative sigh, before continuing: "Ehud Barak has gone crazy. He's gone crazy. He is bombing everywhere and everything. . . . No one is safe."

Explosions are audible in the background. They sound distant and dull over my laptop's speakers but linger like an echo in death's valley. They evoke terrifying memories of my nights in Gaza only two years ago. Nights that to this day haunt my 4-year-old son, who refuses to sleep on his own.

"Can you hear them?" my father continues. "Our house is shaking. We are shaking from the inside out."

My mother comes to the phone. "Hello, hello dear," she mutters, her voice trembling. "I had to go to the bathroom. But I'm afraid to go alone. I wanted to perform *wudu'* before prayer, but I was scared. Remember days when we would go to the bathroom together, because you were too afraid to go alone?" She laughs at the thought. It seems amusing to her now, that she was scared to find her death in a place of relief, that she is now terrified of the same seemingly ridiculous scenario.

It was really the fear of being alone. When you "hear" the news before it becomes news, you panic for clarity—you want someone to make sense of the situation, package it into comprehensible terms and locations. Just to be sure it's not you this time.

"It's strange, my whole body is shaking. Why is that? Why is that?" she rambles on, continuous explosions audible in the background. "There they go again. One boom after another—15. Before that, one or two, maybe 20 total so far."

Counting and systemizing the assaults make them easier to deal with. More technical. More remote.

We speak to each other throughout the day. Last night, she called to let me know there were gunships overhead, as though there was something I could do about it—as though my voice would somehow make them disappear.

Eventually, her panic subsided. . . .

My mother's close friend Yosra was asked to evacuate her building. She and her husband live in a flat near many of the ministry complexes being targeted. They were advised not to go to the mosque for services, lest they were bombed.

Another family friend, an elderly Armenian Palestinian Christian and retired pharmacist, is paralyzed with fear and confined, like many residents, to her home. She lives alone, in front of the Saraya security complex on Omar al-Mukhtar Street. The complex has already been bombed twice.

The rains of death continue to fall in Gaza. And silently, the world watches. And silently, governments plotted: How shall we make the thunder and clouds rain death on to Gaza?

And it will all be made to seem, in the end of the day, as a response to something: rockets, broken truces, irreconcilability . . .

As though the situation were completely acceptable in the period prior to it all. . . . But it is the prisoners' burden to bear: They broke the conditions of their incarceration. Nevertheless, there are concerns for the "humanitarian situation": as long as they do not starve. . . .

The warden improves the living conditions now and then, in varying degrees of relativity, but the prison doors remain sealed. And so when there are 20 hours of power outages in a row, the prisoners wish that they were only eight, or 10, and dream of the days of four.

My friend Safah Joudeh is also in Gaza City. She is a 27-year-old freelance journalist.

"At this point, we don't feel that it is Hamas being targeted—it's the entire population of Gaza," she says. "The strikes have been, and I need to stress this, indiscriminate. They claim that the targets have been buildings and people that are Hamas affiliated, but the employees in these buildings are public-sector employees, not political activists. . . . Other targets include homes, mosques, the university, port, fishing boats, the fish market."

No one has left their home since Saturday, she says.

"The streets were full of people the first day of the attacks, naturally. They were unexpected and came at a time when people were going about their daily business. The streets have been completely empty the past two days. People have closed up shop and are trying to stay close to their families and loved ones. Many homes are without bread—the bakeries stopped working two days before the attack because of lack of fuel and flour."

Monday morning, five sisters from one family were killed when Israeli war planes attacked a mosque next to their home. Four-year-old Jawahir Anwar.

Eight-year-old Dina Anwar. Twelve-year-old Sahar Anwar. Fourteen-year-old Ikram Anwar. Seventeen-year-old Tahrir Anwar.

The small shop down the street from my parents' home, next to the Kinz mosque where many of the Remal neighborhood's affluent residents attend, opens for a little while after prayer. My father goes and gets whatever he can—while he can.

They have one package of bread left but insist they are OK.

"Those with children are the ones who are truly suffering. Umm Ramadan's grandchildren will only sleep in her arms now. They are wetting their pants again."

My son, Yousuf, chimes into the conversation unceremoniously, popping his head into my laptop screen.

"*Seedo?* I like the *fatoosh* you used to make! *Seedo* . . . are you OK?"

"*Habibi*, when we see each other again—if we see each other again—I'll make it for you," he promises. The very possibility seems to comfort him, no matter how illusory.

It is my daughter Noor's birthday on January 1. She will be 1 year old. I cannot help but think: Who was born in bloodied Gaza today?

There Is No "Safe"[4]
Durham, North Carolina, December 31, 2008

My father just called. I have learned to expect that the 9 p.m. call is not a jovial one: It is usually to alert me of some awful thing transpiring around them. It helps, in whatever way, to broadcast this event that has yet to be broadcast to the world, to whomever you can. In this case, that person is me.

I see the number on my caller identification; my heart races. I answer my cell phone.

"We . . . are under . . . heavy bombardment. Heavy bombardment," says my father in terrified, articulated syllables.

"They are bombing the Legislative Council building next to our house. They are bombing just down our street."

"*Baba* . . . are you safe, are you both safe?" I ask, not knowing what else to say.

"I have to go now. . . . I have to go. . . . I just wanted to tell you that . . . but I have to go," he stammers. And the line goes dead.

We have figured out a system. When the electricity is back on in Gaza—which has happened for one hour during the past 48—my parents get on Skype immediately. If I am not around, they give me a quick call from their landline to let me know they are back online; they have two to three hours of back-up generator time after this. They stocked up on fuel during the past few weeks.

Then, it is dark again.

When the bombs are dropped around them, they send me a quick note to inform me of what happened before running to safety. I am still not sure where "safety" is; neither, I think, do they. It is perhaps more a mental state and place than a physical one. In any other situation, people flee to what they perceive as safer locations. In Gaza, there is no "safe." And there is nowhere to flee to, with the borders closed and the sky and sea under siege.

This afternoon, I received these instant messages from them on Skype:

> [1:56:04 PM] moussa.elhaddad says: F-16 and Apaches are in the sky of Gaza now.
> [1:56:16 PM] moussa.elhaddad says: Five new explosions.
> [1:57:58 PM] moussa.elhaddad says: One near Al-Nasr hospital, two behind our house. Money exchangers (Al-Bar'asy and Hirzallah); two other explosions a little bit far away.

Yesterday, my uncle's neighbor's home was leveled. Luckily, no one was hurt. But all 50 occupants were made homeless. They were out on the streets with nothing but the clothes on their backs. Each had to find shelter with a different relative.

This morning, my father and I appeared together on NPR—WUBR's *Here and Now*. There was a surreal quality to it. And for a few moments, we were in that "safe" place together, on some distant, sterile airwaves. It is windy and cold today in Durham. I shiver when the shutters shake. And I think of Gaza. I think of home.

Israeli Shin Bet Recruiter Punked in Gaza![5]
Durham, North Carolina, January 4, 2009

This was a brilliant stunt pulled by *Electronic Intifada* (*EI*). I encourage people the world over to begin doing the same—flood their lines with calls telling them who the *real* terrorists are!

In addition to bombs and missiles that have killed an ever-increasing number of Palestinian civilians, Israel has dropped millions of flyers on the occupied, besieged Gaza Strip.

One such flyer seeks to recruit Palestinian collaborators. Signed by the "Israel Defense Forces Command" and addressed to "the residents of the Gaza Strip," the flyer states, "You hold the responsibility for your own fate!" It invites Palestinians to call or e-mail the Israeli Army "to inform us about the location of rocket-launching sites and the terrorist gangs that made you hostages of their actions." Because collaboration with an occupier is universally viewed as one of the worst forms of betrayal, the flyer warns, "For your own safety, please maintain secrecy when you call us."

EI decided to call the number provided. What follows is a translation of the Arabic conversation between an *EI* editor and an Israeli officer who identified himself using the Arabic name "Abu Ibrahim" (and whose accent begins to slip the more irritated he gets—until he finally goes on an all-out tirade in which he says that Palestinians do not exist as a nation).

Israel has used cash and has sometimes attempted to blackmail desperately sick Palestinians by withholding access to medical care unless they collaborate. Israel may also hope that the humanitarian catastrophe it has deliberately created in the Gaza Strip will make Palestinians more vulnerable to this kind of exploitation.

Excerpt from *EI*'s log of their conversation:[6]

> *EI*: I want to give you names of the biggest terrorist organizations, not just in Gaza, but in all Palestine.
>
> Israeli officer: OK, let's see what you have; go ahead.
>
> *EI*: OK, the first one. . . .
>
> Israeli officer: You mean to tell me they're all from Hamas?
>
> *EI*: All of them are people who . . . you'll see. The first one, his name is Ehud Barak [Israeli minister of defense].
>
> Israeli officer: Ehud Barak? By God there's no one like you. . . .
>
> *EI*: Second, Gabi Ashkenazi [Israeli army chief of staff].
>
> Israeli officer: Do you know him?
>
> *EI*: Of course. The third one is. . . .
>
> Israeli officer: Wait a minute, one at a time. . . .
>
> *EI*: No, write it down, I don't have time. The third one is called Ehud Olmert [Israeli prime minister].
>
> Israeli officer: Look, just a minute. . . .
>
> *EI*: You think that terrorists are only men? There are also women. Terrorist orgnizations have women, too. The fourth is Tzipi Livni [Israeli foreign minister].
>
> Israeli officer: First, I see that you're very clever and very experienced, and you should. . . .
>
> *EI*: And then the fifth's name is Yuval Diskin [head of Israel's "Shin Bet" death squads]. Write it down and record it, my beloved. These are the names of the biggest terrorist leaders in the whole of Palestine and in the whole of the Middle East.
>
> Israeli officer: You know what I think? I think you're not from the Strip.
>
> *EI*: Aaaah. You think I'm not from the Strip? But you take information on terrorists from any place right?
>
> Israeli officer: Now you're not benefiting at all. You're not helping yourself, and you're not helping anyone else. If you were really from the Strip . . .

EI: Didn't I just tell you that there were a number of terrorists in the Strip? Record it. There's a group of terrorists. They're the biggest terrorists in the world. They call themselves the "Israeli Defense Force," but they're not defending anyone. They're a terrorist gang.

My Father's "Story"[7]
Durham, North Carolina, January 2, 2009

Gaza is full of stories. My relative's neighbors—three young children—were all killed today while playing marbles outside their home. Another distant relative was killed in his home. All in the name of making Israel safer and securer.

My father has been doing his part by sharing his individual story with the world.

Yesterday, he spoke with NPR's North Carolina station, WUNC. He was interviewed on *The Story* with Dick Gordon. He recounted his gripping experience in vivid detail, one not unlike my friend Laila Al-Arian's grandfather's own story, published today in the *Nation*.[8]

This is how WUNC introduced the segment:

> Moussa El-Haddad lives in Gaza with his wife. The bombs have fallen as close as 100m from his home. Two nights ago, he was sitting at his desk, and the reverberations from a nearby bomb knocked him right out of his chair. He tells Dick Gordon about what life is like for him now that his city is under siege and about the hope that a new U.S. administration might mean new policies in this troubled region.

Moussa El-Haddad

Note: After my father's interview, the host felt obliged to interview someone living in Sderot—because, after all, the "story" would not be complete without the other view! He ended up interviewing an American Israeli woman who was a settler (read: colonist) in Gush Qatif (a former Israeli settlement area in Gaza) and now lives in Sderot. She reminisced about her wonderful days in Gaza (in illegal, fortified paramilitary complexes) and was nostalgic about living, once again, next to her "Arab neighbors" there! She then went on to complain about how they have little protection, and it's not really safe anywhere (try telling that to the Jabaliya residents, Anita). What really bothered me about this was that not once was she pressed about Israel's assault on Gaza as well as the obvious moral and political equivalencies being implied; however, every time Palestinians are interviewed on American airwaves, they are pressed to take a position on rockets, who to blame, and those they support. . . . But I digress.

Israeli Plan to Topple Hamas, Reinstate Abbas[9]
Durham, North Carolina, January 3, 2009

Here's an excerpt from an article on the Jewish Telegraphic Agency wire summarizing the Israeli National Security Council's (NSC's) assessments for 2009:

> Whatever happens, the NSC says, Israel must continue to pressure and weaken Hamas. If the current Hamas-Israel truce in Gaza breaks down, the NSC recommends that Israel launch a wide-ranging operation to topple Hamas in Gaza. Whether that would mean reoccupying Gaza, and if so, for how long, the NSC does not say. . . . To keep Abbas in power and the two-state solution alive, the NSC recommends that Israel prevent Palestinian elections.

Breaking the truce on November 4, then, was Israel's way of getting the ball rolling for this whole sick game: the toppling of Hamas and the reinstating of the impotent Abbas into Gaza so the "peace process" can remain forever in formaldehyde,[10] to quote wiseass, er, Weisglass.

Israeli spokespersons on *Al Jazeera* and CNN have effectively confirmed this, saying that the "legitimate Palestinian leadership is in the West Bank"; that they must be returned to Gaza; and that if there is an opportunity, they will facilitate this for them.

So the plan is: Destroy infrastructure and government buildings, create chaos and a political vacuum, and reinstate Abbas and his stooges as subcontractors of the occupation.

Jonathan Cooke notes in a recent article on *EI*: "It should come as no surprise that Israel . . . has killed substantial numbers of ordinary policemen, the guarantors of law and order in Gaza."

Land Offensive Begins in Gaza[11]
Durham, North Carolina, January 3, 2009

We just came back from a protest in Durham. . . . Before we left, my father called to let me know that a land invasion was imminent and that a bomb had destroyed a mosque near them, killing 11 civilians.

He just now informed me that a land invasion has begun. The people of Gaza are bracing themselves.

He said Israel destroyed three JAWAL centers (the mobile provider), so many mobile phones, including his own, are down, but his landline is functional.

He tells me that a building behind my cousin's house in Gaza City was destroyed and is now burning down in a voracious fire. It had an orphanage in it.

My mother says she won't lie—they are terrified.

Flares and firebombs are being shot to light up the sky. Propaganda flyers are part of Israel's psychological warfare, telling the people of Gaza that "they chose Hamas, and Hamas has abandoned them"; saying that "Hamas will lead them to catastrophe," superimposed on an image of a bombed-out building; and calling on them to "take charge of their destiny" and call a given phone number or e-mail with tips. It proceeds to warn people to call "in secrecy," much-appreciated advice I'm sure. Israel is also now broadcasting messages on the al-Aqsa television station.

My father tells me Gaza's streets are as "dark as kohl."[12]

Humor under Siege[13]
Durham, North Carolina, January 3, 2009

Yesterday, I wondered had happened to my father's newly acquired bird—the one he purchased from the farmer that tends to my mother's land in southern Gaza.

I feared the poor creature died of a heart attack. My father assured me it was doing just fine, but that instead of chirping the usual tunes that *hasaseen* are famous for singing, it now utters nothing but "boom boom."

Moussa El-Haddad

Trapped, Traumatized, Terrorized: Gaza Update[14]
Durham, North Carolina, January 4, 2009

My father and I made simultaneous, back-to-back appearances on CNN Domestic and CNN International last night. My father spoke calmly, eloquently, in the pitch dark of besieged Gaza, with only the fire of Israeli bombs illuminating his world. "They are destroying everything that is beautiful and living," he told the anchor.

His hands were trembling, he confessed, as my parents lay on the floor of their home, where they moved their mattress far away from the windows, thunderous explosions ripping through the black sky all around them, lighting it up in enormous clouds of fire.

I call them every hour, sometimes every few minutes when I see renewed bombardment on my television. Sometimes he calls me for assurance. "What's going on? What's going on?" he repeats in a weary, hypnotic tone.

"It just felt like they bombed our street from the inside out. I can't see anything. I don't know what's happening. What's the news saying?" he asks frantically, desperate for any morsel of information that can make sense of the terror being wrought upon them.

"The Apaches are right above our house. It's complete darkness outside, complete darkness," he goes on.

Moussa El-Haddad

I ask if he got any sleep. I was up with him a good part of my night until dawn rose as the earth was blasting apart around him.

"Two hours, better than nothing." He went out for a quick breather and took a picture of some children who went out for a few tense minutes to kick a ball around.

He passes the phone to my mother. She tries to make pleasant chitchat, asking about when we will celebrate Noor's birthday, though I already told her a few days ago we had a small party.

"Oh that's right, that's right. Yassine?" she says, addressing my husband.

"I don't know what's wrong with me. It's strange, strange. My body is literally trembling from the inside. From the inside. Why do you think that is? It's strange," she says, distractedly.

I ask how they are doing on food supplies. She says she stood in line for one and a half hours for a parcel of bread yesterday.

My father last night tried to communicate a single message: We keep hearing that Israel is after Hamas, but *we* are the targets here; civilians are the targets here, not Hamas.

An entire refugee family in one fell swoop was killed this morning as they took cover in their home, which took a direct hit from Israeli shells. Their deaths do not make Israel more secure. Their deaths will not stop rocket fire. Their deaths will not cause a popular "overthrow" of Hamas.

Six paramedics and a doctor were also killed as they tried to rescue wounded Palestinians in northern Gaza.

And now, the Associated Press reports that the Gaza phone network is on the verge of shutting down. I do not know how much longer I will be able to communicate with my parents.

Israeli human-rights groups have also just reported that 75 percent of Gaza is without electricity and that the sewage system is on the brink of collapse. In addition, Gaza City, including Shifa hospital, is entirely without electricity. They also say 20 percent of those killed have been children or women. They also note the following:

> More than half a million residents are cut off from a water supply.
>
> Sewage is spilling into streets, causing a risk of more flooding.
>
> No fuel has been permitted into Gaza since the start of the military operation.
>
> A total of 13,000 Palestinians—many of them refugees from 1948—are now internally displaced in Gaza, according to the UN Refugees, three times over.

"Live Free or Die." The motto of the state of New Hampshire, probably one that few Americans are familiar with, has never rung truer. And how similar it is to the feeling of ordinary Palestinians in the Gaza Strip now, trying merely to survive day to day, longing for a life free of Israeli occupation and terror.

Cluster Bombs, Depleted Uraniam (DU), and White Phosphorus Being Used in Gaza[15]
Durham, North Carolina, January 4, 2009

Residents in Gaza have been talking about an unprecedented amount of force being unleashed against them by the Israeli Army—but they have also spoken about new kinds of weaponry. It comes as no surprise. Gaza has always been Israel's "testing ground"—from nerve agents used in Khan Yunis in 2003 to sonic-boom "phantom air raids."[16] Now, there is talk of cluster bombs, DU, and white phosphorus being used over densely populated civilian areas.

And these are only the ones people can identify. CNN correspondents stationed near the borders have also been talking about new kinds of explosions.

Norwegian medics say that some of the victims who have been wounded since Israel began its attacks on the Gaza Strip on December 27 have traces of depleted uranium in their bodies, according to Press TV.

There are also reports that the Israeli Army is using cluster bombs in the northern part of the Strip, as well as white phosphorus, an incendiary weapon used by the United States in Iraq (which would explain the large flarelike explosions unseen before in Gaza).

My father yesterday treated patients in Shifa hospital exposed to some of these ordinances. The description he gave was as follows:

"There were a series of bombs in a row, a large white halo, followed by white smoke, which caused severe irritation and inability to breathe; the exposed areas become red, blistered all over the skin, and itchy."

Israel's Psychological Warfare[17]
Durham, North Carolina, January 4, 2009

We've heard about the flyers the Israeli Army is dumping over Gaza, telling people Hamas is to blame for their woes, not Israel's F-16s and cluster bombs.

Now, they have taken to robo-calling the citizens of Gaza à la Hillary Clinton's campaign ads of days past, at all times of the night and day.

My father has received a number of calls—including one just as we finished another CNN interview, on Skype. He tried to put the phone on speaker for me. The rough translation: "Urgent message: warning to the citizens of Gaza. Hamas is using you as human shields. Do not listen to them. Hamas has abandoned you and are hiding in their shelters. Give up now."

He hung up in disgust, not wanting to hear the rest.

The army has also been calling people to let them know their houses will be bombed.

People have stopped answering their phones now and do not take calls from unknown numbers, my father says.

What Do You Tell Your Daughter?[18]

Durham, North Carolina, January, 6, 2009

Another day, another massacre, more diplomatic deliberation, more silence, more complicity.

The invasion on Gaza has been mentally exhausting. I have tried my best to overcome this feeling of impotence by channeling the energy to action—though we may be powerless to change a government's heinous actions on our own, together our voices rise far above, farther than we can ever imagine.

Last night, we capped off our night with the latest hour of coverage on *Al Jazeera English*, which was reporting on how the United Nations had made shelters out of its schools for those internally displaced.

"I am getting a bad feeling about this—I wouldn't be surprised if this shelter was bombed," I told Yassine.

We woke up in the morning to the heart-rending news that that had indeed happened, as I rushed to make Noor's pediatrician appointment on time, my mind not quite here.

I then appeared on Canadian Broadcasting live with my father.

The anchor asked why my father was still in Gaza City. He replied that it was his home, and no one would kick him out of it. I emphasized that even for those who did want to flee for safety, there was nowhere to flee to—the borders are hermetically sealed, the sea and sky under total blockade.

"Is there anything you'd like to tell your daughter?" the anchor concluded by asking.

"What do I tell her? I honestly don't know if I'll live from one hour to the next," my father replied. "She keeps asking me to describe the casualties for her that I'm seeing, but I can't. What should I tell her? That I've seen bodies with my own eyes reduced to nothing more than pieces of black flesh?"

My father went on to describe accounts of Palestinians being used as human shields—by the Israelis. The Israeli military has been forcing families out of their homes and making them scope out buildings and rooms for the army to enter and for their snipers to nest in. It is a practice they have used before—in Rafah, which I personally reported on during Operation Rainbow in 2004. The practice was also employed in Jenin, and in Nablus in 2007 (where a young girl and boy were abused). B'Tselem has said, "Israeli soldiers routinely used Palestinian civilians as human shields by forcing them to carry out life-threatening military tasks," despite an Israeli High Court Order prohibiting the practice.

He went on to speak about the massacre at the UN school-turned-shelter, which had just occurred, reminding people that these same Palestinians in many cases were told by the Israeli Army to leave their homes through robo-calls and other forms of psychological intimidation—and then were bombed in the only safe place they could find.

I asked if he had gone out at all. He said my mother had not left the house in days, but that they needed some tomatoes to cook supper with. "The stores are empty—there is very little on the shelves—and the Shanti bakery had something like 300 people waiting in line."

Surprisingly, he said people are trying to go on with their lives. It is the mundane and ordinary that often save your sanity, help you live through the terror. It is no small thing to endure: knowing that both in deliberateness and scope, what is being wrought upon you is an unprecedented modern-day assault against an occupied, stateless people—most of them refugees.

How many more massacres until the human consciousness awakens?

Hand in Hand, Gaza Stands[19]
Durham, North Carolina, January 7, 2009

Three hours of this humanitarian "pause," they announced. And each person, family, group had to decide what to do with that time. Some divided the labor: bread, blankets, food. Others rushed to visit loved ones—or simply to get some fresh air.

My parents decided to visit some of the UN schools-cum-shelters, and my father described the scene to me over the phone:

> Every family consisted of at least 10 members, and there was one blanket for the whole lot. We took some donated blankets and clothes with us. Many of these people told me they are well-to-do but now find themselves with little more than the clothes on their backs.
>
> But despite it all—remarkably—everybody is standing hand in hand, supporting one another. Their spirits are remarkably high.

His voice sounded more rested than it had in days.

Farther south, in Rafah, the news was much grimmer. Just as a "pause" was in effect, hundreds of residents there received calls and leaflets from the Israeli Army demanding they leave their homes ahead of an imminent bombardment.

I called my friend Fida Qishta for an update. In the background, a commotion of voices could be heard.

"The announcement was for everyone to leave—the border-area people, half the city left, but many are refusing to go. We are hosting many families—that is all the noise you hear. We have about 30 people here with us," said Fida.

"You have to understand something: It's not about bulldozers anymore. . . . They are bombing with F-16s . . . destroying entire families, Laila . . . entire families," she repeated, driving the point home.

Moussa El-Haddad

Fida was referring to the period during the Second Intifada, when Rafah bore the brunt of Israel's military aggression in the Strip—systematically demolishing homes there en masse with armored Israeli bulldozers under the guise of destroying tunnels. A report by Human Rights Watch at the time found the true intention to be the desire to create a buffer zone. It seems Israel now wants to "finish the job."

Where Do You Hide? The Terror in Gaza Continues.[20]
Durham, North Carolina, January 8, 2009

"You don't know anymore; you don't know who is alive, you feel you are in a trap, you don't know who is a target," said my friend and neighbor in Gaza City, journalist Taghreed El-Khodary, the fear resonating in her voice, over the phone to *Al Jazeera.* Taghreed lives on the street over from my parents'.

"Where to? Where can I go seek refuge to?" she continued. "I live next to the parliament, which was destroyed; next to the police station, which was destroyed; next to the hospitals, which were bombed; and the Israeli Navy is shelling from the sea, the F-16s from the sky, the tanks from the ground . . . where to?" she repeated.

"First your house shakes, and the windows break, and the fear . . . the fear. And when you see all these children around you in the hospital. Some can draw—and what they are drawing is unbelievable. A 6-year old boy in my house drew a picture of boy that was alive and another that was dead. He said the dead boy was his friend, whom the Israelis killed. And the father is unable to protect his child. And the mothers are trying to hide their fear from their kids."

My father today said more flyers were dropped in a bid to intimidate and terrorize an already bludgeoned, starved, and terrified population.

"To residents of the area" read the flyer, which my father scanned and e-mailed to me.

"Due to the terrorist activity that terrorist elements are carrying out from your residential area against the State of Israel, the Israel Defense Force has been forced to respond immediately and operate in your residential area. . . . You are ordered to leave the area immediately."

Taghreed received a copy, too, courtesy of your friendly neighborhood occupying army—just out to watch your backs.

"They are dropping them everywhere—and everyone thinks it's their area being targeted, but in reality, no one knows. And even if they were to leave, where do they go to? To another area where flyers were dropped and where bombs are falling? It's a tactic to induce terror and intimidation," my father told me.

For the first time in weeks, they have a few hours of precious electricity today. And things felt "normal" for a while, as they basked in artificial light and their fridge hummed to life. They took the opportunity to chat with me on Skype. They wanted to talk to me hour after hour, all morning my time, about nothing in particular, before they were immersed in the dark and terror once again.

After speaking to his grandfather, Yousuf looked at me and asked in the inquisitive, matter-of-fact way that he usually does about all things small and big in this world, "Mama—why don't the Israeli soldiers think before they shoot people?"

"Because they don't think like you, *habibi*."

Early in the day, United Nations Relief and Works Agency for Palestine Refugees in the Near East (UNRWA) said it would stop operations after an aid convoy came under direct Israeli attack and two UN drivers were killed by Israeli shells.

In the afternoon, my father learned that a family living in Gaza's Zeitun neighborhood—the Samuni clan—who had already lost dozens of members in previous days, lost an additional 70: Paramedics from the Red Cross were finally able to reach them after days of being prevented from doing so by Israeli forces and discovered bloated rotting corpses and four children clinging to life, lying limp and emaciated from hunger but alive near their slaughtered mother.

Head of the Red Cross Pierre Wettach accused

إلى سكان المنطقة

بسبب الأعمال الإرهابية التي تقوم بها عناصر إرهابية انطلاقا من منطقة سكناكم ضد دولة إسرائيل

اضطر جيش الدفاع الإسرائيلي إلى القيام بالرد الفوري والعمل داخل منطقة سكناكم .

من اجل سلامتكم انكم مطالبون بإخلاء المنطقة فورا.

قيادة جيش الدفاع الإسرائيلي

Moussa El-Haddad

Israel of deliberately ignoring the besieged, dying family: "The Israeli military must have been aware of the situation but did not assist the wounded. Neither did they make it possible for us or the Palestine Red Crescent to assist the wounded."

"It Wasn't Me": The Israeli Guide to Spin Control on Palestinian Massacres[21]

Durham, North Carolina, January 8, 2009

A friend of mine has come up with the following Israeli guide to spin control on Palestinian massacres it "accidentally" perpetrates, such as the Samuni massacre and that at the UN school:[22]

> It wasn't us—one of their bombs exploded by accident or it was their own gunfire.
>
> It was us, but they were shooting from (near) there/storing weapons there.
>
> OK, maybe that's not the case, but our "purity of arms" makes us better than anyone else: No other army in the world takes such care in avoiding civilian casualties.
>
> There's no need for an independent/international investigation, because we are a democracy and conduct our own investigations; and besides, the world hates us.
>
> Why are you still talking about it, you anti-Semite?

This line of argument is also known as: "It wasn't me, and so what if it was, you anti-Semite?"

This Is Gaza[23]

Durham, North Carolina, January 9, 2009

Tonight, Duke University (my alma mater) held a vigil for Gaza. I was invited to speak, even after certain campus groups said they were displeased at the choice of speakers, saying they found my comments offensive the last time I spoke.

Here is some of what I said in my speech:

Imagine if you will a land teeming with refugees: a land of the dispossessed, closed off from the outside world—where smuggling is often the only source of subsistence, where families who [have] not disappeared are on the brink of starvation, surrounded by an army and bombarded by that army.

The year was 1943. The place: the Warsaw Ghetto.

The description is hauntingly familiar. But it is now 2009.

And this is Gaza.

As we speak tonight, more than 800 Palestinians and 14 Israelis have lost their lives over the course of the past two weeks.

Seventeen mosques have been destroyed; a church seriously damaged; more than 12 medics and a journalist have been killed; ambulances; schools; houses; women, men, children.

In fact, entire families—entire families—have been eliminated from existence. This is Gaza.

Roughly the size of this nation's great capital, Washington, D.C., it is closed in on all sides. There is no escape. There is no entry.

And its residents—already stateless after 40 years of occupation, and most of them refugees—are at once being blockaded and bombarded by land, sea, and sky: It is a situation that is unprecedented in modern history. . . .

I have learned that my comments are considered offensive to some. For this, I do *not* apologize.

Sometimes, we need to be offended in order to wake up to the brutal realities around us, realities that we helped create—with our taxes, with our votes, with our silence.

And I say: Occupation is not only offensive; it is lethal.

The United Nations has described what is happening in Gaza as a Crime Against Humanity—in terms of its deliberateness, its scope, and its disproportionality.

That an occupied territory—and, yes, Gaza is still recognized as occupied—is not only subject to a deliberate siege after free and fair elections, depriving an already impoverished and dispossessed people intentionally of electricity, aid trucks, and medicines, but is then bombed, is not only unfathomable; it is indefensible.

It is incumbent upon all of us to speak out for peace and justice for all.

For Israel can achieve only the security it seeks by providing that same security to Palestinians and addressing the underlying cause of it all: We must demand an end to Israel's siege and illegal occupation of Gaza, the West Bank, and East Jerusalem. This is an obligation, not a concession.

We cannot continue to speak of it as an event occurring in a vacuum or as though the firing of rockets onto Israeli towns was simply an event on its own, without context. As though Gazans were not dying a slow death by way of siege before this or suffering under occupation throughout.

It is about the denial of basic Palestinian rights. The right to statehood, the rights of refugees to return to their homes, the rights of families to reside together and to visit one another; the right to travel freely, to receive medical treatment, to education, to a childhood free of violence; the right to worship; the right to live free of occupation and siege.

Palestinians must be allowed to realize their most basic human rights—freedom and self-determination, the same concepts this country was founded on.

The United States must change its longstanding policy of blind support for Israel.

It must become an even-handed broker in this conflict, addressing Palestinian needs for justice, equality, and security just as it does Israel's. It must demand that Israel end its illegal occupation, running on 40 years, of the Gaza Strip, the West Bank, and East Jerusalem.

And friends don't let friends run an occupation.

We Talk in Silence; We Stand Together[24]
Durham, North Carolina, January 11, 2009

We decided to drive to Washington, D.C., yesterday to attend what was a national "Let Gaza Live" march. It was a last-minute decision, weighing the cost of driving a round-trip of eight hours with Yousuf and Noor, and the anticipated inclement weather, against the benefit of standing with Gaza.

Two Duke graduate students accompanied us: one, a Palestinian from Lydd; the other, a Syrian Fulbright scholar.

On the way, Yousuf abruptly interrupts our banter to ask whether his grandfather is going to die in Gaza. He asks me to tell "them" not to shoot him.

"*Seedo rah yimoot? Uleelhum may tukhoo, Mama!*" ("Is Grandpa going to die? Mom, tell them not to shoot him!")

I ask him to make a *dua*, to ask God to keep him—to keep all of Gaza—safe.

"That is stronger than any bullet," I explain.

We arrive a little late and have to march extra quickly to catch up with the group of what was estimated to be 10,000 or so protesters. It is a diverse and civil crowd. Unfortunately, the weather was not so civil. By the end, we are drenched in freezing rain, my fingers as numb as Noor's lips are blue, plastic parkas plastered to our wet faces.

We catch up with my brother and my nephew, Zade, who is carrying a wet sign, its ink bleeding down it as though to simulate Gaza's tears and blood. The sign read, "Obama: I shed tears when your grandmother died. Will you do the same for me? My grandmother lives in Gaza."

After complaining he was freezing, his mother promptly told him, "Freezing is better than dying." He agreed.

Later, he proudly told his grandfather he marched two hours in the freezing rain for Gaza.

We walked by the hotel the president-elect was staying in (though sources say he was busy eating chili) and ended up in front of the White House before heading back to North Carolina.

On the way, I receive the dreaded 9 p.m. call from my father. My heart skipped a beat— late-night calls always bear bad news.

"More bombings, I can't sleep. Israeli Navy gunships are bombarding Gaza City's Tel il Hawa neighborhood—you know, where Amo Musab lives, where he built his new house," he says, referring to his cousin.

"The suburb is in flames. Residents are calling out to the Red Cross, but they can't reach them. They say they are bombing with firebombs or something; there is a thick black smoke descending on them, choking people," he continues calmly.

I immediately have my brother update my Twitter account for me. I feel better, empowered in whatever incremental way, knowing I am broadcasting this piece of information that is at once senseless and meaningful to the world. My brother struggles to condense terror, death, and panic to 140 characters.

We continue speaking.

I learn that my cousin's father-in-law has been hurt. His house in northern Gaza was hit by Israeli forces and then bulldozed to the ground. He was arrested, blindfolded, and tortured—including being made to fall off stairs, fracturing several ribs. He then had to walk an hour to Gaza City's Sheikh Ijleen neighborhood. His wife was also forced to leave in her pajamas in the middle of the night and walk alone to the city.

I talk to my father until the bombing subsides—anther hour. Sometimes we don't say anything at all. We simply hold the phones to our respective ears and talk in silence, as though it were an unfamiliar technology. As though I can shield him from the hell being unleashed around him for those few minutes. However absurd it sounds, we feel safe somehow; reassured that if something happens, it will happen while we stand together.

The Gates of Hell, the Window to Heaven[25]
Durham, North Carolina, USA, January 12, 2009

I have a routine of sorts. I monitor the situation back home all day—I keep *Al Jazeera English* on continuously, as long as I am home, despite Yousuf's nagging to switch to cartoons. He stopped asking several days ago, when, tearful and angry, I told him that Gaza is being bombed, that *Seedo* and *Tete* are in danger.

If I leave home, I make sure my cell phone is near me at all times. This evening, I am at my friend's house, and my father calls me, just before dawn prayers.

"Are you home? Are you there? I don't know what's going on, but our whole house is shaking, the whole house. The windows have blown open, your mother is terrified, it's horrible. I don't know exactly where it is, and the radio hasn't broadcast anything about it yet, either. Just continuous explosions all around and these clouds of white smoke everywhere," he goes on, his words at once weary and weighed.

I rush home to turn on the television again and see what information I can find online. He has the news before they do. Soon, *Al Jazeera* brings my friend Taghreed back on the line. I hear her voice and imagine her sitting next to me, trembling as she usually does in such inexplicably terrifying moments as these, despite having covered Gaza for years.

"People cannot find places to stay anymore. They go from one area they were ordered to leave by the Israelis to another. And there is no more room in these UN schools. . . . I refuse to call them shelters, because they are not shelters. There are like one or two bathrooms for a thousand residents. I met people sleeping in the public garden of Shifa hospital," she says.

My father tells me he has seen people out on the street—entire families, living, sleeping, surviving. That his cousin moved from Tel il Hawa to his brother's house nearby.

One resident in Tel il Hawa describes the evening as Israel having opened the gates of hell unto them—the *shoa* that Deputy War Minister Matan Vilnai said they would unleash unto Gaza last year.

I see an Associated Press picture on my computer of a jovial Israeli soldier posing with two of his weapons with a toothy smile.

I then read an article in *Haaretz* by Amos Harel, writing from the "ruins" of Netzarim, quoting an Israeli tank commander and saying he rather likes it in Gaza, because "it's interesting" there. Other young soldiers say they are "excited," anxious to get in on the action, to shell and snipe to death, this being their first war.

A 1-year-old girl, Rula Salha, was killed today. She was Noor's age. I think of the smiley, war-hungry soldier. I wonder if he got his kick.

My father and I continue speaking. We learn Israeli forces have closed in on Tel il Hawa, and navy gunships are shelling the city again. My parents speak to Yousuf for a while as I hear the explosions echoing over the speaker and machine gun fire and the aftermath of phosphorus bombs over the city on my television. He complains of an ear infection.

The fear is salient; it is suffocating; it is in the air, friends say, and no one knows what's coming next. There is nowhere to turn to except the heavens above.

And so many people in Gaza have taken to doing just that: They are waking up for special predawn prayers *qiyam al layl* in the "last third of the night"—a window of time when believers feel especially close to God and when it is said He is especially close to our calls upon Him, and supplications and prayers are most likely to be answered.

And so they tremble, and they wait, and they pray during this small window to heaven for the gates of hell to be closed—until it is dawn once again.

The Inebriants of Israel's War[26]
Durham, North Carolina, January 14, 2009

During a radio program yesterday, I was asked, "What next?"

In the course of my answer, I said something about how I don't know that the Israeli government has thought that through; it is so drunk with self-conviction, absolute power and military might, racism and nationalism, and perceived "success," all while a media blackout, a well-planned *hasbara* campaign, and a public hungry for "action" fuel the war-terror machine with their blessings and support, that it will blaze ahead, losing sight of why ever the hell it thinks it started this and whatever the hell it was supposed to achieve (the latest line is "increasing their deterrent force").

The herd mentality at its best.

Barack's popularity is through the roof: street parades for the war hero who makes the public *feel* "safe" and "secure."

To quote Gideon Levy, it is "war as child's play":

> . . . pilots bombing unimpeded as if on practice runs, tank and artillery soldiers shelling houses and civilians from their armored vehicles, combat engineering troops destroying entire streets in their ominous protected vehicles without facing serious opposition. A large, broad army is fighting against a helpless population and a weak, ragged organization that has fled the conflict zones and is barely putting up a fight. All this must be said openly, before we begin exulting in our heroism and victory.[27]

Even the name of the "operation" ("Cast Lead"), which is lost on many, exudes innocence and excitement and joy.

My friend Mushon talks of the polarized rendering of events in the Israeli blog-o-sphere in his excellent post:

> The blogs in Israel are divided between covering the terror of life in Sderot and the rest of the Israeli south under the Hamas rocket fire, and the excited coverage of the "glorious" operation titled "Cast Lead"—quoting a Hanukkah song where a child sings about playing with a dreidel of cast lead—a holiday present from an uncle.

. . . Mushon warns the following:

> Also evident is an incipient racism gradually becoming acceptable in Israeli public discourse, as well as an "occupier as enlightener" mentality: Jewish women don't cry like Arab women; Palestinians don't exist as a nation anyway; they are violent; they are inhumane; we gave them the only good things they have; we just want to liberate them—we are on their side; and so on.

I have noticed this, too.

. . . In an article titled "Is Israel Losing the Media War in Gaza?" TIME talks of Israel's "extensively planned *hasbara* campaign" ahead of the war in Gaza and the bluntness with which Israeli officers speak to their domestic audiences. ("We are very violent," the commander of the Israeli Army's elite combat engineering unit, *Yahalom*, told the Israeli press. "We do not balk at any means to protect the lives of our soldiers.")

These factors taken together might also explain the numerous accounts being heard of Palestinians being used as human shields by Israeli soldiers and being shot at (and, in many cases, killed) as they raised white flags—after being ordered to leave their houses by those same soldiers: When there is no accountability and an ingrained lethal ambiguity in "operating procedures," why *not* be "very violent"? Why *not* shoot at "any moving thing," to quote another young Israeli soldier in yesterday's *Haaretz*?

Now Olmert is avoiding meeting with his security cabinet so that a "timeline" can be avoided, and Livni is asking the international community for "more time" to "achieve their goals." (Again, what exactly is the goal here? Human suffering? Destruction of infrastructure so that Abbas can rebuild it? Sowing more anger and destroying hope? All the above?)

. . . Meanwhile, another night of terror and confusion has passed on Gaza, another weary dawn has risen.

I was unable to speak with my parents all day, and so I rang my father just after midnight my time. He sounded wrecked and suffocated, not his usual collected self. "I'm so tired. . . . I'm just so tired. I didn't sleep all night, the bombs are tearing through my head. I really have no idea what's going on outside, nobody has any idea what's going on. . . . *Al Jazeera* in Qatar called to ask me if I knew what was going on . . . and what this is about anymore. I can't even hear anything on the radio anymore, everyone is just praying. I really just want to go now, dear. I'm sorry. Goodbye," he ended abruptly.

"*Seedo?*" piped in Yousuf. "Just remember—the only one who has the power to stop this is God."

The Children of Israel's War, and a "Seize" Fire[28]
Durham, North Carolina, January 16, 2009

My mother, a pediatrician, spent the day yesterday visiting the child victims of Israel's war on Gaza. She distributed some toys bought with donations to try to bring some smiles to their destroyed lives.

My father took these pictures of the children, as well as of ambulances hit by Israeli shells and shrapnel.

They spent what they told me was the most terrorizing night of the past two weeks yesterday—missiles destroying buildings around their house, lighting apartments and towers on fire.

He sent me a brief e-mail around dawn. In terrifying clarity it read:

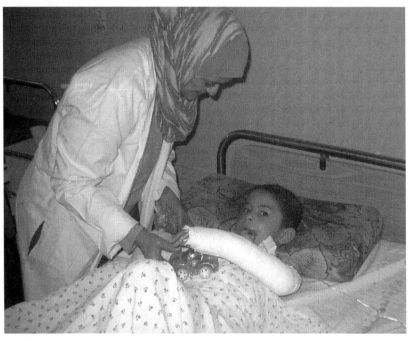

Moussa El-Haddad

Moussa El-Haddad

Loved one:

I thought to take few moments on the generator to write this e-mail to you, it might be our last communication. The Israeli Army has been heavily bombarding everything in Gaza now. They escalated their attack intensively after 4 a.m. Tal El-Hawa is on fire (I will attach photos that I took of smoke from burning buildings); they just fired a missile on one apartment in a huge apartment building in front of our house (Borj Al-Shorook). I guess Laila knows it. Phosphorus bombs now are fired everywhere on houses and on people. UNRWA's main stores in Gaza were hit.

Hundreds of people are trapped in burning buildings in Tal El-Hawa and Al-Sabra and everywhere in Gaza. It is clear now that these people decided now to finish everyone and everything in Gaza Strip. I still have faith in Allah.

This late evening, as I write this post, we hear word of Israel unilaterally ending its offensive—on its own terms—a sinister action in the cloak of benevolence. Such a cease-fire (or "seize fire" as an Israeli journalist friend of mine unintentionally put it) would allow the suffocating siege of Gaza to stay in play and allow the occupation army to reenter and reattack at any moment of its choosing. There is also word of Israel and United States signing a curious agreement to help Egypt end "smuggling on Gaza's border" without any involvement of the people whom the border surrounds. . . .

And as the dust settles and death-drenched streets quiver back to life, it remains to be asked: What has this accomplished exactly? Do Israelis feel safer now, knowing they have eliminated more than 1,000 Palestinian lives, maimed tens of thousands, and destroyed many hundreds of thousands more?

Medics also say a woman and child have been killed in (another) Israeli raid on a UN-run school in the northern Gaza Strip. Eleven other people are wounded.

Moussa El-Haddad

But who's to stop them?

Earlier, in Jabaliya, a mother and her five children—all under the age of 13—were completely eliminated as they huddled together for shelter. These are the victims of Israel's quest for a new equation. They are the factors that are included in the calculation—very clinical, very clean, very defensive.

Gaza Will Rise[29]
Durham, North Carolina, January 18, 2009

There is an unfamiliar stillness in Gaza today, says my father. No F-16s ripping through the sky. No ravaging explosions. There is time to hear yourself think. All a sort of anesthetic. A pause in a sick calculated brutality to allow the caged disposables a moment to contemplate their options—to create the illusion they even have options.

"This siege will endure until we are truly persuaded into choosing a harmless slavery but in total freedom!"

And so the cowering uncover. The homeless return to no homes. The decomposing dead are unearthed from the rubble, only to be buried once again.

The damage is surveyed.

Uprooted trees. Entire groves. A city eviscerated. People burned to a cinder. Disemboweled streets. And more tales of horror on every corner.

A woman's five sons were killed in the assassination of Saeed Siam. They lived in the building over.

Twenty-five more bodies recovered from the Samouni family. An ethnic cleansing.

Reports of executions by young trigger-happy Israeli soldiers, cheerleaders on the borders. A boy, 15 years old. And in between, air force pilots on PlayStation. "I want to destroy the city," one said gleefully. And subcontracts were handed out to further enforce the siege. Hands were shaken. Lives taken.

"They destroyed anything in their path—people, buildings, streets . . . nothing was left untouched," my father said. "It is calm, for now. We sleep, for now. But the siege continues. And make no mistake—Gaza will rise."

CHAPTER NOTES

1. The full original text of this post is archived at http://www.gazamom.com/2008/12/the-rains-of-death-in-gaza/, shortened to http://bit.ly/ajz0uz.
2. Archived at http://bit.ly/asVM8z.
3. Laila El-Haddad, "Bloodied in Gaza," *Guardian Comment Is Free*, December 30, 2008, archived at http://bit.ly/ddD33i.
4. Archived at http://bit.ly/cEXLVa.
5. Archived at http://bit.ly/cceIoJ.

6. Read the full transcript of the call at "Israel Collaborator Recruiter Punked," *Electronic Intifada*, January 4, 2009, archived at http://bit.ly/cahbty.

7. Archived at http://bit.ly/bPGAwy.

8. Listen to Moussa El-Haddad's full interview on *The Story* and see his pictures from Gaza during Israel's offensive, archived at http://bit.ly/a0jNQR. Read Laila al-Arian's account of her grandfather's experiences during the offensive in "To Live and Die in Gaza," *Nation*, January 2, 2009, archived at http://bit.ly/bIEF1F.

9. Archived at http://bit.ly/cJnf6k.

10. Ariel Sharon's top adviser, Dov Weisglass, famously admitted to the leading Israeli newspaper *Haaretz* in an interview on June 10, 2004, that "[t]he disengagement is actually formaldehyde. It supplies the amount of formaldehyde that is necessary so there will not be a political process with the Palestinians." Archived at http://bit.ly/9sdGuH.

11. Archived at http://bit.ly/9RsCvM.

12. Kohl is an Arabic form of dark eyeliner. To view images from Israel's ground offensive in Gaza, see Sameh Habeeb's photos archived at http://bit.ly/a1M9cd (including photos of leaflets being dropped on the city).

13. Archived at http://bit.ly/deOPcV.

14. Archived at http://bit.ly/bigxTo.

15. Archived at http://bit.ly/czl5xb.

16. Darryl Li, "The Gaza Strip as Laboratory: Notes in the Wake of Disengagement," *Journal of Palestine Studies*, January 11, 2006, archived at http://bit.ly/b8WZe3.

17. Archived at http://bit.ly/c0C76L.

18. Archived at http://bit.ly/cMnK6V.

19. Archived at http://bit.ly/bmSrb5.

20. Archived at http://bit.ly/bFDANg.

21. Archived at http://bit.ly/cQt6VV.

22. A similar assessment was given in Robert Fisk, "Why Do They Hate the West So Much, We Will Ask," *Independent*, January 7, 2009, archived at http://bit.ly/9KvAcX.

23. Archived at http://bit.ly/b2RFgg.

24. Archived at http://bit.ly/awTw0k.

25. Archived at http://bit.ly/a01o1c.

26. Archived at http://bit.ly/d96mD1.

27. Gideon Levy, "The IDF Has No Mercy for the Children in Gaza Nursery Schools," *Haaretz*, January 15, 2009, archived at http://bit.ly/8XInQd.

28. Archived at http://bit.ly/dy85oA.

29. Archived at http://bit.ly/9HbEtN.

PART IV

New Avenues for Activism

January 2009–August 2010

Chapter 21

After the Assault: The Emergence of Boycott, Divestment, and Sanctions

Late January through early April 2009

Israel withdrew its forces from Gaza on January 18, 2009, ending its invasion but maintaining its closure and siege of Gaza. President Barack Obama wasted no time after his inauguration a few days later to repeat the refrain of the need for "Israeli security" (he did not follow through on his call to keep Gaza's crossings open), leaving Palestinians wondering who was looking out for their security in the wake of the war. Even before the Israeli invasion began in late December, Hamas had offered to renew its six-month cease-fire with Israel on the condition that the border crossings from Egypt and Israel into Gaza be reopened.

The Gaza assault had another more positive effect: It spurred a global call to action for boycott, divestment, and sanctions (BDS) against the Israeli government. One-fifth of Israeli exporters reported suffering losses and losing foreign markets and customers partly as a result of the boycott, according to the Israel Manufacturers Association.

The BDS efforts culminated in March in what has become known as Israeli Apartheid Week (IAW), an annual series of university lectures and events started in Toronto and now held in more than 55 cities around the world whose aim is to "educate people about the nature of Israel as an apartheid system and to build [BDS] campaigns as part of a growing global BDS movement." I spent two weeks on the road, with Yousuf and Noor in tow, on a speaking tour of Canada during IAW. Yousuf was increasingly concerned for his grandparents' safety back in Gaza and wondered when he could see them again.

Meanwhile, in Gaza, my parents surveyed the damage in the aftermath of the war, visiting the surviving Samouni family and summing it up with "seeing is not like hearing." Following the conclusion of our Canada trip, the kids and I began preparing for a trip back home after a two-year absence.

Occupation: The Elephant in the Room[1]
Durham, North Carolina, January 22, 2009

And so it's done; the curtain has been drawn. After months—by some estimates, a couple of years—of careful preparation, laying the groundwork, massaging public opinion, crafting a Gulf of Tonkin; immaculate timing; *hasbara* campaign: It's a wrap, folks! Just in time to make way for a historic American inauguration, as we are reminded repeatedly.

Intent on proving his critics wrong, Obama wasted no time in reminding them of America's resolve and tenacity: We will defeat you.

But noticeably missing from the talk was any mention of Israel or Palestine.

Fair enough: It was a big moment on its own, no need to weigh it down with a bloody and distant conflict that you will spend the next four to eight years getting mired down in anyway—or miring down further.

And so, as we are told, Obama hit the ground running. The next day, the newly minted president in his first speech talked about the need to open Gaza's crossings because—as any casual observer might have gleaned from this recent "cycle of violence"—to have a "lasting cease-fire," we must give Israel security and open Gaza's crossing (in case you aren't sensing it, I'm being sarcastic here).

But the devil is so often in the details—not in what was said but what was *not*. Notably missing from the call was a need to open the crossing to people as opposed to merely humanitarian aid and commerce, as though tons of food can vanquish the Gaza problem.

It was this very clause that was negotiated to inclusion in the Agreement on Movement and Access, brokered by none other than Condi Rice herself shortly after disengagement: the need to provide access and movement for goods *and* people and to keep the crossings operating on a continuous basis. Of course, this access never materialized, neither in percentage of trucks allowed in or out nor the promised Palestinian control over Rafah within one year. OCHA keeps a good record of weekly violations of the Agreement on Movement and Access as a reference.

. . . Regardless, none of this will matter. If Palestinians are not granted their most basic human right of freedom of movement, the tunnels will continue to thrive.

So I'm going to throw something out here that might sound a bit out there—hold your breath everyone: How about we actually try ending the occupation instead of coming up with a million and one excuses why we shouldn't?

Notice the pattern vis-à-vis any Palestinian group, whether it was Fateh and the PLO before or Hamas now: They are and always will be terrorists (the PLO is still on the U.S. terrorist list). Once you negotiate, it's only a process meant to serve as a cover for continuing settlement expansion and consolidation of the occupation; if that doesn't work, cry foul and say you have no partner for peace—then bomb their security infrastructure and say they have to have better security before they become a partner. If the people elect someone else, start over.

For real change, why not start by saying things like they are: If Israel has the right to defend itself, don't Palestinians have not only the right but the obligation to defend themselves *and* resist against an illegal occupation?

Seeing Is Not Like Hearing[2]
Durham, North Carolina, February 3, 2009

Yesterday, my father joined friend and local activist Fida Qishta and members of the International Solidarity Movement in Gaza to visit the site of the al-Daya home—a four-story house that was leveled by Israeli forces on top of its occupants. My father told me there were still four unburied bodies underneath the rubble.

They then went to visit the area where the Samouni clan lived. Some 15 houses, citrus groves, olive trees, two green houses, one chicken pen (with about 10,000 chickens), a water well, cattle, and other animals—*all* were eviscerated out of existence. The only surviving animal was a donkey. The poor beast was shot in the neck but survived with a battle scar and a bandage on his wound.

Moussa El-Haddad

He sent me pictures (my father, not the donkey) of all that remains of the village; its residents showing their hospitality nonetheless as they served them coffee warmed on a small wood-fired grill. In another picture, surviving family members anxiously accept water donations from a truck.

Moussa El-Haddad

"Seeing is not like hearing," he told me bluntly of the devastation they saw, the livelihoods that were destroyed, and the life that was extinguished.

Remembering a Time[3]
Durham, North Carolina, February 4, 2009

Yousuf keeps bringing up Gaza and his grandfather. Little things will evoke memories of his time growing up in Gaza—fragments he continues to piece together in a sort of nonlinear way, from a time he can barely remember yet is so hauntingly familiar: the turtle we found trying to cross the road from the beach inland that we securely relocated to my father's farm ("Do you think it has a new family now? Is it still there?"); the time he burned his bottom in the ice-cream shop across the street when my mother accidentally sat him on a container of boiled corn (hey, don't call child protective services—it was an accident!).

Today, it was an old manual camera. My father bought it for him from a garage sale during a visit here last year. I dusted it off after Yousuf said he wanted to take his own pictures when we go to Puerto Rico next week, where I am going to be delivering a lecture at the Center for the Freedom of Press in San Juan.

The camera elicited a host of questions and a conversation I can only pretend to answer with any certainty.

"Mama . . . *inshallah*, we'll see them again. But what if they are shot before we go? And how will we get across if the border is still closed?" he asks, knowing full well from years past that going to Gaza is not as easy as hopping on a plane and getting from point A to point B.

"It will all be OK, I promise; don't worry too much about such things. Leave that to me, and take some pictures of the present so you can remember your happy times."

Every time I rub his little almost-5-year-old head after he wakes up from an afternoon nap, when his face is still warm, I remember how we huddled together in my bed in Gaza as our windows shuddered from nightly shelling.

He belongs to that place, and he belongs to this time. He belongs to that time, and he belongs to this place.

A Gazan Feast![4]
Durham, North Carolina, February 4, 2009

I wanted to post these pictures because they made me smile—seeing my parents' glowing faces, happy and well rested, in front of our kitchen table back in Gaza City with a spread that is truly a "Gazan feast": traditional suppertime staples, such as *dagga* (a famous tomato, dill, and hot chili salad); olives from my father's farm; hearty locally baked wheat-bran bread; *zibdiyit gambari* (spicy shrimps baked in a Gazan earthen clay

Darryl Li

Darryl Li

pot); tangy stuffed grape leaves; and *imtaball* (aka baba ghanoush) topped with pomegranate seeds. It was a meal they prepared for my good friend Darryl, who was visiting Gaza on a human-rights fact-finding mission. He took these pictures of them before lapsing into a food coma on the way back to his apartment. Word is that his whole team ate the leftovers he took back with him!

Recipe for Rummaniya[5]

Rummaniya is an unusual Gazan vegetarian dish made from the unlikely combination of sour pomegranates, eggplants, and lentils. It is a seasonal recipe, made when sour pomegranates fill the markets in late summer. It is traditionally considered a "poor man's food," because it is meatless and consists of cheap legumes and vegetables.

Ingredients

1 cup brown lentils
3 cups water
0.5kg [roughly 1 lb.] eggplants, unpeeled and chopped into 2-inch chunks, or 3 sour pomegranates (if you can't find them anywhere, use a few tablespoons of pomegranate molasses, found at most Middle Eastern grocers, mixed with an equal amount of fresh lemon juice and water)
1/2 cup flour
1 small onion, diced
2 tablespoons tahini
3 cloves garlic
2 whole dried red chilies (or dried chili flakes)
1/4 teaspoon ground cumin
1 tablespoon dried dill seed
1 teaspoon salt

Directions

1. Boil lentils in water until soft. Add eggplants, and simmer until cooked thoroughly.

2. Remove pomegranate seeds, and put them in a blender; puree and strain, reserving juice. Set aside.

3. In a mortar and pestle (we call them *zibdiya* in Gaza—basically an unglazed clay/earthen bowl; an equivalent is a Mexican mortar, but if you can't find one, use a mini-food processor), crush salt, dill seed, garlic, and chilies. Set aside.

4. Mix reserved pomegranate juice (or pomegranate molasses diluted in a few tablespoons of water and lemon juice) with flour until well mixed; then, slowly add to stew on stove top while mixing continuously.

5. Add crushed spices to stew, and mix well.

6. Add tahini, mix thoroughly for five minutes or until thickened, and turn off heat.

7. Sauté onion in olive oil until golden brown, then add to stew. Mix well.

8. Pour into bowls, and allow to cool to room temperature. Set bowls in fridge to cool thoroughly.

When ready to eat, top *Rummaniya* with extra-virgin olive oil, and garnish with pomegranate seeds if available. Serve with Kmaj/Arabic bread.

Canada in 8 Days[6]
Durham, North Carolina, March 14, 2009

Well, we're back from my latest speaking tour, to Canada and the northern United States, and I think I've finally caught up on sleep after going through eight different cities in as many days. As I noted to a friend who suggested I was "amazing" for doing this trip with both kids in tow: Some call it amazing. . . . Some call it insane. Thin line.

I should say I feel a little guilty—ever since I've begun Twittering, I've found myself devoting less time to blogging. It's like I'm cheating on my blog! I admit it—I'm having an affair with Twitter!

Back to our trip:

We began our whirlwind in Buffalo, New York, where I was invited to speak at the University of Buffalo fund-raiser for Gaza. . . . From there, we flew to New York City for the night and the following morning to Edmonton, Alberta, Canada, for my first speaking engagement as part of a national (and apparently global event—40 cities worldwide) Israeli Apartheid Week (IAW). It was Edmonton's first IAW and was very well organized.

It was the coldest city of the lot—also the city where Noor had the pleasure of experiencing her first snow (sheer joy for the first 40 seconds—until her fingers began to go numb!).

Yousuf took the opportunity to go sledding (on a cardboard box—an hour before our flight out—see action shot!).

We were hosted by an extraordinarily devoted local group of activists—whose house I fear sustained permanent damage as a result of my offspring. (Who would have thought a 14-month-old could wreak so much havoc?)

From there, we moved on to Calgary, where I addressed a packed auditorium on the realities of the "Gaza Zoo,"[7] emphasizing throughout my talks the consistency and constancy with which Israeli policies have played out there—regardless of who has been in power. Policies that I suggested were aimed at deliberately forestalling any prospect for viable Palestinian statehood—statehood that was never explicitly outlined in the Oslo Accords. We were again met by an enthusiastic group of organizers there, who saw us off to our third stop, Toronto, where IAW was launched in 2005. I caught up with old friends there—including my nursery-school teacher, Um Bashar, now retired (whom I had not seen for 28 years!).

Toronto had the most packed crowd. I spoke there with fellow journalist and photographer Jon Elmer, who was in Gaza reporting at the same time I was and who gave a moving presentation.

One of his pictures, in particular, stands out in my mind—a clearly distraught mother nevertheless tutoring her child, on a cardboard box outside their demolished home.

Toronto was also the city where I was interrupted in the middle of my presentation by staunch Zionists.

From there, I went on to Kingston, where we celebrated Yousuf's 5th birthday, and, finally, Montreal, where I was met by the organizer of the tour, the tireless Laith Marouf, and his lovely family.

After my speech there, a woman stood up to the microphone and made a comment that really touched me. She told me she was a native Canadian/aboriginal and that she was married to a Palestinian. They frequently discussed the similarities between their plights. But she reminded him—and me—how lucky we were to, at the very least, have preserved our language and our culture. She tearfully explained how her native language has essentially been lost, except for a few words, through the brutal segregation and elimination of her people and their social fabric.

I should take this moment to mention that IAW is not your ordinary awareness week. In its few years of existence, it has been met by staunch resistance and a hateful campaign attempting to vilify it and its organizers by status-quo defenders and hypocrites on all levels—a testimony to its significance and its success.

Posters of the event were banned on certain campuses, and donors were urged to condition their funding of universities on banning the week. Even top-ranking politicians have gotten involved—including a former professor of mine at the Kennedy School (now head of Canada's Liberal Party), who, I am sorry to say, I once took a course with.

. . . On our way back to the United States, I was stopped briefly for a secondary security screening. As the two immigration officers were taking care of my paperwork, one asked if I had just come from Palestine after seeing my passport. I told him no, that I hadn't, and that the borders to Gaza were sealed in any case.

"No one can get out either?" asked the second officer.

"No one," I replied. "And if they manage to, it is somewhat of a miracle."

"Damn, if I wasn't allowed out of here, I think I'd kill someone!" he snapped.

In roughly three weeks, we are packing up our things—again—this time leaving Durham for good and moving upward, literally: Yassine will start his cornea fellowship this July in Baltimore. But, in the meantime, the kiddos and I are heading (make that *attempting* to head) to Gaza, while Yassine will go visit his family in Lebanon.

As usual, we will have to play things by ear and gamble on when and whether Rafah crossing might open to Palestinian residents. I will definitely be blogging and tweeting between now and then—and all along the way.

Remote-Control Death[8]
Durham, North Carolina, March 24, 2009

An excellent article titled "Remote-Control Death" was published in the *Nation*; good friend Darryl Li co-authored the piece after a recent fact-finding mission to Gaza. It deals with the now all-too-familiar drone technology employed over Gaza and investigates how "discriminate" they really are (hint: not very), suggesting that no weapon better symbolizes Israel's indirect occupation of the Gaza Strip.

What resonated with me most was the line that attempts to describe the so-called paradox that is Israel's "relationship" to Gaza ("indirect occupation" or, as I like to call it, remote-control occupation); how, despite the fact that Israel has disclaimed responsibility for Gaza, it continues to control every aspect of life there, down to what Gazans can eat and when they can turn on their lights:

> Since removing its military bases and settlers from Gaza in 2005, Israel has disclaimed any responsibility as an occupying power for the well-being of Gaza's populace. But even without permanent garrisons, Israel continues to control Gaza's economy and infrastructure, from its borders and airspace to its power grid and monetary policy. The Israeli blockade of Gaza, tightened in mid-2007 after Hamas took over Palestinian Authority institutions, has created immense hardships on Gaza's civilian population. And just as Israel's control of Gaza's borders allows it to dictate from a safe distance what Gazans can eat, whether they can turn on their lights, and what kinds of medical treatment are available to them, drones give Israel the ability to carry out targeted attacks without having to risk "boots on the ground."[9]

This is Gaza. This is Occupation.

On that note, we are leaving for Cairo on April 6, in hopes of making it across Rafah shortly thereafter.

The Success of BDS[10]
Durham, North Carolina, April 5, 2009

It is always difficult to quantify the success of a grassroots activist movement. It is particularly frustrating in the case of the anti-Israeli-Apartheid BDS movement. Enter this short piece from the *Jerusalem Post* about more than one-fifth of Israeli exporters suffering losses as a result of the boycott. Progress is slow, but the abnormalization of occupation and highlighting its Apartheid-like nature is the way to go:

> Local exporters are losing foreign markets and customers because of the global economic crisis and a growing anti-Israel boycott of locally made products following Operation Cast Lead, the Israel Manufacturers Association said Sunday.
>
> "In addition to the problems and difficulties arising from the global economic crisis, 21 percent of local exporters report that they are facing problems in selling Israeli goods because of an anti-Israel boycott, mainly from the UK and Scandinavian countries," said Yair Rotloi, chairman of the association's foreign-trade committee.
>
> . . . Twenty-nine percent of exporters reduced business travel abroad by more than 30 percent, 11 percent cut it 20 percent, 6.5 percent reduced it 10 percent, and 43 percent reported no change. Twenty-six percent of exporters said business visits by their foreign customers had declined.[11]

Our Pause in Cairo Airport[12]
Cairo, Egypt. April 8, 2009

We have been stuck in Cairo Airport for nearly a day now. We are being allowed neither entry nor exit by Egyptian authorities, who insist that as long as Rafah crossing is closed, they are under strict orders not to allow Palestinians into Egypt.

This is despite a signed letter of consent I received personally from the Egyptian consul-general in Washington, D.C., the day of my travel from the United States.

To quote the Egyptian officials here in the airport, "So sue him!"

I tried to plead that it was not my fault Egypt was in the way of my home—that if I could, I'd parachute in; that I simply wanted to go back home.

For now, we wait and sleep on the roach-ridden floors of the transit hall as our own *Borders* film (a classic Syrian satire by iconic actor Duraid Laham about a man who is stuck between the borders of two fictional countries who speak the same language) unfolds.

We cannot return to the United States because my visa has expired, and I was planning on renewing it in Beirut, where I was to meet up with Yassine after my Gaza stay.

And we are not being allowed entry to Cairo, because Rafah is closed.

No one seems to have an answer, other than what was told to me this morning. No one knows where my file is or what is going to happen. I have an off-again on-again Wi-Fi signal and am trying my best to keep updates on Twitter @gazamom.

The only certainty is uncertainty.

CHAPTER NOTES

1. The full original text of this post is archived at http://www.gazamom.com/2009/01/occupation-the-elephant-in-the-room/, shortened to http://bit.ly/9yGqqB.
2. Archived at http://bit.ly/cAcTbR.
3. Archived at http://bit.ly/bt9QaK.
4. Archived at http://bit.ly/a3j9Lw.
5. In January 2010, I made a short video of my Mom making *Rummaniya*. You can see the video and the blog post I wrote about it, archived at http://bit.ly/ceZyn1.
6. Archived at http://bit.ly/czRn9L.
7. "Gaza Zoo" is a reference to the term coined by good friend and scholar Darryl Li in a piece he wrote for Adalah describing the Gaza Strip: a situation where the freedom of animals is never up for discussion; rather, the objective is to tame them through careful regulation of leash and diet.
8. Archived at http://bit.ly/cXP2Jh.
9. Marc Gariasco and Darryl Li, "Remote Control Death," *Nation*, April 6, 2009, archived at http://bit.ly/bFZluD.
10. Archived at http://bit.ly/axVzYK.
11. Sharon Wrobel, "Exporters Suffer Anti-Israel Boycotts," *Jerusalem Post*, March 30, 2009, archived at http://bit.ly/99xrEs.
12. Archived at http://bit.ly/ahHVLl.

Chapter 22

Traveling and Being

April–August 2009

In early April, after concluding a whirlwind speaking tour that took me to Buffalo, New York, and across Canada, the children and I packed our bags and began our journey back to Gaza just as Yassine got ready to travel to Lebanon to visit his parents. But our plans hit a snag when we were unexpectedly detained in Cairo Airport and eventually deported back to the United States—away from Gaza. This experience was, in the words of Palestinian historian Rashid Khalidi, "the quintessential Palestinian experience." Identity and citizenship remain abstract, tightly bound concepts that we carry in a small satchel around our necks, ready to present and explain in dizzying detail at a moment's notice or ready to be hung by equally as fast, I reflected.

We stayed with my brother in Virginia for the week, because the lease on our North Carolina apartment had ended ahead of our anticipated move to Maryland later that summer. We were forced to revise our travel plans and decided to join Yassine in Lebanon instead. Upon our return to the United States a few months later, we completed our move to Columbia, Maryland, where Yassine was starting his cornea fellowship—still in disbelief that my many attempts to return home were denied, despite all the talk of opening Gaza's borders after the war's end. My parents then attempted to leave Gaza to visit us after I failed to enter it.

President Jimmy Carter, who visited Gaza in mid-June, had this to say about the continuing Israeli blockade there: "I understand even paper and crayons are treated as 'security hazards' and not permitted to enter Gaza. I sought an explanation for this policy in Israel but did not receive a satisfactory answer—because there is none."

My Palestinian Passover[1]
Cairo Airport, April 7–8, 2009; Durham, North Carolina, April 10, 2009 (via Twitter)

April 7, Cairo Airport

4:35 P.M., APRIL 7: Arrived in Cairo—am not being allowed through the airport. Been waiting w/ kids for 4 hours now. Can't go back to United States—visa expired.

4:36 P.M., APRIL 7: Am living a real-life *hdood* (*Borders*—an iconic 1980s satire film by Ghawar).

4:41 P.M., APRIL 7: Thank god for free Wi-Fi in Cairo Airport. Despite the interrogation and detention.

5:11 P.M., APRIL 7: Am now being told I will be deported "somewhere."

5:16 P.M., APRIL 7: Maybe now time to whip out my digital recorder and flip camera.

5:19 P.M., APRIL 7: Sitting next to a snoring Sudanese man and a roach Yousuf just crushed.

5:34 P.M., APRIL 7: This is weird. I am opening Noor's cot in the airport for her to sleep in. I think I'm going to film this.

7:58 P.M., APRIL 7: Hour 6 in Egyptian detention. Low-level official told me they plan to deport me to the United Kingdom—even though I have no visa.

7:59 P.M., APRIL 7: Yousuf asked me: "Why are they not allowing us through? What did we do? Why did they allow Israelis through but not us?"

7:59 P.M., APRIL 7: He asked those questions to the Egyptian officials, who just said, "*Rabina kbeer*" ("God is great").

10 P.M., APRIL 7: Still stuck. Managed to avoid early deportation and buy myself some more time—anyone with connections in the Egyptian government?

April 8, Cairo Airport

9 A.M., APRIL 8: Waiting and waiting. This man has no answers, and my file has disappeared or been cast aside for the moment. Running out of diapers.

10:17 A.M., APRIL 8: Now spiraling into the world of the kafkaesque—no one has answers, and I don't know how to get them.

10:18 A.M., APRIL 8: Thinking of going on a hunger strike.

10:32 A.M., APRIL 8: One officer just asked if I wanted a shelter set up—apparently it's going to be a while.

10:47 A.M., APRIL 8: Now talk of deporting us to the United States tonight.

5 P.M., APRIL 8: I was placed in a detention room with 17 others for 3 hours; then taken to a room and asked "if that's what I wanted for the foreseeable future."

5:01 P.M., APRIL 8: Took my laptop and cameras; everyone was called on by country; 5 South Asians were "Pakistan"; Guinean was "Kenya"; another was "Indonesia."

5:04 P.M., APRIL 8: Then they said, "It's very uncomfortable isn't it? We don't mind keeping you there you know."

5:05 P.M., APRIL 8: I told everyone in the detention room: "I am the only one here because I cannot go home. You are all being deported home, I am denied home."

5:10 P.M., APRIL 8: Unfortunately, could not film there; though could have tried to hide my flip. Oh well.

9:20 P.M., APRIL 8: I don't think I have ever gone such a long stretch with no sleep. I am beginning to hallucinate.

9:22 P.M., APRIL 8: Thank you everyone for your support. I thought I could get in; I exhausted all options. They said I needed "security clearance" (to go home).

April 10, Back in America

7:35 A.M., APRIL 10: Quick tweet to let everyone know we were allowed back into the United States and that I am sick to my stomach (literally and figuratively) and throwing up since 5 a.m.

I Was Born Palestinian[2]
Fairfax, Virginia, April 13, 2009

It was our journey home that began with the standard packing frenzy: squeezing everything precious and dear and useful into two suitcases that would be our sustenance for the course of three months.

This time, I wanted to be ready, I thought to myself—just in case I got stuck at the crossing. The crossing. My presumptuousness is like a dull hit to the back of my head now.

In addition to all the packing of suitcases, we were also packing up our house—my husband was finishing up his residency at Duke University and set to start a medical fellowship in Maryland in July. In the meantime, we were "closing shop," putting our things in storage, selling the rest, and heading overseas: me to Gaza, he to Lebanon to visit his family.

Eventually, I was to meet him there (assuming I could get into Gaza and then assuming I could get out). Yassine is a third-generation Palestinian refugee from the village of Waarit al-Siris in northern historic Palestine; he was born in a refugee camp in Lebanon and holds a *laissez-passer* for Palestinian refugees. Israel denies him return to his own home—despite his marriage to me, a resident of Gaza. So when we go overseas, we often go our separate ways; we cannot live legally as a unit, as a family, in our own homes. The occupation denies us even this.

I hold a Palestinian Authority (PA) passport. It replaced the "temporary two-year Jordanian passport for Gaza residents" that we held until the Oslo Accords and the creation of the PA in the mid-1990s, which itself replaced the Egyptian travel documents we held before that—a progression in a long line of stateless documentation.

It is a passport that allows no passage, a passport that disallows me entry to my own home. This is its purpose: to mark me, brand me, so that I am easily identified and cast aside without questions; it is convenient for those giving the orders. It is a system for the collective identification of those with no identity.

We finished packing as much as we could of the house, leaving the rest to Yassine, who was to leave a week after us, and drove four hours to Washington, D.C., to spend a few days at my brother's house in Virginia before we took off.

First, we headed to the Egyptian embassy.

. . . I did not want to repeat [the ordeal my parents suffered when they last tried to return to Gaza via Egypt], so I called the embassy this time, which assured me the protocol had changed: Now, it was only Palestinian men who were not allowed to fly to or enter Egypt. Women were and would get their visas at the Egyptian port of destination. I was given a signed and dated letter (April 6, 2009) by the consul to take with me in case I encountered any problems:

> The Consular Section of the Embassy of the Arab Republic of Egypt hereby confirms that women who are residents of the Gaza Strip and who hold passports issued by the Palestinian Authority are required to get their visa to enter Egypt at Egyptian ports and *not* at the various Egyptian consulates in the United States on their way to the Gaza Strip for the purpose of reaching their destination (i.e., Gaza Strip).

With letter and bags in hand, we took off, worried only about the possibility of entering Gaza—the thought of not being able to enter Egypt never crossed my mind.

Two long-haul flights and one seven-hour transit later, we made it. I knew the routine by heart. Upon our arrival, I was quick to hit the bank to buy the

$15 visa stamps for Yousuf's and Noor's American passports and exchange some dollars into Egyptian pounds. I figured it would help pass the time while the lines got shorter.

I then went and filled out my entry cards—an officer came and filled them out with me, seeing that my hands were full: a daypack on my back; Noor on my front, strapped to my chest in a baby carrier; and Yousuf holding my hand. . . .

We then submitted our passports. Things seemed to be going smoothly. Just then, the officer explained he needed to run something by his superior: "You have a Palestinian passport; Rafah crossing is closed. . . . "

"I promise it will just be five minutes," he assured me. But I knew I was in for a long wait. It was at this point that I yanked out my laptop and began to tweet and blog about my experience (full progression of tweets here courtesy Hootsbuddy). At first I thought it would simply help pass the time; it developed into a way to pool resources together that could help me and ended as a public-awareness campaign.

The faces were different each time. Three or four different rooms and hallways to navigate down. They refused to give names, and the answers they gave were always in the form of cryptic questions.

They first explained I would not be allowed entry into Egypt, because Palestinians without permanent residency abroad are not allowed in; "Besides— Rafah crossing is closed," one officer said (my response: "So open it"). I was told I was to be deported to the United Kingdom first. "But I have no British visa," I explained. I was ordered to agree to get on the next flight. I refused—I didn't come all this way to turn back.

I was escorted to the "extended transit terminal." It was empty at first, except for a South Asian man in tightly buckled jeans with a small duffel bag who spent the good part of our time there in a deep sleep. During the day, the hall would fill up with local passengers—from villages of cities across Egypt—and we would move our things to the upper waiting area.

Most of the time was spent in this waiting area with low-level guards who knew nothing and could do nothing.

At different intervals, a frustrated Yousuf, fully caped in his black Spiderman outfit and mask, would approach them angrily about why "they wouldn't let him go see his *seedo* and *tete*" and why "they put cockroaches on the floor." When we first arrived, he asked if these were the "*yahood*" ("Jews"), his only experiences with extended closure, delay, and denial of entry being at the hands of the Israeli soldiers and government. I replied, "No, but why don't you ask them why they are allowed through to sunbathe and we aren't to our own homes?"

"*Rabina kbeer*," came the response. They were impotent. God is great.

I was given little access to anyone who had any authority. I seemed to be called in whenever the new person on duty arrived, when they were scheduled for their thrice-daily interrogation and intimidation, their shooting and crying.

Officers came and went as shifts began and ended. But our status was always the same. Our "problem," our case, our issue was always the same. We remained, sitting on our chairs, with our papers and documents in hand, waiting.

Always waiting. For this is what the Palestinians do: We wait. For an answer to be given, for a question to be asked; for a marriage proposal to be made, for a divorce to be finalized; for a border to open, for a permit to be issued; for a war to end; for a war to begin; for a child to be born, for one to die a martyr; for retirement or a new job; for exile to a better place and for return to the only place that knows us; for our prisoners to come home, for our home to no longer be prisons; for our children to be free; for freedom from a time when we no longer have to wait.

We waited for the next shift as we were instructed by those who made their own instructions. Funny how when you need to pass the time, the time does not pass.

"You need to speak with whose in charge—and their shift starts at 10 a.m." So we passed the night and waited until 10. "Well by the time they really get started, it's more like noon." So we waited until noon. "Well, the real work isn't until the evening." And we waited until evening. Then, the cycle started again.

Every now and then, the mysterious phone on the terminal desk would ring requesting me, and a somber voice would ask if I "changed my mind." I insisted that all I wanted to do was go home, that it was not that complicated.

"But Gaza is a special case, we all know that," I was told.

Special, as in expendable, not entitled to rights special, I thought.

Unfamiliar faces who acted as though I were a long-lost friend kept popping in and out to see me, as though I were an amnesiac in a penitentiary. They all kept asking the same cryptic question: "So you are getting on a plane soon, right?"

First, a gentleman from the PLO's embassy in Cairo that someone else whose name I was meant to recognize sent my way. "It'll all be resolved within the hour," he promised confidently, before going on to tell me about his son who worked with Motorola in Florida.

"Helping Israeli drones do their job?"[3]

"That's right!" he beamed.

An hour came and went, and suddenly the issue was "irresolvable," and I was "a journalist up to no good."

Friends and family in Egypt, the United States, and Gaza worked around the clock with me, calling in any favors they had, doing anything they could to get some answers and help me get through. But the answer was always the same:

"*Amn il Dawla* (State Security and Intelligence) says no, and they are the ultimate authorities. No one goes past them."

Later, a second Palestinian representative came to see me.

"So you are not going on that second flight, are you?"

"What are you talking about? Why does everyone speak to me in question form?"

"Answer the question."

"No, I came here to go to Gaza, not to return to the United States."

"OK, that's all I needed to know; there is a convoy of injured Palestinians with security clearance heading to the border with some space; we are trying to get you on there with them; 15 minutes, and it'll all be resolved, we just need clearance, its all over," he assured me.

Yousuf smashed another cockroach.

We were taken down a new hallway. A new room. A new face. The man behind the desk explained how he was "losing sleep" over my case, how I had the whole airport working on it, how he had a son Yousuf's age; and then he offered me an apple and a bottle of water and told me to rest, a command I would hear again and again over the course of 36 hours.

Is this man for real? An apple and a bottle of water? I thought to myself, my eyes nearly popping out of my face.

"I don't want your food. I don't want to rest. I don't want your sympathy. *I just want to go home.* To my country. To my parents. *Is that too difficult to understand?*" I screamed, breaking my level-headed calm of the past 20 hours.

"Please don't yell, just calm down, calm down. Everyone outside will think I am treating you badly, c'mon, and besides its *ayb* (disgraceful) not to accept the apple from me."

"*Ayb?* What's *ayb* is your denying my entry to my own home! And why should I be calm? This situation doesn't call for calm; it makes no sense, and neither should I!"

A distraught Noor furrowed her brows and then comforted me the only way she knew how: by patting me on the back with her little hands and giving me a hug. Yousuf began to cry.

"C'mon lady, don't have a breakdown in front of your kids, please. You know I have a kid your son's age, and it's breaking my heart to do this, to see him in these conditions, to put him in these conditions; so please take the plane."

"So don't see me in these conditions! There's a simple solution you know. *Let me go home.* It's not asking a lot, is it?"

"Hey, now look lady," he said, stiffening suddenly into bad cop, his helpless grimace disappearing.

"Rules are rules; you need a visa to get in here like any other country. Can you go to Jordan without a visa?"

"Don't play the rules game with me. *I had approval from your embassy, from your consul general* to cross into Egypt and go to Gaza; besides, how else am I supposed to get into Gaza?" I shouted, frantically waving the stamped and signed document in front of him as though it were a magic wand.

"So sue him. *Amn il Dawla* supersedes the foreign ministry's orders; he must have outdated protocol."

"The letter was dated April 6, which is two days ago; how outdated could it be? Look—if I could parachute into Gaza, I would, trust me. With all due respect to your country, I'm not here to sightsee. Do you have a parachute for me? If I could sail there, I would do that, too. But last I checked, Israel was ramming and turning those boats back. Do you have another suggestion?"

"What is it you want, lady? Do you want to just live in the airport? Is that it? Because we have no problems letting you live here, really. We can set up a shelter for you. And no one will ever ask about you or know you exist. In any case, you don't have permanent residency abroad; so our government policies say we can't let a Palestinian who does not have permanent residency abroad into the country."

"I have a U.S. visa—it's expired, but my extension of status document is valid until the end of June. And besides—what kind of illogical law is that? You aren't allowing me back home if I don't have permanent residency abroad?"

"I don't read English; please translate. . . . "

"You see, it says here that my status is valid until June 30, 2009."

"Good, so then we *can* deport you back to the United States," he said, picking up the phone and giving a quick order for the Palestinian convoy of injured Palestinians heading to the crossing to go on without me—my only hope of returning home dissipating before my eyes at the hands of this manipulative enforcer.

"You just said if I have permanent residency abroad, I can go home; now you say I can't. Which is it?"

"I'm sorry you are refusing to go on the plane. Take her away, please."

We were ushered back to the extended waiting area, back to our roach-ridden premises that had become our home, along with a newly arrived Luxembourgian and French couple and their two children who had failed to produce their passports and were being sent back home. Here I was, about to be deported away from home, overprepared, with my documents and signed papers, from consulates and universities and governments.

It wasn't long before a new guard came for us, with a request to follow him "to a more isolated room": "It will be better for you—more private. All the African flights are arriving now with all their diseases, you don't want to be here for that! It'll get overcrowded and awful in here."

Given the good wishes that preceded my last interrogation about the "uncomfortableness" I may endure, I somehow had a feeling where we were headed.

We were asked to bring our luggage and were then escorted down a different hallway; this time, we were asked to leave everything behind and to relinquish our cameras, laptops, and mobile phones. We took our seats in the front of a small filthy room, where 17 other men (and one Indonesian woman who was sleeping on the floor in the back, occasionally shouting out in the middle of her interrupted sleep) of varying nationalities were already waiting.

A brute man, illiterate by his own admission, took charge of each of the files, spontaneously blurting out vulgarities and ordering anyone who so much as whispered to shut the hell up or get sent to real prison; the room was referred to as "habs," or a cell; it can best be described as the detention or holding room. A heady man with a protruding belly that seemed at odds with his otherwise lanky body was the door guard.

Officer 1 divided up the room into regions: The five or so South Asians who were there for whatever reason—expired paperwork, illegal documentation—were referred to as "Pakistan" when their attention was needed; the snoozing, sleep-talking woman in the back was "Indonesia"; and the impeccably dressed Guinean businessman, fully decked in a sharp black suit and blue-lined tie, was "Kenya" (despite his persistence to the contrary). There was a group of Egyptian peasants with forged, fake, or wrongly filed identification cards and passports: a 54-year-old man whose identification card said he was born in 1990, another who left his identification card in his village five hours away, and so on.

By this point, I had not slept in 27 hours—40, if one were to count the plane ride. My patience and my energy were wearing thin. My children were filthy and tired and confused; Noor was crying. I tried to set her cot up, but a cell within a cell did not seem to her liking, and she resisted, much as I had earlier.

We took the opportunity to chat when Officer 1 was away. "So what did you do?" asked Kenya, the Guinean.

"I was born Palestinian," I replied. "Everyone in here is being deported back home for one reason or another right? I bet I am the only one being deported *away* from home, the only one denied entry to my home."

Officer 1 returned. This time, he asked me to come with him "with or without your kids." I brought them along, not knowing what was next.

There were two steely-eyed men on either end of a relatively well-furnished room, once again inquiring about my "comfort" level and ordering—in the form of a question—whether I was taking a flight that morning to the United States.

Noor began making a fuss, bellowing at the top of her lungs and swatting anyone that approached her.

"She is stubborn. She takes after her mother, I see," said the man.

Soon, we were escorted back to the waiting area. I knew there was nothing more I could do. We waited for several more hours until my children exhausted themselves and fell asleep. I bathed them in the filthy bathroom sinks with freezing tap water and hand soap and arranged their quarters on the steel chairs of the waiting room, buzzing with what seemed like a thousand gnats. Thank God for the mosquito netting, which I thought to bring with me.

Eventually, dawn broke. We were escorted by two guards to the ticket counter, our $2,500 flights were rerouted, and we were put on a plane back to Washington, D.C.

I noted on one of my tweets that I would be shocked if my children's immune systems survived this jolt. They didn't.

My daughter vomited the entire flight to London as I slipped in and out of delirium, mumbling half-Arabic half-English phrases to the flustered but helpful Englishman sitting next to us. I thank him wherever he is for looking after us.

Yousuf and I caught whatever bug she had in the days that followed—along with an ear and throat infection.

Eventually, we reached Dulles Airport. I walked confidently to the booth when it was my turn.

What was I going to say? How do I explain this? The man took one look at my expired visa and my departure stamps.

"How long have you been gone?"

"Thirty-six hours," I replied bluntly.

"Yes, I see that. Do you want to explain?"

"Sure. Egypt forbade me from returning to Gaza."

"I don't understand—they denied you entry to your own home?"

"I don't either, and if I did, I wouldn't be here."

With that, I was given a stamp and allowed back in the country.

Now that we are warm, clothed, showered, rested, and recovered from whatever awful virus we picked up in the bowels of Cairo Airport, I keep thinking to myself: What more could I have done?

"The quintessential Palestinian experience," historian Rashid Khalidi has written, "takes place at a border, an airport, a checkpoint: in short, at any one of those many modern barriers where identities are checked and verified."

In this place, adds Robyn Creswell, "'connection' turns out to be only another word for separation or quarantine: The loop of airports never ends, like Borges's famous library. The cruelty of the Palestinian situation is that these purgatories are in no way extraordinary but rather the backdrop of daily existence."

Darwish Therapy: Athens Airport[4]
Fairfax, Virginia, April 13, 2009

Yassine sent me this prose poem of Mahmoud Darwish's while I was in Cairo Airport, which he published just after the siege in Beirut. He describes the revolving door nature of Athens Airport and airports in general—which change their residents each day, while "we remain in our seats." Time stands still for the Palestinian. . . .

"Athens Airport"[5]
by Mahmoud Darwish

Athens airport disperses us to other airports. Where can I fight? asks the fighter.
Where can I deliver your child? a pregnant woman shouts back.
Where can I invest my money? asks the officer.
This is none of my business, the intellectual says.
Where did you come from? asks the customs' official.
And we answer: From the sea!
Where are you going?
To the sea, we answer.
What is your address?
A woman of our group says: My village is my bundle on my back.
We have waited in the Athens airport for years.
A young man marries a girl but they have no place for their wedding night.
He asks: Where can I make love to her?
We laugh and say:
This is not the right time for that question.
The analyst says: In order to live, they die by mistake.
The literary man says: Our camp will certainly fall.
What do they want from us?
Athens airport welcomes its visitors without end.
Yet, like the benches in the terminal, we remain, impatiently waiting for the sea.
How many more years longer, O Athens airport?

—Translated by Munir Akash and Carolyn Forché

In Baalbek[6]
Baalbek, Lebanon, May 5, 2009

Well, we aren't in Gaza, but we did manage to make it to Lebanon after more days of drama (this time involving Yassine's refugee passport requiring a British transit visa—though we did not even pass through British immigration, but I digress).

We are currently in Wavel Refugee Camp in Baalbek, enjoying cool mountain weather, *sfeeha Baalbakia* (meat pastries), lots of sumptuous sweets (try an avocado shake mixed with pistachios, honey, and topped with fresh clotted cream and chocolate syrup!), and, best of all, seeing Yassine's family.

Yousuf got his beautiful locks sheared off before I could utter a word—he was whisked away by his grandmother, who said this just wouldn't do! He is running around the camp like a sheep who found its flock.

Noor is enjoying discovering new things, too—she bottle-fed a baby lamb and coated herself in ashes from top to bottom as she explored the roof of the building!

The Internet connection is painstakingly slow here, so I will have a post with pictures later in the week once we make it to Beirut, *inshallah*.

Life Interrupted[7]
Beirut, Lebanon, May 27, 2009

Well, here we are, still in Lebanon . . . nearly two months after attempting to get into Gaza.

I tried, and failed, to get an Egyptian visa from here. So I am slowly facing the fact that I will not be able to return to Gaza, at least not now.

I have torn off my limbs at the final frontier, but there is no passage for the stateless. Where do you reside when you do not exist? What is your address?

Identity and citizenship remain abstract, tightly bound concepts that we carry in a small satchel around our necks, ready to present and explain in dizzying detail at a moment's notice or ready to be hung by equally as fast:

> Where are you from? [What do you mean? What answer do you want to hear? Don't let my accent fool you! Or my scarf!]
> Citizenship, then: [I leave this blank empty, for here I do not exist.]
> National of: PA [An authority over . . . ?]
> So then you cannot enter. . . . [But fear not! This change is based on the political climate.]
> Parents' place of birth: Gaza City

My place of birth: Kuwait [But wait . . . there's more. I lived there
for just one year—then Saudi Arabia, then Bahrain.]
Place of permanent residence: Gaza, with a footnote [a residence
I cannot reach, a permanence that is illusory; does this still count?
Did I pass the test?]
Husband's nationality: Palestinian refugee residing in Lebanon
[but not since 1993]; but *not* PA—this honor is reserved to those
with *hawiyas*, identity cards [the better to track you with, my
dear]; he has never been to Palestine [only smelled and touched it
through an intermediary].

My father goes to the Ministry of Civil Affairs in Gaza maybe once a week. Here,
Palestinian passengers register to leave Gaza through Rafah. But the wait is anywhere from two to four months or more. He registered nearly one-and-a-half
months ago but is in no immediate rush to leave. Nevertheless, he goes to check on
his status anyway. He wants to come visit my brothers and me in the United States
(when I return) since I cannot make it to Gaza.

The ministry updates travelers on the status of their requests via the Web. This
is perhaps the only convenient and "modern" aspect of the entire process. When
the Egyptians announce the border will open, a few days beforehand, a list of
"lucky names" appears on the ministry's website.

You are assigned a bus number. My father's is 66, but it has yet to appear.
During the last opening, they made it to bus 20.

"What does that mean?" I ask of the curious numbers. "Are you at least guaranteed passage eventually?" Rafah's onerous procedures change almost yearly, and
it's difficult to keep track.

"It simply means you have a seat on a bus from Gaza to the border. The rest is
up to the Egyptians. Maybe 40 percent of people are turned back," he explains.

Most travelers go to the ministry in person anyway, like my father, some on an
almost-daily basis. The last time my father went, a few days ago, he described the
heart-wrenching scenes to me.

There was the newlywed, separated from her husband; the newly engaged,
separated from her fiancé for over a year; and then there were those who were simply bawling and begging for some small miracle, to someone who had no "authority" over anything at the end of the day; to somehow clear the brackets of all the
unknowns and get right to the source of the equation; to make things work.

In Gaza, life is interrupted on an hourly basis, in an infinite number of ways.
The most mundane of them are often the cruelest. They go unnoticed.

Images of Palestine in Exile[8]
Baalbek, Lebanon, May 27, 2009

Images from the Wavel Camp in Baalbek, Lebanon; here, Palestine is always within reach, but the residents of the camp can never grasp it, can never meet it; like night and day—there is a brief time where the two overlap, by way of a visitor from abroad, the spouse of a camp resident, with PA papers, and so on.

No Peace from Netanyahu[9]
Baalbek, Lebanon, June 16, 2009, *Guardian Comment Is Free*

"Eight nos, but nothing new." This is the reaction I hear repeatedly from Palestinian refugees here in Lebanon's Wavel Refugee Camp, where four generations wait to return to the homeland from which they were violently evicted more than 60 years ago, in response to Israeli Prime Minister Benjamin Netanyahu's so-called landmark policy speech.

This is from those who even bothered to listen.

The United States and Europe saw his speech as a move toward recognizing two states (while dismissing the right of return, a divided Jerusalem, an end to settlements, and the list goes on) and thus some sort of advance toward peace; others suggested it was a step backward.

Both analyses are flawed. One confuses a call for a Palestinian ghetto as a call for a sovereign, viable Palestinian state. The other is based on the assumption that progress was made over the past (few) decades vis-à-vis Palestinian statehood.

The speech was full of rosy conjectures. The word "peace" was repeated 45 times.

Tellingly, the word occupation was not mentioned once. Neither, for that matter, was international law. Or freedom—except in the context of facilitating some freedom of movement only after Palestinians give up their rights to move freely.

"Peace has always been our people's most ardent desire," Netanyahu explained, citing three "immense" challenges that stood in the way (the Iranian threat, the economic crisis, and the advancement of peace).

In fact, it is an illegal, draconian, and malicious occupation that has stifled peace and continues to pose the biggest threat to Israel's security.

In his speech, Netanyahu called for negotiations without preconditions while simultaneously imposing the conditions that would make a just and viable peace impossible: an undivided Jerusalem, no right of return, no sovereignty, continued settlement expansion.

The demands to recognize Israel as a Jewish state annuls the right of Palestinian refugees to return to their homes from which they were systemically and violently expelled in 1948 from what is now Israel—a right enshrined in international law and at the heart of the Palestinian struggle.

Such a state would promote, subsidize, and allow Jewish-only immigration and rights as it does now, while denying native inhabitants this same right.

Nations are quick to dismiss the Palestinian right of return but equally quick to facilitate the return of Darfuri, Kosovan, or East Timorese refugees in recent years.

This demand also consolidates Israel's discriminatory policies and would dismiss in one fell swoop the rights of the Palestinian minority in Israel, who make up 20 percent of the population. It is effectively saying: We have the right to discriminate against you, to take any measures we deem necessary in order to sustain the Jewish majority. Such measures have already been suggested in the Knesset, like a loyalty oath, even population transfer.

Then there is talk of the illegal settlements. New settlements aren't the issue. Who needs new settlements if Israeli loophole policies in recent years have provided ample room for expansion?

Currently, the illegal annexation barrier, together with settlement-related infrastructure (including settler-only roads, army bases, closed military zones, and more than 600 checkpoints) consume 38 percent of the West Bank, annexing land and livelihoods; dividing villages, towns, and families from one another; and tearing apart the very fabric of Palestinian social and economic life.

So, we have not moved forward. But we are certainly a step backward from the heyday of Oslo, some might say. The fact is, during the Oslo years from 1993 to 2000, four years under Netanyahu's reign, the Israeli settler population expanded by 71 percent.

Such policies are already being implemented in Jerusalem, where land theft and demolitions continue daily, and where Palestinian Christian and Muslim residents are subject to draconian laws that would strip them of their residency rights there if they failed to renew their identification cards regularly.

Netanyahu's vision of a Palestinian state is bereft of the very factors that make a state sovereign: effective control over land, sky, and sea, among other things. But this should come as no surprise. Israel's longstanding policy has been one of repackaging the occupation and postponing viable Palestinian statehood indefinitely by rendering it impossible.

It is a goal summed up by the late Israeli sociologist, Baruch Kimmerling, as politicide: a gradual but systematic attempt to cause the Palestinians' annihilation as an independent political and social entity. In tune with this policy, nowhere in Oslo is there mention of a Palestinian state, only limited self-rule. Netanyahu's own Likud party's charter flatly rejects the establishment of a Palestinian state.

Neither is Hamas the issue, with whom Netanyahu foreswore talks. It was not even elected before 2006. It did not even exist before 1987. But it enjoys broad support among Palestinians; it was rightfully elected in free and fair elections encouraged and unhindered by the United States and Israel, respectively; and it is deeply entrenched within society; it is a reality with which Israel must come to grips.

And long before Hamas, Israel was similarly destroying civilian infrastructure, assassinating Palestinians, closing borders, de-developing the economy, and sowing lawlessness and chaos in Gaza; all punishment for not being "cooperative" enough, "moderate" enough, tame enough.

All this, of course, is leaving aside the 1.5 million human beings consigned to a life of living death by Israel and its allies—and by allies, I also mean the Arab world. Closed in on all sides, deliberately deprived of the most basic rights of life.

. . . But by Netanyahu's estimates, this is peace. Gaza is the model—the vision—for what a so-called Palestinian state would look like. In his article for *Guardian Comment Is Free*, "Progress in the Peace Process," Jeremy Sharon says that if the Palestinian national movement is to make any progress, its "maximalist demands may have to be walked back."[10]

The trouble is, Sharon's maximalist demands are another's minimalism: Palestinians have already conceded 78 percent of their historic homeland in favor of the two-state land for peace deal (I am a proponent of a one-state solution, with equal rights for all, as are increasingly many others).

Netanyahu talked idyllically of a peace in which a tourism-driven economy would draw millions to Nazareth and Bethlehem. He forgot to mention the caveat that tourists would first have to face an apartheid barrier twice the size of the Berlin wall; navigate a kafkaesque matrix of Israeli administrative control; and, if they carry the wrong-color identification cards, scramble through sewers if they desire to visit a family member across the way in East Jerusalem.

Carter in Gaza[11]
Columbia, Maryland, June 18, 2009

Former President Jimmy Carter visited Gaza a few days ago, which six months after its invasion has yet to receive a reprieve from the criminal siege. The situation, he said, is unique in history and a terrible human-rights crime. Speaking in Gaza on June 16 at a graduation ceremony for some 200,000 students who took a special UNRWA Human Rights curriculum, Carter talked earnestly about the absurdity of the Israeli closure regime:

> Last week, a group of Israelis and Americans tried to cross into Gaza through Erez, bringing toys and children's playground equipment—slides, swings, kites, and magic castles for your children. They were stopped at the gate and prevented from coming. I understand even paper and crayons are treated as "security hazards" and not permitted to enter Gaza. I sought an explanation for this policy in Israel but did not receive a satisfactory answer— because there is none. . . .

Gaza Bonanza: The Nuts and Bolts of the Ongoing Occupation[12]
Columbia, Maryland, June 22, 2009

A chilling inside view of how the continued occupation and blockade of Gaza work—the nuts and bolts. This is what I mean when I say that living in Gaza is living in a place where everything—down to the food you put on your table and when and whether you can move—is subject to Israeli control.

The same Israeli Ministry of "Defense" unit—Coordinator of Government Activities in the Territories (COGAT)—also operates in the West Bank. COGAT = occupation administrators in military uniform.

"Gaza Bonanza," Haaretz, June 11, 2009
by Yotam Feldman and Uri Blau

> Every week, about 10 officers from the Israel Defense Force's [COGAT] unit convene in the white Templer building in the Kirya, the Defense Ministry compound in Tel Aviv, *to decide which*

food products will appear on the tables of the 1.5 million inhabitants of the Gaza Strip. . . . Over the past year, these officers were responsible for prohibiting the entry into the Gaza Strip of tinned meat, tomato paste, clothing, shoes and notebooks. All these items are sitting in the giant storerooms rented by Israeli suppliers near the Kerem Shalom crossing, awaiting a change in policy.

. . . Sources involved in COGAT's work say that those at the highest levels, including acting coordinator Amos Gilad, monitor the food brought into Gaza on a daily basis and personally approve the entry of any kind of fruit, vegetable, or processed food product requested by the Palestinians. . . . [13]

Wonderland[14]
Columbia, Maryland, July 27, 2009

I talk to my parents on an almost-daily basis via Skype. Ordinarily, this event would not be noteworthy. And usually, neither are our conversations. But they are in Gaza, and I am here in the United States, giving things a different spin. I sometimes sit and reflect on the absurdity of it all.

We speak normally. Of course, in the back of my mind is the fact that it is impossible for me to go there and see them—having tried and failed twice—although I, like them, am a resident of Gaza. And they have been unable to depart Gaza to see me.

Our conversations almost always start with, "Any news about the border?" And usually, there isn't. If there is, it's a rumor: "Everyone is insisting this weekend, but nothing is confirmed." And "this weekend" comes and goes with the rumor falling flat. And the one time there was "real news," when the border did open for three days, my parents were unable to get out. They have been registered to leave Gaza to come visit us here for more than three months now, to no avail.

"Real news"—what's real anymore when it comes to Palestine? I have always said Gaza resembles Alice's Wonderland, and now more than ever. It is led by a government elected fairly, but which no one outside Gaza recognizes—yet which manages the day-to-day affairs of the residents there in any case, down to daily updates on the Ministry of the Interior's website about whether the border is open and when and where to get your ticket and bus numbers if you've registered to travel.

It's a place that its own residents can no longer access (like myself). Where "space" has a different meaning altogether. Where air and sea and land are off limits; like ants, people burrow below the ground to create an alternate lifeline, an alternate reality—like Gaza altogether.

It is not its own country, nor state, nor sovereign territory. It is just sort of suspended in time, space. . . .

And then, of course, there's the occupied West Bank, the base of the PA—whose so-called president rules in a term that's long expired, just like the accord it's based on but whose authority is recognized as legitimate (solely legitimate), the reverse situation of Gaza.

Makes sense? Welcome to Wonderland.

Lift the Closure—Give Life a Chance![15]
Columbia, Maryland, June 28, 2009

Ah—the Shalit deal. On again. Off again. On again—and, now, off again (according to *Haaretz* and Hamas both, it never existed to start with).

As though Shalit were the end-all and be-all of the Palestinian problem. Never mind the 1.5 million Palestinians trying to survive under siege. Never mind the 11,000 Palestinian prisoners in Israeli jails.

In any case, it appears that there was perhaps something in the works—and in an attempt to pressure Hamas to sign on, Egypt (already sealing Rafah crossing in collusion with Israel for going on two years now) has hindered passage through Gaza's only land crossing to thousands of Palestinians yesterday and today. This despite an announcement that it would open the crossing for 72 hours. Collective punishment.

Of the some 5,000 Palestinians registered to cross, only 250 were allowed out of Gaza on the first day (a total of five buses), and only four buses are scheduled to depart today.

My parents, on bus 16, are waiting along with thousands of others. They registered to travel more than two months ago and keep checking whether their names have appeared on the list of the lucky on the website of the Ministry of the Interior, but nothing is ever guaranteed in Gaza.

On Strange Encounters with the Other Side[16]
Columbia, Maryland, August 27, 2009

You know how sometimes, someone just hands you a blog post on a silver platter?

The other day, I decided to use a coupon Yousuf got from the local library and take the kiddos to a local play place called Playwise Kids. It is pricey, even with the coupon, so we decided to take full advantage of our time and spend the afternoon there.

I noticed a woman with two young boys there, too, around our kids' ages. I noticed her, because she was continuously casting cautious glances at me, which I tried to ignore nevertheless. Eventually, we ended up in the same corner—with the kids stacking large Styrofoam bricks into a make-believe house (insert comment here about whether a toy truck demolished the make-believe house . . .).

I often like to shatter people's stereotypes of what I might sound or look or act like right off the bat. So without thinking twice, I started a conversation with the otherwise reticent, fearful woman.

"How old is he?" I asked of her older child, who was playing with Yousuf.

"Five-and-a-half," she replied, somewhat warily, with a grimace plastered to her face.

Ignoring her body language, I continued, "Tall for his age, eh?"

"Yes, he takes after his father."

"Where are you from?" I asked, detecting an East European accent.

She hesitated a moment, put her head to the ground, and blurted out, "From Israel—*please don't kill me.*"

Stunned, I replied without hesitation, "And . . . *why* exactly would I do that?" I immediately pondered all the smart replies I could have made but decided to stay composed.

Clearly uncomfortable with the situation, she nervously asked, "Well, where are you from?"

"Gaza," I said.

"Well, see, that's why," she declared, as though this single fact clearly explained her irrational, racist outburst.

I pretended I didn't hear that and went on: "My parents just came from there you know, last week. It took them four months of trying and four days to get across the border."

"Oh, why is that?" she responded blankly.

"Because of the siege?" I replied, dumbfounded. "You do know Gaza is under illegal Israeli occupation and siege?"

"Oh, still? I thought that ended."

"Still going strong, I'm afraid," I said, briefing her on the situation—much to her disinterest.

More silence, and then:

"You know it's funny, I've never met a Palestinian from Gaza my whole life. Funny I should have to travel halfway across the world to meet one."

Gee, I wonder why that is, I thought to myself.

I then directed her to my blog. She responded with terrified little nods and finally withdrew, saying she wanted to get something for her younger son from the cafeteria. She left her older son behind. She watched cautiously from afar, making sure I wouldn't take him captive or something.

Looking back, I don't think I would have said or done anything differently. There are always things I imagine saying, in hindsight, such as "Not all Palestinians/

Muslims/Arabs bite" or "Shouldn't it be *me* who's afraid of being killed, given the Israeli track record of violence against Palestinians—1,400 in one month?"

But it was Ramadan, and I was somewhat restrained with my blood sugar so low; I suppose I also always want to make the point that we—Palestinians/Muslims/Arabs, because she was clearly lumping us all together—have no problem with Jews, only illegal occupation, house demolitions, land theft, and so on. A friend of mine in Nazareth once told me her grandmother put it to her like this: "While we were serving our new Jewish neighbors tea and labneh sandwiches in the 1940s, they were stealing our land behind our backs."

I have very little patience for feigned or real stupidity when it comes to what's happening in Palestine, particularly by the occupiers. It's one thing if you really don't know what's going on, but disengagement and willful blindness to a reality you create and support is quite another.

As many of you know, I tweeted about the encounter and asked for the best replies to the woman. I'm going to mention a few of my favorites here:

KABOBFEST: Usually people get really scared when they see my horns and my tail. You're lucky I dress modestly.

JILLYLOVSDURHAM: Tell her you've been hunting down local Israelis one at a time. You even brought your kids to use as human shields!

... NORABF: Did you ask her if she was about to steal your home and bomb the playground?

MUSHON: Respond to Gaza-phobic Israeli women: "*Kol Haolam Kulo, Gesher Tzar Meod. Vehaikar, Vehaikar—Lo Lefached Klal*" (a Hassidic song, very known in Israel and the whole Jewish world, by the rabbi from *Braslew* that says: "The whole wide world is a very narrow bridge, and the most important thing, is not to fear at all.").

CHAPTER NOTES

1. The full original text of this post is archived at http://hootsbuddy.blogspot. com/2009/04/laila-el-haddads-palestinian-passover.html, shortened to http://bit.ly/b9bq45.
2. Archived at http://bit.ly/ajhttF.
3. According to the U.S. Campaign to End the Israeli Occupation, Motorola has close ties with Aeronautics Defense Systems, which makes drone aircraft that the Israeli military used during Operation Cast Lead. Human Rights Watch reported finding debris from Motorola bomb components in the rubble of civilian buildings in the Gaza Strip. Motorola also has the exclusive contract to provide the Israeli military with encrypted mobile phone technology. Archived at http://bit.ly/csiat9.
4. Archived at http://bit.ly/bmyMA6.
5. Mahmoud Darwish, *Unfortunately, It Was Paradise: Selected Poems* (Berkeley: University of California Press, 2003). Reprinted by permission of the publisher.
6. Archived at http://bit.ly/dxBSIe.
7. Archived at http://bit.ly/9GfW5k.
8. Archived at http://bit.ly/axJMdC.
9. Laila El-Haddad, "No Peace from Netanyahu," *Guardian Comment Is Free,* June 16, 2009, archived at http://bit.ly/9YNcn2.
10. Jeremy Sharon, "Progress in the Peace Process," *Guardian Comment Is Free,* June 15, 2009, archived at http://bit.ly/cEQJh9.
11. Archived at http://bit.ly/c4L9Zn.
12. Archived at http://bit.ly/aiNrzZ.
13. Yotam Feldman and Uri Blau, "Gaza Bonanza," *Haaretz,* June 11, 2009.
14. Archived at http://bit.ly/aVpJ9z.
15. Archived at http://bit.ly/bFRDcJ.
16. Archived at http://bit.ly/adNfZz.

Chapter 23

Reliving an Earlier Gaza Massacre

January 2010

I interviewed Joe Sacco about his latest journalistic work, Footnotes in Gaza, *and interviewed my mother about her own recollection of the 1956 Khan Yunis and Rafah massacres, which she revisits in haunting detail.*

Joe Sacco, My Mom, and the 1956 Khan Yunis/Rafah Massacres[1]
Columbia, Maryland, January 20, 2010

I recently had the opportunity to interview cartoonist Joe Sacco about his latest work, *Footnotes in Gaza*, for *Al Jazeera English*. The book is an investigation into two little-known massacres in the 1956 Gaza Strip. I say little-known, because there is almost no record of these two tragedies outside of a short UN document and local eyewitness testimony.

The subject was near and dear to my heart, as I disclosed in my first question to Sacco, because my mother is a survivor and witness to those events in Khan Yunis (her hometown). She was 11 at the time, and I grew up with non sequitur details of what occurred that day—from the harrowing (mass executions) to the hilarious (my mother's jokester of a cousin—while awaiting imminent execution—asked his neighbor, "What do you think they're going to do to us?" The reply: "Make us dance—what do you think?"). My aunt, who showed the soldiers who were about to execute her only son a coat she had purchased in Tel Aviv, explaining how fond of it she was, in hopes they would spare his life (they did, but only because a cease-fire was declared), never quite made sense of it all. Wasn't 1948 the really important date, I thought? And didn't the Israelis occupy Gaza in 1967? So what were they doing there in 1956? And why haven't I read about this anywhere?

"I can't forget Ahmed Bitar—the newlywed they executed just outside the shelter we were staying in, because he pleaded for mercy for his pregnant wife; or the bodies—all those bodies soaking in their own pools of blood along the castle wall in the town center; or my baby sister Mona, who wouldn't stop crying, because she lost her pacifier," my mom kept telling me.

And so when I came across Sacco's book, I was thrilled—in whatever disturbing way one can be thrilled when reading about massacres—to discover that someone had finally bothered to investigate these incidents. I pored through the book's pages one after another. I even showed some to my mother—she recognized many of the faces immediately.

"This is not something you can just forget or [say] 'let's move on' [about]. It has to be acknowledged, it has to be talked about. History has to be written not just by the victors, but by the people being victimized," Sacco said to me in the interview.

Afterward, he made a request of me: that when the interview went live, I would relink it here along with testimony from my mother. That testimony and an exclusive excerpt from the book are available on my original blog post.[2]

Interview with Joe Sacco[3]
Columbia, Maryland, January 18, 2010, *Al Jazeera English*

When it comes to the world of cartooning, Joe Sacco is considered a luminary. Sacco, who is hailed as the creator of war-reportage comics, is the author of such award-winning books as *Palestine and Safe Area Gorazde.*

His latest work, *Footnotes in Gaza,* is an investigation into two little-known and long-forgotten massacres in 1956 in the southern Gaza Strip that left at least 500 Palestinians dead. It is a chilling look back at an unrecorded past and an exploration of how that past haunts and shapes the present—including the beginning of mass home demolitions in 2003 in Rafah.

Sacco navigates the fuzzy lines between memory, experience, and visual interpretation almost seamlessly, all while painting an intimate portrait of life under occupation and despite occupation—a life not only of repression and anger but full of humor and resilience.

> AL JAZEERA: My mother narrowly escaped death during the 1956 massacre in Khan Yunis. Yet I struggled to find any information or record of this event as I grew older. Why do you think that is?
>
> JOE SACCO: I was curious about the same thing.
> What led me to this is a UN document referenced in books about the Suez War according to [which] up to 275 [Palestinians] were killed in Khan Yunis, and then a few days later, about 111 in Rafah.

These are large mass killings the [UN] is alleging. And it was a surprise to me that I had read very little about them.

I thought clearly some of the people who lived [through] this must still be alive. Why not go and try to actually make an attempt to gather their stories?

AL JAZEERA: The book speaks a lot to the inexhaustible nature of this conflict. As you state in the book, headlines written 10 years ago could very well be today's headlines. To what extent do some of the book's theme—exploitation, massacre, subjugation, occupation, disenchantment, survival—repeat themselves till this day?

JS: I think you see a lot of those elements.

Palestinians are very weary of other Arab regimes. They're weary of their own government. And I think you see that in the parts about 1956, about the Egyptian Army not putting up much of a fight and even the *fedayeen* basically coming to the conclusion that the Egyptians were using them, which is probably the case.

And today, you see the fact that a lot of Arab regimes give lip service to the Palestinian cause, but then you see what the Egyptians are doing on the border with the help of the U.S. Army Corps of Engineers; obviously, in their mind, it's clear the Egyptian government has thrown in its walk on the side of the blockaders. So yes, there are certain themes that are repeated.

AL JAZEERA: What is your favorite scene?

JS: The feast (Eid al-Adha). I got a break from drawing soldiers and bodies. But it was also such an amazing experience to see. I kind of wanted to throw the Western reader at this.

I almost passed out—it really made me queasy to see all this, and I wanted to confront the reader with this.

I wanted to show everyone's involved and the beauty of it: the slaughter and kids playing in the blood, the way they divide [the meat] up and give a third to the poor.

For me, that was really an amazing experience actually to [see] something like that and to see how people hang on to their traditions, hang on to what makes them feel like a human being despite everything.

AL JAZEERA: You cite a chilling quote from a 1949 Israeli foreign ministry report predicting what would happen to the Palestinian refugees: that "some will die, but most will turn into human debris and social outcasts."

JS: That seems to have been in some ways a fair prediction, unfortunately.

Look at Gaza today. I mean talk about outcasts—it's as if it dropped off the map. Cut off from everyone. No opportunity to get out. And let it dry out and fall into the sea, as I think [Shimon] Peres [the Israeli president] put it.

AL JAZEERA: Throughout the book, you weave seamlessly between past and present, massacre and house demolitions, as though for the people involved, these events exist in the same plane or time frame. What have you learned about how the past influences the present in this case?

JS: In some ways, the past is sort of swallowed up by the present with the Palestinians, because so much is going on now. Every generation of Palestinians has something that is simply going to stick in [its] claw, as it should.

All these experiences sort of add up. They don't get transmitted as a coherent story. But they do get transmitted as bitterness from the parents. And each generation, I think, picks up that bitterness from the generation before it and has [its] own bitterness from [its] own situation to give to [its] children—and you know that we can't expect more from people in a way. I think we'd all behave in exactly the same way.

This is not something you can just forget or [say] "let's move on" [about]. It has to be acknowledged; it has to be talked about. History has to be written not just by the victors but by the people being victimized.

AL JAZEERA: You were asked this question repeatedly in the book: Why 1956 in particular?

JS: Mainly because it seems like a very large event. This is not to downplay anything [else] that happened. But we're talking about hundreds of people. We're talking about taking people out of their homes, or shooting them in their homes, or lining them up against the wall or in the streets and shooting them.

I just wondered why this wasn't a story I've been able to read about.

And, in the end, you just become attached to getting the story; you go from sort of justifying in your own head why you're doing it to feeling like you are after something, come hell or high water.

And then in a way you become slightly ruthless in your bid to get it, and in some ways you begin to lose sight of. . . . [G]etting the story in some weird way seems to eclipse the story in your mind.

AL JAZEERA: How so?

JS: I think I've written about this in *Christmas with Karadzic*. You get into this mode of being a journalist, so it's something going off in your head when you get "the quote." It's your way of distancing yourself.

You're working to get precise information and line up your facts. It's almost like being a surgeon. In some way, it's necessary to be cold-hearted about how you're going to get the story, but there is sort of a dehumanizing aspect. It was my own commentary on what I was feeling.

AL JAZEERA: Many parts of the book seem non–non sequitur: a heady celebration by seemingly detached Western journalists in Tel Aviv, an Eid al-Adha festivity, the beginning of the Iraq war, checkpoint delays. What was that about?

JS: I think the whole concept of getting the story would be interesting to the reader, because I want to demystify it a little bit and give the reader a sense that [he or she is] traveling along with me trying to find these things out. I want to give the reader a taste of my experiences.

But beyond that, I was there at a very particular time, and I think it's valuable stuff to record.

AL JAZEERA: One segment that stands out in my mind was of a disgruntled man trying to defend his home from demolition. The caption reads: "For the photographers, his house is an image; for the militants, it's cover; for the internationals, it's a cause; for the bulldozer operator, it's a day's work."

JS: Yes, exactly. Even me, he sees [all people] as kind of . . . vultures in their own way. And [they] can explain themselves. I could explain my presence there. But to him, it means so much more, and to him, if I wrote him up in the story, it's still his home if it gets knocked down, that's his life, his money. Everything is invested in there. His memories are invested in there.

AL JAZEERA: Do you think the outcome of Operation Cast Lead would have been any different if it happened in 1956?

JS: I would like to think it would be a big deal. But I mean, we saw what happened during Cast Lead, and what you realize is there were no mainstream Western journalists there. And that sort of says something right away. I mean, Gaza, to me, is a real story, but most journalists are based elsewhere.

I think enough images came out that it definitely didn't make the Israeli version of events seem to add up. Perhaps less so, because I think the mainstream here tries to balance . . . to be so-called objective.

AL JAZEERA: You've said you don't believe in objectivity as it's practiced in American journalism. Can you elaborate?

JS: The reason I came to that conclusion is because when I was in high school, what I saw on [television] news and what I read in the newspapers gave me the impression that Palestinians were terrorists.

And later on, I began to understand why. Every time the word "Palestinian" came up on the news, it was in relationship to a bombing or a hijacking or something else like that. And that is objective journalism: just reporting what's going on. "This is a fact," and leave it there. What it meant was that I had no education from the American mainstream media about what was going on there.

I knew nothing about the Palestinians. I didn't know why they were fighting at all or what they were striving for. It never seemed to come up in the American media.

I want to show things from my point of view, because I think it's more honest in a way to be subjective. Admit your prejudices; admit those points when you feel uncomfortable in a certain situation. Just admit it.

And then beyond all that, I find it very difficult to be objective when to me there is a clear case of a people being oppressed. I'm not sure what objective means in a situation like that. I would rather be honest about what's going on.

Which means perhaps the oppressed aren't all angels—but the fact would remain that they are oppressed.

AL JAZEERA: Your detractors say that your portrayals of the Palestinian conflict are filled with distortion, bias, and hyperbole.

JS: What I would point out is that I don't sugarcoat the Palestinians. I don't sugarcoat their anger, their vitriol. I don't sugarcoat acts they commit that, as far as I'm concerned, don't help their cause. I lay it out.

But what's important to me is to get the context of the situation. What's important to me is to tell the Palestinian viewpoint, because it's not told well.

Maybe we see Palestinian talking heads on [television]. But what about the people on the street? What are they feeling? And it's then you see their humor;

you see their humanity; you see them being angry, and you begin to understand why.

And I think that sort of journalism does a service.

That's what I'm trying to get across. I don't really think of it as biased; I think of it as being honest.

I'd rather put myself in the shoes of someone who's bombed than someone who's the pilot—I know all the glory goes to pilots, and it's very sexy and all that, but ultimately that's not my interest. My interest is the people who are hurt.

AL JAZEERA: What was the most challenging aspect of writing this book?

JS: The most challenging aspect was the sheer length of time it was going to take. When I realize it's a very long and involved book, I just sort of project myself a few years into the future and say, "Do I have what it takes to do this? Is this book going to keep my interest?" The length of time [was] difficult, but the book seemed to be worth that sort of time.

AL JAZEERA: The most rewarding?

JS: The rewarding part comes in fits and starts. When you really have something in your mind's eye and draw it right, and I feel like I'm living and breathing it. That's what's rewarding—when you can sort of really feel it.

I hope at the very least what this has done is elevate the depths of these episodes to some extent so that people are aware of them and that other scholars or historians will get in on this. As far as the West goes, this might be the first attempt to crack this.

AL JAZEERA: There is a section titled "Memory and the Essential Truth." What is the essential truth of this conflict?

JS: Generally speaking, you can fault people for their memory, you can say that all testimony does have problems, and people will put themselves in situations they weren't [in] or exaggerate or whatever, but the essential truth is that many people were killed, and that's what it comes down to, and the overall arc of everyone's story always sticks to that essential truth.

AL JAZEERA: It took you six-and-a-half years to complete this book. Why so long?

JS: I would say the last four years were pretty much spent just drawing.

AL JAZEERA: Given what has happened over the course of the past few years, did you feel frustrated in any way that your work may not be relevant to the here and now?

JS: Yes, frustrating on some level, but then I've stopped thinking of myself as someone who's going to get something out and make an immediate change. What I do think [about] this book [is that] you're recording two things: One is something that happened in 1956, and the other is something that happened when I was there in 2003—the home demolitions.

AL JAZEERA: You devote a fair bit of the book to those home demolitions in Rafah, though the main topic of the book is the massacres of 1956. Why?

JS: I was a witness to what happened in 2003, and I think it's valuable stuff to record.

At the time, all the Palestinians [who] were there were asking me: "Why do you care about what's happened in 1956? What about what's going on now?"

Well, those home demolitions in Rafah aren't going on anymore and have been overtaken by other events. So now, do we just forget the people who had their homes demolished then?

The other important thing is to show that events are continuous. It's almost like another injection into the Palestinian psyche of what's going on—another pummeling basically. This is 2003's pummeling. I'm writing about 1956's pummeling. And in the midst of today's pummeling. And I want to show that.

And that's why I refer to a lot of things that happened in the early 1950s, when there were attacks back and forth, and also what happened in 1967 and how people get all that mixed up.

They can never look back at 1948 and just think about that. There is no closure.

AL JAZEERA: How do you decide how to interpret the memories being relayed visually and what, if any, filters to use?

JS: I try to draw in a pretty representational manner. I did have to decide how much violence I was going to show. And my idea was I would show it pretty straight, I wouldn't try to make it look spectacular or anything like that. Of course, I'm a filter on that; I'm drawing; and I think that's clear, but a film director directs his character, and that's kind of what I'm doing, too.

AL JAZEERA: One of your biggest supporters is Israeli filmmaker Ari Folman (*Waltz with Bashir; Closed Zone*), who has said you've had a tremendous influence on him. Who has been your inspiration?

JS: From a writing perspective, I'd say Edward Said and Christopher Hitchens with their book *Blaming the Victims* as well as Noam Chomsky. Writers like that have helped educate me about what was going on.

In some ways, I felt like I was being thrown through a loop when I was reading their stuff, because I never even considered some of the things. It was all sort of fresh and new to me. Some things felt like a punch in the gut, mainly because I have never thought of it this way. From a cartooning standpoint, I think Robert Crumb.

AL JAZEERA: It has been said that you have set new standards for the use of the comic book as a documentary medium. What in your opinion are its advantages and shortcomings?

JS: It's very labor intensive. Unless you really hone your style to something simple, you can't really talk about what happened just yesterday. I should say I can't. The advantage is that it's a very accessible medium—people open it up, and they are interested right away. How many people would pick something up about an incident that took place in 1956 in Gaza if it [were] in prose?

It has a certain strength in that it can take you back in time, and it can drop you in a place. I can really set the reader right in Rafah or Khan Yunis, and I can do it in the 1950s or in the present day. There is an immediate connection with Gaza when you open the book.

AL JAZEERA: How do the people you interview respond to your method?

JS: When I was first in the Palestinian territories, in the early 1990s, I was a little sheepish about things. But what I soon found was that Palestinians have their own hero, the cartoonist Naji al-Ali, who told their stories with drawing, and he's revered. [Sacco wrote the introduction to *A Child in Palestine: The Cartoons of Naji al-Ali.*] It helped me in a way.

For this book, I was much less self-conscious about what I was doing or how I did it. They could open to the pictures of the Jabaliya refugee camp, and they sort of got it right away. They could see themselves in the drawing.

Pictures are a universal language. There was a direct connection to what I was doing.

AL JAZEERA: What is next for Joe Sacco?

JS: I'm actually finishing up something now—a 48-page piece on African migrants trying to get to Europe and landing in Malta. They are really trying to get to mainland Europe, but they end up in Malta. And Malta is where I was born.

I went there. I talked to Africans, I talked to Maltese. It has more government stuff than I usually do. And half of it is being printed in the *Virginia Quarterly Review.*

CHAPTER NOTES

1. The full original text of this post is archived at http://www.gazamom. com/2010/01/gaza-footnotes-joe-sacco-my-mom-and-the-1956-khanyounisrafah-massacres/, shortened to http://bit.ly/cUjvce.
2. The interview with Joe Sacco, a video of testimony by Laila's mom, and a few preview pages of the graphic novel *Footnotes in Gaza* are all archived at http://bit.ly/cUjvce.
3. Laila El-Haddad, "Interview: Joe Sacco," *Al Jazeera English*, January 18, 2010, archived at http://bit.ly/aimAv5.

Chapter 24

The Battle
of the Narratives Continues

October 2009–June 2010

We settled into our new home in Maryland in the latter part of 2009, as Yousuf settled into kindergarten. This meant less traveling during the year for both of us and a little more stability for all of us. Earlier in the fall, my parents finally made it out of Gaza after a trying few days on the border, which included being herded with more than 500 others by Egyptian military police directly from the border to a deportation facility in the lowest levels of Cairo Airport (where many Palestinians were forced to wait for up to a month being allowed to fly out). They spent the fall recovering, and we rejoiced at finally being reunited. I began to work on other things—chief among them this book—and cast aside any thought of being able to return to Gaza. But on May 31, Israeli naval commandos attacked a flotilla of humanitarian aid destined for the occupied Gaza Strip in international waters in the dead of night, killing nine of its passengers. In the wake of this incident and the international outcry it generated, aging Egyptian President Hosni Mubarak suddenly announced that, effective immediately, Rafah crossing would be reopened.[1] I decided to try my luck again—first at the Egyptian consulate in Washington, D.C., and then in Cairo Airport. This time around, we were successful. For the first time in three years, the children and I were able to return to Gaza.

On Extremists, Moderates, and Us[2]
Columbia, Maryland, October 30, 2009

Last Monday, I was invited to participate in a panel of "progressive" Israel/Palestine bloggers/writers/activists in Washington, D.C. The space for the program was offered by the new lobby J Street, which describes itself as "pro-Israel, pro-peace."

The panel itself, however, was not affiliated with it (J Street did not even include it in the official program of events, fearing it was "too progressive" for donors' tastes). They were in essence independent of one another, cautious but welcoming at the same time, an odd overtone that came to characterize the session itself.

In any case, the panel included an impressive list of some 12 bloggers (academics, writers, and so on), including Phil Weiss of "Mondoweiss," Helena Cobban, Max Blumenthal, Brian Walt, Sydney Levy, and many others.

I arrived a few minutes late to packed conference hallways and an overflowing room and snaked my way to the front. I have to admit, for the first 15 minutes or so, I felt oddly out of place as I tried to sort things out.

When I was asked to introduce myself and speak a little about Gaza, I really didn't know what to say besides how disconnected and remote I have come to feel. "So say that," suggested Richard Silverstein, "because ultimately that is what a siege and total blockade intends to achieve, that's what occupation does." And so I did. My father stood silently in the back of the room. I referred to him, to both my parents, to my family, to everyone in Gaza.

I talked about how difficult it was simply to live there and then to leave or return. You are always feeling like a stranger, always feeling dislocated. And now more than ever. The only thing linking me to Gaza is pictures and memories. I read the news, and I feel so far away.

And then the others chattered, mainly about the role of J Street: Was it bad or good? Did it have potential? What was the lesser of two evils?

Half an hour into the discussion, I was still silent, wondering what I was doing there. Then Ray Hanania joined us via webcam, speaking in deceptive and empty statements that ignored the reality of the situation on the ground, terms that could be uttered by anyone from Ariel Sharon to Gandhi: "We must isolate the extremists on both sides and reach out to the moderates in order to achieve peace, and we all know that is based on the vision of two states for two peoples . . . blahbity blahbity blah. . . . "[3]

"Ray," one of the moderators confessed, "you make it so easy for Jews to speak to you."

OK, I'd had enough. "I'm sorry, I really have to say something here. I've been quietly listening to what everyone has been saying for 20 minutes now—feeling confused and very much out of place, as I hear people talking about moderates and achieving peace and . . . I just have to ask: What is everyone talking about? This is not real. What two states? What 'peace'? Are we living on different planets? Has anyone seen a map of the West Bank lately? Of the settlements? Do you know what the settlements have done? What the wall looks like? Everyone is speaking about 'two states,' about an independent viable Palestine, as if that's real. As though it were something just within our reach. And all I can think about is Gaza. My parents. My husband, a refugee, who can't even go back with me when I was able to go back. The West Bank. Jerusalem. This is not real anymore. I'm really not understanding what we're doing here, and where I fit in to all of this, and what everyone is talking about."

The conversation was way behind the reality. Step off the train tracks and take a look around, I thought.

"We can't continue to speak like this. It's an illusion. I really also have to protest this dichotomous notion of extremists and moderates—who is the extremist here? Are Ray and others suggesting that President Abbas and the PA are the moderates? That they are the ones we need to reach out to? Let me let you in on a little secret: Most Palestinians don't support Abbas. I certainly don't consider him my president—his term expired in January. Where are all the other Palestinian voices? I am an observant Muslim; I also support a democratic one-state solution; but I'm not Fateh or Hamas. I'm certainly pro-justice; do you consider me an extremist then? The Palestinian political spectrum is very diverse and pluralistic—it's high time we recognized that and included these other voices in the conversation. But, of course, that would not be very convenient, would it?"

And, of course, we hadn't even touched on the skewed definition of "moderate" on the Israeli side—"moderates" that support a sustained occupation, expansive illegal settlements, a continuation of the siege, and so on.

Anyway, I'd said my piece. There was applause, and the conversation continued. I never did receive a response from Hanania, because, in his opinion, I would be considered among the "fringe," a voice that the Palestinian leadership does not *want* to include in its conversation.[4]

Tunnel Trade Wins Award![5]

Columbia, Maryland, November 2, 2009

We have just learned that *Tunnel Trade*, the film I co-directed with my friend and colleague Saeed Farouky of Tourist with a Typewriter, Ltd., in 2007 has won a Noor Award for Outstanding Short Documentary at the Arab Film Festival (AFF) in San Francisco.

Michel Shehadeh, executive director of the AFF, says the festival "each year offers inspiring stories and images through films that illuminate Arab lives and present authentic narratives as well as provide insights into the beauty, talent, and diversity of Arab culture. The Noor Awards shine a special light on filmmakers from the Arab world and from the Arab diaspora who break new artistic and cultural grounds. This award recognizes their artistic excellence and their work at building cultural, artistic, and human bridges. These are filmmakers who receive little visibility in the United States."

We finished shooting the film in early June 2007, amid heavy Palestinian infighting that paralyzed Gaza City for days at a time, only a few short days before the Hamas-Fateh tiff came to its ugly conclusion; as Saeed and I like to point out, we filmed the tunnels at a time when filming tunnels was "real"—when even talking about the tunnels was still a very dangerous business. In fact, we had our tapes and gear confiscated on two separate occasions, and Saeed got a gun to his head once (had it not been for the quick thinking and adept skills of our driver and occasional security adviser, Maher, and our dear friend and consultant on the film, Fida, one of us surely would have been dead—or at the very least injured—and the film nonexistent). I did this all while I was pregnant with Noor (I guess that makes the award all the more appropriate!). No one was to be trusted in tunnel territory—not the neighbors, not the tunnel diggers, not the Israelis, not the Palestinian security, and certainly not two random Palestinian filmmakers from abroad.

Nowadays, filming tunnels—or facilitating the filming of tunnels—is as profitable a business as digging them; hand any Ahmed a few greenbacks, and you're good to go. The tunnels themselves have since also become a necessary trade route, what with the ongoing siege, transporting everything from sheep to deconstructed cars and even plastic chairs. (Before, the two most profitable and transported items were cigarettes and spark plugs, with processed cheeses a distant third.)

You Are *Not* Here[6]
Columbia, Maryland, November 17, 2009

A while ago, I blogged about a meta-tourism project created by my friend, Israeli media artist Mushon Zer Aviv, called *You Are Not Here* (YANH), a play on the directional "You are *here*" found on maps everywhere.

YANH is an urban tourism mash-up. It occurs in the streets of one city and invites participants to become meta-tourists of another city. It works like this: You download a map, take your phone with you,

Welcome to **Gaza**

YouAreNotHere.org

and "tour" Gaza through the streets of Tel Aviv. It started as a tour of Baghdad through the streets of New York, a project dreamed up by Mushon and some of his colleagues while graduate students at New York University's Interactive Telecommunications Program.

I collaborated with Mushon on the Gaza iteration of the project, writing and recording the locations in Gaza City. The project was presented in many an exhibit, including Rotterdam's DEAF and Istanbul's Akbank Gallery. During the past few months, we updated the sites and recordings to reflect the current reality and relaunched the tour for a fringe theater exhibition at the (first) ArtTLV biennial in Tel Aviv.

Reuters,[7] *Haaretz*,[8] Abu Dhabi's the *National*,[9] and the Dutch *NOSJOURNAAL*,[10] among others, covered the relaunch.

Rerecording the locations was a very strange, very emotional experience, something that is mirrored in the tour itself. It's been a while since I've been able to return to Gaza, and so much has changed that I feel like a stranger—one who is nevertheless intimately familiar with this city, this place I call home. So relying on my own personal knowledge and experience and filling in the details with the help of my parents, Wikimapia, and some research of our own, we pieced together the most accurate descriptions we could. I tried to make the recordings as intimate and as colorful as possible—I really wanted to disorient the listener, to challenge their commonly held perceptions and their relationship to Gaza, all while reflecting the current reality.

As we made clear to all media outlets we spoke with, this is *not* a normalization initiative. (If you didn't catch it, notice the deliberately broken beach umbrella in the project's logo, created by our colleague Dan Phiffer.) As one of the journalists covering the project put it, the tour serves to "create an association in the mind of the listener—to momentarily disorient the tourist and then reorient them with a new perspective—one that includes Gaza as part of their consciousness."

Gaza, My City[11]
Columbia, Maryland, February 22, 2010

The other day, Yousuf came home from kindergarten with a small project. He was given a paper to fill out to help him learn his address. It listed several categories: street, city, state, zip code. He enthusiastically yanked the paper out of his backpack to show me. He filled it out to the best of his ability (the teacher provided the correct address for them to copy). I tried to make out his elementary phonics-based

handwriting and be encouraging all the while. I noticed, though, that in the blank for "city," he had written something that did not exactly read like Columbia.

"Gosa?" I asked.

"It says 'Gaza,'" he said matter-of-factly.

"Oh, I see. But that's not your physical address, you live in Columbia, Maryland," I instructed him.

"Mama, you don't get it, that *is* my address, it's my hometown, even if I live here, that is my real address!" he insisted.

"But it's not even in the United States," I replied.

"So what? It's my city!" he answered.

OK, obviously this was a losing battle. Forget about explaining geography and the limits of physical boundaries to a 5-year-old. What does it matter in his mind anyway? His "city" is Gaza; he is living Gaza, even though he is physically present in the United States.

That's Yousuf for you. Even though he only spent a short part of his young life there (his first two to three years), Gaza has taken a big part of his heart, and he never forgets it. I think, in some way, that is how we all feel. No matter how far away we are, no matter how young or old, no matter where we are born, and where we end up living, Gaza is in our hearts and is always our city. It casts a spell on you.

The Radical Babes of Gaza[12]
Columbia, Maryland, February 26, 2010

I want another baby. I really do. Yassine—not so much.

But he may not have to worry—at least not if Martin Kramer has his way. The current fellow at Harvard's Weatherhead Center for International Affairs has suggested that I—and other Palestinian women from Gaza—should deliberately be stopped from having babies, because chances are, they will grow up to be radicals.

According to *EI*, which first broke the story last week, Kramer offered this fascinating piece of advice at the annual Herzliya Conference in Israel earlier this month, when he called on "the West" to take measures to limit the births of Muslim Palestinians of Gaza and consider them a form of terrorism, or, as Kramer puts it, "extreme demographic armament." He also praised the unconscionable Israeli siege for getting the ball rolling and reducing the numbers of Palestinian babies there (see infanticide; Gaza Diet). If your skin didn't curl watching the audience clapping at the end of that video, well, save your soul somehow.[13]

Kramer's argument: Gaza is a cauldron of crazy; there is already an excess of aimless young Muslim men loitering around, and all of them will become extremists! Solution: They shouldn't be born to start with. Like I said: brilliant!

How does he suggest they implement this groundbreaking plan? Stop providing "pro-natal subsidies" that encourage these births.

. . . One would think such unapologetic racism need not even warrant discussion. Ever the flag bearer of academic freedoms, Harvard disagrees.

This, despite the fact that Kramer's ideas appear to meet the international legal definition of a call for genocide according to the Geneva Convention (which includes measures "intended to prevent births within" a specific "national, ethnic, racial or religious group").

EI founder Ali Abunimah spread the word about it, trying to force Harvard to take a stand. Instead, it rushed to his defense.

"I wonder how long Mr. Kramer's views would be tolerated if—all other things being equal—he were an Arab scholar who had called for Jews to be placed in a giant, sealed enclosure, which virtually no one is allowed to leave and enter, and deprived of food and schooling for their children in order to reduce their birthrate?" Abunimah asked.

Yassine and I in our Boston apartment. I was eight months pregnant with Yousuf.

NPR, Settlements, and Objective American Journalism[14]
Columbia, Maryland, March 19, 2010

OK, I need to get this off my chest. So I'm listening to NPR the other day on my way back from Yousuf's school. (Note to self: Don't listen to NPR's coverage of the Middle East, even when there is nothing else on.)

It had a piece on the "settlement row" in occupied East Jerusalem, as though this were suddenly some new issue that is threatening to "derail efforts to get the peace process back on track" (what track? and where is it headed? the train analogies never cease).

Its reporter in Jerusalem, Lourdes Garcia-Navarro, proceeds to take us with her on a journey to the settlement colony in question, describing it as a "tranquil" place on a lovely hilltop, the settlers as any other citizens simply facing a "housing crunch." She then goes on to speak to a calm, American-accented settler who says he is oblivious to all that's going on around him, that it really doesn't matter, that they just want to be able to accommodate the increasing numbers of Orthodox Jews in their "neighborhood." By contrast, she says, in the West Bank there is "violence again" as "angry" protesters take to the streets hurling stones. We aren't told why. We don't get a chance to hear from any of them. The next day, the NPR anchor sums up the developments in one statement: "more violence in the Middle East."

I was seething listening to this piece, more than usual, and immediately Joe Sacco's words about "objectivity as practiced in American journalism" being unhelpful, noneducational, and unfair came to mind. If I were an "average Joe," my take-away from this piece would be: those angry violent Palestinians, always up in arms about something. So violent. Those poor calm settlers who just want to live in peace and expand out of their cramped quarters.

I would not learn that, in fact, the settlements are illegal by international law, and they will create an uninterrupted stretch of Jewish-only housing and amenities between the eastern sector of the city and two West Bank settlement blocs.

I would be given no context as to why the settlements are strategically located on hilltops or about the assaulted lives of occupied Palestinians ghettoized around them.

... That the settlements are funded by the Israeli government and by American taxpayers; that colonists who choose to live there are given housing subsidies.

But what does it matter to NPR? After all, we got a supposedly "objective" report, and that's the important point.

Sugar and Spice and Everything . . . Denied: Israel's Blockade List[15]
Columbia, Maryland, May 6, 2010

Today, the Israeli organization Gisha: Legal Center for Freedom of Movement released two lists: one of items that the Israeli authorities prohibit from being taken to Gaza, and the other of permitted items. Gisha caveats that the list is approximate and partial, it changes from time to time, and some of the items are permitted for use only by international organizations.

The list was published alongside a press release informing that after 12 months of unsuccessful attempts by Gisha, Israel has finally admitted that it does indeed possess a list of goods whose admission into the Gaza Strip is prohibited (no surprise there, but now it's official).

Cattle and coffee. Notebooks and newspapers. Sugar, and spice, and shoes. Baby wipes, batteries, blankets. Diapers (back to cloth, I guess? Perhaps another "greenwashing"[16] scheme?). Cilantro, cumin, pomegranates, or ginger. Tinned meat, macaroni, or powdered milk, and on and on.

Once again, we see how invasive the occupation is—how the siege determines not only what food you have on your plate but what you can and cannot read, how you move, what you clothe yourself with. Or, as far as children are concerned, what you play with (yes, toys are on the list, too).

Oh, and it has also surfaced that Israel is calculating how many calories each person needs. Because remember what Dov Weisglass said before this all started: "Think of it like an appointment with a dietitian. The Palestinians will get a lot thinner but won't die."

The Undertaker of Freedom[17]
Columbia, Maryland, May 29, 2010

As the Freedom Flotilla approaches ever closer to besieged Gaza, the *Hasbara* campaign continues full speed ahead.

While Gaza continues to suffer the most methodical asphyxiation of modern-day history, where the most basic rights of child and adult alike—the right to food, to life, to work, to health, to learn, to play—are purposefully denied and where the lists of what shall be denied are crafted and tweaked on a weekly basis and then approved and applauded by friend and foe alike, we continue to hear the naysayers; even the media, misinforming, justifying, questioning why such a flotilla need attempt to sail to Gaza. Why the fuss and the worry?

"We offered them alternative ports and crossings to enter!"

"Israel allows in plenty of aid!"

"The people of Gaza are thriving! No need for an outcry or food!"

To put things in perspective, the latest reports from aid organizations, including the United Nations and the umbrella organization Association of International Development Agencies, give sobering statistics:

> At least a quarter of medical permits for life-threatening conditions have been denied by Israel.
> Seventy percent of the population survives on under $1 a day (with an average family spending just 56 cents on food a day).
> Forty-one percent of the population is unemployed.
> Half the farm land is out of production or inaccessible because of Israeli destruction and the "buffer zones."
> Sixty-one percent of the population and 65 percent of children are food insecure; 65 percent of babies are anemic.
> Fishing catches are down by 72 percent because fishing zones have now been further restricted to only 3 nautical miles at best.
> Allowable exports are at nearly 0 percent, compared with 3,000 tons of strawberries and cherry tomatoes and 55 million carnations that were exported to Europe and elsewhere previously. Imports are 70 trucks *total* since December. This is compared with 118 daily in the past.
> Twelve-hour electricity outages occur.

"But they are run by a terrorist government!"

"Rocket-throwers!"

"Kidnappers!"

"Evil-doers!"

"Arabs!"

Alegra Pachecho, an attorney who worked for an international humanitarian organization in the OPTs for seven years, reminds us that "key principles of humanitarian action include that the aid be delivered with neutrality and impartiality, it should "do no harm" to the people, and that it [should] not be used to advance political objectives. These principles have been severely lacking in the international humanitarian operations in the Gaza Strip."

. . . To quote Darwish:

> *This siege will endure until we are truly persuaded into choosing a harmless slavery, but in total freedom!*

Brutality on Land and at Sea[18]
Columbia, Maryland, June 2, 2010

Early Monday, Israeli Navy commandos attacked a flotilla of humanitarian aid destined for the occupied Gaza Strip in international waters. The ships were carrying 10,000 tons of humanitarian supplies that are banned from Gaza under Israel's directives, including toys, wheelchairs, athletic equipment, and medicines.

The multinational aid convoy to Gaza included a former U.S. ambassador, a U.S. Navy veteran, and 10 other U.S. citizens. The Memorial Day massacre left nine people dead and dozens more injured.

The Freedom Flotilla comprised six ships and carried hundreds of civilian "adversaries," as an Israeli naval lieutenant speaking to Army Radio put it, from more than 40 countries. They had come together to challenge Israel's asphyxiating siege of the occupied Gaza Strip.

This is a siege against 1.6 million stateless people—approximately half of them under 18—who are largely refugees of the 1948 war. They are being blockaded by land, by air, and by sea and granted only the right to remain silent in the face of such unfathomable oppression. It is a situation unprecedented in modern history.

This is a siege that has prevented my children and me from visiting Gaza, my home, for more than three years, though I am a Palestinian national.

This is a siege that killed 19-year-old Gaza resident Fidaa Talal Hijjy, who was diagnosed with Hodgkin's disease in 2007 and was unable to travel to get the bone marrow transplant she so desperately needed.

This is a siege that prevents children's books from reaching Gaza City's largest library, forcing them to resort to smuggling books—yes, smuggling—via Gaza's intricate network of tunnels. A siege that American taxpayers support with their involuntary contribution of roughly $500 annually for each man, woman, and child in Israel.

. . . Contrary to what U.S. and Israeli envoys to the United Nations have said, mechanisms to deliver aid to Gaza are a sham. Imports are less than 1 percent of what they were before, and allowable exports are nearly 0. More important, Israel crafts a weekly list of hundreds of items it forbids from the Gaza Strip.

As U.S. Congressman Keith Ellison discovered on a fact-finding trip to Gaza last year, this list at times included lentils and pasta.

As the occupying power, Israel is obliged to ensure the free and unimpeded passage of humanitarian relief to Gaza without advancing political objectives. Instead, Israel, with the support of the Middle East Quartet (the United States, the United Nations, the European Union, and Russia) and the complicity and complacency of many regional and foreign governments, has been deliberately withholding basic necessities in what one Israeli government adviser referred to as the "Gaza diet."

. . . But in the end, this siege has never been merely about food, as shocking as the statistics may be. Gaza cannot be read as merely a humanitarian case. It is about creating a situation of fear, insecurity, exhaustion, and hopelessness, where Palestinians become willing collaborators in their own imprisonment.

The bottom line is this: This attack on the aid flotilla was an act of piracy. It happened in international waters. Israel's siege of Gaza—and its backing by the international community—is a form of collective punishment that most legal scholars consider illegal and an extension of a much longer closure of the occupied territory going on for more than a decade.

Israel continues to illegally occupy the Gaza Strip, the West Bank, and East Jerusalem, denying Palestinians their rights and statehood. It has continued to control Gaza's borders, airspace, people, and population registry while absolving itself of any legal responsibility, even after it supposedly disengaged from the territory in 2005.

So long as Israel continues to be allowed to act with impunity on the world stage, to remain unaccountable for its actions, to receive unrestricted flows of money with no strings attached (more than any country on earth) from the United States, such massacres will sadly repeat themselves.

Just last week, the U.S. Congress approved by a vote of 410–4 a request from the Obama administration for additional military aid to Israel amounting to $205 million.

When governments fail to act, then the people must. It is time for all Americans to stand united in the face of morally repugnant and illegal actions of the Israeli government, as they did in the face of apartheid in South Africa.

Gaza Bound![19]
Columbia, Maryland, June 17, 2010

I'm happy to announce after a three-year exile, it looks like the kids and I will, *inshallah*, be heading to Gaza next month. If all goes as planned (which, as experience shows, is seldom the case!), we leave in a few weeks. It seems post-flotilla, the Egyptian government has somewhat eased its restrictions on allowing Palestinians into Cairo and the besieged beyond. Although as we also know, government policies regarding Palestinians can change in an instant with no rationale.

If we do make it, besides lots of reportage, I plan to work on my second book in cooperation with Madrid-based journalist Maggie Schmitt—*The Gaza Kitchen: Recipes and Stories from the Gaza Strip.*

Stay tuned!

In Gaza[20]
Gaza City, Palestine, July 23, 2010

We have made it into Gaza safe and sound. Apologies for taking a while to update my blog and Twitter account: I was without Internet access for several days while traveling and then without electricity for 10-hour stretches when we made it through.

On the way, I met a young Palestinian mother (originally from Lydd) who lives in Dubai. She was taking her 1-year-old son with her to Gaza to add him to her *hawiya*, as I was doing with Noor. However, because he had only a "temporary" PA passport issued to him by the Palestinian embassy (with its limited authority) in the UAE, the Egyptians would only grant him a seven-day visa "under security surveillance" (the stamp really said that!).

The border was a breeze—the first time in my life I remember it being so easy (which goes to show that, no surprises, if it were open on a regular basis like most airports and border crossings, there would be no backlog). The Hamas-run Palestinian side of the crossing, now void of EU observers or Fateh presidential guard (just "border security"), was incredibly organized and smooth.

I have yet to reorient myself and adjust my schedule to the long 10-hour rotating electricity outages. At night, our street turns into one large noisy orchestra of generators. My father's plumber joked that we have become "the land of one million generators." The generators have become a fixture of Gaza's streets now and power everything from a single computer to an entire 15-story building, depending on their size and horsepower.

Summer's here, school's out, and summer camps are winding to a close as Ramadan nears. The humid heat burns your eyes at times.

Calling Gaza a Prison Camp Is an Understatement[21]
Gaza City, Palestine, August 5, 2010, *Guardian Comment Is Free*

It's three years since I've been back to Gaza. Much has happened since my last visit. Fateh waged a failed coup and now rules only the West Bank, while Hamas is in charge of Gaza. Israel launched its deadly Cast Lead assault. Fuel shortages. Electricity crises. And so on.

I needed to regain perspective. So I walked and I talked and I listened. I went to the beach where women—skinny jeans and all—were smoking water pipes, swimming, and generally having a good time, irrespective of the purported Hamas ban on women smoking sheesha.

During the eight hours of electricity we get each day, I logged on to the Internet and browsed the English-language papers. It seemed like suddenly many people were experts on Gaza, claiming they knew what it's really like. Zionist apologists and their ilk have been providing us with the same "evidence" that Gaza is burgeoning: The markets are full of produce, fancy restaurants abound, there are pools and parks and malls. . . . All is well in the most isolated place on earth—Gaza, the "prison camp" that is not.

If you take things at face value and set aside for a moment the bizarre idea that the availability of such amenities precludes the existence of hardship, you'll be inclined to believe what you read.

So is there a humanitarian crisis or not? That seems to be the question of the hour. But it is the wrong one to be asking.

The message I've been hearing repeatedly since I returned to Gaza is this: The siege is not a siege on foods; it is a siege on freedoms—freedom to move in and out of Gaza, freedom to fish more than 3 miles out at sea, freedom to learn, to work, to farm, to build, to live, to prosper.

Gaza was never a place with a quantitative food shortage; it is a place where many people lack the means to buy food and other goods because of a closure policy whose tenets are "no development, no prosperity, and no humanitarian crisis," Gisha explained in a press release. The problem is not availability—it is accessibility.

The move from a "white list" of allowable imports to a "black list" might sound good in theory (i.e., everything is banned except xyz to only the following things are banned), but in practice only 40 percent of Gaza's supply needs are being met, according to Gisha. The Palestinian Federation of Industries estimates that only a few hundred of Gaza's 3,900 factories and workshops will be able to start up again under present conditions.

Sure, there are a handful of fancy restaurants in Gaza. And, yes, there is a new mall (infinitely smaller and less glamorous than it has been portrayed).

As for food, it is in good supply, having found its way here either through Israeli crossings or the vast network of tunnels between Gaza and Egypt. Of course, this leaves aside the question of who in Gaza's largely impoverished population (with the income of most at less than $2 a day and 61 percent as food insecure) can really afford mangoes at $2.5 a kilo or grapes, which grow locally, for the same. A recent trip to the grocery store revealed that meat has risen to $13 a kilo. Fish, once a cheap source of protein, goes for $15 to $35 a kilo, and so on.

Prices are on par with those of a developed country, except we are not in a developed country. We are a de-developed occupied territory.[22]

All this information adds up to the erasure of the market economy and its replacement with a system where everyone is turned into some kind of welfare recipient. But people don't want handouts and uncertainty and despair; they want their dignity and freedom, employment, and prosperity and possibility.

Perhaps most significantly, they want to be able to move freely—something they still cannot do.

Let's take the case of Fadi. His father recently had heart surgery. He wanted to seek follow-up care abroad, at his own expense, but he doesn't fall into the specified categories allowed out of Gaza for travel, whether through Egypt or Israel. "He's not considered a level-one priority," Fadi explained. "Can you please tell me why I can't decide when I want to travel and what hospital I can take him to?"

Even the cream of Gazan high-school students must lobby the Israeli authorities long and hard to be allowed out to complete their studies. They literally have to start a campaign in conjunction with human-rights groups to raise enough awareness about their plight and then look for local individuals to blog about their progress, explained Ibrahim, who was approached by one organization to "sponsor a student."

I have no doubt that if [pro-Israeli commentators] Stephanie Gutmann and Melanie Phillips lived in Gaza, their principal worry would not be about "what parts of their bodies they can display"; it would be that they would not be allowed out again. It would be because everything from the kind of food they would have on their plates to when they can turn on the lights to what they can clothe those bodies with and whether they can obtain degrees is determined by an occupying power.

Using the phrase "prison camp" to describe Gaza, as Britain's prime minister did, is not vile rhetoric. It is an understatement and even a misnomer. Prisoners are guilty of a crime, yet they are guaranteed access to certain things—electricity and water, even education—where Gazans are not. What crime did Gazans commit, except, to quote my late grandmother, "being born Palestinian"?

Ketchup and cookies may be flowing to Gaza in slightly greater quantities than before. But so bloody what? Goods for export are not flowing out—nor, for that matter, are people. Although there may be some semblance of civil life and stability in Gaza, there is absolutely no political horizon or true markers of freedom.

And as long as freedom of movement is stifled, whether by Israel or Egypt, and export-quality goods, which account for a large portion of Gaza's manufacturing output, are forbidden from leaving Gaza, all the malls and mangoes in the world won't make a bit of difference.

CHAPTER NOTES

1. The border has remained opened on a daily basis since that time but only for (Israeli-issued) *hawiya*-carrying Gaza residents with foreign visas or permanent residencies abroad. All other categories of passengers, barring some foreign journalists and humanitarian cases, are still excluded from traveling.
2. The full original text of this post is archived at http://www.gazamom.com/2009/10/on-extremists-moderates-and-us/, shortened to http://bit.ly/99A2hA.
3. Hanania is a Palestinian American journalist, columnist, and radio host based in Chicago.
4. Hanania did eventually respond to me on his blog, where he referred to me as an "extremist" who has wrapped herself up "in the suffering of [her] people." . Archived at http://bit.ly/cWYQoW.
5. Archived at http://bit.ly/aSpeNa.
6. Archived at http://bit.ly/9MI65q.
7. Sangwon Yoon, "Tourists 'Visit' Gaza Sites from Tel Aviv Streets," Reuters, October 16, 2009, archived at http://bit.ly/cggetU.
8. Ellie Armon Azoulay, "Art Project Gives Israelis Perspective on Palestinian Life," *Haaretz*, September 29, 2009, archived at http://bit.ly/cvvmiP.
9. Archived at http://bit.ly/dcOuOY.
10. Archived at http://bit.ly/94Tstv.
11. Archived at http://bit.ly/ay0pCc.
12. Archived at http://bit.ly/bZGSP4.
13. See Kramer's presentation at the Herzliya Conference on YouTube, archived at http://bit.ly/9IjK0K.
14. Archived at http://bit.ly/dkcgg4.
15. Archived at http://bit.ly/dBFam6.
16. Archived at http://bit.ly/c9BpkB.
17. Archived at http://bit.ly/aBqACu.
18. Archived at http://bit.ly/cJARF4. Read the original op-ed published in the *Baltimore Sun*, June 2, 2010, archived at http://bit.ly/bCO36H.
19. Archived at http://bit.ly/byhmCD.
20. Archived at http://bit.ly/c4WzmU.
21. Laila El-Haddad, "Calling Gaza a Prison Camp Is an Understatement," *Guardian Comment Is Free*, August 5, 2010, archived at http://bit.ly/9j3Rrz.
22. Harvard scholar Sara Roy concluded that Gaza has been "de-developed" under its decades of Israeli occupation.

Glossary

AFF: Arab Film Festival

AMA: Agreement on Movement and Access

AMB: al-Aqsa Martyrs' Brigades

Amn il Dawla: State Security and Intelligence

ART: Arab Radio and TV

Ayb: Disgraceful

Baba: Daddy

COGAT: Coordinator of Government Activities in the Territories

DEAF: Dutch Electronic Art Festival

DFLP: Democratic Front for the Liberation of Palestine

DU: Depleted uranium

EI: *Electronic Intifada*

Eid: Eid al-Adha (the festival of Sacrifice)

Eid-iyya: Bonus gift money from each visiting relative for children

EU: European Union

FIFA: Fédération Internationale de Football Association

Fijil: Radish

Hajj: Muslim pilgrimage

HBS: Harvard Business School

Hawiya: Identification card

Inshallah: God willing

NIS: New Israeli shekel

NSC: National Security Council

OB/GYN: Obstetrician/gynecologist

OCHA: United Nations Office for the Coordination of Humanitarian Affairs

OPTs: Occupied Palestinian territories

PA: Palestinian Authority

PFLP: Popular Front for the Liberation of Palestine

PLC: Palestinian Legislative Council

PLO: Palestine Liberation Organization

PRC: Popular Resistance Committees

PSF: Preventive Security Forces

Qassif: Shelling

Rabina kbeer: God is great

RPG: Rocket-propelled grenade

Salta'one: Crab

shabeeba or shabeebit Fateh: Young supporters

shawarmas: Middle Eastern wrap sandwich

sfeeha Baalbakia: Meat pastries

shoah: Holocaust

SJF: Special Joint Force

Sumaqiyya: One of Gaza's national dishes often served during Eid al-Adha

Thi'ib: Wolf (as in "Little Red Riding Hood"; in Arabic, *Laila wal thi'ib*)

UNRWA: United Nations Relief and Works Agency for Palestine Refugees in the Near East

waraq inab: Stuffed grape leaves

wasta: Connections

wawa: Hurt

Yallah khalsoona!: Get it over with already!

YANH: You Are Not Here

yahood: Jews

Acknowledgments

"A person who is ungrateful to people is also ungrateful to God." So goes the prophetic Islamic saying. And so it is imperative that I acknowledge those people in my life who have helped make this project a reality.

There was a time when I thought this book would remain a "very good idea" forever. There were innumerable obstacles in the way . . . children, family, and life. But part of it was self-defeatism: I thought that I didn't have anything important, authentic, or harrowing enough to publish—or anything that hadn't been said already. In line with this view, contributing another text about Palestine seemed superfluous, arrogant, and ill placed.

Complicating matters was the continuous nature of the Palestinian conflict. The longer I waited, the more events seemed to change, rendering, I feared, those before them irrelevant. There are ever-increasing layers upon layers of hardship and history, making it difficult to maintain perspective. To quote Joe Sacco from an interview I conducted with him (featured in this book), "Events are continuous, and there is no closure. . . . [T]here is pummeling after pummeling. . . . [H]ome demolitions in Rafah aren't going on anymore and have been overtaken by other events. So now, do we just forget the people who had their homes demolished then?"

I'll admit that, at times, I was also frustrated by my mothering duties and envious of the other journalists around me who had none—those who weren't "tied down," who could jump to cover a story or travel at a moment's notice without having the added burden of making prior arrangements for their children, pumping breast milk, or acquiring the necessary visas and security clearances for their stateless passports.

I am deeply grateful to Helena Cobban for being a mentor and a friend and, mostly, for offering me the opportunity to transform this "idea" into something concrete. But most of all, I am thankful for learning from her to celebrate and be proud of and embrace my life as a mother and journalist, not resist it as so many in our profession have.

I especially have my husband and life partner, Yassine, to thank for encouraging me to think "constructively and proactively" and for insisting I write this book, even when I tried to convince myself otherwise and when the whirlwind of life got in the way. His boundless support for my work and his tolerance for the inconvenient lifestyle that came along with it never ceased to amaze me or those around me. I thank him for being so understanding, for being my sounding board, and for allowing me to live my life even when the oppressors do not allow us to live ours. Gaza is an intimate part of his life, without having ever been allowed to visit it. I know it has not been easy.

I am also eternally indebted to my mother and father, Maii and Moussa: They have always offered their unconditional love and support, even when they never knew exactly what I was working on at various intervals of my life! I thank them for housing and feeding us in Gaza and for being my frequent babysitters and second set of parents to my children, even when their antics would drive them to the edge of madness and beyond.

I thank them also for insisting we return to Palestine as children, even when we loathed the torturous travel routine that was involved, never understanding why this was necessary and never able to keep track of what exactly was going on around us. They have both helped me realize that resistance to oppression comes in many forms—including the seemingly passive kind involved in the staunch commitment to renewing one's identity documents on a yearly basis.

My mother's uncanny memory and ability to recall even the most banal details of her upbringing—and many other personalities—in Khan Yunis filled the void in my own childhood in which I always felt like a stranger, never quite belonging. These memories shaped my attachment to Gaza and colored my pictures of Palestine and Gaza growing up. She also instilled in me the obligation to always speak out in the face of injustice.

A special tribute to "my good friend" Darryl, also known locally as Abdel Ghani Il-Ghazawi, for being my "editor on call" and helping me find "just the word I was looking for" whenever the occasion called for it!

Thank you, too, to my invaluable team of editors who helped transform my writing material into something coherent!

And to the countless others around the world who have encouraged me along the way, via comments on my blog, e-mails in my inbox, or messages on Facebook or Twitter: This book is the cumulative result of your support!

Made in the USA
Charleston, SC
21 January 2011